NON-FICTION
&
PROSE FICTION

NON-FICTION
&
PROSE FICTION

UEA MA
Creative Writing Anthologies
2024

NON-FICTION

MIRANDA FRANCE	Foreword	IX
IAN THOMSON	Introduction	XI
HELEN ADCOCK	The Wartime Rubber Factory	2
MERIEL BEATTIE	Ambidexter	8
CHARLES BLISS	Eyes Wide Shut	14
PENELOPE CODRINGTON	Thanksgiving in Moscow 2014	20
HAZEL COTTEY	Aubade	26
RAVIAKASH DEU	Single Chaffa	32
MAYA GOEL	Blue	38
JULIA HOLLINGSWORTH	Thief	44
HELEN JAEGER	Rogue Brother	50
PETER JORDAN	Death in Stratford	56
ZIXIN LI	Ah Gong and Ah Pa	62
JEAN MACINTYRE	Tea-leaves and Toe-rags	68
ELIN MORGAN	Forest Gate to Leytonstone	74
SHARON NIGHTINGALE	A Flâneuse in Norwich	80
CAROLE PONNIAH	Rebel Woman: Vera Brittain. Dissent and the Second World War	86
JANE RYAN	Two People on a Beach in Norfolk	92
TANTRAVAHI	This piece has no title	98
GINNY THOMAS	A Different Kind of Man	108
	Acknowledgements	417

PROSE FICTION

PRISCILLA MORRIS	Foreword	XIII
JULLIANE PACHICO	Introduction	XV
LW ANDERSON	Soup	116
JENNIFER ARMSTRONG	Keen	122
MUTI'AH BADRUDDEEN	Dreams Lie Awake	128
CHRISTOPHER BRADY	The Hanedean	132
OLIVER GUY WORSTER BRIGGS	Haunted Houses	138
GODESS BVUKUTWA	The Devil Dwells in Douglasdale	146
SOPHIE CHAPMAN	Irene	152
MARK COCKSHUTT	Are You Lonely?	158
NIAMH CONNOLLY	Game Theory	164
CHLOE COOKSON	Wake	170
KIERAN COSTELLO	Hear the Whispers	176
GIULIA DA RE	Lepidoptera	182
PAURIC DANIELS	SkodaLogbook.docx	188
MARK DE ROND	Dean Man can't Even Blink	194
OLIVIA EGGLESTON	nesting in reuleaux	200
RACHEL FUNG	The Home Is a Body	208
DANIEL GLANCY	Soft Bodied Animals	214
ANNA GOLDREICH	The Leveret	220
LAURA GRAHAM	The Grave of the Poet King	226
EVAN STEPHENS HALL	My Report	232
ELLIE HALLIWELL	Nell Robinson	238
KASPER HASSETT	What Parrots Don't Say	244
PIP HIBBERT	The Frogs Are After Us	250
LILY HYLAND	Iteration	256
ROSEENA VERONIKA HUSSAIN	Artefact/s	262
DAWN JELLEY	The Suffolk Merman	268
ALEXANDER KOMLOSI	The Dukes of Canal Street	274
TOM LAKE	The Lover	280
KARINA IC LA'O	Little Things	286
ELSBETH LESLIE	Notes on Equilibrium	292
ALEX LOUIS	Evening at the Fatales	298

MARY LOWTH	The Watchers	304
DARIBHA LYNDEM	Obituaries	310
POLLY MANNING	Did You Hear About Paul	314
CHARLOTTE MARAR	Small Differences	320
REYAH MARTIN	Laid To Rest	326
LUCY MAY	Déjà Vu	332
SAROJINI J. MISRA	The Fall	338
DENISE MONROE	And the Grass Still Grows	344
NIC O'KEEFFE	Starved	350
GAYATHRI SANKAR	Katha Block	356
SAM SAXTON	Binaries	362
ISAAC TAN	Edifice	372
EVA TANG	Lump in the Throat Falling Through to the Stomach	378
ALEXIA TOLAS	Pretty Mollies	384
LIAM VAN DEN HOEK	The Outskirts of Paradise	390
ZABU WAMARA	Find Him First	396
OLIVIA WATSON	SAUSAGE	402
NAYELA WICKRAMASURIYA	This Tender Soil	408
	Acknowledgements	418

MIRANDA FRANCE
Non-Fiction Foreword

I was partly brought up in Norfolk, which makes it a particular pleasure to write the foreword to this wonderful anthology of writing by students at UEA. I remember the excitement of occasional excursions with my parents, which we used to call "going into Norwich". Sometimes we had lunch near the market square in a bistro that had a salad bar. These concepts – the "bistro" and the "salad bar" – were glamorous to a teenager in the 1980s; even "salad" identified an aspiration and at the bar there was a choice of *ten*. Surely it was rare to find such an array outside London. I remember a soundtrack of American jazz, too. The bistro, which we pronounced very Britishly, with a short 'i', offered a window onto another world.

There's a difference, of course, between going "to" and going "into" Norwich. For an explanation of the magic that can be wrought through a change of preposition, please watch William Buckley's interview with the great Argentine writer Jorge Luis Borges. One of the reasons he loved English, Borges said, was because you "can do almost anything with a verb and a preposition". He gave the examples of "dream away", "talk down" and "loom over". The writers collected here show an admirable willingness to go "into" their chosen subjects. Into family, work, love and committee meetings. Into Turkey, China, the rain forest, the ocean. Into race, the Anthropocene, bereavement, the criminal courts. Into Bhangra, mythology, and the Dreamachine.

Barrett Wendell, a professor at Harvard, is sometimes credited as being the first person to introduce "creative writing" into his teaching, in the early 1900s. Before that, the most useful instruction a prospective writer might have had at university would be to read a selection of august predecessors, mostly white and male, usually dead, and try to emulate them. Wendell used to set his students a daily exercise to write one hundred words in a "fluent and agreeable style" about something they had observed during the day. Some mocked the exercise as insufficiently academic, but "the daily theme" proved popular, and soon it was being prescribed in other universities and colleges. At Wellesley College, poet Katherine Lee Bates found it a useful tool "to quicken observation and give as much practice as possible in the sifting and grouping of facts of personal experience". By the 1930s, Virginia Woolf was referring to herself as "a creative writer" in her diary. Twenty years later creative writing courses were well established in the United States. Robert

Lowell might treat his students – who included Sylvia Plath and Anne Sexton – to three hours on one line of William Blake. Jay McInerney recalled fifteen minutes debating one word - "earth" - with his teacher Raymond Carver at Syracuse in the 1980s. Thanks to Malcolm Bradbury and Angus Wilson, in 1970 the University of East Anglia created the UK's first Masters course in Creative Writing.

Writing one hundred words about something that has happened during the day is still the most useful practice for a writer. "I don't know what I think until I write it down," said Joan Didion. The regular writer knows that putting pen to paper can quickly lead to something unexpected: a scene or an image or idea with the potential to grow into a story. To be able to carry out such experiments in the company of fellow writers who understand what you are trying to do and can make useful contributions is immeasurably valuable. I really enjoyed seeing this process in action when I visited the campus on a sunny afternoon earlier this year.

Afterwards I got on the bus and, for old times' sake, went back into Norwich again.

    Miranda France
    26 June, 2024

IAN THOMSON
Non-Fiction Introduction

The trend for non-fiction these days is to assimilate elements of travel, anthropology, art criticism, ornithology, nature writing – and a myriad other disciplines. The genre in all its bracing hybridity has been around for some time. In 1984 *The Periodic Table* by the Italian chemist-writer Primo Levi reached the UK bestseller list alongside Dick Francis, even though the book had been turned down by twenty-seven publishers in the UK before it was finally taken on. Such unclassifiable merchandise would never sell, the editors feared. (Peculiar in construction, audacious in conception, Levi's non-fiction was not exactly autobiography and it was not a scientific treatise either. What *was* it?) Only now, almost four decades on, can we see that Levi was ahead of his time. I am struck by the variety of themes and literary genres on display in this anthology. Included are noirish tales of family malfeasance and drug-induced hallucination (as well as *non* drug-induced hallucination). We have samples of imaginative biography, psychogeography, family reminiscence, historical reconstruction and mystery. One piece looks at the glories of Punjabi folk custom; another at Ankara during World War II. An experimental meditation on the nature of book burning (call it bibliocide) jostles with an evocation of Thanksgiving Day in Putin's Moscow. We even have a piece about Norwich.

    A characteristic of much so called "creative" non-fiction is that it blurs the distinctions between truth and non-truth. Of course, any piece of writing is necessarily a fashioning and re-shaping of events (the etymology of *fiction* is from the Latin *fingere,* to "mould" or "contrive"). We do not expect non-fiction to distort, but of course it *does* distort. Edmund Gosse's Edwardian-era memoir *Father and Son,* written when Gosse was nearly sixty, recounts conversations that purportedly took place when the author was a prepubescent child. Had the conversations been made up? Certainly they had. Accordingly, one contribution here is advertised as an extract from a "non-fiction novel"; another is an excerpt from a "novel". Most good memoirists make life more interesting than it is, blending truth with untruth to create a semi-fictional construct. Only the contributors themselves will know how much (if any) of their writing has been elaborated for the purposes of this anthology. Included are reflections on family heirlooms, family diasporas, family photographs, killer whales and the puzzle of human identity.

    When is a life worth telling? B.S. Johnson, the London-born novelist and tireless chronicler of himself, put the most humdrum of autobiographical details into his "truth-telling" non-fiction novels. His fictionalised memoir *Trawl* (1966), about the time he spent on a deep-sea trawler, routinely fetched up in the Angling section of Foyles bookshop. (It was an early example of an unsaleable non-fiction.) The point is: every life has something of interest in it. Thus one essay here considers a parent's career in a synthetic rubber factory outside London during the Hitler conflict, while another looks at a life lived in the London boondocks of Leytonstone. We also have a memoir of a life of petty crime from the days of Marc Bolan and the Bay City Rollers[1].

Ours is very much the era of Everybody's Autobiography. Bookshops are filled with memoirs (*Never Let Me Go, The Last Time We Cried*) that harp on the miseries of anorexia, autistic spectrum condition, cancer, childhood abuse or bereavement. The books might amount to mere solipsistic spouting, were the writing not up to standard (very often it is not). For some time now I have been writing a family memoir of my own. Unsurprisingly my mother was not always happy to have her past examined by a writer, even one who happened to be her son. ("When a writer is born into a family", warned the Baltic-born poet Czeslaw Milosz, "the family is finished"). I can only hope that my non-fiction effort will be an absorbing amalgam of personal anecdote, travelogue, fiction and family history, in which details from one woman's troubled life provide a documentary authenticity and truthfulness (or semi-truthfulness) in the telling. This anthology is, triumphantly, all of those things, and so much more.

Ian Thomson
19 June, 2024

---

1 I am ashamed to say that the band's drummer was called Ian Thomson.

PRISCILLA MORRIS
Prose Fiction Foreword

The year I spent doing the fabled master's in creative writing at UEA was a turning point in my life. Until then, I'd been writing 'in the dark' for years, not showing my work to anyone. So, even though it was terrifying to have twelve pairs of eyes on my stories, the positive feedback was incredibly affirming. My words were being read at last. It gave me the confidence to carry on writing.

I first knew I wanted to write when I was six. I'd fallen in love with Roald Dahl's stories and thought it would be the finest thing in the world to be the voice in someone's head that gives such pleasure. I saved my pocket money to buy a red plastic typewriter and although at the last minute, and to my almost immediate regret, I bought a doll that cried and wet herself instead, the desire never left me. I wrote several unfinished short stories and first chapters in my twenties, but, with authors on a god-like pedestal, I never felt my attempts were good enough. My inner critic was strong. Get real. Stop wasting your time, it whispered.

In my early thirties, I moved to Rio de Janeiro to teach English. The positive, can-do attitude of the Brazilians freed me and I started writing prolifically, throwing myself into a lengthy narrative poem about the Amazon. I learned a lot about the art of placing one word after another on the page, but lost confidence abruptly three years in. My inner critic crowed that it had been right all along. Fortunately, a close friend suggested an MA in creative writing might help. All right, I bargained with myself, I'll apply to a couple and if I get in, fine. But if not, I'll pack in this writing obsession once and for all.

I did my long-distance UEA phone interview from Rio in my bikini, notes spread out on the coffee table. It was a particularly hot and muggy day. When asked if there was a project I was currently working on, I plucked from the air my artist great-uncle's Sarajevo war story, something I'd tried to write in several forms in my twenties but that had lain dormant for the last few years. To my amazement, I was accepted to both places I applied to. A whole new future opened in that moment. I chose the esteemed UEA course, moved to Norwich, and so started one of the best years of my life, aged thirty-five.

I can't describe the joy and relief of being among other wordsmiths and artists. My parents were accountants, most of my university friends were doctors and lawyers, so being surrounded by people who took the making of fiction seriously, who placed it at the very centre of their lives, was bliss.

The MA intake was smaller back then, around twenty-four for prose, and we were a sociable, supportive lot. The rumour was that some of the previous years had been highly competitive, tearing each other's work down in workshops, but there was a genuinely warm feeling between us and most of us have stayed in touch. I read avidly, auditing all the MA and BA courses I could, with the enthusiasm of someone fourteen years out of education. I wanted to absorb everything. I learned so much about how fiction works from critiquing others' writing and having my own critiqued.

Oh, and then there were the parties! My Brazil-perfected ability to mix vast quantities of caipirinha in saucepans clinking with ice in various Norwich kitchens was renowned. But we also knew how to buckle down and work. UEA invites you to take your writing seriously and most of us embraced this fully.

A third of my cohort have been published over the fifteen years since our MA in 2008-09. I'd say that's an excellent proportion, which will hopefully continue to rise. Some published immediately after, others a few years later, and still others, like myself, only in the last few years. It took me thirteen years to complete my first novel – I had a lot of inner resistance to fight, the topic was not easy – but I got there in the end, in large part through sheer perseverance and the feeling I was too far in to give up now.

Would I have 'packed it all in' if I hadn't done the MA? I doubt it. The compulsion to write is hard to shake. But I also sincerely doubt I would have produced such a layered, accomplished debut novel without the input of my peers and tutors, without the fertile exchange that happens in the magical space of the workshop. I'm extremely grateful to the UEA creative writing school for enabling such a transformative year.

Writers, I hope that your journeys to completing your works-in-progress are swifter than mine, but if they do take a while, just remember: perservere, perservere, persevere. Only you at the end of the day can respond to the question: Is this the best I can do? When the answer is yes, send it off to an agent. I wish you joy and success, grit and equanimity. Bon courage, my friend.

Readers, a glittering bumper collection of diverse voices is in your hands. The stories in the following pages will take you all over the world to Nigeria, Zimbabwe, Uganda, Germany, the US, Hong Kong, India, Australia, Borneo, the Bahamas, India, Sri Lanka, Ireland, Scotland, Wales and England. I adore writing with a strong sense of place, so very much enjoyed being transported as I read. The varied points of view are also exciting. Here, in addition to the human perspective, we have a ghost, a dog, frogs by an Asda carpark and a sperm, no less, leading the way. Kick off your shoes, settle down in a comfy armchair and plunge in.

Happy reading and writing!

Priscilla Morris
July, 2024
@priscillamorriswriter

JULLIANE PACHICO
Prose Fiction Introduction

Inspired by my friend and mentor Andrew Cowan (who taught at UEA for twenty years before his retirement last summer), I have the habit of jotting down and squirreling away quotes about writing that I find helpful. Here is just a small sample of what I've compiled over the years:

"I will try to express myself in some mode of life or art as freely as I can and as wholly as I can, using for my defense the only arms I allow myself to use— silence, exile, and cunning."
  (James Joyce, in *Portrait of the Artist as a Young Man*)

"The only things you must have to become a writer are the stamina to continue and a wily, cagey heart in the face of extremity, failure, and success."
  (Alexander Chee)

"It's not necessarily that I believed in myself, but rather that I believed in the work."
  (Karen Jennings)

"Talent is insignificant. I know a lot of talented ruins. Beyond talent lie all the usual words: discipline, love, luck, but, most of all, endurance."
  (James Baldwin)

If I can pick out any theme in these disparate quotes I've collected, it's a focus on resilience, survival, and endurance (or as Joyce calls it so wonderfully, "cunning"). I like reminding myself of these qualities. They're qualities that many of the writers contained within these pages will also find themselves turning to, as they leave UEA and embark upon the next stages of their careers. UEA is a formative time for many - it certainly was for me - but what lies beyond its doors is often the far more difficult but rewarding stage. I'm very excited to see where these writers will go from here, and I'm sure after reading the stimulating and innovative work contained within these pages, you will be too.

In a time of dramatic cuts to the arts and humanities and the rise of A.I. writing, it can often feel more destabilizing to be a writer than ever. In my favorite essay about writing, 'My Vocation' by Natalia Ginzburg, she talks about the role that writing (the titular 'vocation') plays for her in times of tremendous upheaval: "Only my vocation remained unchanged. At first I hated it, it disgusted me, but I knew very well that I would end up returning to it, and that it would save me." I like this view of writing very much – as a port in a storm that's always there for you, no matter what happens. Picture a scarred and battered tree, rising from the burnt ashes of an apocalyptic landscape – that's writing. I also find calmness and serenity in what William Faulkner said: "Don't be a writer, be writing." What a reassuring thought this is for me! A writer is not something I have to be – I don't have to 'be' anything. But writing, like brushing my teeth or riding my bike, is something I can always do no matter what. It is always there for us. It is the most steadfast and loyal friend we'll ever have. And even if we may abandon it, perhaps for many months or even years, it will always be there.

I hope this introduction provides some reassurance to some of the writers contained within these pages. I've found working with the 2023-2024 MA Prose writers incredibly rewarding and inspiring - I speak on behalf of all my colleagues when I say that working with the students and reading the work they produce over the course of their time here is by far the most rewarding part of our jobs. For the MA Prose teaching team, it has been both an honor and a privilege to have worked with these writers at such a key stage in their personal and artistic development.

I hope that you enjoy reading the pieces in this anthology, and that you find them as surprising, moving, and affecting as I have.

NON-FICTION

HELEN ADCOCK

Helen Adcock has had a long career as a doctor in general practice, public health and medical education. Her writing includes biography, family memoir, psychogeography and historical fiction. She lives near the Norfolk Broads with her husband, son and daughter.

helen.cassie3@gmail.com

The Wartime Rubber Factory

An extract from a piece of creative non-fiction.

I knew my father, Len Adcock, had worked in the Andre Rubber Factory in Surrey during and after the Second World War, but never realised he had been on the shop stewards' committee until I found a notebook containing minutes. Handwritten when he was twenty-five, they cover twelve meetings held during the period May 1945 to May 1946. The maroon book is six by eight inches, and the outer edge of the cover has faded. The centre has retained its colour as if something has been placed on the book while in a sunny spot. Once I had read the contents, I checked again for a smell, half hoping for a whiff of stale tobacco or oil. But there's just the scent of old paper. The cover and spine give no indication of what is inside. Perhaps appearing so unremarkable, it survived the following decades and house moves.

My mother had been unaware of the notebook's existence, when I told her I had found it in a bureau amongst papers and clutter, while clearing her bungalow after she moved to residential care in 2020. It dates from an era before she knew and married my father in 1953.

The minutes start shortly before VE Day in May 1945 and end abruptly in May the following year. All the minutes are signed off by the chair, except for the last. I wonder if my father should have handed the book on to the next secretary of the committee, or whether he had resigned suddenly as many of the stewards seemed to do along the way. It must have been a thankless task trying to liaise with the union and the management about pay and conditions especially as staff and regulations were changing after the War.

After leaving his role in the committee, and later the factory in 1950, I wonder if he had not known what to do with the book. Perhaps he should not have kept it but fortunately, it was not destroyed. I find a frisson of the forbidden in reviewing the pages, like listening at the door or hiding under the table while a meeting is going on.

I am interested to see if I can find out more about both my father's life at that time and the culture of the factory from the minutes. The first reading, I confess, was very dry. At times, the formal and passive language reminds me of a clip of the 1959 comedy film *I'm All Right Jack*. In the film Peter Sellers, as trade union shop steward Fred Kite, walks around the missile factory with his fellow stewards using officious language. This portrayal of workshy men, contrasts markedly with J.B. Priestley's view of the importance of shop stewards during the War. He saw their value, acting as elected representatives of the workforce, in getting disputes settled swiftly. I can only speculate from the minutes how the stewards behaved or how my father was viewed at Andre. In 1980 however, a few days after my father died, my mother received a touching letter from the shop steward committee secretary at the British Aerospace factory in Kingston, where he then worked, describing him as "a well-liked and respected workmate" and offering a small amount of financial assistance.

Reading through the minutes, I think of various committees I sat on or chaired during an earlier career in health service management. It was often challenging to review the record of meetings, especially after someone has insisted something is "not for minuting" or has specifically declared, "I want this recorded in the minutes". How wonderful now to see my father's handwriting and almost hear his voice after so many years.

The handwriting is meticulous, cursive, neat and organised. I know virtually nothing about my father's education, other than he went to school in Hammersmith. My mother said recently he was offered a place at Pitman College, presumably after he left school at fourteen. I discovered evening classes had been held there covering accountancy and secretarial training and it is possible he may have attended, but I don't know. Something about his writing, his ability to summarise, and the absence of errors, makes me wonder if he was asked to take the minutes because of these skills. Did he make shorthand notes first, then write them up? Did he leave the notebook in a locker between meetings?

One meeting, called as an emergency in response to a payment dispute and which my father didn't attend, was minuted by someone else from the committee. This person documents events like a stream of consciousness. There are errors, basic spelling mistakes and crossings out.

Each note is signed off at the following meeting by the chair, and there is often a sentence stating the minutes were agreed by those present. Taking minutes in a tense environment would have required tact and skill, and I have a sense my father got it just right.

The Andre rubber factory was on the Kingston bypass (A3) in Tolworth. As a child in the 1970s, I remember the large metallic building which was about a quarter of a mile along the road from our house in Hook Rise South. Neighbouring factories included Plessey with a company logo like a waveform from a piece of electronic equipment, and the Gala Cosmetic factory. The rubber factory reminded me of an elongated custard cream biscuit, complete with a diamond shaped emblem. On either side of the factories were houses built in the 1930s. Tolworth had developed rapidly from a farming hamlet in the 1900s to a dense residential and industrial area by the late 1930s.

Along the road north of Andre, I remember, stood the Tolworth Tower skyscraper, which during the War had been the site of the Tolworth Odeon. In one direction from the Tower the road went to London; in the other it passed the Ministry of Agriculture and Fisheries buildings towards the factories. A turning by Andre led beyond the back streets to an arcade of shops in Chessington, where my mother would take my brother and me to buy school shoes. Blackberries grew around the wire factory fences in late summer and on Sunday mornings in September, my father and I would go to pick the fruit – especially when he went through a winemaking phase in the late 1970s. The last time I saw the factories was on a visit home during my time at university in the late 1980s. Wooden fencing surrounded the area. I remember a letter box opening near the Andre factory. Peering through at the time, I noticed there was no container in which to drop any post. I doubt anyone would have collected it anyway. Since then, the factories have long gone, replaced today with a Storage Company and an indoor climbing centre. All that remains of Andre are six white flag poles and a pedestrian subway which opens near what was once the factory's entrance.

While my father worked at Andre, he and his parents lived temporarily along the Tolworth Broadway in Ewell Road, having been bombed out of their own house. In 1939 they had moved from Hammersmith to a house along the Kingston bypass, but the house was one of four adjacent properties bombed by high explosive and oil bombs on 17 October 1940. Perhaps like others, his family had moved from the city to avoid bombs only to be bombed out elsewhere. The factories near Andre, particularly the Nash and Thompson arms works and Siebe Gorman diving equipment were themselves a target in a German bombing mission on 2 September 1940. It was not until sometime after 1948, that my father and his parents moved to the house in Hook Rise South that I knew as a child. I only know this, because among my mother's stuff I found a receipt for a very expensive television which still showed the Ewell Road address.

During the period covered in the minutes, I imagine my father cycling to and from Andre, which would have been a couple of miles from where they lived along the Tolworth Broadway – a house they shared with another family, who had also been bombed out.

The factory was due to open in 1939, but the opening was delayed as in August that year, Theodore Bernard Andre, after whom the factory would be named, died suddenly. There's a company annual report for 1940 so the factory must have opened at some point during that year – perhaps under government instruction and requisitioned for the War.

Andre Rubber was a subsidiary company of Silentbloc and during the War produced shock absorbers for aircraft instruments, rubber linings and wheels for tanks. Working at the factory at that time was a reserved occupation; a role considered essential for running the country and the war effort, and workers were generally exempt from conscription. Factories were subject to the Essential Work Order (EWO) 1941; strikes were banned, and employment and dismissal of staff strictly regulated.

Silentbloc in London focused on applications to reduce vibration in aircraft and armoured vehicles and on naval ordnance construction. Meanwhile the Andre company focused on a process where rubber is directly bonded to metal (hence the factory is also sometimes referred to as Silentbond). Andre was reportedly the largest producer of direct-bonded tank bogie wheel tyres in Great Britain. With reduced access to natural rubber due to the War in the Far East, military operations increasingly relied on synthetic rubber produced by factories such as Andre.

In 1945 between four and six hundred people worked at Andre, many of whom I imagine would be bussed-in each day from some distance. Based on advertisements in newspapers at the time, the workforce comprised skilled, semi and unskilled workers; some permanent, some temporary – both men and women.

It was Friday 4 May 1945 and my father notes that the committee met at 6 p.m. so that day and night shift stewards could meet at the end or beginning of their respective duties. The group of eight stewards, seven men and one woman gathered on a warm evening.

Those arriving for the night shift may well have seen the newspaper headlines about VE day or Very Expectant Day as it was dubbed in the *Norwood News*. There was uncertainty in the country about what would happen and when. Hitler was assumed dead, although his body had not yet been found. Prisoners of war were returning to England. There was speculation that the victory celebrations would all start over the weekend.

Not surprisingly the first item on the agenda was how workers would be informed about VE day. The committee decided that an announcement could be made over the loudspeaker during the day but given that the tannoy could not be used at night, a message would have to be put up on the noticeboard if news came through between 11 p.m. and 7 a.m. Mr Atkins representing the metal plating section, seems heated or, in a word my father often used, 'aeriated'. He is reported to have asked whether night shifts were to continue on Saturdays and had been told yes, but others in the same department had been told no.

'*That being the case,* [Mr Atkins continued] *is a worker not within his rights to refuse to come in on another Saturday night when he might have found employment elsewhere? If this firm is in such urgent need of labour, why put workers off for the night?*'

No one seemed to know what was happening.

Other items discussed that evening include backpay owed to workers since Easter and the resignation of the steward from plating.

The unrest I detect even in that first meeting increases over the following year as restrictions on employment and union activity ease after the War. By September my father concludes the minutes with what looks like the following:

'*No satisfactory conclusion to the problem having been found, the* **mutiny** *closed at 7.20 p.m.*'

MERIEL BEATTIE

Meriel Beattie is a former foreign correspondent for Reuters and the BBC. She has lived and worked in Central Europe and the Balkans, Pakistan, Turkey, Greece, Russia, and the United States.

merielbeattie@gmail.com

Ambidexter

The first chapter of a historical investigation

Let me tell you something about Turkish.

The verbs build up from suffixes: you can add all manner of things to the back of a word to indicate mood, or tense, or motion, and one of these is -*mış*. Its purpose is to infer hearsay. Pronounced *'mish' or 'mush'*, it frays at the edges of reliability. There's no direct English equivalent – you need to use 'apparently', 'seemingly' or 'supposedly'.

It's not worth getting too distracted by this as a grammatical point. But it's helpful to bear in mind, when trying to make sense of what follows.

There's a reason, I suspect, why my 1933 edition of *Ankara: Guide Touristique* is in such good condition: nobody ever used it. This is not a reflection on its author, Professor Ernest Mamboury, nor of its neatly comprehensive contents. The slim volume offers sturdy statistics, concertina maps and photographic plates. It's just that for much of the century that Ankara has been Turkey's capital, there's been little need for a guidebook. Few people visit unless they're obliged to.

'Ankara?' said a friend, on learning I would be moving there. 'I guess there are interesting places you can get to *from* there.'

Well, up to a point – and actually, for many years, even that wasn't straightforward. Until 1939 most Orient Express passengers disembarked at Istanbul. Anyone with business in the Near East crossed by ferry to the arched splendour of Hydarpaşa station and caught a train south. Ankara languished on a sluggish branch line out on the Anatolian Plateau. Even today, you can't fly direct from London.

When, in 1923, it was plucked from the chorus line of unremarkable towns for the starring role of capital, Ankara could not have been more different from Istanbul – which was precisely why Mustafa Kemal Atatürk, Turkey's founding father, chose it. Landlocked, sparse, and frowsy, it peddled none of the political promiscuity of Ottoman Constantinople. Atatürk had comelier, racier options, but Ankara was the sensible choice: an arranged marriage where the bride could be told what to do, how to look, what name to take. In its earlier life, Ankara had the more alluring name of Angora. My guidebook illustrates the fluffy goat and cat that are its matronymic heirs.

For several years after the capital was moved, foreign envoys dragged their heels about joining it. In Istanbul they worked from elegant palaces near the Golden Horn. Ankara, by contrast, looked and smelled like a building site. It had a terrible mosquito problem; wolves ran on the plateau. Worst of all, there was *simply nothing to do*. So bad was the tedium in the early days that young diplomats invented their own game of Fox and Hounds. One group ran around the scrublands, making barking or bleating noises, others on horseback pretended to hunt them down.

By the 1930s, most of the Ankara embassies and ministries were established and a racetrack, opera and even a couple of night clubs added to the town. Yet there was still no denying that a posting to Ankara lacked the cachet of Paris, the intellectual challenge of Moscow, the edging threat of Berlin, or the fragrant romance of Cairo.

But then, at the start of 1944, Ankara, the Anatolian wallflower, found itself at the centre of a spy mystery that has still not been solved. Secret documents from the British Embassy arrived in German hands. Was this treason? Theft? A Turkish plot?

Eighty years on, I re-imagine that time.

Wartime Turkey is neutral – and in Ankara, Allied and Axis diplomats, refugees and assorted hangers-on coexist in a small town, while the Turks play everyone off against each other. Britain and Germany field impressive ambassadors: both highly experienced, both aristocratic. The German is Franz von Papen, the Briton is Sir Hughe Knatchbull-Hugessen. Their embassies quickly grow.

There are two main reasons for this new importance. Firstly, each embassy wants to persuade Turkey to enter the war on its side – or at least not on the side of the enemy. It's frustrating work: the Turks agree to much, then go quiet, then let it be known they may be open to inducement. Atatürk's successor, the bristle-moustached Ismet Inönü, is skilled at selective deafness. His Prime Minister is said to be pro-Allied, his Foreign Minister pro-German. But *mish, mush, mish, mush*: who can say for certain?

The second reason is chromite, a mineral essential to manufacture weapons-grade steel. After India, Rhodesia, and the Philippines (all under Allied influence), the next best source is Turkey. When it becomes evident that Germany is getting much of its chromite from Turkey, the British devise a spectacular spoiler, contracting to buy huge stocks of chromite so the Germans cannot. But the Turkish small print proves both expensive and bizarre. Along with the chromite, the buyers must accept an eclectic selection of agricultural produce: pretty much anything where Turkey has a glut. This includes raisins, hazelnuts, and hundreds of thousands of hen's eggs. How (or if) these were ever delivered is not recorded.

Then the British are outwitted. When they attempt to prolong their monopoly, the Turks make inflated demands. London hesitates; Sir Hughe is instructed to wait. And while he does, the Germans step in and agree to everything. Shipments to Germany recommence.

As a duelling ground, Ankara feels cramped. Allied and Axis must share the same pavements, the same dental waiting rooms, tailors, and occasionally (if the railway carriage attendant has not been tipped enough), the same sleeper compartment. Formal events are awkward. Because the diplomatic language is French, *Allemagne* stands uncomfortably close in the receiving line to *Angleterre*. Where possible, the Turks use reception rooms with multiple doors: Allied envoys enter through one side, Axis diplomats via the other. But some collisions are unavoidable, as when a British diplomatic wife snags her gown on a brooch of Frau von Papen, and a neutral Turk has to decouple them.

Still, amid the claustrophobia, there are compensations. While much of the world endures rationing, abundant pleasures can still be bought in Ankara. Coffee, silk lingerie, butter, sugar, milk – and of course there is that glut of eggs. What isn't on the open market can usually be obtained through other, tacit, means. The embassies' Turkish servants mostly know each other; many are related. So the whisky in the German ambassador's drinks cabinet comes from the house of his British counterpart, who in turn can offer a nice crisp hock to senior visitors.

One such visitor arrives in January 1944.

Short, mild-faced and with an improbably low side parting, the man getting off the train at Ankara looks boyish, yet also older than his forty-eight years. He is Sir John Dashwood, Tenth Baronet Dashwood, deputy head of security at the Foreign Office.

From society page photographs I've seen of his pre-war doings at Cowes or Ascot, it's clear that 'Johnny' Dashwood was a tasteful dresser. So when, 80 years later, I gaze along the Ankara station platform, I visualise a well-cut coat and expensive gloves. Met by an Embassy chauffeur, Dashwood must pass through the grand, if slightly pointless station portico to reach the waiting car.

I take a taxi. But with my *Guide Touristique* and a sellotaped 1940s map on my lap, I can reconjure Dashwood's route.

With its four flat lanes neatly hemmed by broad, new pavements, Çankaya Boulevard in 1944 is tailored for the metropolis Ankara hopes to become. A grand avenue through a backward village, it's wide enough to accommodate the broad, American-style cars that are fashionable in this young Republic – a fit too tight for most Istanbul roads. But since Ankara is *not* Istanbul in wealth or style, there are few such vehicles to enjoy it.

To reach the British Embassy, Dashwood's car must cross the administrative part of the capital, a calm, clean district where, in the 1940s, police keep the sellers of lottery tickets, maize cobs and cigarettes at bay. Behind infant hedges and railings too new for rust, stretches the new row of embassies: Yugoslav, Hungarian, Italian, and Russian, each an idealised caricature of domestic design. The German compound, grouped around orderly gardens, resembles the civic offices of a provincial Westphalian town, rather than a nation at war.

Just beyond the Germans, Dashwood's car starts to climb into the hilly district of Çankaya. On the left, tangled up in its neglected garden, lies the empty Polish Embassy. Next comes the Czechoslovak one, now requisitioned to accommodate von Papen. The facade of this stolen villa is smooth and elegant in an Art Deco style. But this serenity is deceptive: two years earlier, an assassin (some say Macedonian, some say Bulgarian) tried to throw a bomb at von Papen here. The ambassador escaped with just a perforated eardrum and torn trousers. What remained of the assassin had to be tugged down from a nearby tree, his bomb having apparently gone off in his hands. This sort of crude violence was quite frequent in other wartime capitals, but in neutral, provincial Ankara, it was unusual.

As Dashwood's car rounds the last curve, the placid, whitewashed front of the British Embassy comes into view. It's chillier here, yet for the British there are advantages. The Turkish President and Prime Minister live a short stroll away: handy for the convivial *tête-a-tête* diplomacy at which Sir Hughe excels. Up here one is also above the dung-coloured fumes that blanket the lower town when the Turks burn lignite. The saplings planted in the embassy garden have come on well. There's even a tennis court, and an almost-level lawn.

But when Dashwood alights on the driveway, the garden is a mess. A higgledy-piggledy hamlet of empty wooden huts obscures what's left of the grass. Until a few days before Dashwood's arrival, these huts housed a British military mission. This hoped to persuade Turkey to stretch its already elastic neutrality so as to allow RAF planes to use its airfields. Negotiations began well, but as the months passed, the Turks prevaricated, obfuscated, and delayed. Patience exhausted, Whitehall cancelled the mission and recalled its senior negotiator.

Which has at least left the nicest embassy guest bedroom free for Dashwood.

Foreign Office papers show that Sir Hughe Knatchbull-Hugessen and Sir John Dashwood met several times, but if there's a photograph of them together, I haven't found it. Both are from noble families. Both were dispatched early to boarding school, where they were found to be clever. Both went to Oxford. Both married beautiful women whom others find 'difficult'. Both realise that their aristocratic lineage is of limited practical use.

Despite the nuance of privilege conferred by that elegantly obsolete -*e* at the end of his first name, and the need-to-read-it-twice challenge of his second, Sir Hughe Knatchbull-Hugessen needs to earn his living. The second son of a second son, his family is a humbler tributary of a wealthy one. His uncle might be Baron Brabourne, but his father is a vicar.

Sir John Dashwood, by contrast, is a first son, inheriting at twelve the Dashwood baronetcy and the gaudy Palladian mansion that goes with it. Shortly before arriving in Ankara, however, Dashwood has signed this property over to a new organisation, the National Trust. He realises that post-war Britain cannot furnish the servants required to keep it going. He never much cared for it, anyway.

Both men work for the Foreign Office: Sir John because he wants to, Sir Hughe because he has to. Both are respected for their judgement and amiability. Yet Sir Hughe has some things that Sir John does not.

One is a Japanese bullet wound in his back.

Another is the burden of the hushed-up suicide of his only, lonely son.

Another is a dependence on a strong sedative.

This may, or may not, be chloral hydrate, which killed his son. It might also be the key to one of the more bizarre spy stories of the Second World War.

Mish, mush, mish, mush.
It's this mystery that Dashwood, and I, would like to solve.

CHARLES BLISS

Charles Bliss is a writer and journalist reporting on the scientific, political and cultural impact of psychedelic compounds. His fiction has appeared in magazines including *Ambit* and *Aesthetica*. Charles is writing a creative non-fiction book about The Beatles, psychedelics and death. He lives in Norwich, UK.

charles@charlesbliss.com

Eyes Wide Shut

A chapter from a creative non-fiction book

On a summer afternoon, I exit the Elizabeth Line station and walk towards Woolwich Public Market in a state of sonder — tuned in to the notion that every passerby is living a life as vivid and complex as my own. I am welcomed into the venue with the peal of a QR code scanner before being asked to stow away my backpack, shoes and smartphone in a small locker. I step into a holding space with twenty other people, who slink down onto the red carpet or balance on accordion benches made of brown paper. We sit, excited yet subdued, before the closed doors of an imposing wooden structure painted with cerulean whorls — and we wait. We are about to plug into the Dreamachine.

Inside, the space is reminiscent of a planetarium. The pink ceiling, green drapery and blue carpet create a gradient of colour and texture into which we are shepherded before being invited to relax on a loop of reclined, cushioned seating. We are given our flight instructions: position yourself between two speakers built into the headrest; decibel levels will reach no higher than a night club; drugs and alcohol are strictly prohibited; you can leave at any time, with no judgement; seek assistance by waving your hands. Staff also provide reassurance that we go through the experience as a collective, even if we arrived alone, as I have. Though we're in it together, we are reminded that each person's experience in the Dreamachine is unique to them and irreproducible. Blankets and eye masks are provided — the masks intended to terminate the visions if they become too intense. I take a deep breath.

As the music washes into my awareness and the first flickering commences, I feel claustrophobic. My heart rate increases and body temperature spikes. But the blush of anxiety disintegrates as my mind is eaten by a kaleidoscope. Geometric shapes warp and dissolve, flash and transform, scintillate and collide, throb and recede. Spiderwebs of golden electricity, exploding clouds, shattering sunbeams, vortexes, fractals, haloes — I see it all in the Dreamachine. But in what sense can I *see* it, if my eyes are closed?

The Dreamachine is an immersive multisensory experience that uses light and sound to conjure a technicolour dreamworld in the space behind our eyes. The contraption was conceived by artist-inventor Brion Gysin and electronics technician Ian Sommerville in 1959.

Gysin was born at the Canadian military hospital in Taplow, Buckinghamshire in 1916. Just eight months later Gysin's father, Leonard, was killed in action while serving as a captain with the Canadian Expeditionary Force. In 1934, Gysin studied painting at the Sorbonne in Paris where he became associated with the Surrealist Group. After serving in World War II, Gysin moved to Morocco and met the American writer William S. Burroughs. The two men began a lifelong friendship and artistic collaboration in which they developed and popularised 'the cut-up technique' — an aleatory creative form whereby words, texts or media are spliced, rearranged and reassembled to reveal new, juxtaposing, often serendipitous and surprising meanings.

In the winter of 1958, Gysin was overcome by 'a transcendental storm of colour visions' while traveling on a bus to Marseilles. 'We ran through a long avenue of trees and I closed my eyes against the setting sun,' he wrote in his diary. 'An overwhelming flood of intensely bright colours exploded behind my eyelids... I was swept out of time. I was out in a world of infinite number. The vision stopped abruptly as we left the trees. Was that a vision? What happened to me?'[1]

Burroughs proffered an explanation after reading *The Living Brain* by neurophysiologist W. Grey Walter. The scientist had employed electroencephalogram (EEG) equipment, which measures electrical activity in the brain via electrodes attached to the scalp, to study how flickering lights affect brainwave frequencies and therefore states of consciousness. Walter claimed that a flicker rate of eight to thirteen pulses of light per second would create a stroboscopic effect that, when projected onto closed eyes, stimulated the same 'alpha rhythms' that occur during rapid eye movement (REM) sleep when most dreams occur. Burroughs concluded that, as the bus drove past, the rhythm of the sun's crepuscular rays knifing through the trees — what Dylan Thomas called 'windfall light', what C.S. Lewis called 'Godlight' and what the Japanese call 'komorebi' — had provoked Gysin's spontaneous visionary experience.

Through Burroughs, Gysin was introduced to Ian Sommerville — a mathematician, sound engineer and computer programmer who was in a relationship with the *Naked Lunch* author. Born in 1940, Sommerville was a precocious working-class child who grew up in the industrial town of Darlington and won a scholarship to study mathematics at Jesus College, Cambridge. He met Burroughs during a summer trip to Paris and the two lovers lived at the Beat Hotel in the Latin Quarter, where Sommerville administered apomorphine injections to Burroughs during a detox for codeine addiction. Sommerville drew upon his university education to programme a random-sequence generator for the cut-up method and worked with Gysin to make the Dreamachine a reality. Gysin described Sommerville as 'skinny and quick as an alleycat with bristly red hair that stuck up all over in pre-punk style. He was crisper than cornflakes and sharp as a tack. He crackled and snapped with static electricity and panicked at the idea of rain on his hair.'[2]

In 1966, Barry Miles, owner of Indica Bookshop and Gallery on Mason's Yard

1 Gysin, Brion, Wilson, Terry, *Here to Go: Planet R-101* (London: Quartet Books, 1985)
2 Burroughs, William S., Gysin, Brion, *The Final Academy: Statements of a Kind* (London: The Final Academy, 1982)

in London[3], recommended that Sommerville fill a tape operator vacancy at Paul McCartney's new demo studio in Marylebone where avant-garde musicians, poets and other innovators could record and exchange experimental tracks. McCartney, Sommerville and Miles discussed the project over dinner and dope. 'In the course of a pleasant evening, Ian explained the principles of free-floating equations and the mechanics of producing hallucinations using flickering lights,' Miles wrote. 'Paul said Ian was clearly the man for the job.'[4]

The studio was installed in Ringo Starr's empty flat at 34 Montagu Square — two Revox A77 reel-to-reel machines, microphones, speakers, tape stock and a mixing desk in a converted basement with purple wallpaper and silk curtains. Except for McCartney, Burroughs was the most dedicated frequenter of the new studio. The Beatle and Beat writer had met at Indica when Burroughs was living on Duke Street, just around the corner from the counterGultural arts institution. In the studio, Burroughs witnessed McCartney writing 'Eleanor Rigby' — a song about the death of a lonely spinster. 'I saw him there several times,' Burroughs said. 'He'd just come in and work on his 'Eleanor Rigby'. Ian recorded his rehearsals so I saw the song taking shape.'[5] Provisional lyrics for the song featured a man 'blowing his mind in the dark' and smoking 'a pipe full of clay' — a possible reference to Burroughs. Though these lines were replaced in the final composition, his influence on The Beatles is evident in the band's use of collage, found sound and tape cut-ups, as well as the decision to include his image on the album cover of *Sgt. Pepper's Lonely Hearts Club Band* alongside other figures including Aldous Huxley, Karlheinz Stockhausen, Carl Jung, Sri Paramahansa Yogananda, Marlene Dietrich and Lewis Carroll. 'William did some little cut-ups and we did some crazy tape recordings in the basement,' McCartney said. 'We used to sit around talking about all these amazing inventions that people were doing; areas that people were getting into like the Dream Machine [sic] that Ian and Brion Gysin had made.'[6]

The Dreamachine was unveiled at the Musée des Arts Decoratifs, Paris in 1962. The original technology comprised a perforated cylinder enveloping a suspended lightbulb, which rotated on a turntable at seventy-eight revolutions per minute to meet Walter's requisite cycle of light. It was designed to be 'the first art object to be seen with the eyes closed'. The frequency and pattern of light dancing off shut eyelids elicited eidetic[7] visual stimuli and induced a trance-like state in the viewer. Gysin hoped that a mass-produced Dreamachine in every home might supplant drugs and television as popular forms of escapism and passive image consumption,

---

3   The bookshop and gallery was named in reference to the psychoactive plant *Cannabis Indica*.
4   Miles, Barry, *Paul McCartney: Many Years from Now* (London: Secker & Warburg, 1997) p239
5   Miles, p241
6   Miles, p242
7   From the Greek *eidētikos*, which is derived from *eidesis* (knowledge) and *eidos* (shape or form), the term eidetic relates to or denotes mental or projected images that have unusual vividness and detail, as if they are actually visible.

awakening humankind from its cultural catatonia and enlightening us to the awesome power of perceptual diversity. This utopian enterprise never came to pass.

But in 2022, artistic director Jennifer Crook resurrected the Dreamachine as part of a nationwide festival titled Unboxed: Creativity in the UK. The government objective invested £120 million to celebrate British innovation and stimulate tourism in the wake of Brexit and the COVID-19 pandemic. Created by Collective Act in collaboration with artists, technologists, scientists and philosophers, the Unboxed tour of the Dreamachine offered visitors in London, Cardiff, Belfast and Edinburgh the opportunity to access free transcendental experiences without mind-altering chemicals. The *Guardian* wrote that the exhibition, which replaced the rotating cylinder with a series of micro-controlled LED lights accompanied by a wraparound soundscape from electronic musician Jon Hopkins, was 'as close to state-funded psychedelic drugs as you can get'.[8]

This is why I am here: to dilate my vantage point, to disturb these ingrained thought patterns, to shake the snow globe. As I sit under the strobes, the most fantastic figment appears before me: an undulating black and white chevron pattern erupting with fountains of rainbows. Inside it I somehow experience a manifestation of string theory — the idea from theoretical physics that reality is composed of infinitesimal vibrating strings, smaller than atoms, electrons or quarks. I feel powerless yet peaceful, overwhelmed yet overjoyed. The tempo of this influx *a prestissimo* of these 'eyelid movies', to borrow Tom Wolfe's phrase, reminds me of 'Jupiter and Beyond the Infinite' — the climactic sequence from Stanley Kubrick's *2001: A Space Odyssey* where the journey to a new dimension collapses the mind in spasms of blistering colours and flumes of light.

When the Dreamachine shuts off, the phosphenes are rinsed away like mandalas of coloured sand poured into the river. I enter the integration space and scratch an interpretation of my hallucinations onto black paper with coloured chalk before recording reflections into a tablet, which generates a digital simulacrum. But the representation does no justice to the lived experience. The word *ineffable* comes to mind. I melt into an orange beanbag chair for a time before pushing through the door, decanted into the midsummer sunlight.

In the afterglow, I find myself wondering: Why is my experience unique to me and not replicable by someone else despite the same stimulus? How can we see things that are not in physical space? How might these transcendental, visionary experiences help us understand the nature of consciousness? Do we share an objective reality or does each brain create our world differently? This carnival of light had ruptured my body of experience and left exit wounds where previous modes of perception and assumptions about the limits of the mind escaped — and fertile, yawning avenues were now open for new material to enter.

8   Jones, Jonathan, 'Dreamachine review – as close to state-funded psychedelic drugs as you can get,' *Guardian*, 9 May 2022 www.theguardian.com/artanddesign/2022/may/09/dreamachine-review-as-close-to-state-funded-psychedelic-drugs-as-you-can-get#:~:text=Well%2C%20almost.,trip%20inside%20your%20own%20head [Accessed 15 March 2024]

PENELOPE CODRINGTON

Penelope Codrington was born in the UK and moved to Barbados when she was nine. She earned her undergraduate and law degrees at Harvard. She writes about parenting and her family history, drawing on her experiences as a single mother and a descendant of people enslaved by the Anglican Church.

pennyelise@gmail.com

Thanksgiving in Moscow 2014

An extract from a memoir

On the day before Thanksgiving in 2014, I traveled to Moscow to visit a man I'd met online. That year I lived with my three sons in a craftsman bungalow on a quiet street near Rock Creek Park in Washington DC. Bushes of pink tea roses bloomed from spring through fall in the front garden, but I rarely sat in the wooden rocker on the porch and admired them. Sometimes when I was rushing up the steps to the house, I longed to linger, inhaling their fragrance, but there was always a child who needed attention: help with homework, a comforting cuddle, a loving reprimand.

I used to tell my sons to calm their bodies when they threw temper tantrums or ran amok at bedtime, but mine was never at rest. At the end of each workday, I hustled from meetings in my office to the metro station, so eager to get home and check on my children that I raced down the steps from surface to tunnel. On weekends I squeezed the boys into our red Prius and deposited them at baseball practices, orchestra rehearsals, birthday parties and bar mitzvahs. Waiting outside, I'd read work documents until a child tapped on the car windows, exhausted and ready to be chauffeured home.

One hot June day, my ex-husband drove to DC from his home in New York, our estrangement abandoned in the face of our parental fears. Yelling 'Black Lives Matter', we marched down Pennsylvania Avenue with thousands of other families protesting police brutality. Adults on the ends, the three boys between us, connected by our clasped hands like a paper cutout of a family, we walked by rows of armed officers, keeping our eyes on the snipers visible on nearby roofs. Red-faced people waving Confederate flags shouted obscenities from roped-off areas on the sidewalks. My children flinched and I regretted bringing them.

The next month, on July 17, a man named Eric Garner was choked to death by a New York policeman. Then on August 9, an officer named Darren Wilson killed an unarmed teenager, Michael Brown, in Ferguson, Missouri. Every night after I tucked the boys into their beds, I searched the internet to see whether these officers would be indicted.

October arrived and I was standing in the checkout line at Costco, purchasing a pumpkin for the boys to carve on Halloween, when I received a message on a dating app. The man, K, introduced himself, saying that he worked in Moscow but was attending a conference in DC. That night at a club in Takoma Park, we danced to go-go, DC's signature funk. As we edged our way into the crowd, seeking a place in front of the stage, the horns were yelping like exclamation points come to life. The bass, snare and hi-hat put down the core beat while the congas and cowbells prinked the rhythm. Hyping the audience which yelled responses to his calls, the front man, his face dripping with sweat, was sending people into a frenzy. Everywhere we looked, folks were dancing and hollering:

'It don't mean a thing if it don't have that go-go swing!'

K was tall, dark brown and shea butter shiny. Dressed in jeans and a tailored shirt, he radiated what my Bajan aunt called 'good brought-upsy'. I initiated a quick round of Negro Geography on the phone from a bathroom stall, kee-keeing as my girlfriends worked our network. Within a few minutes they found someone who studied with him at Wharton and vouched for his bona fides.

As we caught our breath over drinks, he winked, showing off his thick lashes, and perhaps jokingly, invited me to visit. My swift response surprised us both.

'Thanksgiving week OK for you?'

He guffawed, handing me a card from an expediter who sorted my visa.

The timing of this adventure was providential. The boys were to celebrate the holiday with their father and Aeroflot offered an affordable direct flight from Dulles Airport. I imagined a romantic vacation wandering in a storied city. My girlfriends worried about my safety, their concerns stemming from a *Washington Post* article describing protests in Moscow due to Russia's annexation of Crimea in March 2014, and a blog on *AtlantaBlackStar.com*, which deemed Moscow one of the eight worst cities for Black people to visit. A few weeks later, as I disembarked at Sheremetyevo Airport, I thought of my friends saying 'Remember you are a mother' and hoped I would not regret my decision.

Easy to spot among the White people waiting outside baggage claim, K danced over, almost knocking me down with his hug as he sang 'Woman! I am so happy you are here!' in *basso profondo*. Grabbing my luggage, he led me to a Black Mercedes idling outside the terminal. As I greeted his driver, a young Russian named Sergei, I shivered in the cold, no longer pondering why my November fare was so inexpensive.

Sergei opened the back door, barely giving us enough time to slide in and buckle our seatbelts, before he whipped the car around and sped away from the airport. He forced his way through the busy highway by manoeuvering around slower cars, dashing from lane to lane like a deranged downhill skier racing down a crowded slope. When he was not cursing at the traffic shouting 'Fuck, fuck, fuck!' he was yelling what sounded like 'Bleck, bleck, bleck!'

'He's saying *blyad*,' K explained. 'It means "whore" but they use it as a swear, like the F word.'

He laughed at my squinched face: 'Women say it too!'

After Sergei stopped the car and announced our arrival, he turned around and glared at me.

'What is happening in fucking Ferguson?' he said. 'Why you Americans let the police kill that man unpunished?'

I gasped at the news. He was referring to the Missouri grand jury's decision not to indict Darren Wilson for the murder of Michael Brown. The pronouncement had been issued as I slept in the clouds above the Atlantic. Suddenly desperate to leave the warm car, I grabbed the door handle and stepped on to the icy sidewalk. I felt grateful for the mind-numbing chill.

K lived in the penthouse of a newly-renovated building in Moscow's center. I clapped my hands when I saw floor-to-ceiling windows stretching the length of the apartment. Smiling at my delight, he pointed at the onion-domed church steeples sandwiched between pastel residences. Smoke poured from distant industrial chimney stacks and a line of steel skyscrapers, loomed over the landscape like robots in disguise, preparing to unfurl and stomp through the city during the night. The foggy grayish sky hung low above it all.

That first day K insisted that I sleep and left for work. Upon his return, the sound system, activated by his door key, blasted Shep & the Limelites singing 'Daddy's Home'. Pushing an image of my girlfriends rolling their eyes out of my head, I accepted the flowers he offered.

The next day K warned me against going out alone.

'It's not safe for us Black people. What would I tell your children if anything happened?'

Shepherding me through byzantine subway stations and along freezing boulevards, he helped me bargain in a giant flea market, chasing away a vendor trying to sell a T-shirt featuring Putin karate-kicking Obama in the head.

Alas, there was no love affair. K determined I was not his type. I pretended his decision was mutual but each night lying next to him, listening to him breathe, I hoped he would change his mind on waking, although I knew in my heart we were not compatible. He continued to be a kind host serving my breakfast on a tray. Sometimes while he worked at his desk, I sat on the floor in the living room wrapped in a quilt, watching the clouds roll back, buildings taking shape out of the mist, and the city dwellers emerging from their homes.

My sons texted me, raving about their epic seven-hour Monopoly games with Dad or boasting about their Thanksgiving meal. I imagined their father, answering questions like 'Why did the police kill this kid Tamir last week? Is it true he was twelve... like me?' He got to comfort them after their nightmares. He got to wake with a start from his own. Would he allow the six-foot teenager to walk to the movies on a dark evening with his high school friends? Did he say 'yes' when our fourth-grade son asked for a nerf gun? I missed my children but took perverse delight in knowing that, for once, the ex-husband had to struggle with these decisions instead of me.

Sometimes I turned on the television and saw CNN reports about the Ferguson unrest sparked by the grand jury's decision. People crying, fires burning; America appeared a hellscape. Christiane Amanpour stood in front of an angry crowd.

'Doesn't she cover wars?' I thought.

Picturing myself looking away from the television and staring out the apartment windows, I am reminded of my dog Max. He is a coonhound who refuses to turn and face me, when he does not want to leave the garden.

One morning we visited a cluttered chapel in Red Square where a stocky priest chanted and bowed in front of icons of Mary as clouds of incense swirled. Old ladies in fur coats surrounded him, mouthing prayers as they nodded in imitation of their leader. Impressed, I whispered my own incantation seeking to claim some of this foreign religious protection for my sons. I knew that back home Black moms were attempting to ward the evil away by adorning their children with amulets of the hand of Fatima or the Nazar, or tying pungent herbal potions wrapped in cheesecloth around small necks, or muttering prayers each time their babies left the house:

'God before you, God behind you, God beneath you, God beside you.'

On my last day, we went to see Alexander Pushkin's imposing statue in Pushkinskaya Square. I gazed at his stone face and imagined the bravery of this African descendant, opposing serfdom's horrors. I thought of his poem 'Ode to Liberty' in which he bemoaned twisted laws and misused powers. Suddenly, I remembered the Pushkin monument in DC at the corner of H and 22nd Streets. I could feel my heart beating fast and then I smelled the roses growing in front of my house as though I were there, standing on my porch. Despite the cold my body started to sweat and tremble and I bent over, overcome by a sense of impending danger.

I sobbed loudly that evening, destroying any chance of receiving an invitation back to Moscow for my bewildered host looked on in horror.

'Are you in pain? Was your food bad?'

Wailing, I collapsed on his bed, scaring both of us with my outburst.

All the way to the airport the next morning, as the car stopped and started in the sluggish morning traffic, I sniffled and the men exchanged glances in the rear-view mirror. Tears flowed again when we arrived at the bright terminal where K bid me a swift goodbye. He sprinted like Usain for the exit, never to be heard from again.

I imagine he thought my sorrowing sprang from his rejection. It is true that when I sank into the plane seat, I longed for the stillness of our week in the apartment despite its location in frigid Moscow. But as I sat there examining my soul, I recognized that the sadness taking over my body was not due to any feelings for a stranger. No, I was crying because I was convinced there was nothing I could do to protect my children at school, on the street, in the park or at home, despite exhausting vigilance, and I was terrified. I shuddered as I imagined the wall of insurmountable forces pressing down on all Black children. After saying a prayer for Michael Brown's mother, I steeled myself for reentry.

'Spirit of Pushkin be with me,' I whispered as the wheels left the tarmac, and then as we rose above the clouds…

'*Blyad. Blyad!*'

HAZEL COTTEY

Hazel lives in London and studied English and Theatre Arts at Goldsmiths. She was born in Bath to a Malaysian mother, her father was a hoarder. Through her occupation, she discovered the extent of hoarding as a growing modern problem. Her writing explores this and other self-destructive behaviours and their paradoxical relationships with hope.

hazel.cottey@gmail.com

Aubade

An extract from a non-fiction novel

The clock ticks and ticks its awful forever, each tick as long as a match being struck. Alex is sleeping, loudly. I plead into the rumbling darkness for him to stop. Stickily and full of spit, his mouth mumbles something in agreement, but almost at once he starts up again. At first, it's just a whine, almost tuneful; it rises in volume and pitch to the high reedy note of someone blowing on a blade of grass. I try to smooth the tension from my brow with my fingertips, but I cannot shut out the noise. The wet flesh in his nose and throat is vibrating.

There is nothing for it but to have a drink. Absolutely nothing else to be done. Though I have no actual desire for one, the idea has popped into my head as the only route to sleep. I know it is not the only way, that even no sleep would be better, but knowing it is a terrible idea is part of the draw and so my body is getting out of bed and moving towards the door. Trying not to creak the stairs, I crouch over and step with high knees like a pantomime baddie. Driven by something I do not understand, I descend into the kitchen. The moonlight through the garden doors lights the silent setting.

This wasn't the first night like this: they were starting to become a bit too regular. I might sneak downstairs a few times, pour out a drink, then return to bed in the hope sleep would visit; the night's endlessness stretching out before me until the percussive tinkle of bottles in their crates announced the milkman's arrival. His float moving down the conveyor belt of our road, his boots on our steps. Today the bin men arrive right on cue, the high-pitched panic of the van's hydraulic engine, pistons whirring, the waterfall of things thudding towards their end.

One of the children jumps out of the top bunk and crashes down the stairs. The opportunity for sleep before it is time for school is diminishing. Deeply drawing in air to fill my lungs, I push the breath back down through my chest, all the way into my feet. This, and the tone of a jet engine tunnelling through the clouds towards Heathrow, bring today's aubade to a close.

Ten minutes later, I wake with a start. The feeling of someone bearing down on me. The morning is staring me hard in the face. My mouth is stale-bread dry. Alex is asleep next to me, his head under a pillow, a soup of saliva pooled at his mouth. The faint blare of the TV can be heard downstairs. No one knows the events of the night. There is still time to fix this.

I had read that microdosing psychedelics could initiate behaviour change – someone knew someone who could procure psilocybin-steeped rum. Stashed in my bedroom, I rummage around for the tiny spray bottle, take the cap off and spray it, three times, into my mouth. It reaches every crevice: the back of my tongue, in between my lips and teeth. The taste is especially poisonous. Instantly I know I am in trouble.

I hurry through the action of breakfast and plait my daughter's hair. Alex is up and shuffling about, he will take them to school. Once I wave them out of the door, I feel marginally more relaxed, but it's not long until the skin on my face starts to fall in folds. I want a shower but cannot face seeing my body. When I summon up the courage, the water is too cold and too hot. In the bathroom, the plants' colours look at me urgently; I hold their gaze until it is too awkward. The relief is so liberating that I feel a breeze whistle through my head. Avoiding the mirror, I wrap myself in a towel and scuttle down the stairs past the pink strip light that is hanging from its twisted guts at the wall. Splayed flat on my back on the bed, I put an eye mask on, pull a thin sheet over me like a shroud and hope mindful breathing will get me through. The wimp in me starts to panic. I want out but know that I need to let my mind swim freely in the lurid spa of images that are blurring and contorting. I must relax. Aberrations of cats and animals with the hallmarks of dragons morph into one another until I have to sit up and take off my mask. Without it, the bedroom is grainy.

Alex's voice is coming out of the phone. He is not going to work after drop-off. He is coming home and wants to play tennis. He is speaking words about sex. I must regain my composure and divert him from these plans, so I clumsy downstairs to make tea. The cup is slippery, an eel that wriggles from my grip back into the ocean of the sink. I fish it out and am so focused on pouring the boiling water in carefully that I forget the tea bag. When I try again, brown water oozes at its base. I peer at it closely and diagnose a fracture, tip it out, have a third go. There is no time. I am yet to peak, and he will soon be here. These two things cannot collide.

He arrives, angular and yellow. He wants to play tennis – or worse. I back off, muttering 'headache' and run to the bedroom. I sense something earthy and furred. I can feel it in my teeth, glimpse it in my peripheral vision. White noise fizzes a pitch too high to be calming and textures river and shift. I have been transported to a place that has undertones of the familiar. Someone is here. Maybe it is me? Wearing a dressing gown and socks in a bedsit littered with fags in the bleached yellowed vortex of staying up too long; when the drugs overstay their welcome and don't leave. Like that random person still asleep on the sofa, long after the party is over.

Even though I have not chosen this destination, I arrive in an antechamber, a long dawn of cigarettes and illness and lighter gas. Charon has made a terrible mistake and I need to convince him to row me back over the Styx to the land of the living. But in the waiting room there is nothing to do but wait. The bedroom is washed out, everything starts to degenerate into a primitive computer game, digitised and granular.

'Come on, let's play!' Alex's war cry shakes me up but the thought that tennis balls are yellow provides comfort. I open the computer to birth these words out through the pores in my fingertips into the keys. But the screen is pixelated – just the black and white fuzz of an analogue TV long after the channels have stopped airing programmes.

I start rummaging in drawers but forget what for and realise that I am sifting for the act itself; wonder if it might even distract whatever it is that is coming. I'm caught in surges of intensity and must stop and look away. But if I want to give it the slip, I should keep busy.

Up comes the call again that he's ready to play. Another surge. I am losing the pre-match. There is a break between contractions, a shaft of light in which I become curious if I could play and have an inkling that rising to the challenge of going outside might provide some health benefits. I try sorting laundry to build my confidence, but I can only make sad, slumped piles — an installation of failure.

Carried by an abstract conversation, we leave the house without Alex noticing the state I am in. I sit on the child seat on his bike and he rides us towards the courts. Yes! I am a child – maybe even a baby – looking at the world for the first time. I try to process the ways in which everything outside is so interesting. Why have I never noticed before? I start to become proud of how well I am taking this news. Witchy, green-haired women with oversized Toby jug mug-heads wobble down the street. Perspective and colour are no longer reliable friends. The slant of the trees in the park concerns me.

Alex seems to have absolutely no idea that I am in the grip of a strong trip. My hold around the handle of the racket is philosophical. I am unsure of my feet on the ground or why the ruddiness of his cheeks has spread across the sky. Yet the landscape is separated into distinct layers of flat colours: the ground, the middle, the sky. Dangerously leaning trees are felted on and the peculiar, green-fingered quality of their branches piques my interest. I watch us with a wide-angle gaze. It is absurd that Alex is so focused on tennis when there is all of this to see.

He is angry with me for wasting time and, although I think I am only clearing the court of a potentially dangerous ball, I cannot be sure who is right here. I must hide my face from him, so he doesn't see that I am laughing each time he pulls his elbow into his side with a clenched fist in celebratory fashion. The laughter is sewing me back into the tapestry. It is as essential as air.

'C'mon, for fuck's sake, stop trying to psyche me out!'

The anger is making stumps of his legs. He is becoming a long-bodied goose hissing and waggling around the court.

'Stop wasting time. Always have a ball in your pocket! I know you and your mind games. You're doing this on purpose!'

Another game to me and he is swearing and whacking balls out of the court, sometimes missing and rattling the cage. It is all so cartoonish that I cannot take it seriously. The thin thatch of his hair at the front stands up like a limp exclamation mark, making another janky line in my already slanty world.

He wins a game and in comes his celebratory elbow to just above his hip again, the full stop of a fist at the end of a forearm makes another exclamation mark! But this time it is accompanied by a bent knee like a winner at Wimbledon. I scuttle over to clear a ball from by the net, concerned it is a trip hazard while trying to hold the threads of reality together. In my jogging bottoms, I feel puffy and slow but somehow I am hitting the ball, returning it, nicking it into the back corner and with each point I enrage him more. His serves are getting angrier. Often, they are out. But I think it is better not to say.

I could be wearing socks and a dressing gown in a faggy bedsit, but I am hitting the balls that are appearing in front of me like sudden UFOs and returning them as messengers of peace. He is unamused, and I cannot decide if he is more yellow or purple. His head is becoming larger and open mouthed in a scream that has escaped from a comic with symbols coming out for swear words. The air is heavy and pregnant like it is about to rain, and I wonder whether it already is but remind myself not to ask. It is so fucking good to be out in the air and not have the wicker basket inching towards me like a Chinese dragon as I swim in the grainy sea of my bed. I decide not to tell him that what he sees is not actually real.

RAVIAKASH DEU

Raviakash Deu is a Birmingham and Norwich based writer. He graduated in English Literature from The University of Nottingham and completed a short course in Narrative Non-Fiction at City University. His current work delves into Punjab's vibrant cultural heritage to explore themes of love, identity and belonging within a British-Indian context.

raviakash.deu@gmail.com

Single Chaffa

An extract from the third chapter of a novel

Backstage, Madhuri was offering a kind of eyeliner or *soorma* service for those who, already clad in their traditional Bhangra costumes, now sought the final flourish. One of the boys in Vihara's team had borrowed his mum's equipment, but believing this route to be safer, not to mention the added bonus of being touched, or at least painted on, by a beautiful girl, he joined the line. Vihara was already with Bhumi, but after two years together she had started to appear as unexceptional to him as he did to himself. By contrast, Madhuri's facial symmetry reminded him of those Asiana models from the magazines his mum collected. Except she had not been airbrushed; every feature from her almond eyes with their look of wild innocence, to her high cheekbones and bow-shaped lips, was astonishingly real.

Then came all the exquisite finery demanded by this distinctly Punjabi occasion: a golden crown, or *Saggi Phull*, which he would remember for the way it accentuated her similarly gleaming complexion. And a colourful *vardi,* in which Madhuri appeared so comfortable, he suspected she was in some way responsible for its design. As he waited, Vihara imagined her passing hours on the phone to Preet of *Preet's boutique i*n Ludhiana, discussing which fabrics or *kapra* might work best in the ensemble: at this stage worried less about the exorbitant cost of the outfits than them being shipped to the UK on time – if at all. To her relief the package would arrive safely and having tried on each garment, she would finally hand them over to her Indian tailor in Wembley for alteration.

'Look down for me,' Madhuri said softly, drawing the black pencil to his right upper lid.

'That was light work!' he exclaimed a few moments later. But he had spoken too soon because she was yet to tackle the lower lash line.

She moved in again with the instrument when Vihara's eyes began to water. It was not the last time that evening which he would remember as the lowest point in his dance career.

'I thought you said, "light work",' she jested, handing him a tissue.

She allowed him a few seconds to compose himself, then finished off the procedure.

'Anyway,' she said, 'best of luck on stage today, I'm sure you'll do great – who are you dancing for by the way?'

'Thanks, and you,' he responded, and with an unmistakeable sense of pride, 'I'm Gabroo Shokeen.'

Three years later he would meet her again: this time, in the off-season. Madhuri was running some open classes for the public on behalf of her team, *Chakdey*, at a mirrored exercise studio with vinyl flooring, not far from Fulham station. The space held around fifteen people after all the dumbbells and yoga equipment had been cleared away. Sometimes, a few more showed up and everyone had to be careful not to overdo a *chaffa* kick-out or a *phumniya* waddle. Until the video recordings at the end where it became every man and woman, or *Bhangrachi* for themselves.

Madhuri always chose at that juncture to stand on the side-lines and keep count, or shout-out the moves over the music. Vihara once probed her about it.

'Why don't you jump in?' he said nervously. 'It's your choreo, after all.

'No, no,' she responded – attaching her phone to a complex-looking camera stick. 'You execute it much better than I do.'

It wasn't really a compliment but an excuse for her timidness which seemed to him, at other times, to contradict her more assertive nature. Vihara had glimpsed both sides of her through their limited interactions here over the past month: the ten minutes spent waiting downstairs while the Salsa dancers were wrapping up, or the two or three short water breaks she allowed during the sessions. Then afterwards, a small group of them would head to the *Pericos* over the road where, being a strict vegetarian, Madhuri would order something like a halloumi burger with a single side of peri-peri chips. Once done, she delicately employed her little finger to mop up the orange-coloured salt. For Vihara, it would become a defining characteristic.

And then there was her voice. Like his, a little too teacherly for these largely unserious dancers who might've benefitted from fewer complicated words like 'enhance' and 'utilize' and fewer references to the anatomy. Terms like 'scapula' and 'lateral shift' though familiar to Madhuri through her scientific background, tended to bewilder the uninitiated – preferring instead to follow her movements than have them explained in intricate detail.

Clean and precise, Vihara quickly connected these, alongside her strict posture, with the *Jawani* school of Bhangra: a group so fiercely against the whole institution of *nakhra*, including the little head bobbles and facial expressions – those ranging from elation, 'look at what fun we're having'; to seduction, 'keep your eyes on me'; and even, wide-mouthed shock at one's own slick motions, 'get a load of this' – that any students seen to be indulging themselves spent the remainder of the practice dancing with a stick or *khunda* down the back of their shirt.

Whilst she hadn't brought any Bhangra props to the final class, Madhuri possessed something more valuable in the form of a new, unreleased mix by that talented dhol player-turned-Sony Acid Pro whiz kid, Prabh Singh or for commercial purposes, *Prabh Soundz*. Someone from inside the team that finished second at Bhangra Mania had leaked the audio file and, before Prabh had even decided whether to make it public, it had mysteriously made its way into her inbox. Madhuri knew that under these abnormal circumstances, she was expected to show discretion; however, she had so enjoyed the fast-paced segment from minute five of the mix that she selected it for today's routine.

Vihara was having trouble with one of the more acrobatic steps: a 540-degree spin over the left shoulder into a *single chaffa*, when he asked her to run through it again.

'Sorry,' he interrupted, 'can you just slow down the count? I'm not quite getting it.'

She repeated the motion at speed – as though this would help.

'It'll make more sense when we do it to music. You just need to remember to start on the *and* beat.'

'But I don't have a good memory,' Vihara quipped.

Madhuri paused a moment, wondering what exactly he was up to.

'I'm sure it's good enough,' she said, 'C'mon, you've danced in like four competitions, haven't you?'

'Yeah, but you've danced in like eight,' he retorted, 'and I'd say this is an eighth competition move, which makes it twice as complex as anything I'm capable of.'

She shook her head, trying not to laugh – 'Yeah, because that's obviously how it works, isn't it?'

He was so enjoying the teasing back-and-forth that he had forgotten there was a whole studio of folks waiting on Madhuri for their next instruction. Amongst them, in her big, round-framed glasses, wearing a grey scoop-neck t-shirt and a pair of tight, black shorts which stopped at her upper thigh, was Bhumi. Following their recent entanglement, or what had amounted to an accelerated replay of their past relationship, he had not expected to see her again so soon, much less in those bottoms. Vihara, who otherwise acknowledged the enrichment of this traditionally male discipline through the inclusion of women, championed a certain modesty and decorum as it pertained to dress.

She was standing with her back to him in the front left corner of the studio. Between them, Madhuri, and several visiting American Indians from the Toronto-based, all-female team, *TAG*. The Canadians had worked hard to uniform their technique, which was similar to Bhumi's in its emphasis on pinning back the shoulders and shooting the legs up high, but unique in its refusal to compromise on fluidity. At certain moments, Vihara found himself imitating them and adopted the fanciful idea that they were imitating him too – that somehow, he possessed an appeal of international magnitude.

Bhumi might've had a stronger claim to it. Her team, *Kohinoor*, had gone further than any in the UK to establish their reputation abroad, placing first in several overseas competitions. However, for many back home, the exaggerated motions and radical training methods resembled more of an extreme sport than a North Indian folk dance. It was true; Bhumi hit her feet on the ground with no regard whatsoever for her ankles and knees. And by those final *betkeh* at the end of the routine, she had nothing left in them. Or perhaps, for one raised in the more grounded world of *Kathak*, the reality of bouncing in a squat position on the balls of the feet, whilst vigorously flapping the arms back and forth simply didn't appeal. Like a peacock, she was far happier displaying her brilliant feathers than making unnecessary use of them.

As Madhuri glanced over to see her exertions being met with this stylish inertia, she couldn't help but take offense. Since she was not, however, in the business of singling people out, she addressed her gentle disapproval to the whole class: producing an ironic situation where the most diligent students assumed greater responsibility than those who were genuinely culpable. Vihara belonged to neither camp because he realised that, for the first hour and a quarter, it served him best to tread the middle path: to commit to the moves without overcommitting, so that by the final recordings, he felt he had achieved the ultimate goal of becoming one with them, which was also to say they had become one with him: dancer and dance, non-different.

And then unfortunately, the two separated, and he was himself again. The music stopped playing and Vihara untied his *chadar*. It was slightly moist with sweat, but he stuffed it away into his small gym bag before pulling out his jogging bottoms. He slipped them on over his shorts, then tried to remember where he'd left his shoes and socks. Everybody else except Madhuri, who had an unusual ritual of washing her feet immediately after class, was doing the same and talking about how badly they'd messed up this move or that. Partly out of habit, and partly because he wished to display solidarity, Vihara offered his own version of the sentiment, 'Yeah I definitely fucked it.' The studio was now emptying, but to avoid running into Bhumi at reception he wasted a few extra minutes pretending to search for the keys which were already in his pocket. The next group, 'boxercise,' had just begun their capoeira-style warmup when he said that he'd found them.

Downstairs, he watched on as a small crowd of people now gathered around Madhuri to hand over their six pounds for the class.

'Why don't you just round it to a fiver?' said one of the boys, failing to understand that the amount was based on the cost of the studio hire and not an attempt by *Chakdey* to exploit naïve dancers. Too tired to quarrel, Madhuri took his crumpled note and turned to the girl behind, whose no-nonsense middle-parting and darker skin Vihara instantly recognised, along with the folly of his earlier delay, as Bhumi's. He'd just been asked by Harpreet what his plans were next since, if he had none, both of them could travel back together to Southall where he lived and 'smash a mixed grill' at one of the local desi pubs. What Harpreet really wanted to say was, 'let's get on the Jameo's.'

It was an enticing offer, but anxiously focused on the two girls in conversation, he could not as yet give him a straight answer. They shared, if nothing else, a talent for playing niceties. Or was it, Vihara thought, that Madhuri's ability to remain consistently measured, so that one rarely saw a change in her neutral profile, served as the perfect antidote to Bhumi's more animated expression?

MAYA GOEL

Maya grew up in a rainforest in the Western Ghats of India. She did her BA in Literature at Ashoka University, and MPhil in Anthropocene Studies at the University of Cambridge. She is writing a book that blends essay and memoir, titled *What moss can do for a broken heart: notes on nature, literature, queerness, and complexity.*

maya.goel@alumni.ashoka.edu.in

Blue

An excerpt from a memoir

Before leaving home, I painted a pair of orcas on our whitewashed kitchen wall. Another streaked along the maroon counter's edge. A carpenter etched a dolphin into my wardrobe-bookshelf over a decade ago. More recently, my best friend painted a humpback breaching through dark blue and white waves opposite my bed. Escaping out of childhood dreams, there were soon cetaceans swimming all over our landlocked house.

I was leaving my home in the rainforest in southern India to spend a semester studying marine biology at a research centre on San Juan Island, off Washington State. Located in the Salish Sea – the 'jewel of the Pacific Northwest' – this region is famous for its population of killer whales.

One week into the programme our class went on a field trip to study the flora and fauna of Stuart, a neighbouring island in the San Juan archipelago. Equipped with raincoats, clipboards and notebooks made of waterproof paper (I had not known that such a thing existed), we boarded the boat in grey weather. Soon, the wind picked up. Giant waves flew upwards, lashing our jacketed bodies. My new friends felt seasick and most students sheltered inside the cabin. I remained at the prow with another girl, tossed from side to side, clinging to the railing and squinting against stinging spray. The professor who introduced us to the region joked that we were getting a proper immersion *in* the Salish Sea. I had been shivering since my first day there and boat rides were notorious for their chill. With faces whipped by salty wet hair, we looked up at the sun and noticed that it was raining. Keats's line flashed in my mind: *so bright and delicate*. My shoes and socks were soaked through. The wind penetrated my bones. As the island rose into view, I no longer felt the cold.

Later that evening I sat in the overheated library beside the docks and tried to complete the day's assignment. The air was quiet, saturated with soft sunset light. Safe on dry land, we had to record the details of our field trip in the waterproof journal. With a sharp pencil I noted the date, time, coordinates, weather and a list of species encountered. To compensate for my lack of drawings, I cello-taped the pages with pressings of Miner's lettuce, a weed which I had just learned was edible, along with male and female Douglas fir and Madrone flowers, and a tiny pink plant I couldn't identify. But when it came to the narrative section, I had no idea what to write. We were supposed to describe our day. But all I could see was blue.

Rebecca Solnit writes of blue as the colour of distance, horizons, longing. Maggie Nelson falls for the blue of the broken. Blue is the heart of all matter which dissipates as soon as you look at it, the soap-bubble at the corner of your vision. Glinting off sharp edges and pooling at your feet, blue is scorched by light. For all its swirling sensuousness, its stinging colourless drops – to me, blue is not a colour. In the forest, green is not one colour; green is a kaleidoscope. Every leaf casts its own shade. And they are all different from the green of water. That green is a mood of blue. Blue is when a tropical child, freezing from the moment she set foot in the North, stops feeling the cold.

It's not the colour of blue with which I'm in love. It's its allusion to the divine. Perhaps that's why women like us traipse after its receding horizon – its beckoning. The stark fine powder in which we stain our fingers, ourselves, each other. We romanticise darkness because we secretly know its heart is not black, but blue.

Why, in such an idyllic place, is it so hard to write? Is this happiness? Anxiety hasn't churned my stomach in three years. I don't know what to do with the lack of anguish.

***

The San Juan islands are home to two kinds of orcas: Southern Residents, which are critically endangered because they depend on fast-disappearing Chinook salmon, and Transients, which are better off because they feed on abundant porpoises and fat seals. The two ecotypes do not mingle. They have distinct cultures and diets: even a starving Resident (fish-eating orca) that plays with dead porpoises will not take a single bite out of their mammal-meat. Transients, when first brought into captivity, died of hunger before accepting a fish. These whales are the island's flagship species. Every individual's character is known, their behaviour meticulously recorded. Locals and researchers identify them by the shape of their saddle patch – the greyish marking behind the dorsal fin. Visitors flock from around the world, paying hundreds of dollars to glimpse a tall black triangle in the distance. Shops are decked with orca jewellery, orca stickers, stuffed orca toys. But the commercialisation wrought by tourism cannot diminish the whales' magnetic power.

Some individuals are famous, like Tahlequah, who made international headlines in 2018 when she carried the body of her dead calf for over 1,000 miles. When she became emaciated and started falling behind, members of her pod took turns to keep the decomposing carcass afloat. Millions of people worldwide followed the story, sharing in her mourning vigil. On day 17, Tahlequah released her daughter's body.

In the classroom, our introductory lecture focused on the term 'sense of place.' A teacher underlined the phrase 'time immemorial' on the whiteboard and asked the class to explain what it meant. People kept repeating that this region was special. The ecosystem, geology, history and culture entwined to create something unique. But our studies focused on the biodiversity. References to indigenous cultures were extremely respectful, but they (justifiably) carried a sense of over-caution that, for me, only wrought distance. I wanted to appreciate everything, but was sceptical of American enthusiasm. The other students spoke as though they were discovering relationships to the land for the first time. I could not resonate with their excitement. My roots were buried deep in a different forest, far away. I knew the inside of the earth like the inside of my own heart; I didn't need white people to tell me that places hold meaning. The island had not yet wrapped its tendrils around me.

Until, one day, walking across the luxuriant mattresses of moss that covered the landscape – pale green drinking pale blue – I met a yellow-haired girl and a brown-eyed boy. They asked me why my lips were pressed to the sticky bark of a Douglas fir; I said that its resin was sweet and strong. They were students of science. We talked about books and I told them stories of magic. We found a circle of stones. The three of us formed a coven. This coven changed everything.

**

Memory is a stone that you pass around the room: every hand a gentle polishing cloth rubbing it smooth. Places that created something in me have been worn soft by caress, packaging their memories into stories that I repeat. A well-rehearsed assignment of poignancy and place. School, university, childhood, home. Each one a crucible where love and trauma gelled to create a new colour. Representative moments are marbles to treasure. But this island is a rough, lumpy rock. I cannot extract its stories.

I want to record things but words still feel inadequate. Like a wedge between science and art. Adjectives don't work. I can only record the time and weather and coordinates, like they taught us. I noted the number of seconds between each occasion the humpback surfaced. I don't know how it felt to see the whales I'd dreamt of all my life. Somehow, it was more poetic to play the scientist. What better image than mixing sand dollar eggs with sand dollar sperm in a petri dish?

And finally – when I was watching a pod of Southern Residents near the Lime Kiln lighthouse and making notes on J-19's curious hunting technique while fishing boats closed in – finally, it rained on my waterproof notebook. The notebook that made everything worthwhile. Getting wet was the pinnacle of its purpose. But J-19, whom the locals call Shachi? She is a myth. Distant, barely real, entangled with longing. I only saw her that one day, through binoculars. But with her extra-curved black dorsal fin and slight paintbrush roughness around the white eyepatch, I think I'd recognize her again.

***

I spend most of my time with the coven and have grown attached to them. With attachment comes memory. The fear of old demons resurfacing. Anxiety is rushing in. Finally, perhaps I can write.

I miss the days when I felt things deeply. I still cry easily and hope I always will. But what was air before has turned into a column of water between me and the world. Loneliness doesn't quite capture it: it's greater, more nameless, more wasting and wonderful. I don't care what people think – until suddenly, I do. The old and the new wrestle for space in one person. The same girl, closer now to her childhood self. Reckless.

When you romanticise it like this it becomes wild and glamorous. When you don't, it's unbearable. You cannot access the despair: there are a thousand triggers and no real reason. Feeling without words, but not in the way the poets say. Nothingness diluted until the negative loses its negativity. Sadness has no identity.

At the heart of healing is a simple paradox: grief is incurable. Hope got you through like a spot of ink on the universe's fingertip. Hope ruins.

It wasn't hope. It was blind faith. The things that made me insecure are not true – or at least they don't have to be – if I try hard enough. My new friends are not abandoning me. But it's so much easier to rest in the rut of old habit. Repetitive dark fantasies, always for an audience. Always for her.

Everything I love is far away. Even at the edge of this landscape dropping into the ocean. The orcas live in a different realm. They break the surface when they choose, and then they are gone.

**

We swam, one night, a group of us girls. It was pitch dark and freezing. We held a green lamp underwater and thousands of tiny fish swarmed towards the light. Twelve shivering bodies stripped to their underwear and dove off the docks, into electrifying black water that numbed our skins.

I stayed close to the girl from the coven, looking after her when she fell ill. The bioluminescence was our secret. At midnight we snuck out to the weather station, climbed down the rocks, and found sticks to stir the water's edge. It was dim on the first night. But as moon phases changed and plankton multiplied, brilliance radiated from our sticks. Trails of green and yellow sparks fizzed beneath the surface. Blackness carved itself into swirls of light. The water assumed life, surging in flashes of its own volition. Our witchcraft was real.

I was good friends with the kind-eyed boy, and I knew that someday the two of them would end up together. I never confessed my feelings for her. She made paintings for me on bad days, wrote things that dissolved the fortitude I had built. In the weeks before leaving we took long walks and rested in spongy green enclaves, spinning fantastical tales of children who once lived here and were swallowed by moss. She gifted me patterned pebbles worn smooth by waves and I made her a card with seaweed pressings. One of her paintings depicted the cetaceans we saw – humpback, orca, grey whale and porpoise. Another was of a small wooden boat floating in a dark night, stars above and below, a candle burning in its centre.

JULIA HOLLINGSWORTH

Julia Hollingsworth is currently writing a memoir about untangling her identity from her upbringing within far-right American culture. Before relocating to the UK for her Masters, she completed a two-year writing program through the University of Cambridge. In 2019, she received an award from the Texas Association of Creative Writing for best undergraduate essay.

juliabhollingsworth@gmail.com

Thief

A selection of chapters from a memoir

Dust

On a bright spring day, I parked my car outside my childhood home for the last time. I punched the buttons on the keypad, a little grey box so old that certain numbers were rubbed out, making the code painfully obvious; a key to an open door. The heavy metal gate rolled away, revealing an empty garage. By then, I had learned to be more strategic, only going back when I knew no one was home.

I wandered through the house with a hollow backpack on my shoulder, making the rounds. Fridge, pantry, rustle through the drawers for money, scan the shelves for expensive objects. When I walked past the wall-sized portrait of my older brother hanging above the fireplace, I stopped.

He had been dead for three years. I started referring to him as 'more dead than ever' and 'still dead', a habit my partner told me was unreasonable.

'Someone does not become more or less dead,' they said. 'He has always been the same amount of dead.'

Maybe my escapades were some form of magical thinking. I tiptoed around the house, as if at any moment he might jump out and scare me.

I found him! I'd yell. *It was all just a terrible prank!*

Every day that I didn't see him, he died just a little bit more.

When I opened the door to his bedroom, the sun pierced the window like a spotlight, highlighting the dust on his bedspread. His clothes were still colour-coordinated in his closet, his shoes stacked perfectly in a line. Mom kept everything exactly the way he left it. Even the half-empty bottle of shampoo hadn't been removed from his shelf in his shower.

I rummaged through his drawers, furious. If it was the way he liked it, his clothes would've been laundered every other day. If he was still alive, there wouldn't be a speck of dust. When he was a teenager, he washed his hands constantly. He had a habit of vacuuming the inside of his shoes. We teased him, giving him the nickname *Monk* after a germophobic character in a TV show. Some of his quirks might have been attributed to OCD, if my parents believed in that sort of thing.

I left the house with a box of cereal, a few DVDs and a single object from my brother's bedroom. A few weeks later, Mom invited the whole family to a birthday party she was throwing for him. For the last two years, she ordered a cake with his name on it and cooked his favourite meal. The only thing missing was the person we were celebrating.

The party came and went, but I didn't attend. I never attended another family gathering. At first, I made excuses: I was sick, I had work, I was busy. Then I started throwing away my mother's letters before opening them.

A year into my absence, a family friend texted me to ask if we could set up a time to talk. We chatted over the phone about how my parents were doing, how much everyone missed me.

'Your Mom tells people she feels like *two* of her children are dead,' she said.

Perhaps the only thing worse than stealing from the dead is selling the dead's belongings, which is what I did just a few years later when I needed some money. The object I stole was a discontinued video game console from the early 2000s, a collector's item, with half a dozen vintage games. I told myself I would plug it in and play it like we did when we were kids, but when I turned it on, the familiar chime of the power button made me nauseous. I turned it off and yanked the cord, hid it from sight in a closet. My brother occupied a similar place in my mind: in the back, collecting dust.

I posted photos and a short description to Craigslist in a hurry, offering it for a lower price than it deserved. The ad was up for less than ten minutes when half a dozen buyers started asking when they could pick it up. In an hour it was gone.

I like to believe whoever has it now enjoys it. Maybe the person who bought it, a short guy wearing a baseball cap who tried to convince me to let him have it for $20 less (I didn't), gave it to his kid as a present. Maybe the kid was overjoyed, maybe his eyes lit up just like my brother's did when he ripped open the package on Christmas Eve. Maybe the guy is a divorcee and now he has something to do with his kid when he sees him every other weekend.

Maybe the object can finally just be an object. It doesn't need a past. It doesn't need memories. It doesn't feel pain.

Stealing is a Sin!

The first thing I ever stole was a handful of rainbow sequins. I was six years old, in a church classroom on a weekday. There was a short plastic table covered in craft supplies. Thick, white liquid glue, paper plates, glitter and sequins.

The teacher was around my mother's age. She was just slightly taller than the children, with wispy golden hair. I thought she looked like the little robins that pecked worms out of the dirt in the backyard. As we decorated our plates, she tutted around us, retelling the story of Joseph and his Coat of Many Colours. I dumped heaps of glue and glitter like I couldn't get enough. I must have looked like Gollum from *The Lord of the Rings*, eyes wide and sparkling, reflecting the glitter on the table. When the woman's back was turned, I took two fistfuls of the sequins and shoved them in my pockets.

Later that day, I was in my mother's bathroom, watching her paint her toenails.

She always painted her nails the same way: one bare foot propped on the counter, the other planted firmly on the tile to steady herself, like a dancer at a ballet bar. I was digging through a box of nail polish, answering her questions about my morning. When I stood up to put the box back in the cabinet, there was a pile of sequins on the floor.

'What is that?' she asked.

I looked in the direction she was pointing.

'Glitter!' I squealed.

She drew her leg down from the sink and knelt on the ground.

'Where did you get this?'

I told her I had gotten it from the table at church. Then I pulled another fistful out of my pocket.

'Julia, that's stealing!' Her voice rose an octave. 'Stealing is a *sin*!'

She ran out of the room and returned with the broom. She shoved it in my hands and told me to collect every piece.

'We are going to return this to your teacher,' she said.

As I swept, she watched from above, reciting the Ten Commandments. Stealing is number eight. And the premise of number ten.

'If you had just asked, Julia…' she trailed off. 'If you had just asked permission, it wouldn't have been stealing.'

I swept up the shiny bits, now combined with dust and nail clippings. She held open a thin plastic bag and I dumped them in. Then she made a phone call.

Mom stood behind me in the woman's kitchen, ushering me forward. The woman stood with arms crossed tightly over her chest, lips pursed, an angry little bird. I held out the bag, eyes cast down to the floor, asking for her forgiveness. She plucked it out of my hand and smiled.

'Thank you, Julia,' she said. 'I forgive you.'

I sat on her couch while she and Mom sipped coffee, chatting in hushed voices like a couple of schoolgirls. The teacher's name was Margaret, she had two children of her own, boys around my older brother's age. Over the next couple of years, Margaret would become one of my mother's closest friends, eventually moving into a house in our neighborhood. My sin was a bonding moment between them.

On the way home, Mom informed me that it wasn't over. I would have to pray and ask for God's forgiveness as well.

How Unfortunate

There were years when I didn't steal anything. Everything I owned was above board, paid for, earned. I would walk past an aisle in the grocery store and not slip anything into my pockets. I thought the thief inside me had died, but it was only dormant.

I had just moved to Seattle, Washington from Phoenix, Arizona. I watched as the desert melted away in my rearview mirror. The flat landscape unfurled into rolling hills and then sharp, jagged, mountains. It took three days of driving to get there, in a car that was old and untrustworthy. When I finally parked and turned the key, I patted the top of the dashboard, thanking it like an old friend. I unloaded the boxes, promising myself that as soon as I got the money, I would restore it to pristine condition.

A few weeks later, I was on the phone with an old roommate, listening in and out, walking towards the street where my car was parked.

I froze. My dog yanked at the leash.

'Wait, Rebekah,' I mumbled. 'I'm sorry. I have to call you back.'

I hung up before she could respond.

I stood in disbelief, maybe it wasn't my car. It didn't look like my car – most of the windows were bashed in and it was filled with someone else's belongings. But as I got closer, I saw the familiar dark brown stain from a coffee spill on the carpet. Those were my cracked leather seats, my little paper chain hanging from the rearview mirror, fluttering in the wind.

I pulled my dog away from the shattered glass and ran back to the apartment. I burst through the door, sobbing, trying to explain what had just happened to my partner, to myself.

'I have to call my Dad,' I said.

He had given me that car as a surprise, on a random day during my senior year of high school. He taught me how to change the oil and when to take it in for a checkup.

'How unfortunate,' he said over the phone. Then he advised that I sell it for its parts.

Later that night, with the urgency of disposing of a dead body, my partner and I cleaned the car's hollow shell. Our apartment was tiny, 212 square feet to be exact, and the car had become a storage unit. Boxes of winter clothes, pots and pans, a tent and sleeping bag for a camping trip we were planning, luxury luggage we were given as a wedding present. All of it was gone. What was left was broken glass, a filthy blanket and brown-stained pillow, and a half a dozen 100-piece jigsaw puzzles. My car had been robbed and then turned into a shelter for someone I would never know. As I sorted through their garbage, I told myself I was lucky to have ever had a car at all, and grateful for the little extra money we would get from the sale.

It wasn't until a few months later, when I saw the same make and model speeding across the highway, that I realised I'd never received a cheque. The address attached to the car belonged to my parents. Dad must have decided to keep it. I seethed, preparing to call him, to demand a payment and an explanation, but I never went through with it. I knew, despite the number of miles I had driven in it, and the hours I spent crying behind the wheel, it had never really been mine.

HELEN JAEGER

Helen Jaeger, author of twenty commissioned books, teaches marginalized youth. Her writing explores the voice of the outsider. In her memoir, she examines belonging and betrayal, power and lies. Ostracized by family, she's pulled back in after her mother's suspicious death and brother's suicide. It's the start of a new nightmare.

helenjaeger@gmail.com

Rogue Brother

An extract from the opening of a work of non-fiction narrative. Based on true events.

PROLOGUE

'There are only two people in the world, who know how she died, and they're both dead.' (East Midlands Serious Crime Unit, 2016)

October 2016

It's about 9 p.m. I drag myself over to my small, front window. Outside, a slab of solid black sky sucks all the lights from the houses below. Drizzle is hanging like gnats round car headlights on the street. In the gap of glass, where my thin curtains don't meet, a creepy face peers back. I look pale and uncertain. I turn away. Sighing with tiredness, I hobble to the armchair and flop into its worn dip. The old gas fire is wheezing away. I feel myself start to drift off, my book loosening from my grip. It thuds to the floor as the doorbell chimes, like the two are connected somehow.

Surely, it's too late for visitors? Only the devil would call on a night like this.

Rolling my eyes, I open the front door. Two figures are blocking my view of the street. I can make out the shapes of bulky, black jackets. Silver stripes on their high-vis vests catch and bounce the LED streetlights. For a moment, a radio clipped to one burbles, then cuts out. I'm unsurprised. It's not like it's the first time cops have knocked on my door.

Everyone knows a ferret-faced, young guy is cuckooing his old man's house up the road. There's CCTV on the outside wall. Regular visitors ring on their mobiles to get in, smoke from vapes and rollies wisping into the air. At night, their faces flare like Halloween masks. A few weeks ago, a random van had parked in my space on our narrow street. (A space the width of your house is yours, just enough for one car. God help you on a Friday night.) I'd wanted to unpack my weekly shop, so I'd marched up to it, ready to give the driver a piece of my mind. But when a policeman in a bullet-proof vest stepped out, I'd quickly shut my mouth.

Last month police had conducted 'enquiries'. Blue and white tape, fluttering in the breeze, had appeared round a black Audi. The car had been parked at an angle up the pavement, like some drunk had abandoned it. A stabbing. Police said it was routine to ask the neighbours. I'm expecting the same now. A few minutes on the doorstep. Nothing more.

'Good evening. Can we come in, please?'

I nod and frown, turning back into the chilly, dim hallway. We file past pegs with coats that rustle like whispers. 'Sorry about the lack of light,' I mutter, waving my hand towards a lopsided lampshade. 'I need a new bulb.' The familiar worm of shame squirms inside me.

'We've come about your mother,' announces one of the policewomen, as she looks for somewhere to sit. They shuffle about on my shabby sofa, trying to make space, then perch on its edge. I'm unsure what to do. I stand in the middle of the room and shift from leg to leg.

'Tea? Coffee?' I ask, then blush at my stupidity.

The dregs of old respectability.

A brief smile comes from the taller one. She's rummaging in her top pocket. I guess for a notebook. I sit on the arm of my chair, waiting. The second policewoman leans over and hands me a business card. Its glossy surface gleams in the gaslight. I glance down.

'Detective Inspector Kate Bridges, East Midlands Serious Crime Unit (EMSCU)'

Before I can figure out how the hell this relates to me, the first detective chimes in. 'This is my colleague, DI Sally Hawkins. We're here about your mother.'

They must mean Mother... Cynthia. They don't mean my real Mum, do they?

Without pausing, she continues, 'we carried out a post-mortem on your mother after her recent death. There were drug anomalies in her bloodstream. Found at the autopsy. After she died. We wondered if you knew anything about that?'

I exhale like I've been gut-punched. Of all the things I hate most, talking about my adoptive family ranks number one. 'Sorry, I don't know anything about-' I stutter. 'I haven't seen them for years.' I stop for a moment to count in my head. To gather myself. 'Probably about six. They kicked me out of the family when... when I reported someone to the police.'

'We know about that,' says DI Hawkins smoothly. 'It's on public record.'

Slack-jawed, I glance down at the floor. I don't want the police to see the shock on my face. Without thinking, I fiddle with a silver ring on my left hand. It has a Celtic pattern. The news the police have information on me makes me uncomfortable. Prods at me like an insistent child. I thought all that stuff was over long ago. Erased. Like me.

'My adoptive family refuse to have anything to do with me, even though the case was investigated. The person concerned was cautioned.' My voice catches, surprising me.

Dammit, I thought I was over all this stuff.

I grit my teeth and look up. DI Bridges is staring right at me. She seems to be weighing something up. A pause, then she says, 'If I were you, I'd get your mother's and father's wills. Fight tooth and nail for what's yours.'

I try not to laugh. When Dad had died in March, I'd decided I wouldn't break the silence. Why ask about any inheritance? What was the point? My adoptive family was wealthy, but Mother and Marcus would have swallowed it all up. I didn't expect anything. Even so, the knowledge of what they've probably done makes my heart race. I mustn't let it show. I search in my head for something factual to say. Something that won't allow any hidden feelings to hijack me.

'Is this to do with her diabetes? You know she was diabetic?' I ask.

'It might be,' says DI Hawkins. Her tone is non-committal, but I notice that she scribbles in her notebook.

'Have you spoken to my older brother, Marcus?' I continue. 'He might know more. As far as I'm aware, he's living at home, just as he's always done.'

Will they hear the bitterness in my voice?

'Yeah, we've had a chat with him.'

'He recently told people he didn't know where I lived…'

'Oh, your brother was quick enough to tell us your address.'

I shake my head. It's the twitch of an animal when a fly's just landed. The news my brother says what he wants to suit himself, even to authority, is always a shock.

Mind you, there always were double standards for him and me.

The police seem oblivious to my discomfort. 'We should let you know an inquest has been opened and adjourned on your mother. The coroner's office will be in contact in a day or two. We'll be in touch, if necessary,' says DI Bridges, casually, like it's an afterthought. At that, as though at a silent signal, they both stand up. I look up at the detectives and away again. I'm sure there's more I should say or ask. But I can't for the life of me think what. We walk back in the dimness towards the front door. It's then the words tumble out of my mouth.

'You know he has a gun? Marcus has a gun?'

Hamble House, 1979

He was wearing his favourite camouflage jacket, which Mother had bought as a birthday present from the ex-Army store in town. Khaki splodges over a sludge-brown background.

'Careful the wind doesn't blow them over!' she called out from the other end of the lawn. Her brother was lining up six cardboard loo rolls on an empty soap-powder box. He waved his hand dismissively, intent, at work.

'Right, ready,' he shouted, running back to where she was standing. She was holding his air rifle, cocked, over one arm, like a handbag, as he'd told her to do. Behind her – the grey eye of its barrel staring at her – lay a battered, black pistol on the stone step to the terrace.

'Give it to me!' he commanded. She passed the gun over.

He loaded it with an air pellet the size of a peppercorn, taken from a round metal tin. He clicked the air rifle shut and handed it back. Even though she didn't want to be there, she was touched by this small consideration. It hurt her arm just to shut the gun.

'Remember your arm will go up when you shoot,' he barked. 'Make allowance for that. Stand with your feet a couple of feet apart, like this,' – he demonstrated –

'when you're ready, breathe out slowly, aim at the target and pull the trigger. Squeeze. Don't grab at it.'

She raised the scope to her eye and squinted.

'Line it up on the loo roll. Remember to hold steady!' he repeated.

When she thought she was ready, she took a breath and squeezed the trigger. The gun went off with a painful jolt into her armpit.

'Bloody useless.' He grinned.

He took the rifle, reloaded and fired. One of the loo rolls silently fell over.

'Five more to go!' he said, cheerfully.

She tried but missed all of them. With a tut, he grabbed the gun.

Bang! Bang! Bang! Bang! Bang!

He shot with an accuracy that was ruthless and efficient.

Next, he suggested she try the lighter pistol. He told her to hold her arms out straight with a slight bend in the elbow. The loo rolls were resurrected. She squeezed the trigger. It jerked upwards. A pigeon, resting in the dark fir tree, took off with a cry of alarm, frantically beating its wings. He suggested she lie on the ground. It was early Spring. The lawn was wet and fresh damp hung in the air.

He went into the Icebox, which was a sort of outside junk room that smelled of faint cat piss and was filled with old bicycles, shoe shining kits and second-hand freezers that hummed. Dead wasps lay in wire netting over cracked windows. Even in the height of summer, it was so cold, they could see their breath in there. Then he returned, triumphant, waving a flattened, cardboard box. 'Lie on this. You can prop yourself up your elbows. It'll make you steadier.'

She did as he said. Icy groundwater seeped through the seams of her padded anorak. Her *Pink Panther* t-shirt rode up, the cold air goose-pimpling her skin like an uncooked chicken. She forgot her brother's complicated instructions. Shot randomly.

'Bloody hell. You've actually done it!' he crowed.

Later that week, there were voices in the kitchen – Mother asking him if he'd take his air rifle to their aunt's. She was sick of squirrels chewing the bark on the old tree in her garden. He agreed. He started to practise on living things – squirrels, rats, small birds.

A week later, he invited her to the 'playroom', a shared space, now his, next to his bedroom. A window was on the latch, wide open with an extensive view over the garden. Mother's birdfeeders hung on every tree, like mottled fruit. Three birds were clustering round one. Two bluetits and a greenfinch.

He picked up his pistol, aimed and fired.

A bird fell to the ground.

They went outside to look at it. The breeze was lifting its yellow and blue feathers. Its beak was as tiny as a toe clipping.

PART ONE: DENIAL

Chapter one

My brother, Marcus, was always into horror. Films. Books. TV series. Maybe it was genetic, because I wouldn't touch it with a bargepole, though he constantly tried to make me. In his pile of dog-eared paperback books there was one called 'The Rats'. I don't know what possessed me, but one day I promised him I'd do it.

PETER JORDAN

Peter Jordan is a part-time social work lecturer and researcher. His writing encompasses the history of social work in England, including accounts of the reality of social care for both service users and social workers. He is currently writing a memoir about his mother.

peter.jordan5@virginmedia.com

Death in Stratford

An extract from a memoir

Two weeks before my mother died, I lost my sense of smell. Both events were caused by Covid. It might be that one of us infected the other – a smear of saliva fallen on a cheek at a farewell kiss, or a molecule of virus caught in the breath of 'love you'. There is no way to know.

On my desk lies a memory stick containing a recording of Mum's funeral. A bright fluorescent yellow, it glows and glowers at me among the papers and books that litter my workspace. My mother's body was cremated on April 22nd 2020, and at that time and in that place only four people were allowed to attend. She had nine surviving children, so five of us could not be there. I fell into the latter group. As it was, on the day, the funeral directors relented and allowed two of my brothers-in-law to come into the crematorium for the service. This enabled one of them to make a video of the event.

It is four years since then, but I have not watched more than a few frames of the recording. Even so, I know its contents well. My family spread out and mourning in isolation from each other, respecting the social distancing rules in place at the time. The Catholic priest reading a eulogy, written by me, laying out my mother's virtues (kindness, calmness, an ability to connect with people) and making gentle jokes about the relative poverty that we grew up in (adding water to tinned soup to make it go round). Some hymns carefully agreed by us all across a WhatsApp group. And people crying, likely sobbing, in a public display of emotion rarely seen in our family.

The last time I saw Mum was on March 14th 2020. She had been in and out of hospital for the previous nine months with chronic heart failure. At this time she was recovering from a fall that had broken her hip, requiring an operation to pin it. Her physical recovery had gone well but delirium had set in. Waiting to be well enough to be discharged, Mum had been moved to the single-story annex of a hospital in Stratford-upon-Avon, a few miles from her home.

My partner Emma and I were the last to visit Mum that day. As we entered the wood framed building, we read the notice on the door warning people with cold or flu symptoms, or those who had recently been to Italy, to stay away. Inside we were met by a stern-faced nurse sitting behind a desk. She pointed at a deep, white porcelain sink at the side of the area and told us to wash our hands and arms up to the elbows. She radiated anxiety and resentment at our presence. I wonder now how much she knew or suspected about the dangers that were coming, or those that were already present.

We entered a small ward with room for six patients. Mum sat in a chair next to a neatly made bed. She wore a purple dressing gown over a food-stained yellow nightdress. I thought of my eldest sister Tricia who visited every day, bringing clean clothes each time, and of the rota of daughters and sons and grandchildren who came at mealtimes to make sure Mum was fed.

Her eyes were a clouded blue, her skin soft, pink, pale underneath a helmet of unkempt grey and black curly hair. Mum's glasses were missing, but she smiled as she looked our way. There was warmth and welcoming but no recognition. I remember her expression, her faced pulled in darts, lips thin and white, marshmallow padding where her cheekbones had fallen away. One of the acrylic like hairs on her chin curled back in a J as her smile stretched, broadening out, false teeth coming into view as she said hello. Mum looked pleased yet puzzled to see us. it took me a moment to realise that she didn't know who we were.

'It's Peter and Emma, Mum. We've come to see you. From Norwich.'

'That's funny. My son Peter lives in Norwich'.

Emma and I shared a glance, a half-smile, acknowledging the humour in a situation that was otherwise tragic. Mum had shown varying levels of lucidity over the last few visits, but this was the only time that she completely failed to recognise us. There had been one occasion when she had mixed me up with my brother William, but we had always been able to resolve the confusion for her, bring her back to herself. To be recognised is to be seen, and to be known, and from there communication and communion with others follows. On that day, at the last, it felt as if we inhabited different realities.

Even before she was ill, it was often a struggle for me to connect with Mum, and I usually felt that the onus was on me to bridge our worlds. It seemed that it was my job to understand her, and to present an easily digestible version of my life that she could comprehend. It was hard to know what she thought of me, how well she understood me. Hard to see myself fully reflected back in her gaze.

I perched on the end of a bed, watching Mum move invisible crumbs around on a magazine covered table in front of her. She alternated between this fidgeting, picking motion and stopping to gaze at me or at something less obvious in the ward. A sharp warning came from the opposite corner of the room. The uniformed nurse told me not to sit on the bed and gestured towards a stack of chairs at the far end of the room. There is a risk of infection, she explained. And besides, that wasn't my mum's bed. I turned to see a small woman whom I hadn't noticed when I sat down. She looked as if she had been stuffed into a seat in between the wall and the side of her cot.

I pulled the chairs over as gently as I could. We sat either side of Mum, Emma and I forming a triangle with her at the apex. It was easy to just sit and watch her then, the calmness of her gentle bewilderment a counterpoint to the strained, visceral anxieties of the staff. I have a memory of scents: aloe vera, rosewater, Nivea hand cream perhaps? A remnant of institutional food and the ubiquitous smell of bleach too.

We tried to make conversation, but asking her how she was, or whether she wanted anything only elicited wan smiles. Her conversational gambits seemed stranger to us: half-finished sentences about something she'd noticed, pointing vaguely to one of the word search magazines in front of her. She gestured to a place on the floor a few feet away and said 'Look, there's little Peter, under there'. The use of my name showed promise, but it was as if we were speaking past each other. Perhaps we seemed to her like chimeras or ghosts from another plane of existence.

Her tone was the same, familiar one. If anything, it was even softer than usual, her lilting Lothian accent swooping then rising the falling again. The cadence of her voice sang to us as she explained that 'Peter is my youngest'. It was nursery talk, unfettered by knowingness, stripped back to the simplest speech acts. The sounds she made were more than just vocalisations: there was a sense, and intention, behind them. But words were few, and seemingly disconnected from the present. I wondered, if not through spoken language, how to communicate with a mind confounded by illness and institutionalisation.

We soon gave up the struggle to converse and just sat, watching, waiting, as present as we could be. It reminded me of my early childhood. I would often sit on the floor at her feet watching as she slept slumped in a chair, exhausted from work and children.

For a little while, the space we inhabited in that small hospital ward seemed almost timeless. The pull of the outside world was forgotten, pushed away by the compelling kindness of those moments. I wanted to stay, continue to be beside her, and puzzle out, as best I could, what was on her mind.

But staying was not permitted. Visiting hours came to an end and we had to go. Had I known that this would be the last time I saw her, I would have argued to be there longer, to say goodbye properly. Instead, I took comfort in a fictional future where we would see Mum again in a week or so, possibly in a care home or even her own house. There was a sense of assurance that we would see her again. Even so, there was an awkwardness to our farewell, uncertainty as to whether close contact was allowed. A light kiss on Mum's cheek and a brief grasp of her hand stood in for the warmer, more heartfelt hugs we usually shared.

As we got up to leave, I caught a glimpse of the view from a large window at the end of the ward. There was grass and trees and birds, with a concrete multi-storied cap park in the background. The ward felt like a holding place too. Not somewhere for treatment, or even assessment, but a bright and pleasant place to store people until they were ready to be collected.

A few days later I began to feel unwell. There was no way of testing for Covid then, but I guessed that what was I had. The loss of smell followed soon after. News of Mum came daily through conversations on WhatsApp. My sisters saw her regularly until March 23rd when the first lockdown was announced, and visitors were no longer allowed in hospitals in England. From then on, we relied on phone calls to and from the ward.

By March 30th Mum's health had begun to deteriorate. She was having trouble breathing but the doctors treating her were still optimistic that they could stabilise her enough to discharge her to a residential home in the following days. By April 2nd she had deteriorated further and had to be sedated. It was confirmed that day that Mum had tested positive for Covid. As she was a devout Catholic, we asked for a priest to visit her to offer last rites. We were told that no priest would go.

That evening my sister Tricia relayed an offer from the hospital for one of us to go and visit her for ten minutes, but we would be unable to touch her. An hour later – before anyone could have reached her – Mum died. The hospital staff assured us that she was not on her own when she passed away. Tricia rang each of us in turn to let us know. Her own husband had been admitted to hospital with severe breathing problems the day before.

Even at the distance of years, the manner of Mum's death falls hard. She lived a long and, on the face of it, a very unremarkable and ordinary life. I could list worse fates that could have befallen her. Yet that ending, out of sight and touch of her family, feels cruel and sad. In retrospect, the last visit was like an interlude of grace, a respite before the turmoil that was to follow. In my mind, through the time travel that memory affords us, I am still there now, feeling the warmth of her being, marvelling at her, enjoying her in a way that had previously seemed lost to me.

It is this moment, not the unwatched funeral video, that holds my love for her, and my grief at her passing.

ZIXIN LI

Zixin Li used to be a journalist in China. Now he writes about ordinary people's lives in China under the globalization context. He is the founder and editor-in-chief of the nonfiction writing platform Sandwichina.com since 2011.

zixin@sandwichina.com

Ah Gong and Ah Pa

An extract from a memoir about Teochew people's diaspora inside and outside of China.

ONE

On the eve of the Spring Festival in 1986[1], firecrackers echoed throughout the night, scattering red remnants across the ground. While many chose to stay home, an elderly man, clutching a long umbrella beneath his arm, knocked on our apartment door on the fifth floor.

This workers' apartment had no elevator, which meant it would have taken over five minutes for the elderly man to climb up the concrete steps.

'Why are you here, Ah Gong[2]?' I asked, opening the door and seeing him breathing heavily.

'Today is Chinese New Year's Eve! Ah Gong wants to join us for dinner!' Ah Pa[3] exclaimed, ushering Ah Gong in. It seemed they had planned this visit.

Several years ago, we had left the old house built by my great-grandfather and moved to this apartment allocated by Ah Pa's *chousha*[4] factory. Ah Gong remained in the house, after being widowed, for many years. To attend this annual dinner with us, he had to walk for forty minutes.

Ah Gong was silent. When he was smiling, I could see big gaps between his remaining teeth which made it difficult for him to eat. He skipped the goose wings and pork bellies, only went for tofu and vegetables. I thought he just swallowed them whole.

Then, he said to me, 'Boy, I am leaving for your Tai Beh'[5]s home, for another dinner.'

I was surprised. The dishes remained almost untouched on the table. Why had Ah Gong arranged the Spring Festival Eve's dinner this way with his two sons? All I knew is that Ah Pa and Tai Beh, with a seven-year age gap, never got along. Consequently, the two families couldn't join together with Ah Gong to celebrate the Chinese New Year.

'I am leaving. Keep up the good study!' Ah Gong said, descending the steps

---

1 Also called Chinese New Year. The eve of Spring Festival is as important as Christmas Eve for family reunions.
2 "Grandpa" in Teochew dialect.
3 "Dad".
4 The embroidery produced in Teochew.
5 "Uncle". Especially refers to father's elder brother.

slowly, gripping the handrail firmly.

This kind of Spring Festival Eve dinner carried on for about ten years until Ah Gong was too weak to walk over.

Before moving to the workers' apartment, my parents and two sisters, together with me, always had meals in the old house's open courtyard, as our room was too small to fit in a dining table. Tai Beh's family had already moved out by the time I can remember, and he remained distant in both my memory and in his connection with my Ah Pa.

However, the old house was still packed. It accommodated six families—five belonging to my great-grandfather's sons and their families, one for a tenant. Five of us were only allocated to a room of 60 square feet, without a toilet inside.

A bed about two meters wide for five of us to sleep together occupied most of the room. A wardrobe stood near the door, next to it was a desk holding my mom's mirror, creams, and possibly a table lamp. All the furniture was painted in a dark brown hue and exceptionally heavy. My parents insisted that these items were made of high-quality wood, from a place where they spent ten years together – Hainan Island[6].

Ah Gong never dined together with us. Mostly he cooked by himself. Sometimes he would take a bit of steamed rice from our pot, or one or two chopsticks of vegetables from our table, then retreat to his own room to finish the meal. His room was spacious, but full of the unwelcoming smell of mothballs.

His life seemed quite simple to me: an early riser, spending most of his time in his room listening to the radio. Sometimes walking to the shops for essentials. Reciting Tang Dynasty poems occasionally.

'Shishi Mangmang Nan Ziliao,
Chunchou amam do sengmin.'

These two lines are still kept in my mind. They mean: The world is vast, and it's hard to predict one's fate. Spring ignites sorrows, and I have to go to sleep alone.

Ah Pa tried hard to get us out of the tiny room of the old house. One day he finally received the key to the worker's apartment. He was so overjoyed. Upon returning, he even brought home Teochew's specialty, beef balls, which was my favorite and a rare treat.

One couldn't buy property after 1949 in China. Housing was allocated by the government. Each factory called a "unit" provided everything for its workers, from kindergartens to housing. But resources were always scarce. Getting an apartment from the factory was a big deal. Many workers were on the waiting list.

Our new home was a two-bedroom apartment. Situated on the outskirts of the town, we could hear frogs and insects serenade every night from the fields that faced our sitting room. It vastly improved our living conditions. But it also meant that we bid our farewell to the old house.

---

6   The second largest Island in China, about 1000 km away from Teochew.

TWO

It wasn't the first time for Ah Pa to move out of the old house. He did it once when he was young.

Ah Pa's given name is Yuzhao. As a teenager, he was 5'4", with a pale face and an inborn intellectual demeanor. He dropped out of school at fifteen because the family could no longer support him.

At that age, Yuzhao's typical day unfolded as follows: upon waking up, he experienced hunger. But cooking in individual kitchens was forbidden by authorities. Instead, people gathered at the communal dining area for scheduled meals. The person in charge of serving congee held significant power, determining the portion each person received with his ladle. Yuzhao would always politely request, 'Please give me more!'

During this time of the early 1960s, food shortages affected the entire country. The radio proclaimed, 'The People's Commune System is a significant step toward Communism!' Chairman Mao aimed to eliminate the household unit, envisioning a society where people worked, ate, and ultimately lived together within the People's Commune. However, this initiative inadvertently led to a nationwide famine. When individuals worked for an ambiguous collective authority, they tended to be less effective than when working for themselves. An investigation later discovered that 36 million people perished in this famine, marking it as one of the most significant famines in world history.

Yuzhao struggled with a constant feeling of hunger and dissatisfaction during that time. While reading a newspaper, he learned that China was "defending against India's invasion" in the Himalayas. However, he was ineligible to join the army. Only those from poor peasant families, considered most loyal to the power, could send their young members to bear arms. 'I'm from a former business owner's family, and I have no chance.' Yuzhao knew it.

When I was older, I realized that at the time Yuzhao was starving, there was so much going on in the world. The Beatles swept across Europe and America. Khrushchev grappled with the Cuban missile crisis alongside JFK. The U.S. initiated the Apollo Program to reach the moon. And Yuzhao finally found a job to pave the streets inside the ancient city by excavating cobblestones and cementing the roads.

But I also found something remarkable about him. In a monochrome photograph dating back to 1967, he wore an armband, a sign of 'revolutionary student', standing at the far-stretched Tiananmen Square. It was a cold morning, so he was wearing a pair of gloves. Bathed in sunlight at a 45-degree angle, he cast a shadow and was surrounded by fellow comrades whose shadows stretched toward the Tiananmen gate tower. It's astonishing that he journeyed all the way from Teochew to Beijing, a distance of 3000 kilometers.

He told me the story: 'It was early 1967, right after the Cultural Revolution broke out the previous summer. I lost my job since all the factories were disrupted. We were hotheaded, forming a group to appeal to Beijing. If you were a "revolutionary student", all the transportation was free!'

Cold was Yuzhao's first impression of Beijing, a cold that children from southern China seldom experienced. The temporary residence near the Tiananmen Square was bitterly freezing. Yuzhao was one among millions of students gathered there, struggling to catch a glimpse of Chairman Mao. It wasn't until 2008, before the Beijing Olympic Games, that I took him back to Beijing, when he saw Mao closely in his memorial museum, lying there as ja mummy, receiving respect and salutes. 'He has a bigger nose than I thought,' Yuzhao exclaimed. 'He was an excellent revolutionary, but not a good ruler,' he added.

In 1969, Mao summoned all the young people to go to the villages to "learn from the farmers and workers", as the slogan goes. It was a movement that mandated every local council to send young people away from their regions. By that time, Tai Beh had become a doctor, after having luckily enrolled in a free medical school. Yuzhao had to or just wanted to be on the trip.

At the age of 23, Yuzhao bid his first farewell to Teochew. He was the oldest among the hundreds of young people heading to rural Hainan Island. On the same boat was Hongmei, who was 20 at the time. They were strangers then, but six years later, they married.

The journey took two nights, and the route went past Hong Kong. The schedule was meticulously arranged to pass the city then governed by the British at midnight, in fear that someone might attempt to jump into the sea and swim to Hong Kong, to defect to the evil capitalism.

It was a ten-year exile for these young people to endure. They were integrated into a semi-military system, living and working together. Their main work was to plant and harvest rubber trees in the forest. After Mao died in 1976 and Deng Xiaoping seized the power in 1979, the government suddenly announced that everyone could return to their hometown, although many were now in their thirties and with children in tow.

Yuzhao, at the age of 33, accompanied by Hongmei and their two daughters, as well as me, their son in Hongmei's pregnancy, carried their furniture and luggage back home by boat. In the past decade, Yuzhao's mother had passed away, and his father, Ah Gong had retired from the *chousha* factory, creating an opportunity for Yuzhao to inherit the position according to the rules at that time. Yuzhao took the job. His exile came to an end.

THREE

On an early summer night in 1997, Ah Gong collapsed in his room. Discovered by fellow residents in the old house, the doctor diagnosed it as a stroke. No hospitalization was recommended; instead, he was advised to lie peacefully, awaiting the inevitable. Ah Pa and I, together with Tai Beh, gathered by his bedside. I observed him, with his mouth half-open, breathing deeply and slowly, while his eyes remained closed.

Two days later, Ah Gong ceased breathing, and his body underwent cremation. I learned for the first time that human ashes aren't powder-like but resemble the tiny cracks of limestone. Following Ah Gong's passing, Tai Beh seemed to have restored his relationship with Ah Pa. Quietly, the three of us sat in a car back from the crematorium. Tai Beh gazed at Ah Gong's ashes and said, 'Being a doctor, I've seen too many of these. Death is waiting for all of us.'

At the moment Ah Gong's body was pushed into the cremator, Ah Ma told me to shout out: 'Go! Ah Gong!' This is to remind his spirit to get on the road, to the next journey.

The next year, I said goodbye to the worker's apartment and went to Beijing for my college. 26 years have passed, and I am still in exile.

JEAN MACINTYRE

Jean MacIntyre is a museums professional and design historian. She writes mostly about her own experiences and her grandparents' lives. Her grandmother was an English debutante who went to live in Berlin in the twenties and met her grandfather, a Hungarian sculptor. They both fled the Nazis in 1933 and returned to Britain.

macintyrejean25@gmail.com

Tea-leaves and Toe-rags

An extract from a creative non-fiction short story

Tuesday, 14 September 1973, 10pm
The attic room at 13 Dryburgh Road in Putney was just big enough to house a futon and a Biba[1] beanbag. Yet on this particular night, six of us sat cross-legged on the floor, passing around an ancient bong. It was an art: dragging on the pipe, holding your breath long enough to knock you sideways and then exhaling gradually to impress the gang. Once I'd drawn the scorching smoke in, I felt like my lungs were going to explode. Then Woody cracked a joke, and I couldn't help but let it go, spluttering and hacking like the novice they had sussed I was. I lay back on the beanbag and my head swam. Whisps of blue-grey smoke floated across the room, interlaced with fragments of conversation.

From the outside, 13 Dryburgh Road was an impressive Arts and Crafts mansion, but it was converted into bedsits in the early sixties. By the seventies the inside had become a den of bleedin' iniquity inhabited by a succession of dope dealers and assorted lowlife. That evening me, Woody, Justin, Scott, Frank and Gary were squashed into Frank's bedsit staring up at the fluorescent stars Frank had inexpertly Pritt-sticked to the ceiling to make it more 'trippy'. In one corner, vamping it up, stood a life-size cardboard cut-out of Ziggy Stardust, aka David Bowie, who looked down on us with a brazen disdain. I do not remember most of what was said that evening but a recurring theme, sustained by Woody, was the fate of his precious motor car.

Four months earlier – May 1973
My boyfriend Woody and his best friend Frank had decided they deserved a holiday. 'From what?' you enquire. If I had to describe their profession now, I would say they were grifters not grafters, small time thieves – 'tea-leaves,' they would have said – and oh such petty drug dealers. This must have been a tiring business, what with the police being on their case pretty much constantly. In 1973, the Wandsworth Police were a tad unpredictable. They were part Dixon of Dock Green[2], your friendly neighbourhood copper, and part Sweeney[3], your high speed, half-bent harasser of the criminal classes. And you never knew which one you were going to get.

---

1   Biba was an Art Deco styled department store.
2   *Dixon of Dock Green* (1955–1976) was a TV series that featured a friendly neighbourhood policeman.
3   *The Sweeney* (1975–1978) was a TV series about two members of the flying squad chasing down criminals in London.

Anyways, Frank and Woody had resolved to get away from all the aggro and drive to sunny Scotland. Neither of them had a driving licence and Woody's Morris Minor had no MOT, tax, insurance or seatbelts. The day Woody bought the car we climbed inside and, as we slammed the doors shut, my passenger side door fell off its hinges and onto the pavement. The previous owner legged it down the street.

I should describe the boys.

Woody was a poor man's Rod Stewart. His feather haircut framed a ferret face with a crow's-beak nose. His navy Ben Sherman[4] button-down shirt was tucked into an ancient pair of Levi's which were smeared with garage grease. He had customised his Levi's with his sister's sewing shears and some scraps of Laura Ashley fabric, so now triangles of floral cord separated the seams on each outside trouser leg. Not so much bell-bottoms as swinging skirts that hung above his boots. Woody was not a friend to personal hygiene. He lived with his parents in a Rachmanesque[5] hovel off the Queenstown Road where there was no bathroom, so once a month he'd visit the Latchmere Baths and come out smelling of chlorine and cheese-and-onion crisps. Woody had read three books in his life. The first two were by Richard Allen – *Skinhead* and its sequel *Suedehead* – and these books had particularly influenced his footwear. He hammered Blakey's into his Monkey Boots, no doubt hoping to give some unsuspecting toe-rag a good kicking. By the time I met him, he was a skinhead turned hippie who worked part-time as a milkman. He delivered to the estate opposite my school which was, without a doubt, the worst comp in the whole of 'Saaaff Lundun'. After school I used to sit in the cab of his milk cart smoking Rothmans while he serenaded me with classics like 'I dream of Jeanie with the light brown teeth'. To say Woody was light-fingered was an understatement. He once pinched a giant plaster toadstool from Santa's Grotto in Selfridges. He just tucked it under his arm and swaggered past the security guards. We took turns sitting on it on the tube home. His idea of a date was to take me to his favourite caff so I could watch him shovel the full Tooting grease-up down his gullet. The sight of that congealed fried egg, flabby bacon and crusted baked beans swimming in pork lard made me gag, and the tin ashtray next to his plate, brimming with fag ash with the odd gob of bubblegum stuck on the side, wasn't none too appetising neither. I used to sit opposite him picking the crusty bits off the red plastic tomato-shaped ketchup dispenser to take my mind off his plate. If he was feeling flush, he'd stand me a Pepsi. You can see why I was smitten.

Frank was short and muscular with shoulder-length red hair. His white cheesecloth shirt was cut close to his freckled London-Irish skin. It was deliberately a size too small so that his tattoo bulged out to proclaim his hard boy credentials. That is, until you took a proper look at the tattoo, which turned out to be a heart and the name of his ex-bird Sharon. If you looked even closer, you could see where

---

4   'Ben Sherman is a legendary name in menswear, creating iconic wardrobe staples since 1963. Adopted by the Mod movement of the 60s and beyond, subcultural style runs through every stitch.' Ben Sherman marketing campaign (2023).
5   Peter Rachman was a landlord with a reputation for exploiting his tenants.

he'd tried to rub letters out on the request of the next love of his life. He had what was known then as a schoolboy grin, though in his case it was reform school. At the age of 15, Frank and his mate had beaten up the cashier of the local bingo hall to get their hands on the till. Trouble was, the cashier was an old lady and in his cups Frank regretted it and would sob: 'I'm a naasty bastard like my uncle Eric – don't have nothing to do with me.' At one point he'd persuaded my mate Julie's parents to let him doss in their back bedroom. Then one night he offered to get a round in for her family at the Spotted Horse on Putney High Street. While they were all out necking their pints of Young's Special, Frank sent his friend Budgie round to burgle their house. Julie reckoned that when the family got home and discovered the break-in, nobody, but *nobody*, was more surprised than Frank. Now that was gratitude for you.

David Bowie was a massive influence on Frank. He was such a humongous fan that he used to sing 'The Laughing Gnome'[6] in the shower, the song Bowie hoped we'd all forget. In honour of his idol, Frank wore platform shoes and Maybelline Ultra-Lash Mascara whenever he got the chance, though in all honesty he looked more like the bassist in The Sweet[7] than Aladdin Sane[8].

David and Rod, as the two lads saw themselves, had met at a Battersea secondary modern and bonded over their addiction to bunking off[9] and LSD. 'Take it,' they chorused, 'Find your inner chi-uld,' 'Don't be a fuckin chicken'. Eventually I dropped a tab in the art deco café on Biba's fifth floor, while eating a Knickerbocker Glory. I felt like I had walked inside a rainbow. They ran off laughing, leaving me to pay, which was hard because I thought the money in my pocket was gold doubloons. I opened my mouth to speak to the waitress and realised I couldn't remember any words. I ran out into the labyrinthine roof garden thinking it must be a figment of my spaced-out imagination.

 Anyway, one fine May morning, they set off on their hardly-deserved-at-all holiday. It was pissing down with rain and the windscreen wipers were knackered, so they tied two bits of string to the wiper ends and Frank worked them from the front seat. As they drove through Hertfordshire, they were clocked by the Old Bill[10] who pulled them over and nicked them for the state the car was in and for their total absence of documentation. The Hertfordshire constabulary then alerted every other police force in the kingdom. And so, by the time Frank and Woody reached Scotland, they had acquired not one but six official demands that they bring in their documentation within the next seven days at six different police stations across England. No chance. Once they were over the border, they went on a nicking spree somewhere south of East Kilbride. Then they packed the car boot with

---

6   'The Laughing Gnome' was a song by David Bowie released in 1967. It was a pastiche of songs by Antony Newly whom Bowie admired.
7   The Sweet were a glam rock band in the 1970s. Steven Priest was their bassist.
8   *Aladdin Sane* is an album by David Bowie released in April 1973.
9   *Bunking off* refers to skipping school or playing truant.
10 Old Bill became the nickname for the Metropolitan Police following the Great War.

their contraband and legged it to the nearest pub to boast about their exploits to a couple of likely lassies who, half cut, were moderately impressed. According to Frank, the initial conversation with the girls had gone something like this:

'Rum and black, is it?'

'I have nae a scooby wat yer on aboot.'

'Laaager and lime? Snowball? Babycham?'[11]

'Go on then.'

'Which one, love?'

'That lot ull do fe now pal.'

By the time they made their way back down the country, they were brassic[12]. What were they to do? Woody vaguely remembered a mate telling him that if you ran out of readies you could pop into your nearest police station and ask for help. Given the contents of their car boot, it is hard to believe that they chose this option, but then they were both, in South London parlance, a few sandwiches short of a picnic. So that is how they ended up at Huntingdon nick on a Tuesday morning in May asking for some bread[13] from their good friends, the boys in blue. Once the Duty Sergeant had explained that the station was not a community bank, he took the precaution of searching and then impounding Woody's car and taking into evidence the stolen goods found therein. The Sergeant presented our heroes with a lengthy charge sheet and bailed them.

And how did these likely lads[14] get home? I think they hitch-hiked all the way down the M11. I can see them now, in my mind's eye, two helpless, hopeless cockneys with their thumbs out on some debris-strewn slip road on the edge of the fens. What passing motorist could resist?

11 A snowball is a cocktail – a mixture of advocaat and lemonade – popular in the 1970s, while Babycham is a sparkling perry that was marketed at women during this time.
12 The term *brassic* refers to having no money or being *skint*. Boracic lint was a dressing for leg ulcers in the 19th century.
13 *Bread and honey* is Cockney rhyming slang for *money*.
14 The phrase was popular in the 1970s partly because of the comedy series *The Likely Lads* (1964–1966).

ELIN MORGAN

Elin Morgan grew up in East London. Her writing focuses on the relationship between place and people, peeling back layers of history and memory to find stories. Before returning to study, Elin worked for a number of years in PR and communications with a specialism in theatre and dance.
elinjmorgan@gmail.com

Forest Gate to Leytonstone

An extract from a project where I walk between everywhere I've ever lived in London

She is standing on the platform at Walthamstow Queens Road when her sister calls. Her sister wants to tell her about her recent trip to Paris. They continue to talk as the train comes into the platform and she boards it, heading in the direction of Forest Gate, where they both grew up and where her sister still lives. As the train trundles along past the chimney stacks of Victorian terraces, her sister tells her that it is raining there, where she is going. She is still two stops away and there the sky outside the train window is blue. As she passes through the next station, a light shower starts falling. They're still on the phone as she disembarks and it turns out her sister is about to pass the station she's just arrived at, on her way to an appointment. It's no longer raining. They meet at the bottom of the metal steps to say hello. Her sister looks askance at her coat, a beige slimline Puffa she bought in TK Maxx a few weeks ago. She knew her sister wouldn't approve. 'You were never meant to see me in this!' she explains. 'It's the one I use to blend in when I do my walks. No one notices me in it.' Her sister laughs, stylish as ever in a vintage tan suede jacket and black trousers. There is something of their mother about both of them. They kiss and say goodbye, and she starts her walk.

As I reach the edge of Wanstead Flats, I'm greeted by wild borders of blue borage. Leaves are beaded with the just-fallen rain. A bramble bush to my right is spattered with white paint, likely the victim of one of the Flats' regular fly-tippers. On a branch that's budding for spring, a coal tit trills– jer-by-jerby jerby jer – it tells me. I see a magpie, that familiar bird which always seems to guide me on my walks. I'm pleased it's here even though it's solo, for sorrow. The lake is boggy with reeds and the ring of trees next to it – where once in Victorian times, a bandstand stood – is overgrown. I feel the featherlight first drops of another shower coming in. Although there are wildflowers and birdsong, the hum of the road, the flights overhead, and the houses that border the grassland remind me I'm still in the city. As a child, I learned to ride my bike here (a copper-coloured Raleigh), and spent long days exploring the paths and copses of our own corner of wild East London.

On the far side of the pond, I spot a pile of what I take for builders' rubbish, before I realise it's someone's home, constructed from bits of wood and plastic sheeting. I'm reminded of a time when my Dad, keen to test a new bivouac bag he'd bought, got my brother and I, about seven and nine at the time, to try it out – only for a storm to break out. We were relatively safe, far from trees in the middle of one of the football pitches, though I watched terrified (but dry) inside the orange plastic shell, peering through the opening as lightning flashed and thunder rang around us. It gives me pause to realise that now, people are finding shelter here, full time, in not much more than we had that afternoon.

A group of children, around twelve or thirteen years old, stomp past me in single file, headed for the crossing on Centre Road, as once my friends and I stomped here. Looking in the direction they're heading, I hear screams through the trees, but I'm not alarmed. The whirling lights above the bushes tell me that the fair is still in town, the one I visited each Easter with Mum and Dad – and later with my friends, daring one another to go on the scariest ride – and screaming. There also used to be a circus too, every so often, and we'd see camels and other exotic creatures grazing on the grass, as though they were no different to the resident cows.

This part of the Flats has hosted a fair for centuries but during the Second World War, it had a darker purpose, as the site of a prisoner-of-war camp. One of two that were sited on Wanstead Flats. The only remnants of that time are two rusted iron posts, around a metre high, that barrage balloons used to be tied to.

The rain is coming down hard now and as I try to type a message to a friend, drops hit the keys and compose words I didn't intend. I pass what used to be a model boating lake, now green and rewilded. Where small motorised boats once whizzed and whirred, there are now nesting beds for geese and ducks. As I stand on a jetty and watch the birds, screams still ring out behind me.

I cross the road on to the Bushwood side of the Flats. Two magpies, this time – for joy – caw me onwards.

Cutting a path across the plain I am confronted by a waist-deep ditch full of water that I've never seen before, a result of the recent storms I imagine. Blocked on all sides, I'll have to walk a longer way round. Ahead of me those brother blocks of flats, Fred Wigg and John Walsh Towers, and further away, the silver of Canary Wharf and its siren-sister towers. By now birdsong is drowning out the driving rhythms of the fair. I find the end of the ditch and it's almost brimming over. One more shower and there'll be a breach.

As I look ahead to the long grass, I have a memory of lying in it with a good friend, an Easter bank holiday in a heatwave, looking up at the sky, sunglasses on. Laughing and swigging from a bottle of rosé, having not bothered to bring any cups.

I smell something sour which I suspect is rotting grass. Water is seeping into my trainers. It occurs to me I'm not thinking about Mum.

And then I am. Thinking about Mum.

Ten years ago this year, my parents came to visit me and my husband in a flat we'd just moved into, in Leytonstone. They set off from their home in Forest Gate and walked across Wanstead Flats. They arrived with bread, salad and some other bits and we shared lunch together. Mum gave me a card to say how happy she was that we'd moved back closer to home.

A few days later, I got a call from my Dad at around 5 a.m. He told me that Mum had been hit by a car the night before, while going out to meet friends. She was in a coma at a hospital in Whitechapel. She sustained serious brain damage and was in and out of a coma for the next two and a half years. And then she died. That lunch in Leytonstone was the last time I ever saw her complete.

The walk I am doing traces the one they took to get to us that day. It's a walk I've done many times, for many reasons, though not recently.

I find myself plucking at the head of a long stem of grass, as she used to do, taking pleasure from the sensation of beheading it and scattering its seeds, feeling them between my fingers. I stand for a minute among the grass and the puddles and I stare at a gorse bush and feel the hot burn of tears behind my eyes.

At the edge of the long grass is a football field which I'll walk across to get to where I lived for five years. At one of the goalposts, two boys are playing football with their Mum and laughing uproariously, play-tackling each other.

Looking around me, the blocks, the bushes, the fields, all mean something to me, meaning forged in time I've spent here, in layers from childhood to the time I returned. I loved this place and I cry for the pain, but also the lost pleasure of those times. I cry for wasted time, time wasted, snatched time, more wasted time, time that's just slipped away, and I know I can't waste more time.

I meet Ros, who lives nearby, at 12.30. She doesn't have a mobile phone so we've made an appointment to meet in a café. It's her birthday and we share some pastries to celebrate before making the ten-minute walk back to her house.

Ros was a friend of my Mum's, and we've kept up with each other over the years. They met in the 1980s, initially on the circuit of parents' forums, women's centres and left-leaning political groups that were a mainstay of East London culture at the time 'When West Ham Lane had a bookshop and a health food shop where Benjamin Zephaniah used to work. Those were the days,' Ros tells me.

Later, they were colleagues at the Newham branch of the mental health charity, Mind. 'There was always a feeling she was so good at what she did,' Ros says, 'and my desk was here and her desk was there so we were opposite each other. And she was just such a calming and amiable presence.'

After they stopped working together, Ros and Mum stayed in touch as part of a small group of women who met fortnightly in one another's houses to talk honestly about their lives. Keeping this regular date in the diary when partners and children were banished for the evening was a small but radical act of sisterhood, and the group continued over a number of years.

Ros has lived in Leytonstone since around 1970, when she moved into a house on Hainault Road. A big house with a lot of people living there. An anarchist activist (married to a friend of hers) whose brother was a folk singer. His ex-wife lived upstairs with their daughter. A couple from Israel who were peace activists. Eventually, in 1974, Ros teamed up with a friend to buy the house we're in now. It's where Ros brought up her daughter, who recently become a mother herself. Lots of people have moved in and out of this place, most recently, her lodgers, some of whom have been more compatible than others, she tells me, in a voice which crackles with wry humour and sincerity all at once.

Sitting in the yellow-painted kitchen surrounded by potted plants and posters for arts and political events gone by, Ros tells me about the people who live, and have lived round and about her street: musicians, writers, tramps, activists. 'The road is getting very gentrified now though,' she says, 'and I don't necessarily like that. My daughter could never afford to live around here.'

And then we talk some more about Mum. I want to know what she remembers. We talk about her kindness, what she was like as a friend, her love of having guests over. Her fondness for decorating rooms in bright and unusual colour schemes. 'I wish I had more distinct memories,' Ros says.

Finishing our tea, we say goodbye and I wander back towards Leytonstone High Road. I find I'm asking myself – how do you hold a mother (my mother) in memory? What fragments can I piece together that will keep her complete as the years pass? What she taught me (how to wire a plug, among other things)? The songs she loved (David Bowie)? Her love of the absurd (Monty Python)? The things we talked about over Baileys on Christmas Eve as we wrapped presents until 2 a.m.? The things she said? The things she didn't say? The things she disapproved of that would go missing from my room? That she lived her politics through the way she treated others?

The card she gave me on that day, when she walked from Forest Gate to Leytonstone.

SHARON NIGHTINGALE

Sharon Nightingale is based in East Anglia, and inspired by its land, water and people she intertwines the challenges of our world with memories and the depths of human emotions. Exploring with a sense of wonder and reflection, her journeys are both fun and thought-provoking. She is a wild swimmer, artist and collector of hagstones, sea glass and stories.

Sharonjb17@yahoo.com

A Flâneuse in Norwich

An extract from a project on walking in cities

Flâneuse [flanne-euhze] – the feminine form of flâneur [flanne-euhr]. An imaginary definition of one who wanders, or dawdles, usually in cities.[1]

I had slept badly, rising just after sunrise to a palette of frosted white grass, blue sky and a hint of pink warming the highest branches. Exhaustion delayed me and the sun was already loosening the frost on the car windscreen as I prepared to leave. I intended spending the morning flâneusing the city but an internal voice was nagging. The longer I spent there the less time I would have with my son later, and I see him quite rarely. Then there is my fear; can I wander into places I know nothing of? Can I trust my instinct? I wondered if a flâneur would be feeling this way.

I don't 'know' Norwich well but I have an idea where the main streets take me so I was unsure how to begin being aimless. The sun glinting on the river drew me to it and I began following its route. The only surviving Swan Pit on my right. Intriguing. And two swans in the river on the left. Coincidence? Then I had to stop. The route was flooded. I exchanged pleasantries with a couple on the other side of the divide, then we each turned back and retreated. I reached my starting point and followed the river in the opposite direction.

Sunshine, reflections, swans and cormorants, willows and crocuses.

Four people had spoken to me in the space of 200 metres. All friendly, but the sight of a tent pitched by the river had me pausing with a sudden fear. The door of the tent was slightly open. But was the fear for me or them? After all, they were on the edge of a flooded riverbank. I caught myself wondering if it was someone who was homeless, such a stereotype view ingrained in me, but then it may just as easily be someone on a long pilgrimage-type walk. The drift of a sweet, flowery scent on the air had me sniffing and searching the bushes along the bank until I found the source, an evergreen with tiny white star like flowers. I closed my eyes to savour it. When I opened them I noticed, behind the shrubs, another tent, this time pitched up close to a wall for shelter. I began to think my first assumptions had been correct. The two sides of most cities were displayed here on the banks of the river, tents of the homeless on one side and, on the other, the gated blocks of

---

1   Paraphrased from Elkin, L. (2016) Flaneuse *Chatto and Windus*

river-front apartments, their chrome-gleaming balconies absorbing the warmth of the early spring sunshine.

Passing St James Quay I ascended the steps onto a bridge and wondered where to head next. I knew there was a café at the end of the road to the right of the river so turned in that direction. After all, a mid-life flâneuse is going to need a toilet before long. A green 'Viking Norwich' plaque (partly funded by the North Sea Viking Legacy Programme – who knew!) alerted me to the fact that St Edmund (once King Edmund) was killed by Danes in 869. I supposed I could follow these plaques, but then that would be with a purpose and so against my flaneuse rules. A faded Churches Trust plaque on the church wall cautioned me, 'in using this building, remember its origin with thanksgiving', but the door was locked so I was excused from using it at all. A second 'Viking Norwich' plaque announced that Colegate may derive from a Scandinavian personal name. But then, I thought, it may not. Opposite this a temporary fence stood, but I noticed a clematis twisted through the fence and a three-foot-high buddleia growing behind it from a pavement crack. The fence was not so temporary then. Looking up I could see the golden gleam of the clock on Norwich City Hall's tower which made it a little difficult now to believe I didn't know where I was. I followed a ginger cat as it slinked around a shady corner into a courtyard of modern houses but it had disappeared, apparently into thin air, and there was no exit for me. Turning back the clock was now out of sight and I was disoriented. Flints covered the buildings to my left and right and I stood looking at the tool marks on these for a while. One building was five hundred years old and I touched the marks on the flints wondering if the makers had been appreciated for the undoubted skill they had. To feel the passage of time through the centuries in such a small insignificant thing was a little humbling. What will I leave the world when I go?

The café was closed and I paused; a flâneur may be able to use a bush or duck behind a wall but this is not an option for a flâneuse. The sound of music coming from the left drew me in that direction. A tiny play park was fenced in on St George's Green, a graffiti artist named 'Sock' had been at work, and there was a busker playing on the bridge. To the sound of 'Wild World' I crossed the bridge back towards the city. Four different church bells chimed ten o'clock: at 09.57, 10.00, 10.02 and 10.04 by my watch. I was stopped in my tracks by violets growing out of a wall, opposite 'BENSON, BASS & SLATTERY Ltd REGISTERED OFFICE', and by the eclectic items in Whistle Dixie's window. Past St Peter Hungate, I did a U-turn in Plumbers Arms Alley as it seemed to go nowhere, entered Tombland and felt like a giant by tiny ancient front doors. Relief that Blue Bear café was open and had a toilet. A tea sipped in the sun, in front of its window, gave me an excuse to watch the world go by and gather snatches of chat.

Tiger print fur blouson jacket with purple tartan trousers emerged from the gateway and headed right. Flint walls opposite and a tiny window way up high. A secret room?

'They turned a corner at reasonable speed. Guess what happened?' I will never know.

The cathedral entrance bathed in sun, its weather worn statues were passed by electric buses humming their route. No belching fumes to cloud my view. Thick tyred electric bikes whirred by, Just Eat and Deliveroo. Inevitably, a car backfired. A plane trailed across the sky, deceptively heading for the spire, passed behind and chequerboarded with earlier trails.

'You say what categories you want and I will set it up.'

Double pom-pom hatted woman taking a photo of the emerging blossom on a small shrub by the cathedral wall. A celebration of returning warmth.

'I ain't going in there.'

Finger pointing, navy quilted jacket. Mansplaining in the direction of the cathedral. So knowledgeable. Then a leopard print fur coat, fake I'm sure, with matching hat and bright red scarf crossed the road. Opposite, a shoulder carried tripod and camera on a walking booted, khaki rucksacked, slim outdoorsy man. So serious about his photography and his walking. He paused, let the camera slip into his hand, pointed, shot and slung it back across his shoulder as he marched off. No flaneur, then, this was a man with a purpose. I turned to the left as I rose from the café's seat, for no other reason than the fact that the bin was that way. As I deposited my cup, the bell above the café rang its old-school-yard sound as a customer entered, I continued walking with the sound echoing in my ears.

Waggon and Horses Lane, named after a pub of course, had the feel of a waiting Victorian film set, but the double yellow lines dragged it back into the present. St Simon and St Jude's pre-Norman plot sat in the shadow of a double-trunked yew whose branches almost reached to Wetherspoons across the road. In Elm Hill, brunchers dined in the Sunday sun of Olive's, while I read of the loss of the last elm from Henry VIII's era to Dutch Elm Disease in the 1970s. Rumbling announced the approach of a car through this narrow way, across cobbles unable to envisage this method of travel when they were first laid. I wobbled across the stones to investigate shining from within Truman's Barbershop, which turned out to be the glint of chrome from the row of sleek 1950s style chairs ready for Monday's customers. The window display showed that Billy had this barbershop in 1900 and it was used as a snowy film set for Netflix in 2019. Roaches Court led to Pub and Paddle, traffic cones topped a plastic sheeted wardrobe in the churchyard and Stoned and Hammered's window held pearls and flowers. A tiny courtyard behind a wrought iron gate was filled with a jumble of windows, doors and steps.

I paused and heard the same busker again. Where was he? Where was I? I looked up and saw a mannequin in a window. The Arts University; so I had to be near the river. I turned a corner and saw the Pub and Paddle sign again. I knew where I was. I was learning how the city is connected, how the alleys and lanes link and how the river really does run through its heart. Stepping down onto the quayside, wood and iron bales along the quay represent packages discharged from barges. They bear the names of some of the people who lived and worked at Quayside over the past 200 years.

Another tent on the opposite bank sat just above a white boat reflected in the still river, its bright pink buoys echoed the tent colour and were doubled from five to ten by the water.

I stood to one side to let a large group pass me, and eavesdropped again 'I know I find that a bit weird, don't you?'

'I'm going to listen to, like, positive tunes.'

A row of terraced houses faced new apartments and the last one had a shady, lush green front garden set behind wrought iron fence and gate. A small grey painted bench to the left of the path suggested a sunset perch for summer evenings and the white of snowdrops and hellebores nestled in green swathes of leaves. A grey leafed buddleia stood sentinel on the right while the tiniest, tentative white petals were braving the chill spring day on the miniature magnolia centre stage. A few houses further on and, in a window, I was startled by the movement of a black cat statue. Flanked by a photo frame and a jar of jelly beans it had a blue collar and a silver bell. It watched me writing and then blinked and looked away, haughtily as only a cat can.

'It was quite good to remind her of the good times.' I glanced after the speaker and wondered why?

'It wasn't going to be completely dead in winter,' said one of a group of women walking towards me. Clad in long puffer coats, wearing trainers and rucksack bags. I assumed they were a walking group, but maybe they were on a hen do, it could have been either. A small white dog wearing a royal blue jumper with four sleeves trotted past me, its legs all warmed by the knitted fabric. I didn't notice what its owner was wearing. I was now back at St James Quay and retracing my steps. The scented bush, three white-barked birches, wide open large iron gates,

Fatsia Japonica, tent, and lilac graffiti. The sound of a jogger's feet from behind me, I stood to one side and she passed by. I had settled into this aimless wander and would do it again. I had enjoyed the noticing. Without reason.

CAROLE PONNIAH

Carole Ponniah is interested in telling the stories of less well-known figures in history, religion and literature. Her first proper job was in TV as a scriptwriter. She has also worked in a Somerset vineyard, taught in Eastern Turkey, and tested samples for infectious diseases. She has degrees in Literature and Biology.

caroleponniah@hotmail.co.uk

Rebel Woman: Vera Brittain. *Dissent and the Second World War*

Extract from Chapter 1

1935: THE SADDEST YEAR SINCE THE WAR

The six-year-old was afraid of the dark. Perhaps telling stories out loud at night helped.[1] Fragments climbed out of her room, stole across the passage, and fell over her younger brother, Edward, half-asleep, half-listening in his nursery bed. In the daytime, singing and tinkling piano music filled the house in Cheshire. But for the young Vera Brittain, the impulse to tell stories was ever pulsating, thickening, gnawing at her. By the time she was eleven, she had written five 'novels' on thick wastepaper from the family mill that her governess had cut, shaped, and stitched into little books.[2] When she turned twenty in December 1913, she yearned to earn a living through writing. It put her out of kilter with her wealthy, middle-class parents, and a patriarchal society. Fortunately, she was her father's favourite. In the summer of 1914, she won a place to study at Oxford.

When war was declared just a few months later, her brother Edward and their close friends, Roland, Victor, and Geoffrey, volunteered to fight. 1915 saw her engaged to Roland and in the summer, leaving Oxford to train as a nurse. This would take her to army hospitals in London, Malta, and northern France. The war was not so kind to her young men. By 1918 they were all dead.

About a year later, the twenty-six-year-old returned to Oxford. Brittain was depressed and felt guilty at surviving the war. By chance, she struck up a friendship with Winifred Holtby, a fellow History student. Holtby helped Brittain navigate herself out of the darkness. After university, they lived together in London, both set on pursuing literary careers. Despite their aspirations to financial independence, their parents paved the way with a flat and a maid.

Brittain's first novel *The Dark Tide*, soon trotted out of the gates. Its caricature of varsity life caused a public scandal but was not well-received in literary circles. But she was making a name for herself in articles and reviews. The clear voice that used to tell stories at night became a sought-after presence at meetings and lecture halls. Here she talked ardently about women's rights and canvassed for the League of Nations, a peace-keeping organisation.

Unexpectedly *The Dark Tide* initiated a courtship through letters from a fan, George Edward Gordon Catlin. He was a professor of political science at Cornell

---

1 Vera Brittain, *Testament of Youth* (London: Orion Books, 2014), 9.
2 Brittain, *Testament of Youth*, 12

University in North America. When they married in 1925, Brittain tried to be a dutiful faculty wife. But she hated the stifling life and returned to England where she felt she could entirely submerge herself in writing her war book.

In August 1933, on the threshold of turning forty, she became famous. Her autobiography, *Testament of Youth*, was an instant hit. A haunting elegy to the young men she lost to the war, it is also a vivid testimony of war suffering. No detail is spared. Victor shot through the head and blinded, hanging on for weeks. Geoffrey hit in his left lung, slowly suffocating. A wait for a telephone call to announce Roland's arrival for Christmas, turning into a call from his father to say he had been killed. The blood-covered nurses. The suffering from severe burns because of mustard gas. Holding the hand of a dying German soldier and thinking it is Roland's hand she is holding. Even French mud is analysed: it is not fresh and earthy but sodden and saturated with the dead. The narrative carries a bitter denouncement of the statesmen and popular press who peddled false ideas about the nobility and glamour of war. And like a sword, the book cleaved a male perspective of the war that dominated the 'war books boom' of the late 1920s.[3]

Today *Testament of Youth* remains one of the most authoritative narratives about disillusionment with war, ranking alongside war classics' such as Siegfried Sassoon's *Memoirs of a Fox-Hunting Man*, Erich Remarque's *All Quiet on the Western Front*, and Robert Graves's memoir, *Goodbye to All That*. In a diary entry, Virginia Woolf may have mocked "...how she lost lover and brother, and dabbled her hands in entrails..." but she stayed up all night to finish reading it. Woolf wrote to her soon after to say how much she liked *Testament of Youth*.[4]

Once the autobiography hit the shops, Vera Brittain was not just busy, she was roller-coaster busy, right into the spring of 1934.

Diminutive at five foot three, impeccably dressed and coiffured, she travelled across the country to speak at over-warm assembly rooms and wind-swept church halls. Perhaps she was a beacon of hope amidst the shadow cast by talk of another impending war.

That autumn, she sailed to the United States for a gruelling three-month lecture tour through seventeen states. Everywhere she went in the US, she was dined and feted. She was excited. She was exhausted. Then she fell in love with her attentive American publisher, the handsome and married, George Brett.

Since their marriage, Brittain and her husband, Catlin, had slipped into a routine of Atlantic-wide separations. The relationship had become a 'semi-detached' marriage. It was also a ménage à trois[5]- with Holtby.

As singletons, Brittain and Holtby had agreed to live experimentally in family

---

3 Brittain, *Testament of Youth*, xiii, Introduction.
4 Anne Olivier Bell and Andrew McNeillie, ed., *The Diary of Virginia Woolf, Volume Four, 1931–1935* (New York: Harcourt Brace & Company, 1983), 177.
5 Elaine Showalter and English Showalter, ed., *Between Friends. Letters of Vera Brittain and Winifred Holtby* (London: Virago, 2022), 147–148.

settings of their own choosing.[6] Brittain was short, dark and anxious. Holtby was tall, blonde and laid-back, despite suffering from a painful and debilitating kidney condition that involved long periods of convalescence. Holtby was popular with other female writers and feminists like Lady Rhondda, founder of the feminist magazine, *Time and Tide*. The insecure and prickly Brittain was not popular. The writer Stella Benson called Brittain 'a bloodsucking friend' and Holtby a saint who liked being leeched.[7]

To the end of her life, Brittain asserted that Holtby was a beloved friend, not a lover.

When the North American tour ended in 1934, she returned home in time for Christmas to a round of familial duties: caring for two children with mumps, helping her mother find a new house, and soothing a depressed and infirm father.

At the start of 1935, Brittain confessed to Holtby that Brett was continually on her mind.[8] Holtby herself was in love with an ex-soldier, Harry Pearsons. Their non-sexual relationship teetered between the romantic and the platonic.

The women agreed that 'work' was the only effective remedy to unrequited love and illness. When Holtby went home to her family in Yorkshire, she wrote letters to Brittain, chivvying her to continue *Honourable Estate*, a story to be loosely based on the Brittain and Catlin families. In turn, Brittain hoped her letters neutralised Harry's unannounced visits and kept her pal working on *South Riding*, a novel about a rural community in Yorkshire. A year later *South Riding* would go on to win the James Tait Black fiction prize.

Perhaps because she was describing the effect of war on her characters in *Honourable Estate*, Brittain may have been dwelling on what she had learnt the previous summer about her brother, Edward. On the day before Edward had died, his Commanding Officer, Colonel Hudson, had warned Edward that letters to and from fellow officers were being read and censored. Edward had turned pale suggesting he understood Hudson's meaning.[9] Edward's homosexuality was not a surprise, but Brittain was shocked at the suggestion that Edward may have deliberately put himself in danger to avoid public disgrace. The incident seeps into *Honourable Estate* when an officer, Richard Alleydene, deliberately seeks death in battle to avoid a court martial for homosexuality. Richard's sexuality is presented as a romantic friendship between schoolboys, an aberration during war due to the lack of 'decent' women, meaning prostitutes.

There were other distractions in 1935. No writer could miss the celebrations around King George V's Silver Jubilee. On the 6th of May, a swirling wave of red,

6   Showalter and Showalter, ed., *Between Friends. Letters of Vera Brittain and Winifred Holtby*, 150–152.
7   Showalter and Showalter, ed., *Between Friends. Letters of Vera Brittain and Winifred Holtby*, 150.
8   Showalter and Showalter, ed., *Between Friends. Letters of Vera Brittain and Winifred Holtby*, 389.
9   Paul Berry and Mark Bostridge, *Vera Brittain. A Life* (London: Chatto & Windus, 1995), 130–135.

white and blue flags decked the streets of London. Garlands of paper flowers looped from one building to the next. Men's peaked caps and women's wide-brimmed hats gave some relief from the shimmering sun. People gathered on pavements and grass verges to watch as the procession made its way from the Palace to St Paul's Cathedral and back. Loudspeakers broadcasted the service. Those lucky enough to have indoor seats by windows in shops and banks, like Brittain, Holtby and the children, looked out in some comfort on the troops on horses and those on foot. They watched the royal carriage with a tired-looking King and his Queen, in her silver cloak and pink turban, going by at a swift trot.[10] By 3 p.m. it was over. Once home, the children rushed to play soldiers and royal figures. Brittain lamented the difficulty of teaching children about peace against the attraction of carriages, horses and uniforms.

By the end of July, fatigue, bouts of illness and the never-ending round of family demands were beginning to take effect. The bitterest blow was a visit in June from the tall, athletic, and sun-tanned Brett. They would meet at her tenth wedding anniversary party. She wore a delicate blue and mauve chiffon dress to match the mauve orchids that Brett had sent beforehand. But when they were alone, Brett only asked about *Honourable Estate*.

To get away from it all, at the end of July, she took the children, seven-year-old John and five-year-old Shirley, and Fraulein, their German governess on holiday. Wimereux was a popular family resort in northern France with a beach nearby and the port of Boulogne just minutes away by taxi. The garden at the Grand Hôtel des Anglais et des Bains was fringed with flowering trees and dusty shrubs, shading her from the noise and eyes of fellow holidaymakers. Scarlet nasturtiums overhung a shallow ornamental pool, their faint spicy scent a companion to the August heat percolating over the French coastal town. On one side the sound of the sea and shifting dunes, and on the other, the hay-scented countryside. It is easy to imagine Brittain eagerly bent over a table in the garden, scribbling in the shade, feeling the warm, salty breeze from the English Channel, gently nudging the sheets of paper, and in the distance, snatches of adult chatter and the muted shrieks of children. Minor domestic demands were swatted away because Fraulein was a godsend. This holiday was a perfect opportunity to throw herself into *Honourable Estate*.

On her second night, a large moth flew into her room unsettling her. The following evening was spent at a French military cemetery, watching a beautiful sunset.

The next day at luncheon, when she was expecting her husband, she looked up to see instead, a pale and haggard Holtby in her tweed coat standing in the lobby.

---

10 Vera Brittain, *Diary of the Thirties. 1932–1939. Chronicle of Friendship,* ed. Alan Bishop (London: Gollancz, 1986), 178.

BIBLIOGRAPHY

Bell, Anne Olivier, and Andrew McNeillie, ed., *The Diary of Virginia Woolf, Volume Four, 1931–1935*. New York: Harcourt Brace & Company, 1983.
Berry, Paul, and Mark Bostridge. *Vera Brittain. A Life*. London: Chatto & Windus, 1995.
Brittain, Vera. *Diary of the Thirties. 1932–1939. Chronicle of Friendship*, Edited by Alan Bishop. London: Gollancz, 1986.
Brittain, Vera. *Testament of Experience*. Bath: Victor Gollancz Ltd, 1957.
Brittain, Vera. *Testament of Youth*. London: Orion, 2014.
Showalter, Elaine, and English Showalter, ed. *Between Friends. Letters of Vera Brittain and Winifred Holtby*. London: Virago, 2022.

JANE RYAN

Jane Ryan trained as a psychotherapist in the 1990s. She was the founder and, for twenty-two years, Director of Confer, an independent organisation providing cutting-edge conferences for psychotherapists. She was the co-founder of the publishing imprint Confer Books, and Creative Director of Karnac Books, 2020–22. She is the editor of three psychotherapy books. www.confer.uk.com/biogs/biog_ryan.html

suffolkisbeautiful@gmail.com

Two People on a Beach in Norfolk

Recently, while searching for my grandfather's unpublished memoirs, I found a photo that was taken when my son was sixteen months old. It was captured by my friend Mark on a beach in Norfolk one day in January, a long time ago. The three of us had gone up there to stay in a rickety cottage with iron bedsteads and brick floors that belonged to someone he knew. I remember cloud-soaked skies and skeletal trees, wondering what might relieve my melancholy that New Year. Yet this photo shows a scene of happiness that reminds me that hopelessness couldn't have been my only state of mind at that time. I was smiling with delight.

Mark and I had met the previous summer while staying in a Cornish fishing village on the Roseland Peninsula. I'd driven there from London in my rickety Morris Traveller to join him and one of my closest friends, his sometime-partner Rowena. I was looking forward to seeing her and meeting him for the first time – to being a guest in an unknown house. With my baby son strapped into a makeshift car seat, his buggy packed in the boot with my rucksack, I eagerly set off to join them. Ash was a patient passenger, watching southern England blur by from his perch. It was going to be his first birthday that week.

Eventually descending the final steep lane, the harbour opened before us: a silver sea enfolded by shiny brown rocks and grassy cliffs; a fishing boat reclining on the slipway by a heap of lobster pots; a scattering of stone houses that straddled the pathways. I released Ash from his seat, and we stood for a while soaking in the ozone and cry of seagulls. The cottage was easy to find, squeezed between the hill and an alley of stone buildings that huddled the quay. 'We're here!' I called up to Rowena and Mark, who I soon spotted reading in a patch of garden. Unlatching the back door, I let myself into a dark kitchen. The room smelt of damp plaster, and tar from blackened beams.

'Hi, it's great to meet you,' grinned Mark as they came down the stairs. He was a small man – agile, tanned, with peephole blue eyes. 'How was your drive?' he asked, offering me a snappy handshake.

'It was fine. And long!'

Rowena and I half-hugged, Ash perched on my hip, the throbbing of the car's engine still pulsing through my body. 'Hi Ash!' she greeted, planting a kiss on his forehead. She had come to look after me following his birth, fetching supplies and making food while I contemplated the new being breathing in my arms, wondering who he was and who he would be. She said she would never have children of her own; the world was too unsafe. Rowena was always conflicted: a psychiatrist who was anti-psychiatry, a feminist who longed for rescue. She agonised over the crude medications she was trained to prescribe; worked with patients on hospital wards while worrying about those who were homeless; brooded over her boss's indifference to the emotional world of her patients and countered this by writing papers on the uniqueness of each psychotic mind.

'I'll make some tea while you show Jane around,' she told Mark, darting to the kettle in brown bare feet, her curly hair bobbing, searching for clean mugs. I followed Mark upstairs to a bright living room with a wide salt-sprayed view. He chatted about the history of the village, how he'd been coming here since he was eight when his uncle had bought the cottage from a fisherman's widow. We stood quietly for a moment watching two walkers pushing their way up the cliff path beyond.

'Look at the sea!' I said to Ash. 'Isn't it big!'

'Doh' he said, pointing intently at a spaniel racing into the water. It was his first word. I slept deeply that night, the sound of the waves rumbling in the walls of the house, peaceful as the guest of this new couple: the outsider without responsibilities.

'He's nice,' I said to Rowena the next day when Mark had gone ahead to make supper after a walk along the beach at low tide. We were sitting outside *The Lugger's Inn*, a red ball of sun sinking behind the hills, the sea evening-still.

'Yes, but I don't love him,' she said, sipping her beer. 'I can't quite find his edge, his limits. His real feelings.' She speculated that he was burdened by the niceness that his parents had insisted upon as he grew up. They were Jewish refugees from Europe who'd raised him to be as undemanding as possible. Later, when Mark cheerfully served up wine and a big bowl of pasta, I wondered if he knew about Rowena's reservations. I suspected that he didn't and that he would avoid that knowledge for as long as possible.

Over the week that followed, the three of slept, strolled, or gazed at Ash while he played with shells or wooden spoons and took his first steps. Walking single file along the narrow cliff paths, taking turns in carrying him in a sling my mother had sewn one sleepless night, we paused from time to time to gaze down at foaming brown rocks or bathers below. We talked about the things that concerned us most: Rowena's boss, Mark's research into echolocation of bats. The impending miners' strike. The Troubles in Northern Ireland. Thatcher. They smiled at each other but didn't touch. One morning when I went to offer them a cup of tea in bed, I found them reading into their own worlds, like random travellers, side-by-side on a train. I suspected that, at least in her imagination, Rowena was already onto her next relationship, on the stepping-stones of men and women who eventually led her to someone as suitably interrogating as herself.

Shortly after that Cornish holiday, when Rowena had discharged Mark from her life, and he and his camera found a small place in ours. Initially, he took up the habit of cycling over to my place from his lab for an occasional supper and to talk about the loss of this relationship. He wrote to her, he said, but the letters fell into a black hole. Gradually, these visits became more frequent. I was grateful for his company even though I couldn't share his fascination for cycling technology or the neurobiology of bats. Nor could I quite bring myself to desire him, much as I wished I could. But nonetheless an intimacy was growing between us that lingered somewhere between friendship and romance.

'How would you feel about coming away at New Year?' he asked whilst giving me a back massage with a knowing touch. I looked up at our reflection in the kitchen window. It seemed a good idea.

Just after Christmas, we packed the Morris Traveller and set off to a flint cottage somewhere near the coast of Norfolk. I can't remember where it was exactly, but I do recall my melancholy. Motherhood had given me a precious son, but since Ash's birth I had become an outsider in my family. My father didn't want me to go home, so deep was his shame at my child's illegitimacy. While I was unhappy for both of us, I was also worried about Dad's health: not long before he'd had a stroke that was causing hallucinations.

'Your father's been questioning me about a brown dog he can see in the living room', my bewildered mother had told me just before we left for Norfolk. 'And marvelling at the brilliant blue of a river he says has appeared in the garden'.

I fretted that they wouldn't be able to contact me if they needed to, but Mark said there was a phone box in the village anytime I wanted to call. We made the beds, opened a can of soup, and dried off some kindling in the oven. 'He was stable when we left,' he reassured. 'Try not to worry'. We eventually lit a fire and studied the map for possible walks by the sea.

Now, decades later, I hold the photo that Mark took the next day on a wide beach of hard damp sand in Norfolk. What surprises me is that the person I see inside the frame is not the delinquent I have been told I was but a surprisingly normal young woman smiling at her child. I'm crouching low, poised to take a photo of him. In the same moment Ash turns towards me, puzzled, caught between the gaze of two cameras. His dungarees and little blue-shod feet poke out under a woollen coat my mother made for him. His hands look cold – perhaps he took off his gloves – but his face peers out from a warm woolly hat. I too am wearing a hotchpotch of clothes. I remember the sheepy smell of that hand-knitted sweater and the feel of those purple brogues that bulged around my toe bone. In our small triangle of gazes, this is a scene of happiness in a cold, windswept place.

That night Mark and I slept together, consolingly, fondly. And over the next year, we saw each other regularly, either at my place or when I visited him in Hastings where he'd moved to live with friends. The relationship lasted contentedly until the inevitable and painful conversation in which I had to acknowledge I wasn't in love. 'I thought that bit was alright,' he said, confused. I shook my head, wishing that it was. He accepted my rejection with typical equanimity and we stayed friends for a while until he started dating a woman from work. Eventually, they and her children moved to Devon. Very occasionally I pop his name into google to see what he's doing. He is publishing books on echolocation.

There is, I know – somewhere – another photo, the one I took of Ash on the beach in Norfolk while Mark photo'd us. But to find this would involve the daunting task of opening the wooden trunk containing all the pictures I have accumulated in my life so far: albums of unremembered relatives, vanity shots of my father's boat, pouches of glossy prints, negatives and slides, a reel of film, tinted studio photographs parents took of various children. Snapshots of houses and pets, weddings, hills, snow, and seascapes. I can't afford the time to swim in those memories. For now, I can imagine that image: Ash turning his questioning face towards me, the icy northeast wind pinking his brown skin, looking so small against that vast slick of beach – the subject of another person's adoring gaze.

'I thought you might like to see this,' I message him at his London office with a copy, 'You and me years ago on a cold beach in Norfolk. Do you remember falling in the sea? Just after we took those photos you wandered towards the water, transfixed by the way the sea foam crept towards us. A bigger wave suddenly came from nowhere and surprised us all. In your astonishment you sat down and were soaked. I whipped you up into my arms and we ran to the car to take off your wet clothes and to wrap you in our coats.'

Somewhere there's a photo of that too, of Ash sitting in his car seat, swaddled in our sweaters and jackets, lost in some sleepy thought.

TANTRAVAHI

Tantravahi is obsessed with burning libraries. As a Disputes attorney from India, she has always enjoyed arguing from both sides of any legal issue. She is now working on a collection of essays on the themes of archival silencing, censorship, and libricide, titled *Do You Ever Read the Books You Burn.*

tantravahimanasa@gmail.com

The piece has no title.

Excerpt from the opening pages.

What if…

    You had to burn a book.

A *book* book.

A hard-bound. Ink and paper. Cardboard and satin!
A golden imprint of the title on its cover. The author's name on the side.

A *bookmark* sticking out of it, three-quarters of the way through.

If you had to.

    Burn it *completely*.
    -charred remains!
    -an ashy lump
    -a pile of soot

How would you do it?
Where would you begin?

                  You don't *have* to do it.[1]

                  But what if you had to?

---

[1] I think my friend up there – you know, the one talking to you – just wants to know *how* you'd do it. If you must. A question for the day, let's say… And it's okay if you can't think of any reason why you *must* burn a book. I get it. I mean who burns a book because they *must*… as if there's a diktat? I could have a chat with him if you'd like. You don't *have* to listen to him.

Unless… you *want* to burn a book.

Do you? Is that something you—

Say no one's watching you.² You know… In case you're wondering about the *where* and the *when,* and you're not one of those who's ready with a plan the minute I said, 'Let's burn some books!' If you *are* one of those, just skip to the next section: there's a special plan for *you* there. In the meanwhile, let my other readers take a second here. Now… *you*. The other you. How would you do it?

Say no one's watching you.

You'll do it in the parking lot of some department store, maybe. One of those huge, crowded – yet isolating – capitalist by-products which can give you all the privacy you need when you need it… picture this: the copy first doused in cooking oil and sparked. Then the floundering orange flames flung on the grey gravel of number 451, the parking lot. Yeah?

It'd catch the eye of *none* of the hundred orange plastic bags busy squeezing themselves into their cars, a grey gravel frame speckled with orange dots, your little arsonous venture lost in the saffro—*orange* throng – the flame and the bags, the perfect orange camouflage.

How does that sound?³

Or you could do it in your backyard.

While-your-partner's-at-work-and-your-children-are-off-at-school-and-your-ailing-father's-settled-into-his-couch-for-the-day. There. How about that?

I'm not *all* riddles and imagery, you know.⁴
You could do it in the evening, too!

When it's not so well-lit.
How about that? No?⁵

2 I was still talking!
3 It *sounds* like… my friend's dangerously close to making this about something else altogether. It would help my friend to remember that that imagery – a-a-a *saffron* fire fitting in 'perfectly' in a sea of vapid orange plastic bags, and in a 'capitalist' backdrop too (he's not very subtle, is he) – is the sort of imagery that'd work only if the reader knows *exactly* what he's talking about. Let's stick to the original idea – he only wants to know what you feel about *burning a book* and nothing else.
4 Smooth. Also, this is starting to reek of a hidden agenda.
5 No! If it's not so well-lit, the *fire* would be seen! You idiot. Do it in the afternoon if you must. Also, the department store idea – assuming you're actually going along with this madness – makes even *less* sense in the night.

Maybe you could lean against the side of your car, your mini-van, your vehicle-of-choice – at the department store – and hide further from view. Or you could do it on your back torch—*porch,* sorry, one that runs around your building and ends at the back door... you know... flanked by low brick-walls on either side, or iron grills, a back garden verandah*,* a sit-out. There.

Anywhere.

Any of these.

You're *fine*.

No one can see you and no one can know what you're up to.

Now.

                  How would you do it? The actual burning, I mean.
                              Where would you begin?[6]

---

[6] I think what he (probably) means – with all these suggestions – is... It's not a crime anyway. Just burning a book. It's not the Constitution, it's not a flag; it's just a book. There's no punishment for that. For example, here in India, it's not even an "offence" burning books out in the open! As per the Indian Penal Code. We've looked it up. We'd know. Besides, a *lot* of people have done it already. They burned copies of Rohinton Mistry's *Such a Long Journey* in 2010 (it was obscene and had "vulgar" language) out on the streets. They ransacked a library and burned copies of a history book on the Maratha warrior king, Shivaji, in 2004 (it was full of "lies"). They did Perumal Murugan's *Madhorubagan* in 2015 (it was blasphemous, it insulted the temple at Tiruchengode in Tamil Nadu, it was in "bad taste"). And nobody said a word about penalties. It's not an offence, merely burning a book. He means you're fine, as far as the law is concerned.

It's not the law. So, this is (probably) only about the aesthetics. Maybe he actually wants to know how you'd do it? Uniquely you?

Wait.

Why *is* it fine, as far as the law is concerned?

Or would you prefer if you did it in a crowd instead? You, who's *excited* at the possibility of setting a text alit, you. This here is for you. Do you have any friends?

I *have* thought about asking this in the first instance… I mean I'm clearly not one to shy away from such things.⁷ Except… it's icky, no? No, not icky. Uncomfortable? Not uncomfortable. Just. Delicate. Delicate? I don't want to come across as judgemental. A mob circling a biblio-pyre, watching it smoulder, turn clinker. Even a mob that is whimsical, not diabolical. Experimental, not sadistic. Like-like *you* lot. It might still be a delicate topic, no? It's a resurrected scene, not one fresh out of our imaginations.

But… if you're comfortable, then that's what we go with?

Maybe it is perfectly okay, doing this in a crowd.⁸ Maybe it is thrilling, in some ways. Maybe it's like role-playing. Maybe it's like the Stanford Prison experiment, you turn perpetrators for a—sorry, you turn *guards* for a moment. You wield power, you hold all the torches, you have the capacity to turn a collection of words, fifty thousand words, eighty thousand words, a hundred thousand, and thousands and thousands, words into *nothing* with the slightest movement of your collective hands. You get that second of deliberation, you get to stand at the mouth of a library, the air still except for the crackling of the flames in your hands, the air smelling of nothing at all, nothing's burning just yet – it's you lot and the flames, alone and united – and *whoosh…* you bend the spines of a thousand books to you in reverence, each of you is a conductor of that orchestra.

Isn't that intoxicating? ⁹

---

7 Clearly.
8 Maybe it is. You know… a band of workers belonging to the Rashtriya Swayamsevak Sangh (RSS) – maybe a part of the Bharatiya Janata Party (BJP) too – broke into the AKG Memorial Library, in Malappuram district, Kerala, in 2016, and set it on fire in the middle of the night. About five thousand books were powdered within an hour. And then a swarm of a thousand *Hindutvavadis* – Hindu extremists – invaded a 113-year old library in Nalanda district, Bihar, in 2023 and razed it to the ground. It had housed about 4500 books, which included 250 *kalmi* (handwritten) manuscripts, before it was destroyed. You *could* do it by yourself, like he suggested up there, or you could do it in a crowd like *they* did. You get to choose. You always get to choose.
9 I remember what Guy Montag, in Ray Bradbury's *Fahrenheit 451* said: "It was a pleasure to burn. It was a special pleasure to see things eaten, to see things blackened and changed." And then Susan Orlean burnt a new copy of that book on a "windless, warm day and climbed to the top of the hill in my backyard", by dressing the book in an aluminium cookie sheet and holding a match to its cover. She recorded it in *The Library Book* as: "As soon as it was over, I felt like I'd just jumped out of an airplane, which is perhaps the natural reaction to doing something I'd resisted so mightily—there was the elation at overriding my own instincts, elation at the fluid beauty of fire, and terrible fright at the seductiveness of it and the realization of how fast a thing full of human stories can be made to disappear." Maybe it *is* intoxicating? Maybe it is…

Don't you feel... huge? Don't you feel like you could do *anything* if you didn't really care for what lies between those covers? Don't you feel like no idea could hurt you again, no one's opinion could bring you down, make you feel stupid, illiterate, make you feel small, incapable, dismissed... nothing. *You* get to convert those ideas into nothing, *you* get to win, you get to defeat what could have owned you, you get t—

if you knew what it was, of course, inside those books...

you wouldn't unless you *read* those books, but that's a minor issue, no?

Is it necessary to truly know what you're defeating before you go about defeating it? Is that win, the finishing off of a *possibility,* without knowing exactly the future consequences, any different from the finishing off of a well-defined enemy? Nip a flower while it's still a bud, no?[10] Minor issues, anyway.

This though. This power.

Between you and me, you think that's why they did it? Those mobs. In Kerala. And Bihar. Would you then prefer doing it in a crowd?

Not that you need convincing twice on all of this. Don't worry. I haven't forgotten the excitement of *you* lot. I guess I'm just thinking out loud.

But what if, in the midst of all of that, you forget to tell me – you forget to notice – what you actually feel about the *burning*? What if you get consumed by the power – it can happen, obviously, it's understandable – and forget the original question. Then the question wouldn't make sense, would it. Or it would. I just wouldn't get my answer.

Let's stick to you, for now. Just you.

And me.[11]

What do you think?

---

[10] As a part of prison rules in Nabokov's *Invitation to a Beheading,* the protagonist Cincinnatus C is told "It is desirable that the inmate should not have at all or, if he does, should immediately himself suppress nocturnal dreams whose content might be incompatible with the condition and status of the prisoner [such as: resplendent landscapes, outings with friends, family dinners, as well as sexual intercourse with persons who in real life and in the waking state would not suffer said individual to come near, which individual will therefore be considered by the law to be guilty of rape]." You cross a line in your *dreams,* and you are guilty of rape because an illegal *dream* has the potential for the actual commitment of a crime in the future. Thus burn a book – illegitimise and then destroy its potential – before its ideas spread and commit crimes. The principle is the same.

[11] And me!

Now, what fuel would you use? I doubt you'd use much quantity, whatever it be. Is it kerosene?[12] I *did* mention cooking oil. Something inexpensive, maybe. Easily procurable at a local mart. No acids and complicated chemicals. Or you're not into catalysts. Or theatrics. You wouldn't want to hasten the act, maybe? I'd get that. I'd understand. But how else would you do it?

---

[12] My friend seems to have a *lot* of ideas on how to do this... why does he need *your* method? I don't get it.

I could have asked you something else, you know. I could have asked: 'What if you had to drown a book?' Kill it off in other ways. How would you do *that?* Would you waterboard it? Hold it inside a tub filled with water until the pages—

GINNY THOMAS

Ginny Thomas is a psychoanalyst and writer from Cambridge, with a background in art. Her work combines memoir, biography and art history, often through a psychoanalytic frame. She is currently writing a family history of trans-generational melancholia, as well as exploring public mourning via a piece of memorial land art in Sicily.

ginny.thomas@yahoo.co.uk

A Different Kind of Man
A Piece of Memoir

I've finally had enough of the frail old man, so I've taken him down, covered him in a white sheet and consigned him to the attic.

We've looked at each other for years, the two of us. He's been hanging on one wall or another for my entire life. But recently, in the wake of my mother's death, I realised I didn't want to see him anymore. I think I mainly liked the picture because my father gave it to me when I was twenty-one, just a handful of years before *he* died. For the thirty-eight years that he has been mine, this unknown, painted man has followed me wherever and whenever I have moved. In some ways he's been a heavy weight to carry.

The subject of the painting saw everything that those my mother termed 'the men' did, much of which felt to me as a child exciting and even a bit dangerous. A lot of it also felt alien, in an environment that was all boys and men with the exception of my mother and me. The picture hung above the fireplace in the sitting room where my father and his friends would often drink whisky, smoke cigarettes, play poker and tell rude jokes. From the age of around eight and for the next few years, I was desperate to be allowed into this adult, male, other world. I'd sit on the rug by the fire with the dog, hoping not to be noticed and told to go to bed, while the room got warmer, the air thicker and the ash trays filled. When there was an east wind, even the fire would smoke. The painted man was a wordless witness to all the dirty richness in that room, perhaps some of which lingers still between the yellowing layers of the picture's aged varnish.

The painting looks Dutch and is most likely a Victorian copy of a seventeenth-century work, as both style and sitter – male, white, wealthy, like the majority of portrait subjects at the time – evoke Rembrandt and his contemporaries. The man appears frail with his pale, lined skin and his face is somewhat overshadowed by a thick, fur-rimmed cape and large black cloth cap. Beautifully dressed, serious and silent, he was so different from the loud men in the room that back then he seemed from another species altogether. He was also a different kind of man in that he was of course only a representation, held in and held back, suspended within the two-dimensional form of oil on canvas.

If portraits could speak, this one would surely emit, if not a 'champagne and cigar' voice, one of Bell's whisky and Player's non-filtered cigarettes. In Dutch. I wonder what he'd have to say about what he saw and heard. Were he a religious man, I imagine he may have been as disapproving of my father's jokes, with their 'cunt' punchlines, as my mother tried hard to appear to be. But she was often too busy in the kitchen, too sick of the same old talk to want to see or to listen to what went on. 'I've heard it all before', she'd say.

Sometimes I'd watch the man in the painting as I moved. I'd see his eyes following me, that unnerving ability portraits have when their subject's gaze is directed outwards. I didn't mind being under his eye. Perhaps I liked it, even.

A little later, as I moved into teenage years, I did mind being under my father's eye. I became aware of this, his noticing of my body, only via the words of my mother. 'Dad doesn't like it when you get *big up here*' she used to say, vaguely waving towards the area between her breasts and her chin. My father said nothing directly to me about my shamefully developing form, but he would often criticise his 'big-bosomed' half-sister: 'I'm afraid she's let herself get *fat*,' and in that I heard a message that I thought was meant for me. This conflation of fatness and femaleness was confusing, but what to do? There was no stopping the advance of puberty, even though I used to lie in my bed looking out of the window at the tall trees and willing it away, wishing I was the girl to whom it wouldn't happen. Whatever 'big up here' meant, I knew I didn't want it.

My looks were also commented on by others, as was my name, 'She's a well-built lass' and 'How's Virginia-Vagina?' – the latter by a particularly unpleasant, smirking son-in-law of friends of my parents. And yet this man was challenged not about his words but about his dark green velvet jacket. The perceived flamboyance of such a garment was something of an anomaly in this northern culture: any man wearing clothes that suggested his appearance mattered to him invited suspicion and ridicule. Had the man in the painting been present, in the 1970s equivalent of his rich cape and soft cap, he would also have been mocked. I like to think *his* words would have been very different from those of the intrusive and embarrassing son-in-law. Released from his painted suspension, maybe the Dutchman might even have called him out.

Throughout my childhood one of the noisy men in the sitting room – I'll call him J – whom I did not like, often joined us for Christmas Day. He would otherwise have been on his own following his divorce, and my parents, or my father at least, were happy to include him. His presence may be why I developed the slightly strange habit, on the odd occasion that we ate out, of nagging my parents to invite any solitary older man to join us. However much I might have disliked J, I had perhaps absorbed the message that a man could not be alone. After my father's first wife died when he was forty, leaving him as well as their three young sons behind, it was a matter of months before he and my mother, then a twenty-four-year-old nurse, started seeing each other. The scraps of knowledge I must have gleaned about this were perhaps the first iteration of the impossibility of a man being left on his own.

My thoughts about solitary men even reached as far as television characters. My mother told me that when I was about eight or nine, I wanted us to look after the leading men in two long-running detective series with which I became obsessed: *Cannon* and *Ironside*. I wonder whether the man in the portrait may have elicited a similar response in me in my adult life. I certainly took care of him for long enough.

J brought the same offering for my mother each Christmas. The choice should have been easy: he, like everyone around her, knew that she loved dark chocolate. Any dark chocolate, but particularly Bournville, Bendicks Bittermints and red Bounty bars. And yet every year J presented her with a box of Cadbury's Milk Tray, known since the late sixties for melodramatic tv commercials in which a dark-haired man would ski down mountains, fight fires or swim past sharks to deliver chocolates, 'all because the lady loves Milk Tray'. Perhaps J identified with the James Bond-esque figure in the ads, although his own journey to hand his box over was a somewhat less spectacular ten-minute drive across the Wolds in his beige Ford.

Every year, J would consult my mother about what he should buy for *me*.

It was Christmas 1977. I was thirteen, self-conscious, and just starting to like boys and music. In the summer I'd bought my first single, ABBA's 'Dancing Queen' and all I wanted – apart from to be the sweet, young seventeen-year-old in the song – were records. There was nobody else staying with us that year. All four of my grandparents had died, and my three much older half-brothers were away with friends or fiancées. It was just me, my parents and J, an odd little foursome.

I was standing by the record-player in a corner of the sitting room when J handed me a present, flat and square, surely an LP. Our family was not given to kissing each other on the cheek – I didn't know anyone who did that, not in North Yorkshire, although I was occasionally subjected to uncomfortable 'bear hugs' from a godfather or uncle – so I was surprised when he leant towards me as if to do so. But instead he kissed me on the mouth. It lasted long enough for his eager tongue to dart wetly in between my lips and out again.

Sometime afterwards I wondered how he'd got away with it. I wondered where my parents were. Why didn't they see? Was my mother in the kitchen, or in the sitting room unwrapping a present of her own, or stroking the dog? Was my father pouring a drink or lighting a cigarette? Putting a log on the fire? I don't think I made a sound. If I had glanced at the man in the portrait in those moments, and I can't remember if I did, he would have been looking back, would have witnessed this impingement. I suppose that if I didn't glance at him, he would have been looking elsewhere, like my parents, and he'd have missed it too.

The album was the eponymous *The Sound of Bread*, a compilation of greatest hits that seemed to be played relentlessly on the radio for months afterwards. For many years the memory of the kiss disappeared from my conscious mind although, as Freud tells us is often the case with repression, there were effects: I was aware of strange sensations when I heard any of the tracks and I couldn't understand why some of the lyrics made me feel sick.

Decades later the thought of the album, or the very rare occasions when I hear one of the songs, still unsettles me. Also uncomfortable is the memory of the colours on the cover: a warm yellowy-cream background with brownish swirly letters, not unlike the sickly Banana and Toffee Whirl sweets that added to that bad taste of the seventies.

The recollection of the experience itself is, however, free of feeling. As if it happened to someone else, with me as onlooker, as though I were the man in the painting.

When, in my late twenties, I finally told my mother about it, she expressed shock, and regret that she had not known at the time. But she found it difficult not to think of it as something – albeit something wrong, uninvited, clumsy – from which I just needed to move on. She didn't see the value in returning to anyone's past, and mine and hers were no exceptions. She couldn't understand why anyone would go into psychoanalysis, never mind become an analyst oneself, as I did. 'How can you bear to listen to people all day?' she'd ask. We differed there: bearing witness is one of the things in life that makes most sense to me.

And so the painted man is in the attic, the sheet over his face. While I don't attribute the significance to his gaze that I did as a child, there is still a weight. However benign his presence might have been, it remains attached to a set of memories. Log fires, cigarette smoke, dirty jokes, warm whisky. The seventies, the men. *The Sound of Bread.*

I'm not sorry that this particular painted man – such a different kind of man – was part of my life for so many years, but it was time for him to move on. The room already feels lighter for his absence.

PROSE FICTION

LW ANDERSON

LW Anderson was born in Cambridgeshire to Irish parents. She takes inspiration from the postmodernist styles of Vonnegut and Saunders, applying them to her own flowered fiction, predominantly in novel form. She is also completing a second master's in Irish Mythology and Folklore and has a keen interest in exploring the orality of legend-storytelling, particularly regarding feminist theory.

lilyanderson@hotmail.co.uk

Soup

A short story

Today is an inside day.

The wind is beating at the windows of our small, rented cottage, rain coming down in great sheets and rattling the panes, and the plants lining the sill outside are bending under the weight of the water, their stems desperately trying to remain upright. One turns its face towards me, bobbled middle weeping and petals starting to detach themselves from the head. I give it a commiserating look, the kind of look that says *better you than me*, and it droops further, flattening until leaves and stem become indistinguishable.

Another gust pours through the valley, thrashing at the surface of the sea-lake and pivoting to beeline straight back for our windows again. I take an involuntary step back as it pounds at the glass, a malevolent chill seeping through the stones around the creaking frame. Two steps back. One more, just to be safe. The weather wants in.

My knees give way as the backs of them hit the dated wooden armchair on my next step and it occurs to me that standing here staring at the squall will only anger it further, like the monkeys at the zoo, so I turn tail and shuffle back to the bedroom we're staying in. It's the only other option besides braving the outside; the tiny kitchen is occupied by my wife, and I think better of crowding her between me, the crockery, and the storm.

The bedroom isn't much, the cottage long past its glory days – teetering between neglect and disrepair – with the scuffed and threadbare carpet haphazardly laid over the cement floor, completely cold to the touch, for anyone stupid enough to step out of bed in bare feet. An earwig climbs the peeling wall next to me and I sigh, silently urging it to get out of sight before Maggie sees, and I'm forced to do something about its presence.

The bed, a wooden monstrosity that invites stubbed toes and bruised shins, creaks under my weight when I sit on it, sinking too low to be entirely comfortable, and I shuffle back until my legs aren't so crooked. The wind sounds muted here, like it hasn't quite figured out how to get around the back of the house, contenting itself with wearing the front down until it collapses.

There's a pistachio-coloured sink in the far corner of the room. Maggie had done a doubletake when she saw it, pointing at it in confusion until I shrugged and told her it'd always been there. Back when I was a kid, and I'd come here with Michael and our mother, it had been an awful, pink-toned beige. The bed had been the same, though, and the carpet and the striped wallpaper. Even the earwig inhabitants strike as familiar.

Back then, we'd come every summer. We'd take a train and a bus, and lug our suitcases the rest of the way, stopping only for a few scant necessities on the way, and as soon as we'd managed to navigate the uneven flint drive, our mother would fling the doors open to let the cold sea air chase away the dust, dumping our bags in our room and taking to her bed as soon as she could see it was liveable. She'd say it was migraines if anyone from the village came up to check on us, or peered in on a stroll past the cottage, but Michael used to say that it was the loneliness. He'd say that for some people, the weight of their own life kept piling onto their bodies like pennies in an arcade machine, and when he'd rouse my mother to shower or eat, lifting her from the bed so he could change her sweat-soaked sheets, he'd take a moment to stare at the crater her body had left in the stiff mattress, as if he could see the heaviness himself. Those were the only moments Michael didn't smile in this place, the only times during the summers that I saw just how much older he was than me, despite there only being a few years between us.

Both of their lives stretch out in this room and the other three, the past and the present merging over one another until it almost feels as though the wind and rain are my brother and mother, desperate to be let in, so we can be together again, relive what I'm sure my own memory has warped. My feet itch, wanting to stretch the windows wide, accept the fate that would befall the stone walls and tiled floors under the onslaught of the storm, if only so I could feel the touch of them against my skin.

My breath comes quicker, and I heave, my mouth filling with saliva and my stomach cramping as the loss of them sinks me further into the bed. I wait for the tears, wish for them, but nothing comes – my eyes stay dry and open, the rain pelting the window a mockery of what refuses to fall, and I ball the woollen covers up in my fists.

A knock. My head shoots up, forgetting for a moment where I am and why, slides of my own life blinking across my eyelids until I reach here and now, dizziness pressing in at my temples and darkening the edges of the room. I turn towards the door and my gaze snags on the metal urn sitting on the bedside table, the stark silver of it so out of place with the worn wood of the cottage. It's tiny, barely bigger than my fist, the sum total of a huge life packed into small metal jar. My chest constricts, and the dizziness fades into the flatness of reality.

When I look up again, Maggie is leaning against the glass door to the bedroom, having waited patiently for me to notice her. Sorrow etches lines into a face only vaguely reminiscent of the one I fell in love with, the natural blonde now straying grey at the roots and the full mouth, lined by decades of secret smiles and roaring laughter, her body rounded by our late-night snacking and stolen dates at late night street vendors. Watching her features crumple and stretch now, lips rubbing together, worrying at the skin there as she tries to keep her thoughts from her face, to stay strong for me, I think I love this one more. I give her what I hope is a reassuring nod, my lips tipped.

'Lunch is ready,' she murmurs, glancing warily at the space between us, like she doesn't want to disturb whatever spectres are floating there. I nod and, taking her outstretched hand, follow her through to the rickety table set up at the far corner of the living room, mismatched chairs forced to fit under and around it.

Soup sits in a shallow bowl at the two settings, mushroom, and crusted rolls next to it on a cracked earthenware plate the butter dish open, its contents glistening. A teapot rests in a threadbare cosy on a mat in the centre, steeping, chipped Easter-egg mugs waiting patiently beside it to be filled. The milk is still in the fridge when I sit and Maggie takes a minute to get it, plonking the bottle in front of me and popping the top, the glass cold enough to drip with condensation and cool our drinks, to stop us from burning our over-eager tongues.

I leave the tea, but break open a roll, swiping butter across its soft middle and dipping it into the soup. It doesn't soak, only slips off the buttered surface, coagulating back in the bowl, a gelatinous sheen glinting at me as it resettles. I wrinkle my nose. Twisting the bread and dipping it back in, using it to scoop the reluctant grey liquid instead of soak, I manage to get a mouthful.

It sits there for a moment, coating my cheeks and gums in filmy goop, until my tongue pushes through it, encouraging it to the back of my throat. I swallow, and go back in for another – a spoonful, this time – the bread abandoned on the stained side plate.

Cream. Salt. Pepper. Tarragon. More pepper. A hint of poorly washed crockery.

Essence of mushroom.

Nostalgia burns at my tastebuds, tightening the muscles where my tongue meets my jaw and burning at my eyes. It tastes exactly how I remember.

'Peter.'

I can hear my brother laughing, feel the chill of the Atlantic creeping up my legs as my wellies are submerged, the boggy sand holding them hostage as the tide still sweeps in. He's calling my name, and I'm laughing, too, trying to free myself, trying to get to him on the shore, waves now hitting my knees and kelp creating a skirt of my jeans.

'Pete.'

We're inside, and Michael is tugging at my boots, the water clogging the sides having sealed them to my feet. He braces himself against the bench I'm on, and I hold onto the sides, pushing back as he pulls. *Schhhhqquuueellch*. One comes off, and Michael goes flying, hitting the wall and tipping the welly-water all over himself in the process. I can't help it, I cackle. He only snarls, mischief and love warring for ownership of the sparkle in his baby blues, and he yanks the other boot clean off, tipping the water over my head this time. I squeal and duck for the bedroom, glass door almost shattering as I shove through it, his laughter following me all the way to the bathroom.

'*Peter.*'

I'm clean and dry, and Michael has made us soup for tea, using an old packet he found in the ill-fitting cupboard and adding whatever we had the money to buy as groceries into it. Milk, some herbs from the garden and a lot of pepper – too much pepper. It tastes amazing, though, after hours of being hunted by the tide, even as he mutters complaints onto his spoon, lips caught between a grumble and a sip, scrunching his nose when the pepper hits the back of his throat. I grin at him, and his lips twitch up, taking a whole slurp and trying – failing – to dunk his bread into it. We're laughing again, we always are, and the rain is dancing across the bay outside, my lungs full of something that I want to feel for the rest of my life.

A hand lands on my arm, startling me from the memory, and the sudden warmth chafes against the frost of goosebumps pricking my skin. Maggie is watching me closely, her eyes darting between my cheeks and the half-lifted spoon, still dripping soup back into my bowl. I put the spoon back, hunching and rubbing at my chest, the emptiness stark there in the chilled cottage. The rain isn't dancing, anymore, the wind pelting it at us in a tantrum, screaming across the surface of the lake.

'You're crying,' she says, and I touch trembling fingertips to my cheeks, finding them hot and damp and rough.

Eventually I nod, dropping one hand back to my lap and taking another mouthful of soup, the salt on my lips easing the bite of pepper. She goes back to hers, too, sifting it through her spoon and pretending to lift it to her lips, concern painting golden starbursts in her hazel eyes even as she lets me sit on the shore of my own grief, the waves crashing and ebbing with each swallow.

Today is an inside day, and we're having soup.

JENNIFER ARMSTRONG

Jennifer is an Irish writer, previously shortlisted in the Bournemouth Short Story Prize. *Keen* tells the story of three sisters named after mythical Irish queens. It seeks to explore the isolation of rural life, the complex nature of sisterhood, and how easy it is to harm those we love.

Jenniferarm92@gmail.com

Keen

The opening of a novel

My first one.

Out she came two weeks early in the baking heat of a lazy June, when I was dozing away on a collapsible chair bought in the winter sales, helicopters from the sycamore falling at my feet and her impatient to meet me, tapping and then knocking then clawing her way out, leaving me spill the hot tea all over my sunburnt belly.

Emer the schemer, even as a babe always up to no good, but how could one resist those green eyes almost threatening, when she looked at you with rage, if you stained her dress or broke her crayon, or god forbid lost a piece of the ten piece puzzle, she would nuzzle then into my side until slowly, slowly the tears came down and like a clown I begged forgiveness, begged and pleaded for the tears to halt, promising I would buy her a new jigsaw as soon as I was able but such fables worthless on Emer, nothing being enough to entertain the entertainer, who ruled the roost. Ruled our roost, even when Deirdre came along, requiring more attention from the very first day but still Louis and I had no say, no matter the matter, we could only acquiesce to her behest, always Emer who decided who and what and when and where. Emer who came up to me, aged four and hobbling, and me pregnant leaned over the counter cooking Sunday dinner, for a treat for Louis to cheer him up, and Emer clambered her way up on the chair and onto the counter to look in at what I was doing, and said to me emphatically, mammy you're doing it all wrong, Colm's mammy cuts it lengthways, then sears then stews, and Colm's mammy has done away altogether with mash, it's not the done thing you see, the done thing is new potatoes tossed in oil and salt and slow roasted in the top oven, for maximum flavouuuuur, and she held her wee mouth open saying the word slow, letting the sound rattle on her lips and wiggling her finger and hips, as though telling me off, and I said that's fascinating Emer love, and would you shell some peas for me, and she said of course not Mammy, I have business to attend to.

Emer always had business to attend to up in the room with the girls before Maeve was even walking and Deirdre only small, and Emer conducting inspections, and I said to Louis, well, she got that from your side anyway, and he grunted as if to say, what's that, and I whispered, the Catholic *austerity*.

Austere was the only word for Emer, running a tight ship, checking the girls had tidied their rooms and washed their faces, advising the girls don't need more Barbies because any more would only lead to clutter, and like butter the girls melted at her feet, Maeve and Deirdre only babes but listening to Emer like she was their mammy, inciting the fear of god in them and the fear of God that might take away the Polly Pockets, that might give the Beanie Babies to the dogs.

For a time I was wondering if all wee girls were the same, if Deirdre and Maeve might go through such a phase, watching Emer in a haze storming into the rural country primary school where there were only two teachers teaching the lot of them and wee Emer, on her first day, demanding to see lesson plans.

Lesson plans? The teachers whispered and stared.

Where on earth did she learn the words, lesson plans?

I could only cough and shrug and try hide behind the shrubbery, backing away slowly, while Emer told them she would need to review schedules, the order of things, would numbers or letters come first because she was itching to read and write and count and already knew her daddy's farm had fifty sheep and fifteen chickens and a field of cowslip that could be smelled from the back window. Poor teachers only left to stare speechless watching the little curly demon count the chalk on the board and the pencils in the pot. Would there be enough for all of them – all four of the wee children in her infant class – would there be enough for them all to have their own? She needed one of every colour or how else would she draw and write what was required? How else would she grow to be the leader of the pack?

Leading firmly since then, scaring full grown men, bossing her sisters about the place, and them like moths to a flame, drinking up every word, only pleased to please Emer, delegating her chores when my back was turned and her father asleep, exhausted from all those mornings in the field and the numbers and exhausted just from life, and me gone to do the books for the tennis club down the road and the pub on the corner just for the few extra pennies, pennies Emer would take as pocket money for managing the household, divvying out the tasks so she could oversee and inspect, making sure everyone was performing up to scratch. That's all it is Mammy, you see, she said so sweet and low, I am only making sure everything gets done. I am only taking charge to make sure they do their jobs.

It was a job alright to manage Emer, and me wondering had I done something wrong – did I have too many Nescafe's with her in utero, did I make her this way? I said to Louis, only joking, despairingly, and he, tired and needing a holiday, the holiday we had put off for decades, he only squeezed my shoulder and said, ah she is only a wee girl.

Our wee girl indeed, passing no heed, when poor Deirdre Dee awoke desperately in need.

Eight-year-old lungs wheezing away and the breeze coming through the window Emer left open, and the inhaler left out downstairs on the grass by the treehouse, forgotten after a game of 'Doctor'. What in god's name were you thinking, Emer love? I said, running up the stairs with my feet wet and cold, holding the inhaler, holding my tongue, wanting to run and wring her neck.

It was only a game, Mammy, she said to me then. Only a game of Doctor with Dee the patient and Maeve the nurse and Doctor Emer arriving just in time to save them all from the deadly disease. And what about your sister's deadly disease? Silence then with all three of them staring up at me, and Deirdre still holding the inhaler to her mouth, pulling it away slowly and asking me with her eyes what I had meant. What did I mean at all, I wondered, and I tried to say oh nothing girls, silly mammy using silly serious words. I tried to say don't heed me, don't listen at all to what I say.

And really they were already away, my growing gangly girls, the three of them always off and about the place. Emer leading them down through the forest past the farm, where I told her she should never go alone. But then I was back at work, their father trying to keep an eye and supposedly he was minding them, doing the best he could really but then he was not so well himself and how are you supposed to watch them every minute of every day?

How can you ever be sure they are safe?

Emer with her head held high singing follow me I'm the leader, leading them astray, having them traipse behind her in their new school shoes well into the overgrown woodland, full of foxes and hares and mink, mink with teeth like sharks ready to nip, and the dips in the treacherous hills, the girls going over and under rolling and laughing and sure it was all harmless fun until Deirdre tripped and fell. Deirdre trying to say wait for me, trying to say hang on there a minute girls.

Deirdre always getting lost and losing things, most often her breath, lungs full of laughter until suddenly her chest was sore and heavy, unable to keep up with them really, unable to keep up with Emer and poor wee Maeve only a babe at six years old doing as she was told, and Deirdre falling and tripping on the tree roots rising from soil, cutting her chin on the thorns. Poor Deirdre, spending her life just trying to breathe, left behind struggling to get free, rashes from the nettles across her bony knee.

Emer and Maeve were sat on the back step, their father taking his afternoon nap and still sound asleep and dreaming. The two of them well aware, looking up at me innocently as I got out of the car. I counted them there quickly in my head and I thought two out of three ain't bad, to only be missing one isn't bad, but then wee Deirdre Dee is the sick one, my fragile one, and where is she? I shouted, and Emer, turning to me so sweet to say I'm sorry Mammy, like Deirdre was a new puppy they had been trying to train, we've lost her, she's ran away, she's missing mammy.

I yelled from down deep such violent words I'd never said before and never would again, and me and Louis running off as the sun went down with torches on our heads and in our hands, whistles used for the sheep and the dog and using them then for our girl, so she might hear us coming and shout and say mammy I'm here by the big stone where we carved our names, or maybe by the river where we dip our toes, or the clearing of daisies where the gorse once caught alight.

And you've had quite the fright I said to her, comforting her, finding her waiting by the gate at the end of the field, dragging herself that far through the plants and ants, waiting for her sisters, waiting hours for her big sister, sprained ankle the size of her head, hair matted into knots as though she had been gone weeks and a look in her eyes, even when only a child, knowing something had changed, something cruel had been done to her and she wouldn't forget and I wouldn't forget, the shape of her doe eyes gone angry and fearful.

And I didn't know which were worse, Deirdre's eyes or Emer's, when I went in to tell her goodnight and that in time I would forgive her, and her sister would forgive her, and not to worry too much these things happen, and I was sorry for all those words I had said. Those awful words I had uttered that I'll never say again.

The look she gave me then, eyes with no warmth at all, moonlight fracturing through the window making them glaze and glisten, looking at me like it was my fault, my wrongdoing, looking at me as though I had let this happen. As though she, *Queen Emer*, might never forgive me.

MUTI'AH BADRUDDEEN

Muti'ah, a Nigerian mum and reproductive health physician, is the author of 'Rekiya & Z,' winner of the 2022 SprinNG Women Author Prize. Longlisted for the 2022 Commonwealth short story prize and nominated for the 2023 Pushcart prize, Muti'ah has been published in 'the other side of hope', Brittle Paper, and The Shallow Tales Review, among others.

Email: mutiabdeen@gmail.com
Twitter: @/deenprogress
Instagram: @/deenprogress

Dreams Lie Awake

A historical fiction exploring African feminism and Yoruba mythology

The girl's earliest formed memory is of surviving òrò with her grandmother.

Everything else before that night – she must have been four or five years old – remains a blank slate that nothing, not even her parents' multitude of stories of alleged toddler impishness, fills. The next few years, too, are spotty; a mish-mash product of her mind's hazy recollections and those parental stories.

But that one incident, that night, is sharp in her mind's eye. Refined by countless visits in the realm of dreams; every detail is preserved.

They never spoke about it, so she could never test its veracity. Could never be sure that it wasn't the fanciful imaginings of a young girl's overactive mind. She could never bring herself to ask her grandmother, never told anyone.

What would she even say?! No female witnesses òrò and lives to tell the tale.

Years would pass after that night before the girl learnt what òrò was. To her young mind, òrò was the presumably naked spirit of some long-gone ancestor turned into a god. Because, as many women had intoned in her presence, why else would there be such stringent rules about females not seeing òrò? Why the almost fanatical zeal to keep women and girls from learning about it, never mind witnessing it? All the girl knew even as she grew into adulthood was that òrò roamed the land for certain days annually, and sometimes following a momentous event.

And that no female, or foreign male, was allowed outdoors when òrò was loose – at night in Èrè – for entire days on end in some villages. To defy that convention was to face consequences so heinous, no one ever mentioned exactly what they were. After that night and until date, the girl only witnessed a few òrò festivals, all from the safety of her grandmother's cavernous new house, walled in its six-foot fence.

For a long time though, her dreams played a trick on her. One where she is back there, a little girl waking up abruptly from slumber in the bed of a bolekaja, those rickety lorries with wooden sidebars, to find Màámi's arms wound tightly around her. They were on their way back from one of Màámi's markets, much later than usual. The bolekaja didn't start' for a long time after they dropped the last woman traveling with them, at her home three villages away.

The day was already fading when the girl fell asleep, but it was so dark everywhere, she couldn't see anything. She knew Màámi was the one holding her, from her unique scent, a mix of òrí, àdí-àgbon and epo pupa. Her grandmother's daily beauty routine – with shea butter, coconut oil and red palm oil – were well known in Èrè, yet her scent was never achieved by anyone else, no matter how hard the other women tried.

Distinct and familiar, the smell comforted the girl, and she relaxed for a moment, finally registering the reason it was so dark. Màámi had covered them both, head to toe, in the heavy òfì cloth she tied as protection over her ankara wrapper while sorting and trading her wares. The thick cloth was mildly pungent, a not-entirely-unpleasant mix borne from its numerous exposures to obì and orógbó juices, lingering traces of the chemicals used in cleaning them and the dusty motes of travel. The weight of darkness enclosed within it was more oppressive.

The girl stirred then, restless as any little child confined, but Màámi's arms tightened into a vice, cutting off movement and deep breaths. Her fierce, whispered 'Dákẹ́!' settled her granddaughter into the stillness and silence she was commanded.

The fear descended then. Quite suddenly, it settled on the girl, the sense that something wasn't right. An unmistakable sensation of being in the path of danger permeated the protective cocoon her grandmother had swaddled her in. She heard it, too. Fear makes a deceptively sibilant sound, swishing *vroom-vroom-vroooooom* across the night. Like the very air was wailing, warning them that this was not safe.

They were not safe.

Piercing, chilling, the sound got closer. Steadily. The fear pressed down, harder.

The bolekaja was barely moving at this point. *Did someone command the driver to stop?* In no time at all, the sound was upon it, surrounding its passengers with a ferociousness that was amplified by the stillness of silence so palpable beyond it. Looking back, or in her dreams, the girl's flesh always rose up in unison, she remembered the cold infusing her entire being.

'Who goes there? Which woman is it who dares venture into the streets with the òrò loose?!' The voice is raised, its address pointed.

A whimper sounded, *probably the bolekaja driver.*

'I am Abibatu Àbẹ̀kẹ́, Ìyálaje of Erè village.' Màámi's voice matched the volume of the questioner, its steady cadence belying her tightening grip on her granddaughter. 'With me is my grandchild, the only daughter of my only son. Fathers of our fathers, I beseech you. We mean no disrespect. We were detained on our way back from Ọjà-Ọ̀dàn market because the bolekaja did not work. We did not know that the streets belonged to you this night. We beg you, Father of our fathers, for safe passage.'

'Daughter of Erè! Your name precedes you. But you know the consequences for violating òrò.' It was not a question.

'Indeed I do, Father of our fathers – no female who sees òrò lives to tell the tale. But consider that neither of us have seen anything. The child was asleep long before we got here. And I am lying here with her under this òfì. Both of us have been covered up, head to toe like corpses on their way to eternal rest, from the moment I was made aware that you roam the streets tonight, long before we heard you. We have seen nothing, Father of our fathers. I assure you; we will speak of nothing.'

There was a moment of silence. 'What will be your penance?'

'My bàǹtẹ́ is in the smallest basket next to our feet. It contains all the money

I was blessed with at the market today. May it appease the ancestors. And if we arrive home safely tonight, I promise to have seven of the fattest goats I can find in Erè driven to the òrò shrine here in Iwide tomorrow, before the sun reaches its place of rest.'

An even longer silence – try as she does over the years, the girl never heard anyone get into the bolekaja bed – then, 'Go, Daughter of Erè, and do not speak of this to anyone!'

They drove a considerable distance, enough that they no longer heard the whistling of òrò. The girl waited an even longer time before turning to her grandmother. 'Màámi –'

'Dákẹ́!' Her response was swift, equally fierce, still whispered.

Màámi's arms did not loosen their grip. Neither got up from their position, lying wrapped as they were in the smothering swaddle of the òfì cloth. Not until they were back in the safety of the raffia-fenced compound on the edge of the iga.

Until she died, Màámi never spoke about that night; the girl continues to call it a dream.

CHRISTOPHER BRADY

Christopher studies the Anglo-Japanese as a style, culture, and relationship. In addition to a novella that provides an obsessive examination of detachment and sensibility, his debut novel uncovers the Japanese elements of Edwardian London through the stay of the first Japanese Ambassador and his family.

csvmk@outlook.com

The Hanedean

The opening of a novella

It was late on Sunday evening when I squeezed the last of my soothing toner, one to two per cent succinic acid distilled from amber, onto the tip of my index finger. Touching it to each cheek would have ignored the crease on my forehead while a line from forehead to nose would have left my chin dry. Rubbing it into my neck might have pre-empted the morning shave, which often left it with a red glaze, specks of blood streaking from top to bottom as though my jaw were stuck with thorns, but there was a great deal of skin to cover. I touched my finger to my nose and then pulled the drop of toner apart, crossing the bags beneath my eyes. There was nothing left by the time I reached cheekbone.

The bathroom mirror scattered my reflection about its cracks. I angled my head this way and that, inspecting each shard for changes in contrast or soreness. In one, the cool glimmer that I had just dragged below my eyes looked wet, in another, it glittered. Beneath the white bathroom light, seemingly ripped from a shared office space, those two wings of one to two per cent succinic acid, distilled from amber, speckled like a starry night. While staring at this shard, which was landlocked and shaped like a narrowed eye, I took the one-hundred-and-seventy-millilitre bottle of soothing toner and then peeled away its informational wrapper. The glitter beneath my eyes began to dull. I glanced between each of the other shards. I needed more. I needed to cut open the bottle and then trace its insides with my fingers.

It being the limbo between Christmas Day and the New Year, each of my housemates had long since returned to their family homes. It would have been easy, irrelevant, to take and return the pair of kitchen scissors with them being none the wiser. I struggled around the thought. The butter knife, the only knife I owned, could never have pierced the bottle, but borrowing the scissors would introduce a degree of uncertainty that made it difficult to consider at all. On the slim chance that I was to leave a bottle, carton, pouch, stand-up pouch, or any other type of skincare container in the bathroom, the thought that any of them could do the same – 'borrow' some face cream as they often did milk and sugar – made me want to retch. I had never considered myself a part of their communal management of the kitchen. I had never used as much as another's cutlery.

I reached towards the windowsill, to the left of the sink and mirror, and took one of the tiny cardboard boxes from the stack. With the house empty, I had started leaving one thing after another in the bathroom. It was unintentional at first, the result of wandering through rooms without needing to open and close doors, but it had evolved, devolved, into something sluggish and far removed from my previous eleven months in the house. I no longer dressed up for the kitchen. I no longer filled a bag with my belongings when moving from one room to the next. Each little cardboard box contained five individually wrapped double-edged razor blades, but I no longer marked them with a pen to keep stock.

I undressed one of the blades and then, gripping it between my thumb, index, and middle fingers, began sawing down the centre of the one-hundred-and-seventy-millilitre bottle of toner. It was the softest part of the bottle. Before long, it punctured, but cutting a clean line that would split the bottle in vertical halves proved too great a challenge. I supported my working fingers with the others, careful not to place the point of each fingerprint near the naked edge. Whether it was through moments of carelessness or the difficulty of cutting hard plastic with a double-edged razor blade, I began to feel the occasional prick. When I tensed after a few nasty bites, and when blood threatened to drip from the razor and taint the sliced bottle of toner, I dropped the blade into the sink and then submerged my hand in warm water.

Despite having removed the cap, it was not possible for the razor to cut through the hardened plastic of the bottle's lip, nor its bottom. I had, at least, made a line, the length of my little finger, down the centre of the bottle. My final act had been to dash each end of the vertical slice as if it were the capital letter 'I', opening the possibility of pushing or pulling on the folds and then slipping something inside. I could have continued and cut something of a torso from the bottle, opening it up to be scoured by multiple fingers at once. Watching my hand in the lukewarm water, however, and the red ribbons that continued to swirl from the tips of my fingers, I gathered that continuing would only serve to draw more blood.

Heat radiated from my neck, cheeks, and forehead as I lay in bed. I could feel the red blotches, untouched by toner, as they squirmed within my skin and crawled towards the furthest reaches of my face. I had not as much as grazed it since returning from my failed routine in the bathroom. If I could not complete the first step, the rest, naturally, could not follow. I lay on my back, as was routine, staring up at the white plasterboard. The backdoor light from the neighbour opposite flicked on the moment that the sun went down and shot into my room at an upwards angle, courtesy of the ill-fitting curtains. I wondered about it and its wider implications, about whether to apply sun cream multiple times each day rather than once within my morning routine. These idle thoughts, any idle thoughts, returned me to my failed routine. I made straight to the bathroom.

Different parts of the mirror gave me different impressions: in the largest shard, shaped like a Wellington boot in the bottom left, there were pink streaks like grill marks on each cheek; in the stalactite from top to middle, there was nothing but an empty room; and in the narrowed eye, there was a reminiscence of the glimmer from before. I picked up the one-hundred-and-seventy-millilitre bottle that I had left beside the tap. Inside were the dregs of one to two per cent succinic acid, distilled from amber. The vertical slice remained. The realisation that I had violated this gift began to settle like stones in my stomach.

Stuffed into K's carry-on bag had been an embarrassment of skincare products, more than enough to lather this sleepy city, purchased, in a hurry, at Haneda Airport. I could not figure out if they had been meant as introductory gifts, potential favours, or were simply the result of his spilling the lot on the floor of our living room and then proceeding to hand them out as part of a prolonged apology. He made sure that each of us had several unique products without doubling up, though his explanation of each one passed me by. Much of what he attempted to explain passed me by. I quickly developed the habit of sounding out key words and mirroring his enthusiasm with the breadth of my smile without ever stepping too far over the mark. The others, however, must not have taken to the products, as I began to find them scattered unopen about the house. I scooped each of them up without a second thought. Should it have been the first bottle, the one that K had handed to me while recovering from being half-prostrate on the hardwood floor, I could never have cut it with a razor. I had kept the empty bottle in my cupboard until I was swayed by the natural order of things – a bottle sporting the recycling logo, or a foreign equivalent, desired to be recycled. That K saw me with the empty bottle as I placed it neatly within the kitchen's recycling bin was not a coincidence, but it would be some time before he returned with any more.

My neck began to sting. I swallowed hard as I looked at the slice in the bottle, pulsing the muscles in my throat and momentarily empowering the inflammation. The mirror gave me nothing. Most of the shards reflected flat, painless skin. Only the narrowed eye's reminiscence, stuck in that starry-eyed stare, gave me something more. I took the bottle and then started back to my room. When I pictured the scene to come in the few steps that I took from bathroom to bedroom, I imagined it in complete darkness, detached from the rest of the room, the world, like the experience of eating the ortolan songbird. What I was to do should not need to be hidden from God, yet the stutter in my step before I slunk beneath the duvet gave my mind pause. At the very least, complete darkness was an impossibility; I would have to make do with the intruding light above my curtains..

I lay on my back, as was routine, staring up at the white plasterboard which had been interposed by the one-hundred-and-seventy-millilitre bottle of soothing toner. It quickly became all-encompassing. The thin streak of light showed through the bottle, outlining the few specks and drabs of toner that remained glued to the bottle's insides. I traced the slit with my middle finger. Despite the care with which I had wielded the razor, each of my thumb, index, and middle fingers were littered with little red marks. I supported my middle with my ring finger and then applied pressure wherever the 'I'-shaped fold allowed for an opening. After a time of testing, retreating, then testing again, I made through. I prised the slit wider before pressing further inside. I scraped the inner walls of the bottle, collected toner, fractions of a drop each time, then smoothed it onto the dry parts of my face. I became hurried. I threw my two fingers in with abandon. The cut plastic grazed me, creating a red-raw ring that extended down the deeper I made. When I was no longer content with the dregs, I began curling my fingers and scooping toner towards the opening. I rocked the bottle, gently, with both hands, urging gravity to pull the last of it towards me. I waited. I mouthed something. The one to two per cent succinic acid, distilled from amber, fell, in a single, stringy drop, onto my bottom lip. I smoothed it down my chin and then onto my neck. I felt as though I were drowning, my head barely above water. With my hands to my throat, I applied a little pressure, embedding the toner deeper within my skin and tilting my chin upwards, towards safety. The coolness made me wince and smile both.

In the bathroom, each of the shards reflected in unison. Even the narrowed eye, which alone had been fixed on the momentary sparkle beneath my eyes, reflected swathes of shimmering skin. I watched from beginning to end, flicking between shards as if I were changing channels, except, rather than being underwhelmed and switching to find something new, I was switching to absorb as much, and as frequently, as possible. I raised my head to the white ceiling light and looked at the mirror through my peripheral vision. It being more difficult to perceive the cracks in the mirror, the different shards, different reflections, I, instead, saw myself as one. It was only once the sensation had completely faded that I applied the following two parts of my night-time routine.

OLIVER GUY WORSTER BRIGGS

Oliver Briggs was born in London. He is drawn to ergodic and epistolary writing, and considers formal experimentation to be a central tenet of his own work. His stories explore technological uncertainty and alternate histories, injected with dark humour. Much of his writing incorporates illustrations and hand-drawn graphics.

oliverguyworsterbriggs@gmail.com

Haunted Houses

An extract from a novel

[extract from Edward Belgrave's diary]

FEBRUARY 28TH, 2001 — *PETER HEWITT DIES, AGED 102*

Maria and I had dinner with Lewis Hardt on Monday. I did not think our evening substantial enough to note yesterday, but with today's news of Peter Hewitt's passing, have found myself revisiting the dinner table in my mind. I am deluded in deeming an evening where we are afforded the privileges of civility 'insubstantial'.

Monday was the first time we had seen one another since Lucas Garner-Lake's funeral, six months ago. I had proposed a vague plan to catch up outside of the typical weddings and funerals, and only later realised I actually wanted to do it. I owe a lot to his mentorship.

He served halibut and leek with creamed potatoes, and we had wine from somewhere in Kent. He asked us to try and guess where it was from; in his asking I immediately assumed someplace unconventional and went for Iceland. He asked if I meant the country or the shop.

Maria and I were enamoured by his apartment and much of the evening was spent discussing the artwork he 'played caretaker for'. Amongst the landscape pieces in his drawing room was a tiny Turner, which I joked I would happily play caretaker for whensoever that position needed fulfilling. Lewis told me that since I liked it, I ought to visit Peter Hewitt and sidle up to him before he croaked. Probably a coincidence timing-wise, and in any case, I doubt I could've gone from 'pupil of an estranged pupil' to 'inheritor of fine art collection' in forty-eight hours.

Fifteen minutes after Hewitt's name was raised, Maria pointedly remarked that the time was approaching ten. Lewis offered to call a cab on his expenses card; 'the only good thing the government had left him with', but Maria insisted I stay and talk about the things we had been avoiding in front of her. She said this pointedly too, as if she wanted me to want her to leave.

Something of a wall fell when Maria left. Only now did we speak as old colleagues, rather than old friends.

A bottle of whisky was procured — Lewis explained it had been gifted by Garner-Lake's son at the funeral.

'Lucas left a bottle for each of us[1] but Knight,' Lewis said, sliding me a glass. I found this hard to believe; Lucas Garner-Lake and Herbert Knight had been closer to one another than the rest of the department put together.

'Had they fallen out?' I furrowed my brow.

'Lucas left him the distillery.' Lewis smiled.

We drank in Lucas's memory.

'Lovely, isn't it?' Lewis topped our glasses up. 'Almost makes you forget how much of a prick he was.'

I laughed politely. I suddenly felt much younger than sixty, uncomfortable in disrespecting a senior. Lewis recognised this.

'He *was*. Posh bastard. Though I don't imagine you saw much of him.'

'I certainly felt his presence,' I said.

'He and Herbert were proof that though you can take the boy out of Harrow...' He raised his eyebrows at me.

'You can't take the Harrow out of the boy.'

'Quite right. As far as I'm concerned, his ilk are best confined to... running our whisky distilleries; kept as far away from Department Sixteen as possible.'

'Do you keep much in touch with anyone else?' This was the first time either of us had mentioned the department by name; curiosity got the better of me.

'From Sixteen?' He twisted his mouth. 'Not if I can help it— present company excluded, of course. And I imagine it's rather like Theseus' Ship there now, surely?'

'Everyone's flown the coop,' I began. Any information about the current runnings of the Department was, I admit, highly classified. I explained, in some detail, how the current roster of active agents was no longer confined to Department Sixteen.

---

1   I'm guessing 'us' here refers to each of Lewis Hardt's cohort
    (the now-retired 'Overseers') rather than everyone at the funeral.

How other government bodies would assign D16 agents to their own activities with handlers acting as auxiliary support. That my own understudy, Jacob Fortescue, was currently in ▮▮▮ — I had to stop myself here.

'We all thought *we* would be doing that sort of thing,' Lewis said bemusedly. 'Gordonstone's probably spinning in his grave. Cathal, too. The most action I ever saw was training you.' He laughed, then.

'A little early to be going for the understatement of the millennia,' I said.

We spoke tactfully about Jacob for a while, and his peers. Lewis told me he had brought up the Department because he had heard that someone was in the midst of writing a book.

'The understudy of one of Herbert Knight's understudies,' he said, gesticulating in such a way that implied his own separation from both the information and the source of it. I furrowed my brow; asked who. Lewis recalled midway through a sip, snapping his finger and pointing at me.

'Arthur Lloyd-Ford,' he said. 'At Garner-Lake's funeral. He told me that what's-his-name[2] was writing a book.'

I didn't follow up on this, frustratingly — I became waylaid in telling an anecdote about a training exercise Lloyd-Ford and I had ruined in the early seventies.

It was conversation of this calibre that rounded out the evening. I left in the usual way. Though I didn't have my cassette player on me, Lewis had a vast collection of digitised albums on his computer. Very state-of-the-art. Before I left, Lewis implored me to catch up with Arthur; I now realise Lewis may have been suggesting I sniff around that whole book thing. I told Lewis I would certainly think about it, and moments later I was standing in my study.

MARCH 1ST, 2001

Wrote an e-mail to Lewis expressing condolences about Peter. I'm sure he found out before me — I suppose it's possible he knew on Monday.

I wasn't keen on going into work, and I'd already sent one e-mail today, so I sent another one to the office informing them I was taking the rest of the week off for vague 'personal reasons'. I thought I'd wake Maria with a tea, and I watched

---

2   Ostensibly Lloyd-Ford's understudy, Orville MacLeod.

my inbox as the kettle boiled. A reply came in quickly — the first line contained the words 'absolutely understandable', and I switched the computer off without bothering to read the rest.

I am constantly being encouraged to make 'adventures' of any quotidian task, in the interest of not killing myself (paraphrasing Dr. Northmoor here, but it was his idea).[3] As such, I left to find Maria something pastry-based and interesting for breakfast. The further afield, the greater the adventure, I assumed, and set off in the direction of Mayfair.

Jacob often says that after weeks of training he finds it incredibly difficult to walk. Whether this is some kind of Ritual side effect is debatable, but the younger lot never have to walk to work, and covert photography has come leaps and bounds since I was his age. Gone are the days of digging through illicitly-acquired holiday snaps, I suppose. Even then you'd have to find people who hadn't just stuck to the tourist spots, lest you materialise in the middle of Pariser Platz.

I thought about Jacob as I walked. I ended up in a small, independent bakery that he'd certainly hate. I thought about what, if anything, he'd be eating now — and left with a couple of pain-aux-raisins and something Danish and heavy-looking.

I didn't rush back — that tea was definitely cold by now — and meandered through the little gardens off Portman Square. Several of the benches were taken up by gaggles of grey-suited grey men, probably bunking off work too. My father once told me he 'came here to quit smoking'; he had sat at one of these benches and forced himself to smoke a packet one-by-one. The things we put our bodies through!

Two women crowded around a pushchair were blocking the gate, one coaxing the baby to summarise a holiday they'd been on. They moved when I approached but didn't break character; the baby's mother cooing *And tell auntie Hilly what you did in Whitchurch... we ate*— and I was out of earshot. Took me back, to hear someone say Whitchurch — and still odd to think I could be standing there at a moment's notice, my bag of pastries suspended for a moment before dropping to the ground.[4]

---

3   Never heard of a Dr. Northmoor but he sounds like a psychiatrist or counsellor. Will investigate.
4   Didn't work out the Whitchurch connection until last night. You're lucky I couldn't sleep! Give this a read — Penelope

[*extract from classified Departmental material*]

With these candidates thoroughly vetted, the Department now needed somewhere to train them. Derby's initial journey to the Lake District was seen as too great an undertaking to be a template for training exercises, and for a long time, agents practised travelling between the floors of D16's London offices or from there to their homes. Practising outside of such private environments brought with it the risk of witnesses to insertions, as well as the more practical difficulties of verifying the success of a Ritual Repositioning from London to another part of the country. Equally, D16 needed training environments that more closely resembled the field.

It was Rupert Godolphin's new understudy, Felix Tarrant, who proposed the ingenious idea to hold field practice at locations with a history of supernatural folklore. There was already a counter-argument that a member of the public witnessing a person vanish into — or appear out of — thin air would either doubt their own account, or be subject to ridicule. Practising insertions and exits at, say, a haunted house simply added to this dynamic.

Twelve locations were proposed in line with this suggestion, before a fairly straightforward and cost-efficient vetting process. The first three 'Forward Operating Sites' were established between late 1965 and early 1966.

FOS1 — The Chapel at Whitchurch

A ruined chapel to the north of the Dorset town of Whitchurch Canonicorum was the first location put forward as a potential FOS. It had several reports, spanning multiple centuries, of typical 'hauntings'; ghosts seen in the bell-tower, unseen dogs baying during the nights, and so on and so forth. It was not quite infamous enough to be a tourist site and therefore saw little public traffic.

FOS2 — Southing Pier, Suffolk

The coastal village of Southing has two piers, the newer Suffolk Cob and the older, dilapidated Southing Pier. The supports of the older pier had been designated as unfit to support the weight of the buildings atop it — a café and a museum — and the pier itself had been the subject of some paranormal folklore after the museum's curator had died in a similar fashion to John Whister, the infamous poet whose remains were kept on the pier.

D16 was given adequate funding to discreetly reinforce the structural platform and renovate the inside of the buildings whilst keeping the pier closed to the public. Office space was also purchased from a hotel on the seafront, officially to observe the emissions of the Lodestone Oil Rig in the North Sea, as a means to explain the higher number of government workers now living and working in the small town.

FOS3 — Barch Quarry, Berwick-Upon-Tweed

This location was in theory a dream come true — it was miles from any actual town, contained plenty of underground space to convert into work-space, and had seen a mining disaster popularly attributed to a vengeful spirit from beneath the earth. However, its substantial distance from London and the other FOSs meant it saw the least use and was only staffed between March and October. Only by 1970 was it regularly used, when the standard examination for field work was to travel from FOS1 to London, then to FOS2, and then FOS3 in under fifteen minutes.

Not everybody in the Department was enthused with the locations, however.

> the
> Hotel Northcliffe
> Fleet Street
>
> Morgan,
> Hope you're well. Just wanted to raise a minor concern. Next week five of us are heading to the West Country to prepare a training site in a 'haunted' church, per Rupert's suggestion. Now I don't believe in ghosts but two years ago I didn't believe you could use music and photographs to teleport. You know? I'm not taking the piss or anything but what if people say the church is haunted because it actually *is* haunted? Just something to think about.
>   Declan

Nonetheless, it was the work undertaken across these four sites that revealed some of the most important discoveries about the nature of Ritual Repositioning.

GODESS BVUKUTWA

Godess Bvukutwa is a Zimbabwean writer and a feminist development practitioner. She won the Konrad Adneur Stiftung Best Short Story Award in 2018 and the Norma Kitson Short Story Award in 2012. She's the Zimbabwean project lead for the British Council-funded project When Women Write. She has also published narrative poetry.

gbvukutwa@gmail.com

The Devil Dwells in Douglasdale

An extract from the first chapter of a novel

Nancy and Precious flanked Letwin's sides. A few textbooks were spread open in front of them. Exercise books and pens were strategically placed next to the set books — just in case Matron ambled in without warning. Agatha sat across from them as usual. Writing. They were waiting for her to finish the page she was on. As soon as she finished, they would grab it from her, lapping up the words with unashamed greed, and then wait for another. The love-hate relationships in her stories drew their eyes to her large cursive writing like a magnet. The kisses and caresses titillated them. They would giggle behind their hands. The other students in the dining hall where they studied would turn to give them annoyed looks. But not during the last week of the school term though; there were cautious chitchats and controlled cackles throughout the dining hall instead of the usual manufactured silence.

Agatha slid the page she had been writing on across the table as if she didn't care much about it. Nancy lunged for it and placed it in front of Letwin who sat in the middle. Agatha's love stories were much like the Mills and Boons which were a staple food across the whole dorm, except Agatha replaced the blonde hair with braids or kinky afros. Slim figures with curvy ones just like the writer's own. Thin lips with full lips. The characters at times ate sadza and maguru and came from places like Guruve and even Zaka. The men remained the same; tall, dark and handsome. The stereotype worked both ways.

'Kikiki!'

'Shh, Precious!' Letwin and Nancy chorused their shushing.

Precious always forgot to muffle her titters. Last time a prefect punished them except for Agatha, who was safely across the table. All because of Precious' high-pitched giggles.

After finishing the page, Letwin signalled to her friends that she was going to try to study, and they looked at her as if she was a UFO. Ignoring their eyes Letwin chose a Physical Geography textbook from the books splayed on the table. Face down, she rested her head on the table supported by her right arm and randomly opened with her left hand a page with diagrams showing the infiltration stage of the water cycle.

The challenge with this position was that it always managed to unlock the floodgates of tears that would otherwise have remained plugged in a more upright position. She shut her eyes hoping to discourage them, the tears. Hoping the black blank space that comes when one closes their eyes would swallow the hideousness of the memories. But it had been two months of her blocking out That Sunday Afternoon. The black-blank-space trick was losing its effect. The images were beginning to penetrate through; they were poking holes into the pitch-black blanket in which that afternoon lay, tightly wrapped.

What could happen though? If she dared to exhume That Sunday Afternoon from the shallow grave where she had hurriedly buried it? Her friends were there. Nancy, the reasonable one, was there; she would explain and make it all make sense. Precious would hold her hand, put arms around her and squeeze her hard. Agie would fix her eyes on her as if using her eyes to absorb Letwin's pain and make it her own. She had seen Agie do this the day she told them that her mother had died the previous year of a heart attack.

The term was ending. In a few days, she was going back to that road with its trees and grass standing stiffly by the side. The only difference was she would be on a school bus with excitable students around her; delirious because they were going home after three months inside the cage, as boarding school was often referred to. And there she would be, pinching her arm to stop the tears from coming out just like she was doing now. She couldn't afford to travel the road again the following week before she travelled it in her mind. The first tear fell onto the open book on her lap and infiltrated the page...

***

She had just got into Mr Lloyd's car. The road was bumpy. He was driving with one hand. He stretched his left arm towards her and slipped it under her skirt. Bewildered, she tried to push his hand off.

The trees watched the white truck as they moved past, casting their eyes to the side and pretending not to see. They gasped when they saw his hand feeling her thighs with a casualness she couldn't grasp. They heard her let out a little scream; as if the scream itself was too afraid to come out. They saw her fight his hand off with her slight frame and how it turned into heavy iron, immovable as it gripped her vulva through her pink panties.

The grass saw too and turned to its neighbours, speaking in hurried, hushed tones. Together they witnessed her head turning to him, eyes pleading with him amidst a cloud of confusion. His eyes were bright and shiny in an odd kind of way. On his lips, a toothy garish smile was plastered. As if, as if this was a game.

The dusty road heard her pleading. 'Mr Lloyd, please stop. Please stop. I want to get out of your car. I beg of you, please, please, please.' The desperation made her voice sound foreign to her ears.

'Are you not the one who stopped my car? Waving your little arm nonstop.' He broke into guffaws of laughter and the wildflowers hidden in the savanna swards shrivelled and shrunk into themselves. 'Don't worry, I'm not going to do too much. I'm driving, you see.'

He groped the inside of her thighs. Roughly. With a precision and quickness that terrified the wind blowing past the open windows.

She tried the door and of course, it was locked. Again, she tried to shove his hand away, but it had become a large granite rock with her vulva squeezed in its palm. She bit his upper arm.

He laughed. 'I like what you are doing. Stop tempting me to stop the car and do the real thing.'

The Savannah had chosen to stay on the fringes, in typical Zimbabwean style, so she stopped lobbying its woodland for help. No saviour was coming.

She steeled herself for the worst and felt his fingers creep inside her panties like a tarantula. Her skin crawled. Her body coiled. She shrieked out loud, thumping him with tightly rolled fists on his arm and right-side upper body. She felt the dirt road getting bumpier, slowing him down a little, forcing his eyes back on the road when it felt too uneven. Was the road trying to help her?

She could punch his face or gouge his eyes out, she thought. But what would happen if they veered off the road and hit a tree or grazing cow? She felt nauseated at the thought of dying with his hand in her panties. That would torment her even in her death. She stifled a sob.

The trees and the grass, they saw. They saw his lips curving down on the ends. His eyes half closing and his fingers slackening. A sharp bump slipped them out. Slimy. Disgusting.

He wiped his fingers on her maroon skirt and switched the radio on. Beyonce's singing voice blurted out. Letwin's vagina throbbed.

'Who knew you looked like Beyonce under your skirt?' The stupid grin was back on his face. Through her teary eyes, she could tell he thought it was a witty thing to say.

'My father is waiting to see the truck,' he announced when they got to the school. It was his way of telling her to get off. He had stopped in front of the administration block. She gathered the broken pieces that were Her, fearing that some of them would fall off onto the floor of his car and in his sudden impatience he would drive off and she would never piece herself together again.

***

Letwin had no idea how many teardrops had permeated the unfortunate page in the geography textbook. She blew her nose into her maroon cardigan and wiped her eyes with it too. Nancy and Precious were chatting in whispers.

Letwin wasn't sure if she could ever glue herself together and go back to before. Everything had changed. Even Agatha's stories remained letters huddled in clusters on the lines of an Eversharp notebook. They didn't jump out at her like popcorn in a pan in excitement, as they used to. The romantic scenes had faded in colour, lost their sweet and sour taste and their occasional spiciness. Now the same scenes sounded silly and stupid.

The bell rang. It was over; the pretence of studying.

'Lettie, what's wrong? Your eyes are red, and they look swollen.'

'Yes, Lettie what is it?'

'Were you thinking about your mother?'

Letwin nodded. The three girls made a human fort around her like they had done twice after That Sunday Afternoon, and like those two times, when she had failed to hem in her tears, she told them she was missing her mother. Chairs scraped the cement floor, and books slammed shut. Zips on backpacks zzzzzed all around. Some of the girls lingered, of course. The boys, who studied in the classrooms, made sure they left the classrooms five minutes early to hang around the dining room windows like ghosts before proceeding to their hostels. They used the extra few minutes to chat with their girls through the windows. To steal some kisses.

Letwin, Agatha, Precious and Nancy walked to their dorms with the rest of the girls in a noisy crowd. They didn't have love interests searching for them through burglar-barred windows. Theirs were still on Agatha's pages, yet to jump out and come to life.

That night, Letwin lay awake on her sunken bed replacing the wide, weird grin with her mother's hearty laugh. She chased the glinty eyes with her mother's closed eyes when she had sung her Methodist hymns.

She heard Agatha tossing and turning on the bed next to hers. She had not told her aunt that the cubicles they saw in the dorm close to the admin block were nowhere else at the school.

'Agie. Agie,' she whispered.

Agatha turned to face her even though it was pitch dark and they couldn't see each other's faces.

'You can't sleep again.' It was more of a statement than a question.

'Yes,' Agie whispered back.

A pause. A hesitation.

'Agie.'

'Yes.'

'Do you think we were wrong about the girls who said, you know, who said, umm, that Mr. Lloyd had done something to them? Remember, the girls during the first and second terms? And those before I came. Do you think we were wrong in not believing them?'

Agatha didn't say anything. For a second, Letwin thought she had dozed off. 'Agie.'

'Yes.' She sniffed a little.

'Are you okay?'

'Yes.'

'Do you remember when I came back after falling sick?'

'I remember.'

A pause. 'I never told you all that the person I got a lift from was Mr Lloyd.'

Agie lifted her head off the pillow. 'What?' Her whisper sounded broken like it was bleeding and no one had put a bandage on it yet.

'Yes.'

A moment of silence. Then Letwin heard fidgeting sounds coming from Agatha's bed.

'Lettie, come and sleep here.'

Letwin chuckled. 'The matron will die if she sees us.'

'You can go back to your bed later. Come, I've made space for you.'

Letwin leapt out of bed and joined Agatha on her single bed. Agatha helped to cover her up with blankets.

'Your pillow is wet, Agie.'

'Let's turn it to the other side.'

They turned the flower-patterned pillow to the side where the blue petunias were still dry. They laid their shaved heads on them.

'He's a monster, Lettie.'

Letwin nodded her head against the pillow.

'Yes.'

'He's the devil himself.'

'Yes.'

SOPHIE CHAPMAN

Sophie Chapman is a Welsh writer and the 2023/24 Malcolm Bradbury Memorial Scholar at UEA. She is currently working on a novel about generational trauma, maternal instinct and 'unlikeable' female characters.

sophc1999@outlook.com

Irene

The opening of a novel

She stands in the rush of the train. She breathes out in its wake.

Irene has always liked trains that do not stop at stations. Trains that fly by so fast they make her unsettled. The itch in the back of her mind that wonders what would happen if she just took a few steps forward, if she just jumped. She likes that they are not at their destination. They are continuing on to somewhere else.

She gets on the next train that arrives, chooses a seat with a table even though she is by herself, even though she is only going two stops. Even though there is a family with two young children who now have to sit separately. She wants to take up space.

She is going to visit her mother. She does this once a month although they live a fifteen-minute train ride apart. As the train pulls out the station, Irene finds herself curling both hands into fists, digging her long fingernails into her palms. Through the window, she watches as the lines of uniform grey houses give way to fields lined with wind-bent trees. When the train arrives at her mother's station, she unfurls both hands and notices the violent red half-moon indents she has left on her skin. She stands and runs her hands down the front of her skirt.

Her mother's house is up the hill from the station. It is a steep enough climb to cause a sweat to form on her top lip. She sees her sister's bike resting against the house and is relieved she won't have to be alone with their mother. When she pushes the front door, it opens easily under her hands. She can hear them, her sister's careless laughter and her mother's monotone. The house smells of baking, mixed with the same undertones it's always had, of disinfectant and old carpets. Irene makes her way towards the kitchen, clenching her hands into fists again. Both her mother and sister have their backs to her, staring at something on the hob. Their heads are pressed together, elbow to elbow, breathing in, quietly appraising their work. On hearing her enter they turn, two bodies swivelling simultaneously. A bubbling quiche sits between them, yellow liquid oozing over the white ceramic.

'Irene!' Her sister smiles.

Mother grunts.

Even after all these years, her mother's face still comes as a shock to Irene. It is a glimpse into her future. As if someone has taken her face, crumpled it up in their fist and placed it upon her mother.

'It's ham and cheese.' It takes her a moment to realise Jane is talking about the quiche.

'Your sister brought a salad.' Mother looks pointedly at Irene's empty hands.

Irene flexes them, presses them deeply into the folds of her skirt.

'It's only small, I had some things about to go off.' Her sister's tone is halfway between an apology and excuse.

'That's thoughtful.' Irene barely keeps the distain out her voice.

'Why don't you go and lay the table,' Mother suggests. She gestures to the plates sitting on the side, beside a large wooden salad bowl.

Irene takes the cling film off the top of the bowl; finds inside freshly chopped lettuce, diced tomatoes, black olives and feta. She feels a sudden and violent hatred towards her sister. It lingers acrid and warm in her mouth.

'Wait!' Jane appears with a jar. 'Let me put the dressing on, I didn't want it to go soggy.'

Irene presses her lips together in a thin, grey line. Jane pours the dressing. Irene carries the bowl to the dining room.

'Don't forget to toss it,' Mother calls after her. Irene imagines throwing the bowl on the floor, bits of lettuce and olive scattering across the wood.

Once the table is laid, Jane comes in carrying the quiche like a prize chicken, arms extended, checkered tea towels wrapped around both hands. Their mother is smiling. They sit around the table, Mother beside Irene, and Jane opposite them. The seat at the head of the table remains empty. In the centre the quiche sits hot and expectant.

'Jane, do you want to serve?' Mother asks. Jane's eyes dart to Irene, who stares hard at the shelf of antique ceramic hens above Jane's head – she won't give her sister the acceptance she knows Jane desperately wants. Jane picks up the knife and begins slicing the quiche. Irene counts the hens. There are seven. When she was a child there were eight. She can remember the sound it made when it shattered.

Once Mother's quiche and Jane's salad are plated, they sit in silence. Irene knows Jane will be the one to break it.

'How's James?'

'He's fine.'

'We would love to meet him,' Jane perseveres, twisting a string of grated carrots rapidly round her fork, not meeting Irene's eye.

'Maybe another time, he's very busy at the moment.'

'Irene's embarrassed of us.' Mother spits out flakes of crumbled pastry as she speaks.

Irene doesn't deny it, although it is not entirely true.

She thinks of James sitting alone in their flat. When she left, he was reading a newspaper in the living room, feet propped up on the coffee table, one leg crossed over the other. He hadn't bothered to look up as she was leaving but called out, 'Have a nice time with Amanda.' She guesses he will be in a similar position when she returns, maybe he'll have moved onto whatever book he is working his way through at the moment.

'How about work, anything exciting going on?' Jane is now using her fork to shred the pastry crust with a determined brutality. She doesn't bring her eyes up from her plate.

'Same as normal.' Irene nods, puts a forkful of quiche in her mouth.

'Have you asked Jane about her holiday?'

A piece of pastry catches in her throat as she tries to swallow. Irene chokes it down in a painful gulp, tears gathering in her eyes. Her mother's gaze is unrelenting.

Irene can sense her sister looking back and forth between them with apprehension. Jane interrupts the heavy silence with talk of her trip: the Greek salads and crazy drivers and the lovely English family she met. Irene is exhausted already. Tired of all the pleasantries and fake niceties. Though, she considers, maybe they aren't fake from her sister, always so sincere.

Jane had called Irene from her little Greek island getaway. *Oh, it's simply gorgeous, Irene. You would just love it here. Maybe we could go together someday, even bring Mother. She would like that, don't you think? Did I tell you about the seafood?* Irene had pictured Jane on the other end of the line, chewing a hangnail and wrapping the hotel's phone cord around her little finger over and over.

Irene notices her mother is still watching her, anticipating her reaction.

'Sounds nice.'

'I really think we should try to go away somewhere, the three of us,' Jane ventures. Irene is pleased to see Mother looks startled by the suggestion.

'Go where?' Mother asks. She picks up her napkin and dabs the edges of her mouth.

'Abroad, I'm not sure, France maybe. We could get the ferry over.' Jane seems genuinely excited by the prospect.

'Oh, I don't know.' Mother shakes her head. 'I wouldn't want to leave...' She gestures around at the room, the house.

'I have work,' Irene adds.

'Just for a few days,' Jane persists.

'We'll see.' Mother's tone closes that conversation. She places her knife and fork down diagonally across her plate, carefully straightens them. 'I was hoping today we would all go and visit–' she begins, watches their expressions and stops, adjusts the cutlery.

'Ok,' says Jane at the same time Irene says, 'No.'

Irene watches her mother's face fall. She doesn't know why they must go through this routine every time. Mother shouldn't be surprised any more.

Letting her chair scrape loudly on the floor as she pushes it back, Irene stands up from the table. 'You both go, I'll do the washing up.' She starts collecting the plates and retreats into the kitchen.

She doesn't have to look back to know Jane will now be getting up from the table, placing a consoling squeeze on their mother's shoulder before following her out the room. This is a routine they have practised; they all have their choreographed steps. Irene shoves her hands into waiting washing up gloves and slides them right up to the elbows.

'You upset her when you do that.' Her sister leans back on the counter beside the sink. She picks up a tea towel and starts drying the plates absentmindedly. Every time Irene sees Jane, she seems to get smaller.

Irene lets her impatience seep into her voice. 'She is very capable of going without me.'

Jane stacks the dry plates on her other side. She starts twisting and knotting the tea towel round her fingers and wrists. 'Can't you just go for her? Not for his benefit, just for hers.'

'Maybe next time.' Irene lifts her hands out of the sink, streams of water running down her arms and dripping steadily off her elbows onto the clean linoleum. They both know she is lying.

'We won't be too long.'

Irene nods, turns her face away so she is staring out the kitchen window and doesn't have to look at her sister's pitiful expression. She remains like that until she sees the pair of heads bowed against the wind, two sets of coat collars turned up and arms linked tightly together, heading down the front path, through the gate and turning left towards town.

Irene takes off the yellow gloves, places them behind the sink, finds her feet taking her upstairs. She pushes open the door to her childhood bedroom without intending to. The walls have been repainted, a soft yellow, the colour of milky scrambled eggs. Gone are the posters and postcards and drawings she had blue-tacked to the walls in her teenage years. A painting of a farmhouse hangs above the bare desk and a canvas of an embroidered hen rests on the chest of drawers. She finds herself standing before the window. Her shins press against the frame of the single bed she once slept in.

She waits for them to appear. One head of permed grey curls and one of mousy brown frizz. They are still arm in arm. She can just see them through a gap in the houses behind. For a moment, they disappear behind the Jones's then reappear a little further up the hill. She waits for them to find it, waits for them to stop. Her knees bend, forcing her skin so deep into the harsh wooden bed frame it begins to sting.

She watches Mother unlatch herself from Jane and lean down to brush something off the stone, a fallen leaf maybe, it's too far away for Irene to tell. Jane tilts her head down; it's a position that could suggest respect or fear.

It looks like Mother is saying something, a prayer she presumes. Irene turns her head away and stares down at the off-white bedsheets, the sharp, tucked in corners. When she glances back up, they have linked arms again and are walking together back down the hill. She stares at the stone for a moment, there are no flowers resting on it like some of the others, no wreath or bouquet. She does not need to be nearby to know what the words on the stone say.

Irene takes a step back, the sudden relief makes her throat bob, she looks down and sees two dark lines indented into her shins. The feeling of her blood pulsing underneath is urgent. She leans down and rubs a finger over each dent, marbled purple against her fingers. She is sure it will bruise.

MARK COCKSHUTT

Mark Cockshutt is a writer of weird fiction. He is working on a novel – *The Noise* – and has previously been published as Mark Bardwell with his children's novel *Dylan and the Deadly Dimension* (Everything with Words, 2017).

markcockshutt@yahoo.co.uk

Are You Lonely?

A short story

Rebecca had woken feeling sunken and stale. She jumped when the bell above the bakery door tinkled for the first time that morning. The customer's eyes were down as he entered, his brow furrowed. He shuffled forward, his pace slowing as he neared the counter. When he stopped it was sudden, as if he was surprised to have found it in front of him.

He looked up at Rebecca and said, 'Are you lonely?'

She frowned and shifted from one foot to another. 'What can I get you?' she said.

He looked at her for a second longer than was comfortable, before asking for a sourdough bloomer. He thanked her, his gaze making Rebecca blush a little, much to her annoyance, before he broke eye contact, turned and left.

Once the bell had let out a laugh and the door rattled shut, Rebecca felt guilty for ignoring his question, but it only lasted until the bell went again, letting in a stretch of sunlight and a new customer.

The next morning, Rebecca tore a paper bag sliding a loaf into it and swore under her breath when she tore the next one. The customer she was serving, a cheerful old lady, asked with concern as to whether she was OK, and, commenting on the shadows under her eyes, if there was anything on her mind?

Rebecca tried to keep a cheerful face on after that and took a deep breath whenever the sleepless hours crept into her hands and made her clumsy. The man from the previous day came in at eleven to eleven. He walked in briskly this time, and did not look at the floor, quickly finding her eyes. He looked at her with interest, not concern, as the old lady had.

'Tell, me,' he said, 'are you lonely?'

She sighed and asked what he wanted.

Once he had his purchase under his arm, he paused.

'Lemmon,' he said.

She looked at him for a moment, before pointing at the lemon drizzle cake under the glass of the counter. 'How many slices?'

He smiled and shook his head. 'Terrence Lemmon. I thought you might be less lonely if I told you my name.'

'I'm not lonely.'

Terrence Lemmon nodded. Still smiling, he turned and left the shop.

Things were worse for Rebecca the following day. She was late to get going and didn't have all the loaves out on the shelves when two of the early regulars entered the shop and acted cold and hurt when Rebecca was not responsive to their normal chatter.

The door flung open at nine to nine, bell flailing ecstatically. Terrence Lemmon bustled in, a wide smile upon his face. He laughed as he looked around the shop. It came out in a short crescendo, as if he had been trying to keep it in but was unable to. He joked with the other customers, who put their hands up to their mouths and laughed when he made a risqué comment about a baguette. His eyes searched for Rebecca's, his lips curving upwards into his grey moustache.

'Are you lonely?' he said, once the other customers had left the bakery.

Rebecca folded her arms and looked at him. 'I'm not lonely.'

The smile remained on Terrence Lemmon's face as he continued looking at her. He was holding his trilby against his chest with his right hand, drumming his fingers lightly on its crown. Rebecca looked at him properly for the first time. He was largely bald, but the grey hair that remained around the sides of his head was thick and put Rebecca in mind of vegetation, of plant life that you could get lost in. Dense hairs protruded from his nostrils like unearthed roots. He had a greenish-brown wax jacket on, that looked like it may once have been another colour entirely.

'Are *you* lonely?' Rebecca said to him. 'Why do you keep asking?'

'Because I'm concerned that you…?' he held out the trilby expansively.

'Rebecca.' Rebecca hadn't meant to say her name. It popped out of her mouth of its own accord. Terrence Lemmon looked at her encouragingly. She felt her tongue forming her surname before she said it, tried to stop it, but out it came – 'Crisp.'

He looked delighted. 'Rebecca Crisp! How marvellous. A sourdough bloomer, if you please, Rebecca Crisp.'

She felt uneasy. She had not intended to give her name to him, but it had felt like she had no power to stop it. She got him the loaf and bagged it and charged him. He was one of the only customers to still pay by cash. He slowly and deliberately placed the coins on the counter and pushed them one by one towards her.

'You didn't answer,' she said.

'I didn't?'

The way his smile rose up against the bristles of his moustache hairs made her angry.

'Either of my questions.'

'Which one would you prefer that I answer?'

'Both!'

'You can't ask that of me.' The smile did not fall for a moment.

'I can.'

'I was lonely, until I met you.'

'Gross!'

Terrence Lemmon laughed and started to walk backwards.

'Good day, Rebecca Crisp!' he said. 'Until tomorrow!'

That evening, Rebecca was making herself some tea – a quick dal with tinned lentils and toast made with slices of a leftover loaf from the bakers – when she pondered Terrence Lemmon's question. *Was* she lonely?

She thought about it. She tallied up the number of times she had met up with friends so far in the past six months. Four. None of those times involved anyone visiting her flat. It was too small to entertain properly, and she liked keeping it separate from the other parts of her life. A cat would be nice but, again, the flat was too small for her to keep one. She had her fantasy novels and her jigsaw puzzles. In any case, her small friendship group had mostly become absorbed in the business of settling down and having children and rarely had time to spend with those who weren't. If she found herself in need of company, she would turn on the radio and not really listen to what was being said.

When the dal was ready, she spooned half of it into a plastic container and left it to cool on the side with the lid balanced loosely at an angle on top. The rest she spooned into a pasta bowl and placed the buttered slices of toast next it. She sat down at the kitchen table and took a bite. She closed her eyes for a moment while she chewed her food. She opened them once she had swallowed and said, 'I'm not lonely,' aloud to the kitchen. 'I'm just a bit tired.'

The next day, Terrence Lemmon stood outside the bakery door without entering. Rebecca could see him watching her through the glass, his moustache hovering over the reversed lettering of the door like a caterpillar, nose and eyes balanced above. She did her best to ignore him, pretending to be busy, adjusting the displays and moving the bread around, hoping he would either go away or come in. A trio of knocks rapped against the door. Resisting this call for attention, she slipped into the back room and took a deep breath before heading over to the window that overlooked the back yard where the deliveries came in.

Another knock sounded on the front door. Rebecca counted to twenty-seven in her head, at which point she got bored and thought about what she would do after work that afternoon. She took her phone out of her apron pocket. Maybe she would see if anyone wanted to meet up for a drink. She typed out a message in the group chat. Her finger hovered over the send button before moving over and holding down delete, the cursor rushing backwards, removing her unsent words from existence. She heard the bell at the front of the shop.

She went back to find Terrence Lemmon standing in front of the counter, staring at her. There was a smile under the moustache that propped up its ends, but his eyes were wide and fierce. He waited until she was in her usual position behind the till before saying anything.

'Are you lonely?' he said. The friendly tone now had an urgency running beneath.
'What can I get you?' Rebecca said blankly.
'Who?' Terrence Lemmon's fists curled up by his sides.
'You. Obviously.'
'And who am I?'
Rebecca folded her arms. 'Terrence Lemmon. What can I get Terrence Lemmon?'

'All I want is for you to answer my question, Rebecca Crisp.'

'Which question is that?'

Terrence Lemmon stuck the nib of his tongue between his teeth and bit down so hard that blood seeped through his bottom teeth. 'Are. You. Lonely?'

'Will you stop bothering me if I tell you? Again.'

'If you answer honestly.'

Rebecca considered this for a moment. 'Fine. Ask me again.'

Terrence Lemmon smiled and straightened his posture. His fists unclenched and he put his hands on his hips. He looked like he should be wearing a cape.

'Are you lonely?'

'No,' said Rebecca.

His eyes unfocused. His face flooded a deep red and his cheeks rose, lips becoming a rigid square around the bloodied teeth. A growl crept up his throat.

'Are *you* lonely?' she asked him.

Terrence Lemmon began to stalk around the shop in a circle, beating his hands against his legs and chest. The growl stopped when he opened his mouth. He looked like he was roaring, but no sound was coming out. He stood still and continued silently trying to roar in the middle of the shop, mouth gaping as Rebecca watched him. He looked like he was about to burst.

'Are you lonely?' she asked him again.

He closed his mouth and looked at her, startled, and in that moment rapidly shrank down until his clothes were heaped into a pile on the floor. Terrence Lemmon stepped out of the neck of his jumper, naked and four inches tall. His body was obscured by his moustache, which had remained the same size as it was. 'Yes,' he said, voice a high squeak. He became still, rooted to the spot. Panic entered his eyes as tremor passed through his body. His flesh rapidly expanded and turned a pale green as it stretched out his human form into something that resembled a succulent, his head splitting and peeling out into thick leaves.

Terrence Lemmon was now very much a plant.

Rebecca gathered his clothes up and thought about whether to donate them to the charity shop across the road. There was an odd earthy odour coming off them, though. Not unpleasant exactly, but it made her uncomfortable. She bagged them up in a bin liner and stuck them in the back to take out later and got on with the day, moving the plant to a shelf out back.

As she served the customers, her thoughts kept returning to the plant. In the lull after lunch, she went and looked at it. It looked lonely, so she picked it up. It had a sort of charm, despite the straggly remains of moustache dotted about the leaves. She put it back down and left the bakery, turning the sign on the door to *Closed*. She headed to the garden centre bought a small plant pot and some soil. On the return walk, she thought about where she would keep it – the kitchen window got a lot of sunlight, and it would keep her company as she cooked and ate her meals. At the bakery, she froze in the doorway of the back room and stared at the empty spot where the plant had been, the soil and the empty pot clasped in her hands.

NIAMH CONNOLLY

Niamh is an Irish writer with a BA in English and history. She has written several features for *Life* magazine of the *Sunday Independent*. Her novel, *Game Theory*, is a decades-spanning love story dealing with miscommunication, bereavement, financial disparity, and loneliness; this novel-in-progress won the Women's Prize Trust Discoveries 2024 award. Niamh is represented by Rosie Pierce at Curtis Brown.

niamh546@hotmail.com

Game Theory

An extract from a novel

The coolness of the marble tiles felt good against my sunburnt cheek. An unidentifiable insect scurried past my face; I did not have the energy to react. My back ached, curled, and pressed against the bath's exterior. The T-shirt I wore was stained with sweat. A piercing cramp warned me that the next wave was coming. I peeled my body from the floor, lifted the ceramic lid off the toilet, and hunched my body over the bowl. It took seven seconds for the retching to begin. There was too much for my mouth to handle, so chunks of bile charged through my nostrils. Everything burned: my throat, my nose, and my eyes. When the exodus finally stopped, I flushed the toilet, closed the lid, and placed my cheek back down on the tiles.

The bottom half of my body was bare and cold. The terracotta bathroom no longer smelt of aloe vera and sun cream. I wanted to open the window to let some air in, but my body would not move. Lying on the ground, I had the sensation of being back on the boat. The tiled floor began to rock; it felt like a malleable surface breaking beneath my limbs, and so I closed my eyes to make it stop – to make it stand still.

I woke with a start. Someone was shouting. My body was shaking. 'Hello!' the voice echoed. It was getting closer. A hard crust had formed along my eyelids. I couldn't make out where I was. 'Dolly!' The voice belonged to a man. 'Frances!'

As the door swung open, hitting my foot, I saw my shorts crumpled on the terracotta tiles, and instantly remembered where I was.

'Jesus –'

'Get out!'

Callum ignored me, kneeling down by my side. 'Frances –'

'Seriously, please leave.' I didn't have the energy to sit up.

He rolled me onto my back. Of all the ways in which I'd imagined Callum seeing my vagina for the first time, this was not it. He reached for a towel and placed it over me like a blanket. 'Frances.' He held a hand to my sweaty forehead.

'Please don't touch me.' I was almost in tears.

'I'm going to try sit you up –'

'Callum, please, you being here is making this worse –'

'I'm not going anywhere,' he said, his voice tense. 'Do you think you can sit up?'

I closed my eyes and nodded.

He reached his hand behind my back and helped me manoeuvre my body so that I was resting up against the bath. I opened my eyes. He wore pale blue jeans and a white shirt.

'Honestly, I'm fine –'

'You are not fine.' He stood up, and then ran a towel under the tap before kneeling back down in front of me. We stared at each other for four seconds.

I could feel the tears pooling and so I closed my eyes again.

Callum moved the damp towel over my face in soft strokes. Then with his finger wrapped in the towel, he ran it along my dry lips; the moisture was gone as quickly as it met my skin. 'I'm going to get you some water,' he said. 'Don't move.'

I heard a tap turning; the water pressure was strong and the bath vibrated against my body as it filled. Within thirty seconds, he was back in the bathroom holding a plastic cup to my lips. I didn't want to swallow, scared it would come back up, but it felt good to wash away the sour taste in my mouth. Callum held the cup as I drank, his eyes on mine the entire time.

While I sipped, I studied his face. There were pock marks on his chin from the cystic acne he had during fifth year. His nose was red from the sun. There were little clusters of freckles over his eyebrows and along his rounded cheekbones. His lips looked as dry as mine felt – the skin pink and peeling.

He raised his eyebrows, 'You enjoying yourself there?'

I pulled my mouth from the empty cup and said, 'You've aged.'

'Thanks,' he said, dryly, rolling back onto his heels and placing the cup on the sink.

'Not in a bad way per se.'

'Right,' he said, turning off the tap and testing the bath's temperature with his hand.

'I mean you look mature, but like' – I gestured to his face – 'in a dehydrated way.'

He laughed, 'You know you could just say, *Thank you, Callum, for helping me.*'

I looked up at him and mouthed the words *Thank you*. More tears pooled in my eyes; I'd lost the strength to keep them in check.

He crouched back down and said, 'The bath is ready. Do you think you can stand?'

I nodded as I knotted the towel around my waist. Every movement hurt.

Callum held out his hands and I took them. 'Whoa,' he said as I tried to stand. 'Slowly.'

'I'm fine from here,' I said, my feet on the ground, my calves resting against the bath.

He shook his head, motioning towards the floor, 'I'm not leaving you after that –'

'I'm fine –'

'You can barely stand,' he said, looking at my hand clasping his arm. My knuckles were as white as the skin along his wrist where my fingers dug in.

I could feel my body buckling, and so I gave in, instructing Callum to shut his eyes.

He rolled them before closing them.

There were freckles on his eyelids.

With one hand holding onto Callum, I loosened the towel around my waist and let it drop to the floor. 'I'm going to need help with this next part –'

His eyes opened.

'Keep them closed!'

His eyes snapped shut, 'Jesus, relax. You're forgetting I've just seen –'

'Do not remind me.'

He smiled a big smile, 'It's an image that's ingrained in my mind forever –'

'You're being an asshole.'

'I'm just teasing,' he laughed. 'What do you need?'

I moved his two hands to the hem of my T-shirt and said, 'Could you pull this up?'

He was trying not to smirk, 'Certainly.'

It took all my strength to lift my arms over my head and as soon as the T-shirt was on the floor, I grasped back onto Callum to steady myself.

'You okay?'

'Yeah.' I smiled at the absurdity of standing naked in front of Callum with his eyes closed. 'I'm going to get in now.' The water was warm, almost too hot, but it felt good to sink below its weight. Callum had added an oil to the water that smelt like rosemary, and it gathered in small pools on the surface.

'You in?'

'Yes,' I said, pulling my knees up to my chest. 'It feels good, thank you.'

'Can I open my eyes now?'

I laughed, 'Okay, but if you're going to stay, you have to sit behind the bath. This is too embarrassing –'

'You're forgetting I already –'

I splashed water at him, 'Shut up!'

'So sensitive,' he said, settling himself down on the floor between the bath and the sink.

I rested my head on my knees, imagining what we must look like – picturing the scene from above. My back arched, the grooves of my spine protruding like those on a whelk shell. Callum sitting on the terracotta tiles, behind me, his long legs crammed and curled into such a small space.

I turned to see if he was looking at me, but his head was resting against the wall, his eyes on the ceiling. I faced forward and said, 'I didn't think you were arriving until tomorrow.'

'The lads left this morning, so I got an earlier boat. Thought I'd surprise you guys.'

I lifted my fingers from the water; the skin was bright red and wrinkled.

'Where are the others?' he asked.

'They're at this full-moon party.'

'Did you go and come back?'

'No, my stomach started feeling off after lunch. I'd advise you not to try the clams from the street vendor.'

He didn't laugh. 'So what did you tell Dolly?'

Cupping water in my hand, I splashed my face and said, 'What?'

'I mean did you tell her you were feeling sick?'

'I just said I was tired.'

'Right.'

'Why?'

'And were you going to message anyone to tell them when you started vomiting –'

'I was a bit preoccupied with the vomiting part,' I said, goose bumps appearing along my forearms.

In a strained voice, he said, 'So you'd still be on the floor if I didn't get an earlier –'

'I didn't plan this, Callum –'

'I know that –'

'Then what are you getting at?'

He sighed, 'It's like you refuse to let anyone see you needing help.'

There was a gentle ringing in my ears. 'That's bullshit –'

'It's not,' he said. 'Dolly is your best friend and you didn't even tell her you were feeling sick. You never let anyone help you –'

'Stop.' My head felt dizzy. The nausea had returned. I started counting, hoping he would let this go – I didn't have the energy to fight him.

But he wasn't done.

'I'm not trying to be a dick. It's just, you should know it's okay to ask for help.' His voice sounded tired. 'And, like, I'm always here for you. I' – he breathed out heavily – 'I worry about you.'

'You pitying me is the last thing I want –'

'Jesus, there you go. You see a friend telling you they're worried about you as some kind of pity. You're impossible –'

'Then leave me alone. No one is making you stay here.'

I counted to seven before he said, 'For the last time, I'm not going anywhere.'

'Fine, then can we stop talking. I have a headache.'

He didn't respond. There was silence except for the fan spinning in the adjoining bedroom. I pulled my knees tighter into my chest and let the tears that I'd been holding in fall. My arms started to tremble as they fell, and I couldn't stop the heaving in my body. I tried to pretend he wasn't there, witnessing this. I bit down on my bottom lip to make it stop, but it didn't work.

I waited for him to say something; to ask why I was crying, but he remained silent, sitting behind me. He just let me cry. And it felt like the kindest thing he'd ever done. He didn't ask me to stop or explain. He just let me be, while not leaving me alone.

I cried until there were no more tears, and when my body finally stopped shaking, I felt a sponge move across my shoulders.

'Put your head back,' he said, gently.

I followed his instructions. I was done resisting. Water ran through my hair and down my neck; this action was repeated four times. I heard the click of a bottle opening and then his hands were on my scalp, rubbing a shampoo that smelt of ginger and lemongrass into my hair.

'Close your eyes,' he said as he rinsed the shampoo out.

I was acutely aware that he could see everything at this point: the stretch marks along my breasts; the heat rash on the back of my neck; the broken blood vessels on my upper arms. But I no longer cared.

'The water's getting cool,' he eventually said. 'Let's get you out.'

I held onto the edge of the bath as I got to my feet. Callum stood with a large orange towel stretched between his arms. I stepped out of the bath and he wrapped the towel around my body, softly rubbing my shoulders. His shirt cuffs and breast pocket were soaked through.

'Better?' he asked. I nodded.

CHLOE COOKSON

Chloe Cookson is a British-Canadian writer from the west coast of British Columbia. She has an undergraduate degree in Writing and English from the University of Victoria and has been published in the university's magazine *This Side of West*. Her fiction is both strange and tender, historical and relevant.

chloecookson73@gmail.com

Wake

An extract from the opening of a novel

The charcoal wagon trundled down the closely wooded track, the trees on either side the varied shades of rotting fruit. Tom and Cecil sat on the wagon's bench in a settled silence, shoulders hunched. Ahead, the sun pulled its last pale rays below the horizon, and a woman walked in the road.

Her hair glowed like a candle wick in the bruising November evening; it was Anna Wake. Tom imagined, not for the first time, taking the heavy warmth of that hair in his hands, letting it knot around his fingers. She held her hat in a gloved hand: a black-trimmed felt hat, festooned with three dark feather plumes. She swung the hat idly, like a rich lady with the luxury to be careless, Tom thought. The feathers bobbed; the brim brushed against her skirts. The hat was new: he had first seen her wearing it the week before, the feathers creating complicated shadows over Anna's face, a silver monogrammed pin affixed to the band declaring her first initial — his mother hissing beside him, 'how can she ever afford it, at four-fifty a week!'

'Anna!' Tom cried out, straightening.

The horse drew even with her. She turned and smiled. Was she smiling at *him*, Tom wondered?

'Evening,' Cecil called from his place beside Tom, as he slowed the horse to pass.

'Aren't you out late, Anna?' Tom said. 'You shouldn't be out here alone.'

She didn't reply, just nodded in greeting, smile still fastened to her face. The wagon slid by. Tom twisted around. They had already passed her interest; she was swinging her hat again, gazing out into the trees at the hem of the road.

'That's old man Wake's eldest daughter,' Tom confided. He had a desire, suddenly, to create distance between himself and Anna.

'That drunkard?' said Cecil. 'You'd never have thought. A diamond, sired by a rough.' He coughed a laugh.

Tom chuckled as well, on instinct, then stopped himself. He looked off into the trees. A flash of water — they were passing Grey's Pond. Tom had gone there with some of the other farmhands, once, to fish. He'd been the only one who hadn't caught anything and the others had teased him. 'Tom can't catch anyone,' they'd crowed, 'not even a fish.'

'You should hurry,' he said to Cecil, 'it's getting dark.'

'He has another daughter, doesn't he?' Cecil asked, holding the reins slackly. Every line in his hands was darkly etched by the charcoal he sold, and the beds of his nails were black. Tom rubbed at his own hands, knowing they were not much better; scoured with dirt which never seemed to wash away, roughened with calluses, smelling like earth and rot. He knew Anna's hands would be soft as a donkey's coat, and smell like lilacs, and the river on a cool day.

'Yes.'

'What's her name, then?'

Tom pressed his teeth together. 'Irene.'

'Is she just as pretty?'

He curled his fingers around the wooden bench. *Pretty* was too small a word to describe Anna. 'I wouldn't know. I've never met her.'

Cecil scoffed. He glanced at Tom. 'Fancy lady, for the daughter of a no good drunk who can hold a job as well as a rusted out bucket can hold water. She's bettered herself, I suppose?'

'She works for a family in town.' Tom had visited her at their residence twice. A tall, intricate house, quieter than the homes Tom knew, where there was always shouting and laughter and arguing pouring out of the windows. He'd brought Anna an apple plucked from one of the trees at the farm; 'to sweeten your day,' he told her when she met him at the back door. She hadn't smiled. As she closed the door, Tom vowed he would study to be more charming.

'Does she have a sweetheart?' Cecil asked.

'Can't you make your horse go any faster? It would be quicker to walk at this pace.' Tom sniffed. The air was dirty with the smell of coal, from the heap in the back of the wagon, and from Cecil himself. Coal dust had settled into the sweaty hollow of his throat, showing stark white lines where the skin creased as he talked.

Cecil smirked. 'Do you have someplace to be? Are you meeting a *lady*?' The word curved with insinuation from his mouth.

'I would just prefer to get to town before nightfall.' Already the sky was purpling above them.

'This is my wagon, and it goes at my pace. I'm doing you a favour, letting you ride with me.' Cecil slanted his head towards Tom. 'I bet you'd like to be meeting that Wake girl, wouldn't you.'

'I think I will walk,' Tom said primly. 'Slow up.'

Cecil grinned but did not adjust his grip on the reins. The horse snorted, as if in on the joke.

'Slow—' Tom huffed, but stopped himself. Cecil didn't deserve the respect of a full sentence. What a small, dirty creature he was, his only connection to Tom the fact that he had sold Tom's family charcoal for years. Cecil should show more deference, Tom thought, to one of his most loyal customers. He would tell his mother to stop buying from Cecil, and he felt stronger from the resolution, even though she would likely not heed his advice.

He pushed himself up and leapt from the moving wagon, twisting his ankle as he landed. The wagon seemed to gain speed as soon as he'd fallen from it, and Cecil's laughter faded in extended loops as it pulled away. Tom scowled and felt his ankle: it was only sore, not broken. His cap had fallen into the mud and he stooped to pick it up, attempting to dust it off. He looked behind him. They had only passed Anna about ten minutes before. He could walk back, catch up with her. He should have offered to escort her, like a gentleman would. Tom beat the cap repeatedly against his leg, trying to get the dirt out. This was why no girls ever showed interest in him, why Essie had pushed him hard on the shoulder when he'd tried to get close to her; because he didn't think of the things a gentleman would.

But he would now. He would give Anna his arm and she would take it, and he would talk and she would smile.

A light rain had started, spotting Tom's shirt. He turned back and started scuffing up the road, holding Anna in his mind.

He recalled first seeing her at the farm, a bright blue spring day when she had come to visit her aunt and uncle, the sun ice white, the wind playful. The three of them had walked out to see the new heifers Anna's uncle had acquired, Anna lagging behind, and they passed Tom where he knelt repairing a fence post. The wind picked the hat off Anna's head — not the black feathered one, but a more humble blue toque-style hat, without adornment — and it had drifted, landing near Tom's feet. He crouched to pick it up, and when he looked up, Anna's hair had torn loose from its tight knot and was rippling around her head, as long and golden as the dry grass at the end of summer. He had not really looked at her until he saw her hair.

Another gust built up strength and blew Tom's own cap off his head, and he was forced to chase after it, snatching it out of the air just before it settled in a pile of cow dung.

The sound of Anna's laughter carried over to Tom as her hat had. He wasn't sure if she was laughing at him or not. He stumbled over, clutching both hats awkwardly in his hands.

'Thank you,' she said, before he'd even presented the hat to her, her mouth still laughing.

He handed her the hat, realising a beat too late that it was not the blue toque he had given her, but his own tattered and filthy cap. But she was already placing it on her head, grinning knowingly. It sat on top of her wind-tangled hair like an overused rag, shapeless and discoloured from years of absorbed grime. A flake of dried mud shed itself from the cap to catch in a golden strand. And yet she still looked like an illustration in a catalogue, Tom thought, with apple cheeks and long neck, like the kind of pictures the other farmhands tore out and tacked above their beds.

'Go on,' she nodded to her hat, still clasped in his grip. 'Put it on.'

Tom grinned shyly and lifted the toque to his head. He had expected it to be too small for him, but it fit snugly perched on his dishwater hair, the velvet soft where it brushed his ears. He wished he had a mirror or even a puddle to examine his reflection. He wanted to know how he looked to her.

Anna's smile stretched. 'It suits you.'

'Anna!' Her uncle — Mr Spicer — strode towards them.

Tom expected her to take the cap off, but she didn't, just gazed at her uncle as he approached, her grin gone.

'What have you got on your head?' Mr Spicer asked. Tom thought his face was even redder than usual. 'It looks like a cow pat.'

'It's a hat, Uncle Roy.'

'But it's not *your* hat.' Mr Spicer glanced towards Tom for the first time and stiffened. 'What are you doing?'

Tom snatched the toque from his head and lowered his eyes. He had forgotten he was wearing it. His heart juddered in his chest and his eyes grew hot. He could already see the turned down look on his mother's face when he told her Mr Spicer had let him go. He kept his eyes fixed on the thinning toes of his mud caked shoes.

'It's my fault,' Anna said. 'I asked him to try it on. He has a similar complexion to a friend of mine and I wanted to see whether the colour would suit her.'

Tom's eyes widened. Why had she said that? She had *lied* to Mr Spicer. The truth felt equally innocent. He did not understand.

Anna turned to Tom before Mr Spicer could respond. 'Thank you for being my model. I don't think I know your name yet. I'm sure Uncle Roy was just about to introduce us.'

'Tom,' he stammered, still hanging his head.

'Anna Wake. Here's your cap.' They exchanged hats but Tom was too afraid to put his on again. He couldn't look at Mr Spicer or Anna. He stared down at the cap in his hand, his fingers pulling at the loose band. There was a single thin strand of gold caught in the fabric. Then it, too, was seized by the wind and lost in the wider world.

When Tom looked up, Anna and Mr Spicer were small in the distance, walking into the blue horizon, Anna's hands raised to her head as she re-pinned her hair.

Mr Spicer had not mentioned the incident afterwards, and continued to treat Tom as he had before: like a runt of a herding dog who had to be taught what should have been inherent to him. But it didn't matter, because he had met Anna.

The hollow cry of a loon broke Tom's reverie. There was Grey's Pond, on his left. Surely it had been only moments after seeing Anna that they had passed it? He should have caught up to her by now. Maybe she'd stopped to shelter from the rain. Tom squinted. The purple light of evening had turned to a soft, faded grey. He was about to call out Anna's name when he heard something, farther up the road: a soft jingling and rhythmic clopping, faint but steadily increasing. He stopped.

KIERAN COSTELLO

Kieran is a British-Irish writer. His first published short story appeared in Writers' Forum in 2017. He writes about lives on the margins, digital isolation and fractured identities. He is currently working on a novel that explores our evolving relationship with nature, and what happens when it pushes back.

kjscostello@gmail.com

Hear the Whispers

An excerpt from an early chapter of a novel.

Where is she now. In a dipped furrow, contemplating the break of day. Waiting for the man to move; for the clouds to gather and flatten the landscape. Setting shadows in motion. And she amongst them, indivisible from the reeds and sedges, the bowed alders. Silent through the hush of the wind.

But the insects are about her: mosquitoes on her flesh. Swarming gnats filling her vision with a thousand flecks of black. So that it's hard to see beyond. Hard to see the man as he finally rises, shivering in the early mist, rubbing at the bites on his skin. Studying the treeline ahead and craning his neck behind. Where the sun is rising, stretching apparitions across the flats.

Anika breathes; the peat and foetid water fills her lungs, and she holds the smells inside. Finds the place where the earth meets the soles of her feet. Cold sunlight draws upon her, and she lowers herself to the tarp that parts the reeds, crests the shallow bog. And through the sounds – the birds in the sky, the whir of insects – she listens for the breaking of water. His first step sending bitterns booming from their beds, spoonbills craning in formation to the reaches of the swamp.

She waits some minutes, and quietly packs the tarpaulin and thermals. Michael's button eyes flash from the recesses of her backpack, and she takes him out and squeezes him to her face, inhaling deep the faded smells. Something of lilacs, her mother brewing tea, her father digging. She blinks at the teddy. And it's in her mind that she speaks: we can't go on. And that a reply comes: yes, we must.

There's the laptop, too, and then her thoughts are on the group, the battery. The growing distance between them, too far now to track. But reminding her of her purpose. Which isn't here; it isn't this man, who goes blindly, reading signs that aren't there. Inching closer to the waters that swallow stories whole, receptacles entire.

But he's survived. Finding passage through a sinking world, and him sinking into it. Not eating enough, letting the mosquitoes have their fill. Past the boy that drew steel to his belly. Saying there's no way through; that this is the end. And Anika watching from the window as the man stood calm, smiling beyond fear, but shaking all the same. Waiting for deliverance.

The days pass, and he is her study. She sleeps when he sleeps, eats when he eats. Leaving shallow footprints in the grass, dimples in the overgrowth. Her own feet calloused, broken and mended, hardened by endless journeys, worn soles meeting edges where they lie. At times he kneels to the floor, as if studying something found there, then looks up, to the sides, taking in the air. Perfumed with the flowers that bloom even as they walk. Clasped heads suddenly opening, angling upwards, petals like arms to the waking forest.

Ahead now: skeins of bog, varicose thickening. Bursting forth with the rains, so that water meets water, and the pathways vanish. And where there were fields lie pellucid lakes, flat mirrors to the sheer sky. So that looking in she's at once rising above, falling below. There she stands before a changed face: features flowing into shallow valleys of gentle skin, green eyes. She pulls out Michael and holds it next to her, still staring into the waters, into the sky, caught in mirrors.

I'm different, she says.

You're older.

I don't look like me.

She holds the teddy closer to the surface, as though to get a better look, and in doing so her face rises to meet them.

Everybody changes, he says, and she lowers her hand to touch the perfect symmetry, where her fingers pierce through, sending distortions rippling outwards. For a moment she forgets, and only when the last ripple fades does she look to the horizon, intuit the path, and follow.

The man finds new dangers. Across the peat marshes his legs sink deep into the earth, panic clear even from afar: flailing limbs reaching to the distended sky. From her position she observes, waits, knowing that to survive is a choice. And sure enough, his mind calms. He sees his path and slowly, ever slower, seizes the weeds – stalks thick, buried deep – and pulls himself forwards. And there he pants on the peat, and though she cannot see it, and though she cannot hear it, she feels his breath. Rapid and glad, imbibing the putrid earth.

She has learnt to sleep most places. To fix her body down, shielded as best she can, tarp writhing, and wait the hours. Riding the world's arc to the break of day.

Over the wrinkled flats she can see to the ends of the world: pimples of dipped brick, swelling forests that blow seed into fallowed fields, spreading further. Splitting roads. And before the night she is naked before the stars. Thinking often of the peaks, the valley, the great winding crags. Monolithic sentinels standing firm. Pulling her back into memory. To Esther's face, and that of the other children that dissolve in the waking light.

She watches the man begin to disappear. Over mounds of wet earth and swollen hedgerows, between copses. His smell and footprints fading. For the rains have finally come. And they compress the land, drawing a curtain on the world.

Into the forest, then. Where roots join, share minerals, shed time. Past hushed willows that dip fingered branches into the murky waters. Through glades of purple heather and wet ferns, where ash, birch and sycamore close in, crowd the taller oaks like acolytes.

For a moment she loses him to the rhododendrons. Delicate with every step, she slows until they're everywhere: the pink buds, the splayed leaves, climbing to the light.

But then there are no more tracks, and she finds him huddled in an opening with his knees drawn to his chest. And here he sleeps, watched by the towering flowers.

She wakes and picks whatever she can, wild garlic where she finds it, and runs her fingers through clumps of hair before tying it back. Then her usual rituals: caressing her hand over the teddy, the nametag, the laptop. Breathing them in. Taking in the knowledge of who she is, where she is, as the forest canopy thickens, threading needles of early sun. Already warm, and she knows what's to come: the heat smothering the life it creates, setting alight the dry underbrush.

In an opening she finds red haw berries: beads of blood at the end of thorned fingers, having already shed their white flowers. And it's her father before her. Eating them, clasping his hands to his throat, pretending to die. Then smiling just as her tears became real. His face suddenly serious: too much of anything can kill, he said. And then he spat out the little hearts. The poison sealed in the seed.

The next day they walk in a circle, and at its end the man sits beneath a familiar canopy. Whimpering, drawing in, coaxing the flame he's started. The orange glow wavering as it licks the moist logs. And Anika watching from beneath the tongued fronds. I'm sorry, I'm sorry, I'm sorry, he says to the shadows, as a crescent moon flashes between the treetops. And he cooks noodles, and the unfamiliar scents reach her, filling her empty stomach. So she retreats until the fire is a distant glow – and drawing her woollen blanket to her, her teddy, she drifts to the sound of splitting wood.

Before daylight he's away. Gone before she can roll her groundsheet. Lit up, coaxed by the billowing wind, headed east, towards the acid seas. She bundles her items and sets off after him. Keeping low, angling her body to the docile rhododendrons.

But it's his scream that finds her. Punctured like a wound. And the echo stills the forest. So she doesn't know exactly where to go. And not knowing, not seeing, she takes her knife. Crouching low, letting the sap-lacquered stems brush across her face and arms. And as she parts the forest the ground opens up. The ravine dark and wide, roots clawed inwards like broken sutures. Where she finds him. A shadow steeped in the dark aperture, unnaturally seated, still.

The rains come. She covers herself with the tarp and waits, checking the laptop's seal, her food, her water. The herbs she's gathered – poultices of lavender. Her arms are freckled with mosquito bites, and she sticks them out so that the rain splashes her bare skin. And about the waters gather: a sheen forming in the belly of the fissure, glinting with daggered sunlight.

As the rain ends the shadows divide to dusk, and the man does not wake. Looking over, she can see his twisted leg. The colour of his hair. Bones jutted, skin drawn against the peaks of his body, ridged veins. Already a different face. Broken and hungered, lifeless. Anika leans further, her palms pressed to the ledge. And it's here that their eyes meet. That his mouth opens in surprise, groping for words that do not come. Teeth flashing, whites vast. Then coughing, spluttering. Wailing into the forest, calling to her dormant fear. So she runs until she cannot. Until she's lying flat with the earth alive around her: rustling, scuttling. Blanketed by the soughing wind. She covers herself, waits, contemplates going back. But she's tired; the day's spent, and the night's already here.

Raindrops tremble in the stream. She cups water to her face. Hearing the man cry, pleading into the distance. Sounds that burrow inside her, winnowing the dirt from her veins, the ash from her heart. All that has been, passed, settled. New life compacting old, and the earth's turning, the sun's rising.

She wakes as the wind sweeps in, bending the flowers. Cold, she wraps herself. Hungry, she eats what's left. And all the while something claws at her insides. And as she turns to walk – to leave the forest, and skirt the edges of the marsh – she feels herself sinking. Drawn back, pulled in. With the wind to the ravine. If only to confirm what she already knows.

 At first, stillness. Wrens chime. Squirrels race. The scent of dew and flowers. And with this awakening the man's eyes open, alert but subdued, pooled in night.
 I thought I imagined you.
 She says nothing. Seized by his voice, her own breaking from its chrysalis.
 Then: You didn't.
 You were floating.
 I wasn't, she says.
 No, he says. Help me.
 You will die.
 Not if you help.
 I can't.
 Why?
 I don't know how.
 The forest shivers. Seconds pass. Then minutes, as they find each other, and the girl watches his eyes close, softening to fitful sleep.
 Don't leave me, he whispers.
 But she does. She leaves because words fall through her, and too long it's been since she's talked to anybody. There's Michael, yes. But that's different. Speaking without speaking. Easily understanding what's meant. But to another? The last were quiet words in the cave, and she wasn't sure if Esther heard as she shut her eyes. Sealing herself away with her body. Which Anika laid to be the ground, digging at the silt and hard soil. And then waiting until morning, dragging her to where the earth would yield.

What are the days. What's happening to the night, cowering on the crust of the world. Anika runs until her limbs tire; until her body gives in, and her mind contracts. And all she can see is what's ahead: the blistering light she cannot reach. The man's screams in the air. Until they're no more. Snuffed, silenced, she falls to her knees. Zephyrs across the plains. Dancing in the sedges, spinning dead leaves. Cumulus clouds fleeing the warming sky. And before it all she is lost. She sits and blinks through still tears. Watching for any sign on the flat horizon. Listening for her own breath.

GIULIA DA RE

Giulia Da Re is an Australian lawyer working in London. While at UEA, she's been writing two Australian Gothic novels – a short historical novel about eerie murders in a remote town, and a novel about a woman who succumbs to a cult while grieving her sister's death.

gydare@gmail.com

Lepidoptera

The opening of a short story

Maybe it starts many years ago, when her mother blinks out like a light. Maybe it starts during the two-week break in between spring and summer term, as her brother gets quieter and quieter. Or maybe it starts today, this morning, as she and her brother get ready for their first day back at St Christopher's. The days are hot. Mirages shimmer and vanish on the highway. The bush is dark and silent – the gum trees have blossomed, and the blossoms are dying. Apples ripen in the orchards. Wasps hover over the front patio, lantana curls in through the laundry door, and black blow flies bump against the kitchen window. She and her brother sit at the dining table, having cornflakes for breakfast. Her brother reads a book, one of his books that is thicker than the Bible. His face is blotchy. The telephone rings and their father rushes into the kitchen to answer it. He says, It's codling moth, you reckon? Christ. And then a little while later, he says, Right-o, well, I'm coming in now. He picks his work bag off the floor, ruffles her hair, says to her brother, You'll be right today, won't you, mate? and slams the flywire shut on his way out. Her brother looks out of the window, watching their father disappear down the driveway, then watching the dust from the ute hang in the air. She says, What's a codling moth? and for a moment she worries that he will stay silent, as he does so often now. But instead he looks at her, leans forward, and smiles a little. He says, The Codling Moth is an ancient and mythical creature. It starts off as a yellow caterpillar as round as a cow, and it roams the land, eating apple trees whole. She says, What else? He says, When it needs to rest, it makes a green chrysalis, big as a coffin, high in a tall tree, like the jacaranda outside your bedroom window. Then, it goes inside and seals the chrysalis closed. She says, Does it ever come out – is it gone forever? He says, No, it's not gone. Inside, it digests itself down to goo, and then it re-makes itself. And when it comes out, it has the body of a human, and big white feathers on its wings – but it doesn't have a mouth, so it communicates with its mates like submarines do, using sonar, which sounds like when Dad circles his fingertip around the inside of a glass to make a ringing sound. She says, Is it Evil? He says, I don't think so. People say it shouldn't eat the apple trees, but it can't help how it's made. It's been a long time since he told her a story, and now she hears that his voice is sometimes deeper, but sometimes how it's always been. She says, Why is your face all blotchy? He says, It's not, and he punches her on the arm.

* * *

At recess, her brother is sitting on the Blue Seat outside Father Joseph's office. Kids look at him as they walk past. He swings his feet, scuffing them on the floor. She wants to sit next to him, to make him promise that he'll be good from now on – he knows what might happen if he keeps getting in trouble. But he looks so sad – even though, when he sees her, he rolls his eyes and grins to let her know he's okay – that she just grins back and keeps walking, as if she were going to the drinking fountains all along. Later on, Emily says that Mrs Hogarth asked him to answer a sum in Retard Maths, and he tried to escape through the classroom window, but he must have grown over the break, so when he was only halfway out he got stuck, and while he was stuck there, the whole class stood and clapped.

* * *

It's forty degrees. When their father disappears into his shed, she and her brother slip away through the dry paddocks to the river. There's been no rain this month, so it's now only a dazed stream, rust-coloured by tannins from the gum trees. They make their way down-river without getting wet by jumping from stone to stone to the sandy parts of the riverbank. They know a spot where, even at this time of year, the water wakes up – running through the narrow channel between two smooth rocks, leaping and spindrifting, before falling, tumbling – only a meter or so – into a sandy pool. They sit on the rocks in the feathery shadows of the gum trees. They race crisp leaves through the channel, down the waterfall, into the pool's idle water – disappearing for a moment, bobbing up, floating giddily to the edge. They dip their hot feet in the pool, and then their ankles, and then they wade in, waist deep. Her brother says, Hey! and points. At the bottom, among the gum leaves slippery with scum and the flickering black tadpoles, a gilgie is watching them, ridged body still, feelers twitching. This is a lucky find – a treasure. She says, Let's catch him and take him home. Her brother says, No, leave him there. He'll die if you take him out of the river.

* * *

It's nearly time to leave for the school bus, and she sits on the family room floor, rushing to finish her homework. On the patio outside, her brother says to her father, I might have a temperature, Dad, do I have to go to school? She knows – but her father does not – that today St Christopher's gives out their school reports. Her father puts his hand to her brother's forehead. He says, You do feel a bit warm. All right. You rest up, then, mate. She smiles at her brother as she leaves, but he doesn't look at her.

* * *

At lunchtime, she is sitting in the shade of the cypress trees behind the library, reading, when she sees Mrs Hogarth looking at her through the staff room window. Mrs Hogarth comes huffing out of the staff room door, down the ramp, across the bitumen. She says, The other girls are playing hopscotch in the quadrangle, you know. For a moment they are both silent. Then, Mrs Hogarth holds out a sheet of stiff paper that's been folded in thirds and says, Here's your brother's report. You'll have to give it to your father. Without waiting, she huffs back across the bitumen, back up the ramp, and back into the staff room. Her brother's report. Without opening it, she tears it into pieces, and puts it in the bin.

* * *

After school, she gets off the bus, walks along the gravel road, through the bush, to the bottom of the driveway, alone. A police car and a shiny blue four-wheel drive are parked next to her father's ute. Her father and a policeman – it's Sergeant Gibbs – are standing under the jacaranda. Sergeant Gibbs has a hand on her father's shoulder, and they are staring up at something high in the tree, but when she looks, she can't see anything but pale grey branches and clouds of purple flowers. As she gets closer, she can hear they are talking softly. Her father's voice is hoarse, and he says, I should have sent him up to Maria's sister when I had the chance. Her father sees her – his face has faded to white and the whites of his eyes are red – he turns away and falls silent. A woman opens the flywire and comes out towards her, calling her name. It's her aunt, her mother's sister, who lives in the city, two hours away. Her aunt takes her backpack – her hands are shaking – and leads her into the house, into her bedroom, and sits her on her bed. Through the window, her father and Sergeant Gibbs are still standing under the tree. Her aunt tells her a story. In the story, her brother has gone, has gone to rest, has gone forever. She listens, but she knows the story can't really be true, just like her brother's story about the Codling Moth. For a start, her brother wouldn't go away without letting her know that he's okay. Her aunt says, I'll stay here awhile to look after you. We can pray together. Bow your head, Mia. Almighty God.

* * *

There are women in the kitchen and bathroom and laundry and they are murmuring to her aunt and to one another and they are cleaning. She's seen them at school, picking their kids up after class. She's never been to their houses. She stands against the wall in the hallway to let them past. She gets off the couch and goes outside so they can vacuum. They bring her peanut butter sandwiches on brown bread and a glass of apple juice for lunch. By the afternoon they are gone.

* * *

The family room carpet is dark orange and thick up to her first knuckle. There used to be a layer of dust in it that she could see when she pushed the pile aside. When she was younger, she thought the carpet grew out of the dust, like grass grows out of the ground. Now the dust is gone. So are the apple cores and wishbones that her father lined up on the kitchen windowsill. Cold and dark, winding its way upwards, hairy tendril after hairy tendril, is the fear that she and her father and her brother have been doing things some secret way, some wrong way, and now everybody knows.

* * *

They are home from the cemetery. She sits on the patio with her back to the wall and her face to the sun. The grass growing up between the bricks tickles her back. She closes her eyes. Behind her eyelids, a coffin sinks down into a dark hole. She wishes that she, too, could sink down into the dark. Inside the house, her aunt says to her father, I can't understand why you wouldn't have it at church. But surely her aunt knows that her father doesn't say God's name anymore? Her aunt says that her brother has gone. Maybe God has gone, too. She sits in the heat, eyes closed, and she feels around for Him, she tries to brush up against Him. If He's there, He's scuttled into a corner and is keeping very quiet. There is nothing but air at the tips of her fingers, the red insides of her eyelids as the sun shines through them, her blood roaring in her ears, and the honey smell of the jacaranda flowers.

* * *

She stands at her bedroom window. A cloud moves away from the moon. In the jacaranda, high up, through the leaves and flowers, she sees. Something is hanging there. A chrysalis, twisting in the air. As tall as her father, green, wrinkled as skin, it swings to-and-fro, creaking. And there is something inside it. She holds her breath. There is a ringing sound inside her head, bright and clear. Near the top, in a seam, a tear appears. The tear opens slowly, like a zip down the back of a dress. The something inside is pulsing. The something inside is slowly working. The something inside is patiently, carefully, stretching itself out. It peels the skin of the chrysalis back, it unfurls its damp soft wings. The wings expand as they dry, and, after a while, she can see they are big, the size of doors, covered in white feathers that are sharp as knives. The winged thing drops – straight down – she waits for the thud, but at the last second – whoosh! – it soars up, a foaming rush of white, so close to her window that she gasps and closes her eyes. When she opens them again, it is morning.

PAURIC DANIELS

Pauric Daniels is a writer from Dublin, Ireland.

pauric.daniels.pd@gmail.com

SkodaLogbook.docx

An excerpt from a novel

LOG #2 – ANNA

It's been three days since my first log, which I'm not happy about, because I've actually wanted to write. But here's what happened: I arrived home on Friday, around midnight, and was ready to go straight upstairs to my desk and start typing while the night was still fresh in my mind. When I came in the front door, Linda was asleep with her mouth open, on the couch, with a half empty Milk Tray beside her. The TV was on low volume, playing an ad for some sort of medicine for heartburn or indigestion. She woke when I came in, and through a yawn asked me how it had been. Well, I said, not great, to be honest. Nothing major to complain about, just a little boring. Anything to write about for your log? she asked. Yeah, I said, I think I'm going to write about these two old ladies who were pretty nice. They didn't say much but they were sweet. Then Linda sat up and said, What, no, don't do that. Why write about it if it was boring? There's no rush. Save the write-ups for the good ones, because otherwise what's the point?

And honestly, I was in two minds about this. I'll admit it, though, that realistically she was right, and so I followed her advice. I didn't write about the two old ladies and instead just went to bed. That was Friday night, and I didn't log on Saturday either, and Sundays are my days off. So today is Monday and that means I haven't written in three whole days.

Two things: firstly, I should write every day, at least while I'm starting out, as I need to get better at writing, find my voice, figure out what style is most appropriate for the logs, etc. Secondly, and this is the main thing: isn't everyone equally interesting, in their own way? Well, okay, that's probably not entirely true, but what I'm saying is this: it'd be a shame to speak to someone like, for example, Alan, the guy from Log #1, and then just forget about him. The thought of that makes me sad. Because Alan, actually, was interesting and cool, wasn't he? Okay, again, maybe not really, but I liked him. I really did. And reading back over the log, I was glad I'd written about him. So there's that.

Linda read the entry. When she was finished, she closed the laptop and said, But, like, nothing happens? And I said, What do you mean? I made it interesting, I asked some questions, tried to connect with him. And it was only a short cab ride on a Thursday evening? What did she want me to do? Pretend that Alan had revealed he was actually a secret agent for America and that he'd come to recruit me, or that there was a UFO landing on O'Connell Street and Alan got abducted, or– I don't know. I'm not sure I have a head for that sort of thing, anyway. I told her that, and that the reason I started writing this log was to literally *log* my real life customers, not to start fabricating stories to make my life sound like a wild, thickly plotted novel. She had shrugged, then, and said that *I* was the one who'd mentioned that maybe my logs could be turned into a book one day.

But anyway. The next night, then, pulling the Škoda into the driveway, I was ready to go straight to the laptop, even though I had just finished a shift during which, by Linda's definition, nothing had happened. I was planning to write about a couple with whom I'd had a brief conversation about breakfast, the main discussion topics being the cholesterol-related benefits of porridge, whether you should brush your teeth before or after you eat, how easy it is to be put off eggs when you get a bit psychological about it, and so on. And but so when I sat and stared at the blank Word doc, I just felt tired and bored by it all. I closed the laptop and went up to bed, where Linda was already asleep and snoring. I got in beside her and lay awake for a while, listening to the rain on the window, hoping tomorrow would bring me something more interesting to write about.

Here is tonight's log.

Date: Monday, 27th Nov. / **Pickup time:** 19:12 / **Conditions:** Damp, cold, blustery, 5°C

I accepted a fare from the app: someone named Anna, in Smithfield, had requested a taxi from a hotel. I pulled up at the entrance and watched her come out through the revolving doors, into the wind, dragging her small suitcase, her hair going everywhere. I took her suitcase and opened the back door but it immediately blew shut. I opened it again and this time held it while she sat in. Once I had put her case in the boot, I got into the front seat and rubbed my hands together.

'Wow,' I said. 'Mad wind.'

'Certainly,' she said.

'I'm glad that door didn't take your fingers off.'

'Hah,' she said, smoothing her tousled hair. 'Me too.'

I pressed *Start ride* on my phone screen and *Destination: Dublin Airport* flashed up, then *Estimated arrival time: 19:34*.

'We're going to the airport?' I said. 'Is that right?'

'Yes please.'

I turned onto Constitution Hill and she sat back in her seat. In the mirror I watched her rub her eyes and yawn.

'So,' I said. 'Where are you heading to? Somewhere nice?'

'No. Well, yes, I mean. I'm just going home.'

'Home?'

'Yes. I'm Austrian.'

'Oh. I didn't pick up on an accent.'

'No?' she said, then shrugged. 'But it is definitely there.'

The radio was playing at a low volume. I turned it off.

'Will you say something else?' I said.

'Oh. Yes. Okay.' She cleared her throat. 'Hello. Um. I am Anna. I am from Austria. Hello. This is my voice. I am speaking. Yes.'

I listened closely. 'I can hear it now.'

She laughed. 'Yes. I only arrived in Ireland yesterday. So it would be crazy if I was already speaking like a Dublin person.'

'Only yesterday?'

'Yes. I had only a very short trip.'

'Way too short. Were you here for work?'

'Ah.' She cleared her throat. 'It is a long story. It was for a funeral.'

'Oh. I'm sorry to hear that.'

I looked at her in the mirror. She was looking out the window.

'Yes. Thank you. It's okay. He was an old colleague who I had not seen for many years.'

'Had you come here before? To see him?'

'No. This is my first time in Dublin. I meant to visit him for a long time. We worked together in Munich, then he was transferred back to Dublin. He became sick maybe two years ago. I meant to come and visit him, but– Yes.'

She shifted in her seat, then sighed and rested her temple against the window.

'Well,' I said. 'I'm sorry to hear that.'

'Hm. He was a– I don't know how to say it. He was a person who some people liked and some people did not like. I have to say though that I liked him very much. Very much.'

I nodded as solemnly as I could, though she wasn't even looking at me.

'Hah,' she said. 'Yes. You know that word you use here, *chancer*. *He was such a chancer*. Yes, James used to say that all the time about other people. But, as I understand it, James was a chancer. In a nice way. I don't know if that word's supposed to be nice or not.'

She laughed. I did too.

'Was he from Dublin?' I asked.

'Yes. Rathgar? I think that is the name of the place.'

I nodded. We crossed the Binns Bridge. All day it had been threatening to rain and now was starting to drizzle. I twisted the windscreen wiper dial to LO.

'Do you know the church in Rathgar?' asked Anna.

'Yeah.'

'That was where the funeral was. It was– Actually, it was awkward. It felt strange because he was not religious. I remember very well that he was not religious. But the funeral was in a church and it was led by a priest? This is crazy.'

'I know. That's just how we do it here. Is it different in Austria?'

Anna didn't respond. She didn't seem to have heard me.

'And I could not understand everything the priest was saying,' she continued. 'Because he mumbled a lot and his accent was strong. But one thing he was saying again and again was that James would return to God's Kingdom, or into God's loving arms, all things like this. And that he would return to his late mother and father in Heaven. It was all about returning, returning to this or that. But actually he is leaving, no? That is how I see it, that he has left. And–' She stopped for a breath and sat forward. 'The craziest thing of all. I am absolutely sure that James was not religious. Not one bit. He did not believe in Heaven. So, it all just seemed so strange.'

I waited to see if Anna would continue. She didn't.

'It might have been for his family,' I said. 'They're probably religious, or at least still in touch with the Catholic tradition. You know?'

'Maybe. But for me, I have to say, I still did not understand it. The funeral was not sad. Sad would be the wrong word even though I saw some people crying. Especially his sister. But the church as a whole was not, how would you say, full of emotion? It was– I'm not sure what the word is in English but in German we say *angespannt*. It was a little bit tense? I don't know why.'

We were going through Drumcondra now, past St Pat's, and the road was quiet. Someone wearing black almost walked out in front of the car and I had to brake to avoid flattening them.

'But yes,' Anna said. 'You don't need to hear all of this. But thank you for listening. I do not understand it. But I think the reason I am still talking about it is because it did not seem like *his* funeral. It was just like a general funeral that could have been for anyone if you swapped his name for someone else's. Do you know what I mean?'

'Yeah. I get you.'

'When I think of him, in the future, I don't want to remember this strange funeral that could have been for anyone.'

We drove up the Swords Road and passed the big redbrick church in Whitehall. I looked in the mirror and saw she'd closed her eyes and was resting her head against the glass again.

After about ten minutes, we arrived at the airport and I pulled up outside Departures. Anna sat up and yawned. I got out and took her suitcase while she stood out of the car and stretched.

'That payment's gone through on the app,' I said. 'So you're all good to go.'

'Ah. Thank you.'

I pulled up the handle of her suitcase and handed it to her.

'I hope you have a safe flight.'

'Thank you.' She laughed and shook her head.

I sat back into the Škoda as Anna turned and went towards the building, rolling the suitcase behind her. The automatic doors opened and she went through. I turned the car and joined the rank where people were queuing to head back into the city.

MARK DE ROND

Mark de Rond uses fictional techniques to explore the peculiarities of our human condition. His stories are rooted in his ethnographies of people who live challenging circumstances on their own terms: doctors and nurses at war, a psychiatrist to the Taliban, a ragtag band rowing the Amazon, and citizens who made it their life's work to expose paedophiles in spectacles of public humiliation.

mejd3@cam.ac.uk

Dead Man Can't Even Blink

A short story

As the dog days of summer elongated, and with school out and everyone who is someone having been moved on, and with nothing to do and nothing whatsoever to look forward to, two teenagers killed a pizza delivery guy and didn't eat the pizza.

They stood in silence for a while after as the adrenaline metabolised. I turned off the radio and moved nearer the cracked window.

'Yo, wagwan; what's the move?'
'Dunno, bruv.'
'That's mad peak.'
A wasp seemed to have landed on one of the dead man's eyes.
'Bruv that's grim.'
'Dat's how you clock someone's gone.'
'What you saying?'
'Cuz a dead man can't even blink, innit.'
'Dat's some next ting.'
The delivery man was dead alright and still wearing his helmet and backpack because that's how quick the teenagers had been to the draw.
'Who you reckon got there first?'
'I reckon we was both equally quick.'
'Which one you reckon is yours?'
'Dat one up top, innit. What was you tryna hit?'
'His ticker innit.'
'Someone shanked him in the nuts, and it wasn't me.'
'Dat ain't what finished him still.'
'But you *was* tryna off him and dat's what the feds care about – *in-ten-tio-na-li-ty* – and dem don't care if you're a dead aim or not.'

The summer had been a beast. Whatever moisture the sun hadn't already burned off was sucked out of the air by neo-brutalist high-rises linked by walkways. There was so little vegetation left on the estate that nothing could absorb the heat except for those living on it: tradesmen and single mums, the jobless and ex-soldiers like me, all of us thrown together in a utopian experiment in the midst of strikes, stagflation and class-wars. Not even the hardiest of us escaped the madness the heat and unrest bred. Visitors began to stay away as did the summer winds, and without winds there wasn't anything to cleanse our estate from the sourness it secreted.

Couples took to sleeping separately for that's how warm and listless nights were to reunite over breakfast and sigh with the concrete at Southwark Council's decision to cancel the estate and everyone in it. And so, our homes became a holding pen as we waited for our relocation briefs.

It wasn't the waiting so much as not knowing when the waiting would end that had stopped life in its tracks and transformed the estate into a chaos of nothing: life was empty as was the soul. Pessoa's curse had become ours too.

The experience took me back to my time on the Kosovo-Serbia border as a young man, and how we'd pray for firefights to lift the boredom. Of how one day our sergeant said, 'let's kill a fucking cow' and made a spear out of a broom stick and zombie knife and pinned this cow into a corner and stabbed it. Of how the cow looked at him and then us and couldn't understand why anyone would hurt her. Of how the sergeant passed the spear to someone else and so on until we all shared in the shame and of how she ultimately went down. Of how we decapitated her with a saw and then didn't know how to gut the rest of her except to mind the bladder but how we figured it out in the end. Of how Johnny cooked us up some steaks and a farmer walked up while we were cooking and said he'd seen us kill his cow and of how we said we didn't kill her but that she got caught in the crossfire. Of how he wanted compensation and our sergeant said there's no fucking way we were going to give him any cash but that he could have potatoes to the value of his cow, and of how we decided that hers was the best steak we'd ever had.

'So, what we gonna do with him?'
'It's calm, innit. We'll fix this. Let's bury him.'
'Nah, bruv, that's long. It's bare hot out here.'
'If we leave it, the body's gonna start ponging.'
'Let's lob him in the river.'
'He's gonna float, innit bruv.'
'Nah, not if we slap bricks on him.'
'No way we gonna move him to the river without the ends knowing. People gonna ring the feds for sure.'
'We could burn him.'
'You reckon man will burn, bruv?'
'It's like a crem, innit?'

The waiting caused unease and suspicion on the estate and before long the overhead telephone wires were said to give off a buzzing noise; and because of this some now only ever went out with heads wrapped in silver foil. Others said the noise came from an electrical charge going through the wires and how they had it on good authority that the birds sitting on them weren't birds at all but drones with cameras made to look like birds.

The teenagers' barrister, who happened to also be a lay preacher, would point the finger at Southwark Council for its persistent lies and contempt. The teenagers, he would say, had 'diminished responsibility', that is, if the prosecution were even able to prove that they'd had a role in the death. Residents had been afflicted with a psychosis, is how he would put it, and submit in evidence how two mutts from the same family had been skinned and strung up from one of the walkways, and how the family whose pets they were packed up to leave what they said was – and I quote – 'a godforsaken hellhole'. Several others reported cats with heads removed that some said was the work of urban foxes, but others said couldn't be as the cut was too clean and because one had been found halfway down a mayonnaise jar and there's no way a fox could do that. The Londis around the corner had gone up in flames and the owner's wife, Bev, of how she had to be committed afterwards to keep her from hurting herself, and how none of these things had any obvious cause except that they were inspired by Southwark Council. The estate, the barrister would say, was cursed, and the killing of a pizza guy fit a pattern of senseless slaughter. What this estate needs isn't a show trial, he would say, but an exorcist.

The barrister would heap evidence on evidence to show how this psychosis gave rise to other strange occurrences: of an alien script written in paint on walls and into the softening asphalt; of Mrs Merkle's mobility scooter displaced as if by magic from her front door and onto the roof of the local Montessori; of all the water on the estate have turned a dirty brown overnight; of cars catching fire without apparent cause; of clowns stalking kids; of blood running down concrete walls; all of which had residents calling for police and firemen to be defunded. When that failed to materialise, they trained their resentment on those outside the estate instead – academics and doctors and lawyers – until they had so internalised their bitterness that they wished for nothing other than for everyone to be as angry and as bored as they were.

Suspecting that teenagers might have been co-opted in Southwark Council's work, some residents took it upon themselves to burn down an arthouse cinema. The barrister himself once used the pulpit to claim it was used to manipulate the minds of impressionable teenagers with subliminal messages and to coerce them into depravity. Others took to decoding strange events as messages from a great leader who kept his identity a secret. They would meet sharpish at 6:30pm every night in Mrs Merkle's flat to discuss their findings, and reasoned that if the Council had cursed their estate, they might as well scorch the entire city and have front-row seats to a world on fire as they waited for the storm. For the storm would come and bring with it relief at last from the infernal heat and boredom. It would carry powerful winds and rains to end the drought and rid the estate of an evil beyond anything in living memory.

'Bossman ain't bunning.'
'Check his garms, fam.'
'Dem don't bun either.'
'Burn his hair then, innit.'
'....'

'....'
'So his hair's gone, but there ain't no fire yet.'
'He looks proper mad with no hair.'
'Innit, fam, proper mad.'
'Does your mum have any bits to spark up the fire?'
'Like what?'
'Like petrol, gas, white spirit.'
'Nah, bruv.'
'How 'bout the guy's ped? Bare petrol in there.'
'But how we gonna get it out though?'
'You suck it, ya get me? Find me a rubber hose or something.'
'We ain't got nothin' like that in our yard.'
'Grab me the shower hose and a big blade then.'
'What for, bruv?'
'To chop the hose.'
'A're you mad, fam? My mum's gonna clock that the hose is shorter, innit.'
'You got any better plans?'
'Nah, bruv. It's calm. Let's do the hose ting.'

The barrister would also offer his own hypothesis for the cause of death: that it'd been a rare case of backward lightning shot from deep below the concrete, at which those residents present in court would murmur agreement for they remembered hearing thunder; and he would say that the pizza delivery guy happened to be in the wrong place at the wrong time, and – and here he would raise a hand and cite scientific evidence – that while it looked like he'd been defending himself when attacked, it wasn't that at all. It was the natural result of his muscles contracting and causing his joints to flex, leading to – and here he would pause for effect – the *pugilistic pose,* widely found among bodies recovered from Pompeii following Vesuvius.

I walked from my kitchen to the bedroom window to put faces to voices and saw that these had been students of mine a few years back. The boy reminded me even then of a young De Niro in *The Gang That Couldn't Shoot Straight* but with tats and fairer. Natasha wasn't any longer the harmless 13-year-old of my English Comp class and a strong writer. The death of her child by a crackhead mum, and living with a gangster brother, had hardened her features.

'So, his legs are on fire but the rest of him ain't burnin,' said the young De Niro.
'Didn't I say start pouring from his head, bruv? Now all the petrol's done.'
'So, what we gonna do?'
'Dunno. Maybe fold him.'
'How we gonna fold him?'
'Ya lift his back and push, innit? Get his head down to his knees so it can bun up.'
'He's proper stiff,' De Niro said.

'You're bare weak.'

'Maybe we get some of the youts to lend a hand.'

'Don't be daft, bruv. Use your bulk.'

'He ain't staying folded.'

'Siddown on him till he stays folded then.'

'Bruv, I'll bun up if I do that.'

'Don't be a wasteman.' Natasha sucked her teeth. 'You push and I'll drop the ped on him to weigh him down.'

The barrister would call on me as a witness for the defence seeing how I was the only one to have seen and heard everything. Did I recognise the teenagers in the dock as having been on the scene, the barrister would ask while reminding me of the penalty for perjury and telling the jury of how upstanding a citizen I was being a teacher and former soldier and all, and I would take a deep breath and give the court my answer. The barrister would then say that it is true that he couldn't explain how the man's moped had ended up on top of him but that life's weird sometimes.

OLIVIA EGGLESTON

Olivia is a German, Assyrian and English writer. She is currently working on a novel.

olivia.s.eggleston@gmail.com

nesting in reuleaux

excerpt from a short story

&
what we do
what we do is this:
convene at our convergence.
and then we go home and i don't know where
they go, and they don't know where i go, and i don't see them
there, and they don't see me here. but clear
as day i see them in our warm room,
and suspended, for a time, are
all the evils of the
world
&

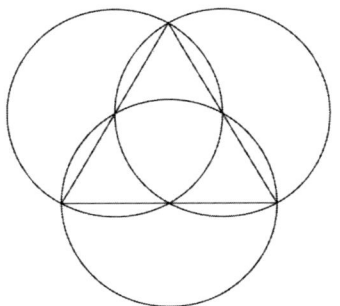

Bobby has been at the house an awful lot lately. This seems reasonable to both myself and Alice, because Bobby's father died two weeks ago. We were here, the three of us, in the front room, and he said, 'my dad's died,' and Alice and I looked at each other and looked at him and maybe or probably we both thought, no, no, that can't be true, that can't be true.

'What?' we said, 'what?'

'Yeah.' Bobby nodded. 'My dad's died.'

'God,' we said, 'God, Bobby.'

'Yeah.' He rubbed his eyes. 'It feels, you know, pretty bad.'

Later Bobby went to the bathroom and Alice and I had a moment in private to agree that a) we would do anything for Bobby, and b) it must indeed feel pretty bad.

Know, please, that the house is not a house, nor are we there in the way that you would think, and you might not understand, but we do. And today Bobby is here again, recumbent on the sofa, with his shoes on, and usually I would tell him to take them off – he was wet when he came in – but lately, of course, I am 'cutting him slack.'

In the kitchen, I cook something or other which he, for sure, will like, and Alice is not there until she arrives, and when she does she's there, and we all are, and the house becomes the ground it's meant to be.

Front room. The table is hefty, mahogany; a dozen tea lights, their uncertain flames. We sit down. There is wine. We start to drink it.

'Bobby,' says Alice, 'should we ask how you are?'

Bobby shakes his head. 'No,' he says. 'But I'll tell you this. Every day I feel that I might cry. But I never do. Instead—' He laughs. 'Instead, you know what happens? My nose starts to bleed.'

Alice and I exchange a glance. 'Bobby,' she says.

Bobby takes a sip. 'Christ,' he says. 'Anyway.'

'Alright,' Alice says. 'Maybe later.'

'Yes, maybe later,' I say. And then we sit and drink and get all swept up and some things are said and others are not and all of them matter a lot. And then we've all had three glasses and Bobby jumps up and tells us he wants to dance — 'I want to dance,' he says, 'dance with me.' He makes for the living room. We follow.

Alice flits from corner to corner, waking the little orange lamps. Their light refracts through the patterns in the glass shades and it seeps across the whole room, breaking over the brass trinkets and the big empty vases and illuminating raggedly all the framed tarantulas and butterflies and sepia portraits of strange women and men. Then she lets herself fall onto the terracotta futon, crossing her feet. Her lace skirt clings like a film to her long legs, sweeping over the bend of her knees, and is depressed in her lap by a crystal ashtray. The giant Areca palm throws a jagged shadow over her face. She lights a cigarette.

Bobby is looking through the records. 'What do you want to dance to?' he asks.
'Do you know how to waltz?' I reply.
'No. Will you teach me?'
'I'll teach you.'
'What are we waltzing to?'
'Hm,' I say. 'What's a good Waltz?'
'Moon River!' Alice calls over.
'Oh!' I say, 'yes! Moon River, Bobby, find Moon River.'
'Okay,' he says. 'Which version?'
'The Andy Williams,' I reply.
He flicks through the records. 'I've got Andy Williams here,' he says.
'That's it.'

He puts the record on. We bring our bodies close. I feel his bare feet against mine and stand on his toes for a moment. He laughs. I take one of his hands in mine and put the other on my waist. 'My hand goes here,' I say, placing it on his shoulder. We both turn to look at Alice. She is smiling, watching us. The cigarette is in her mouth.

'Okay,' I say to Bobby. 'I'll lead to teach you.'
'Mrs. man of the house,' he says.
'That's correct.'

I show him the steps: back, side, together, forward, side, together, et cetera, et cetera. We start slowly and he gets it wrong a few times, but only a few times, and then he gets it right and we start to dance and begin naturally to turn around ourselves. Alice laughs and claps. My dress furls and unfurls around my calves with each turn. Bobby and I dance and Alice jumps up and starts twirling around us, holding the cigarette to my mouth, then to Bobby's. Bobby blows the smoke into my face, a gentle, thin stream. All the while we dance, dance, dance. Moon River plays over and over again, or perhaps it hasn't ended at all. We step faster and the turns become bigger and Bobby is leading now and he twirls me around two or three times so that I am almost dizzy, and I am laughing, laughing hard, and the splintered orange light cuts a pattern into Bobby's face and probably onto mine, too.

Only when I step away to catch my breath and let Alice dance with Bobby do I notice the blood streaming from his nose. Over his mouth it runs and onto his white shirt and there the capillaries of the lace fabric suck it in. He notices, too, and looks down at his shirt, and then at me. We both know it doesn't matter.

Bobby teaches Alice to waltz and they dance for, I think, a long time, and then Alice and I dance and Bobby lies on the sofa with his bare feet over the armrest and he watches us and smokes and smiles. We listen for hours or days to Williams' Moon River. Then there comes a moment when Alice and I both feel tired, and we go over to the sofa and drop down to our knees, our skirts pooling around us. Bobby touches the skin below my eye with a fingertip. Alice puts her cheek against his leg.

'Will you put on a record for me?' he asks.
'Whatever you want,' I say.
'Will you find that Jackson Frank?'
'Sure, Bobby.'
I go to the shelf and pull out the Frank record. I know where it is.
'It's the first side,' Bobby calls. 'Track three, I think.'
I gently lower the needle into the right groove. Jackson Frank starts to sing Kimbie and I kneel back down by Alice and Bobby. We sit like that for some time. I feel a bit drunk but not terribly. Just enough to ache a little in different corners of myself. Alice and I both have our cheeks against the sofa. We look at each other and smile and then I watch her eyes move up to Bobby.
After a while, Bobby tells us that he wants to stay the night.
'We'll all stay,' Alice says.
'Yes,' I say, 'we'll all stay.'

We switch off all but one of the lamps and go to the pile of Persian rugs. 'I love sleeping on these,' I say. Alice and I climb on, leaving space in the middle for Bobby. He comes up and says nothing and lies down between us. Frank sings Kimbie. We lie shoulder to shoulder to shoulder. Time passes. Kimbie plays.
'I don't want to grow up,' Bobby whispers, 'even more than I have.'
I breathe, in, out. Then I say, 'we have to.'
'But you don't know what it is.'
'I think I know a little bit.'
'This is it,' he says. 'You grow up when life shows you how fickle it is. And if you're a real grown-up, a good grown-up, you avoid spending your days expecting the worst.'
I don't really know what to say, so I turn over and look at him. He turns too. The blood on his face has dried. I lick my thumb and try to rub it off.
'It's okay,' he says. 'It doesn't matter.'
I turn my gaze from his nose to his eyes. They look slick and full. I watch a tear fall from his right eye, across the bridge of his nose, into his other eye. I touch his arm. I can tell from Alice's breathing that she has fallen asleep already. 'Goodnight,' I say to Bobby.
'Don't tell anyone I cried.'
'Come on.'
'Whenever I see you two,' he whispers, 'I remember I need to call my grandmother, or pick up the book I put down, or listen to more than two songs on an album.'
'You really do need to listen to more than two songs on an album.'
'I know.'
'Goodnight, Bobby.'
'Goodnight.'

I wake just before sunrise. The heavy embroidered curtains were never drawn and the first thing I see is a tense purple sky, the sun somewhere behind it, toiling away to crack it open. I sit up, rub my eyes, smooth my hair, smooth my dress. I reach over Bobby and touch Alice's arm. She wakes immediately. Quietly.

'Is it the morning?' she says.

I nod. 'We should make him breakfast,' I whisper.

We get up and creep, bleary-eyed, to the kitchen. Alice puts the percolator on the stove and I make something historically nice like pancakes or eggs and bacon. By the time we've set the table, Bobby is awake, between the sliding doors, rubbing his face.

'Morning,' he says. 'What time is it?'

'Early enough,' I say.

'I want to go back to sleep.'

'You can't, Bobby,' I say. 'You need to be in Marlow at eleven.'

'God,' he says, 'I do. Thank you.'

I put a cup of coffee in his hand (milk, two sugars) and push him to the table. We all eat enough and then it is time to go.

We stand in the middle of the garden. It is vast and overgrown and ends only because of the horizon. We are barefoot still and the dew is cool on our soles and beneath them each blade of grass bends for us palpably. The sky is slowly relenting to the sun, swelling with it, the purple bursting at the seams. We stand for a few moments, holding Bobby's hands. Then we kiss him and he takes a step back. His hair begins to fall in wet strands onto his forehead, even though it isn't raining. Alice and I kiss him again. His cheeks are cold and damp. It's early, very early, but it's good he's leaving now. It can take a long time to get back from the house.

There is no more to say. Bobby turns on his heel. The light is still so low that he is soon swallowed up, though we still hear his steps in the wet earth for a minute or so. I wish I could follow him, but I know that I can't. It is hard to let him go.

Alice and I stand hand in hand for a while, looking into the dark, endless garden, both, probably, wondering what world Bobby is walking into. You never see totally, do you. You never see someone beyond the house you build between you.

I turn to face Alice. We'll be together again in a few hours. We embrace and she goes off, southbound.

I start down my path, through the orchard, up the hill. When I get to the top I turn back to look at our house. For a few moments I watch it stand still.

Then I start to hurry. Need to be in Marlow at eleven. To bury Bobby's dad.

RACHEL FUNG

Rachel Fung grew up between the islands of Borneo and Singapore. After reading law at King's College London, she worked as an intellectual property lawyer. Her debut novel deals with reverse migration, the burdens of displacement, and a search for identity through one woman's occupation of her abandoned childhood home.

rachelfungwc@gmail.com

The Home Is a Body
An extract from a novel

DAY ONE

The house stood before her, silent and contained, as the taxi pulled up to its cracked driveway.

Located at the end of a cul-de-sac, the winding road they had followed ended at the foot of the compound's ornate black iron gates. To the left stood another house which belonged to Lily's old neighbours, the Huangs. Lily glanced over at their property, but there was no car in its driveway and all the windows and doors of the house were shut tight. She wondered if they too had moved out. There were always certain signs, particularly for the houses in this neighbourhood. Overgrown weeds and grass. Barren porches and shuttered windows.

She looked back at her old house; there could be no confusion as to its state. Paint had faded in irregular places and dark streaks ran down along its body; a patchwork of neglect visible amidst the creepers that were swallowing the house whole. The gardens had grown amuck and seemed to press up against the large iron gates, as if forbidding its use as entry.

The houses were positioned on the western side of Signal Hill. The land to the right of Lily's home sloped down an incline of dense jungle. Living on this boundary, they had always needed to be careful of the animals, which sometimes found their way inside. Monkeys that left fruit half-eaten, rotting on a counter. Or the snakes – silent, coiled, nestled in shared warmth and tight spaces.

The taxi driver got out of the car to give Lily a hand with her suitcase. After taking in the properties and land around them, he let out a low whistle. 'You confirm this house correct kah?' Lily nodded and tipped him RM5. He accepted this with a nod and then with a short wave got back into his taxi. She watched him manoeuvre out of the cul-de-sac, inching and breaking, before the car disappeared down the road, and she turned to face the house alone.

On a bright day, the interior of the house appeared settled and serene in its disuse. Such that when she paused at its doorway, watching dust motes swirl in rays caught around her, she felt like she was interrupting.

She took her time to reacquaint herself with the house room by room. The front entrance opened into a large living area, which flowed seamlessly on to the dining room. A baby grand piano shrouded under a dirty white fabric straddled the two areas, two legs in the dining room and a leg by the living room sofa. It was imposing in its position and size and seemed to cast a watchful air over the space around it from beneath its milky veil. To the left of the living room was a dark wooden staircase, which curved right and led to three bedrooms on the next floor.

Lily started with the staircase, a hand on the banister. She moved slowly upwards as the steps creaked and groaned under her. Somewhere above a house lizard screeched, which triggered a response from another lizard in a different part of the house. They were sending warning signals to each other; there was an intruder in their home.

The middle of the staircase was one of the darkest parts of the house. No light from the windows on the ground floor or the first floor ever reached it. It was at this point that she felt a particular give in the step before her, which carried a threat of breaking, so that she stepped back without proceeding further. She fumbled for her phone before crouching down and turned on its light to inspect the stair in greater detail.

It looked smoother and slightly lighter in colour in the middle where years of feet had worn the wood. At the joint where this step ended and the next began, Lily caught sight of a flash of white that burrowed into a tiny gap in the joint before disappearing completely. Running her phone's light across the length of the step, she saw an entire line of tiny white bodies crawling, quivering in silence along it. She turned off the light and felt her insides curl at the sudden thought of them marching up and along her body. The stairwell was infested with termites. They were eating the house from the inside out.

She quickly slipped the phone into her pocket. With her back to the banister, she inched the rest of her way up, along the less-worn sides of the steps, praying that they would not give way.

The staircase led to a long corridor on the next floor. Her own childhood bedroom was the one closest to the stairs. Her parents' bedroom was located at the end of the corridor, whilst Nick's old bedroom was opposite hers, a little further down. She paused for a moment before entering her room. Its door still carried Blu Tack markings and tiny holes from signs and Christmas decorations put up and taken down over the years.

The door was stiff and difficult to open; over the years the wood had warped, become misshapen. Its bottom scraped along the wooden floor, lodging itself against the grain, and Lily had to apply her body weight to it, partially then fully, until it opened in a rush and she was in her room.

Pale pink walls and white cupboards. Soft toys which stared out along a shelf, some with eyes half-opened or closed, balls of dust gathering on their heads and seams. A tiny library in the corner, lined with Nancy Drew, Enid Blyton, and Ge Mei Lia comics, their edges yellowed and foxed with time. In the middle stood a single bed with a rosewood headboard, behind which was carved with a box cutter, her name, another's, and the date: 15.03.99.

She had forgotten how soft girlhood bedrooms could be. Before their passing, Lily knew her parents had kept hers and Nick's rooms as they had always been, apart from a regular cleaning every month or so. Looking at the state it was in now, she felt there was something particularly sad about seeing something so tender, yet so untended. She walked over to open the one window in the room to let in some air.

When she was fourteen, she had become very interested in watercolour painting. Her art teacher at the time, Mrs Chopra, had advised them to pick a particular subject and paint it, repeatedly, over the course of their July holidays. Lily chose her bedroom window.

Her paintings captured the bough of a tree that looped along the top left corner of the window; the crown of a banana tree that peeked along its bottom edge, with its fronds that waved and beat against the glass when the wind was particularly strong. A brick wall cut across the frame, topped by jagged pieces of coloured glass that glinted in the height of day. And beyond that lay the jungle, monolithic and unbroachable.

She painted this scene every day obsessively for three weeks such that she started noticing when particular leaves of the tree had fallen and new ones had sprouted. Or when the shade of a banana leaf was shifting into a more verdant hue. From this exercise, she became convinced that no two views could ever be the same. If one looked close enough, there was always a differentiating detail. The angle of a branch that morning or the crust on a stain of bird dropping. It was just a matter of what one noticed.

Since then, the banana tree had grown taller and its fronds dominated the bottom left half of her window. With the window open, they spilled – one above the other – into her room, clamouring to fill the space.

She stood before this window now, superimposing upon it all the views of it she had known before and committed to memory, noting every detail that had changed, planning every new stroke she would make.

DAY TWO

Lily watched Nick reverse out of the driveway and speed down the road outside; his frustration and anger palpable in the breaks and movements of the car. The stems and leaves of plants collapsed back to their natural resting positions after the car sped past.

Standing by the front door, Lily crouched to her feet in relief. Then she got up slowly and went to pull the heavy black gates shut. She had won a few more days in the house at least.

After trying and failing to convince her for about an hour to leave, Nick had stood up abruptly and walked right out of the house and back into his car without another word. Lily recognised this as a technique he had learnt from his anger management therapist – to take a step back or leave a situation if it got too agitating. Somewhere deep in the house, the old grandfather clock struck noon, two hours too late.

But perhaps he had come with an understanding of the stubbornness embedded deep within Lily as well. *You make me so mad, you're just so unbelievably…* Because he had brought a packet of duck noodles, which remained hanging in a clear plastic bag by the front door handle. *Selfish.*

Lily picked the bag up and carried it to the kitchen, where she placed it on the table. She sat before the bone-white polystyrene packet which now half-covered the dark burn mark on the table and opened its lid to a glistening mound of stringy yellow wanton noodles, topped with five pieces of duck flesh covered by thin layers of crispy brown skin. The noodles and meat appeared fixed in place, cocooned in a congealed layer of fat from sitting for so long. She picked up the pair of disposable bamboo chopsticks that came with the packet and started untangling the noodles from its nucleus of fat, feeling its strain then eventual loosening at the point of breakage. A shaft of light came through a kitchen window and fell upon Lily's hands and the packet of noodles, and the burn mark, as if highlighting this simple act of sustenance, of repair and disrepair in one brush of light. Then she gave thanks, and tasting the first silky bite of the egg noodles in duck sauce on her tongue, she began eating with a hunger embedded deep within her cells.

DANIEL GLANCY

Daniel is a London-based writer, raised in Cornwall. In *Soft Bodied Animals*, an infamous local ghost narrates the story of a Cornish community struggling with disaster fatigue and inertia, as a tsunami hurtles towards the South Coast of Britain.

bensonglancy@gmail.com

Soft Bodied Animals

An extract from the opening of a novel

Many years ago, I'd haunted a Swedish banker named Lasse. He lived in a renovated monastery on a tidal island, far up the River Lynher. It had been built by monks at the turn of the first millennium and for a thousand years it had survived everything that mother nature and mankind had thrown its way. Shortly before the turn of the second millennium, Lasse paid for it to be reinforced for another thousand years.

Naturally, Lasse wasn't fond of my presence. I never revealed myself to him, but he understood what I was, if not exactly who. Most of the people I'd ever haunted were never quite sure what was happening, but Lasse knew. Bankers often knew in a way the average person didn't, something, perhaps, to do with all the Faustian pacts they'd made. Knowing what I was, however, didn't help him cope and I spooked him deeply. The day Ennis came to view the property I had just finished a lengthy assault on Lasse's nerves. Every night, moments before he fell asleep, I'd whisper into his ear and he'd sit bolt upright in bed until the morning came. I rearranged the furniture, unplugged the fridge, redirected the drainpipes into open windows. The house went up for sale, but not before it all came to a crescendo after I'd found some photos of his mother and strewn them around the house. I knew once I had done this, what a terrible son he must have been. He begged for her to leave him alone, for her to stop tormenting him.

Lasse was a shell of a man when Ennis came to visit, but that didn't faze him. He barely noticed Lasse's nervous twitches, instead, he read the storm-proofing plans, judged they were to be trusted and bought the island without a second thought.

I watched him from a distance at first, but I could see early on that there was something different about him. Something sad. His wealth seemed a result of his pain, as if he'd accrued it only to bury some past horror. And although I must admit getting rich does seem to go a long way towards muffling the pain of the past, most people can't muffle it forever.

I decided to reveal myself to him after months of deliberation. I can't recall the catalyst, if indeed there was one, only the fact that after all these centuries I had become a little lonely. And I could see he was lonely too, and kind, if not a little unusual.

So, I picked my moment. One night, while he was enjoying some private, tender time to himself, I snuck under the sheets and revealed myself. *Voila!*

When I was alive, apparitions were common enough, but by the standards of the day, it was hard for poor Ennis to process. For a man zealous in his opposition to all things hocus pocus it was quite the twist of events. He screamed and lashed and tried to fight me, but what can a man do against a disembodied spirit? That being said, I'd have made light work of him in my prime.

He believed he'd gone mad for quite some time, and I'm not sure he ever truly believed in me. But he relaxed into it after a while, allowed himself to trust me, to enjoy my company. It was certainly my view of madness in the olden days, the fear of losing your mind was worse than the madness itself. I worked with many a person that society had deemed *mad,* but they were far happier working for me than being locked up in an institution. I loved my work. Dishonest, honest work, and I slept well because of it.

Poor old Ennis, on the other hand, did not sleep well. Tumours of regret in every sinew. Sometimes, I watched him at night. He lay with his eyes closed for hours on end, but I knew he was awake, drifting through time, through his past. Whatever it was that haunted him, I wished he would've let it go, but alas, when you live alone separated from the mainland, that voice of inner doom can howl. Perhaps when I revealed myself to him, I thought I could help, perhaps I thought with two centuries of experience I could reason with him, but it's hard to reason with a mind that's been left alone to cannibalise itself.

The day before catastrophe struck, I watched him staring from the window. There wasn't a cloud in the sky, but there were birds, plenty of them. Almost a murmuration, dancing and diving, swooping down to feast on jellyfish stranded in the mud. Not the mud you'd find in a field though – estuary mud, boggy and thick, a quicksand of sorts. Birdwatchers loved this mud, but Ennis was no twitcher. No, Ennis had taken the threat of seagulls far too personally to love birds for their innate *birdness.* He'd known many twitchers and how they loved birds in all their variety, but he did not. He couldn't accept the way that mallards procreated or how cuckoos nested, not to mention the cannibalistic tendencies of chickens, and as he stood at the window, looking down at the sweet, wading birds, hobbling through the mud, he was certain, even if he didn't know what exactly, that there must be something deeply sick within their nature that disqualified them from his love.

The mud though, this boggy, thick sludge of estuary mud, had a beauty of its own. Especially at low tide when it teemed with hidden life. Although he watched the birds feasting on the jellyfish, he knew this was only a fleeting delicacy. Ordinarily, it was full of alternative delights. Molluscs and mud snails, bristle worms and bivalves, not to mention the nearby sea lavender and the samphire, that would lure the butterflies, that would lure the birds.

It had a beauty certainly, but it was brutish too if you took time to consider it. All those birds gorging themselves on tiny, defenceless beings. Ennis spent a lot of time considering it and he found the birds' behaviour harder to accept than most.

It was unusual to have so many jellyfish that far up the estuary at any time of year, let alone December, but the storms had scooped them up from the tropics and dumped them there in the brackish water, thousands of miles from their hot, salty homes.

I could see Ennis considering their fates with pity from the window as he looked down at them.

'Jellyfish don't have central nervous systems,' I said, making him jump. 'So, they're not in pain.'

'It's a nasty business, nonetheless,' he replied.

'It is.'

Ennis had told me once that there had been an earthquake in his village when he was a child. It was the reason he had returned to Cornwall years later and bought the island. The early shake had changed him. He'd spent time living on fault lines across the planet hoping to scratch that early itch, but it had never felt the same. There was something about it happening in England, in Cornwall. The unexpectedness, the absurdity. So, he moved onto Lasse's island and installed his gear. It was advanced stuff for a hobbyist, but he could afford it. And so, he sat, and he waited, but the tremors never came. They twitched and teased from time to time, flirted, titillated, threatened but never shook. But Ennis feared the day the tectonic plates would move. That the ground would not shake enough. That the dogs wouldn't bark, paintings would still hang from the walls, the glasses wouldn't smash and that it would be a mere feature on the news, trivial and forgettable. What Ennis wanted, but never spoke aloud, was catastrophe, life altering catastrophe, and everything that came with it. From the outside he looked as though he had led a charmed life, but on the inside, he was a man lusting after its collapse.

But it's not often one suffers the catastrophe they fear, let alone the one they crave. So, if you think I'm about to tell you how this handsome, lonely man's house shook, giving him just what he wanted, then you are mistaken. No, Ennis sat up in his attic, staring at the charts, waiting for the ground to shake, whilst all around him the weather began to change. The once occasional winter storms began to arrive in droves. Tidal surges, landslides, flooding. From October to April, relentless wind and rain battered the county. All the while, Ennis sat in his attic, obliviously checking his equipment. There was plenty of seismic activity in all the usual places, but nothing near him. Some mornings he'd clear branches from the lawn, other times, when he had to visit the mainland for food, he'd grab a sandbag or two to help the locals, but his mind was always elsewhere. He barely noticed the decline happen. The working week became shorter, the police disappeared and although the healthcare remained free, waiting lists had become so long that talk of visiting a doctor became hypothetical.

Perhaps it was everyone's cheerful optimism that allowed him the comfort of his ignorance, but likely it was his obsession. Whatever it was, not even he was able to ignore the most recent hurricane.

'Shall we clear the carcasses then?' he said, turning away from the window.

'Well, I can watch you clear them.' I had thought it prudent to pretend that I was incapable of moving things, you never know what you could become embroiled in.

'That's what I meant. I'm aware of your limitations.'

Ennis shouldered the front door open with force. It had become swollen after months of rain. There was a granite path from the doorway that led directly to the mainland when the tide was low. The house, the outhouse and the path were all built from Cornish granite, a superb material when it came to storm proofing. The trees and the shrubs in the garden were bent in accordance with the prevailing southwesterly winds. At some point, someone had planted an orchard at the most exposed point of the island. It looked rather abstract at the best of times, but especially so as it had stood then, covered in jellyfish from the night before. All shapes, sizes and colours, hanging from the branches like discarded kites.

'Quite the selection,' I said.

'I don't even recognise half of these.'

'I recognise a few from the Caribbean.'

'I'm surprised you can remember.'

'As clear as the waters themselves, Ennis.'

'Moon jellies, a Man of War,' he poked them with a stick. 'What are these?'

I hadn't noticed them at first; they were tiny, the size of a thumbnail, I'd never seen them so small.

'Are any of them still alive?' Ennis asked.

'Not many, I would've thought. I think we should return them to the water, leave them for the beasts of the ocean. Who knows what else that storm has brought with it.'

'I dread to think.'

'Haha! We took these waters for granted didn't we. Careful not to touch, Ennis, I think some of these are lethal.'

He poked his stick underneath them and twisted the tendrils round like noodles, lifting them one by one from the tree, he launched them into the shallow, low tide water.

'Do you think they still sting?' he asked.

'I wouldn't take the risk.'

After an hour or so, he launched the final tree-jellyfish into the water, along with the stick.

'What about the one's on the lawn?' I asked.

'I'll do it tomorrow, I'm jellied out. Besides, there's some activity in the Azores I'd like to keep an eye on.'

'What are you doing for food?'

'I haven't thought about it.' He placed his hands on his midriff, considering the question.

'You can't keep having Armagnac for dinner, Ennis.'

His eyes darted around as he weighed up my comment.

'I have been craving vermicelli.'

ANNA GOLDREICH

Anna is a writer living in Norwich. She was shortlisted for the Bridport Short Story Award in 2022 and has gone on to adapt this short story into her debut novel, *The Leveret*. The novel explores queerness, grief, and relationships between people and animals.

a.e.goldreich@gmail.com

The Leveret

The opening of a novel

I move, foot and root and rock and dirt. Hair left on branches, skin pricked by brambles, my right shin stung up and down by nettles. Phoebe chews on doc leaves, she's all mouth. Shaping like this and that, forming around the leaves, a tongue and teeth. Chewing, chewing and spitting out, and she is rubbing the green stuff into my skin, turning me into something. And talking as she does this, always talking, she is. Giving me little pieces of how it was to grow up in a place like this. The hardness and the softness that comes with it. I watch her face for small movements, see that there are pieces of green in her teeth. When I tell her, she sticks out her tongue.

Phoebe talks at me while her hand points at things. There, a tree she might have climbed up when she and it were smaller; there, a collared dove, a pair of them, and there a little stream. I am learning the place. I am learning it with my nose and my ears and my eyes and my feet. I am walking and looking and placing things. I'm trying not to think. And the days have bled into each other, yes, unmarked by plans or by work, just the slow unpacking, making calls from the landline phone, getting the internet set up. No signal, Phoebe had warned, in the car ride over, she'd said, let's buy some DVDs for the evening because there'll be no internet until we get it put in. But didn't I try to find some anyway? Didn't I stand in the bedroom that first day, there, holding my phone to the eaves?

She shows me how to touch the nettles so they don't sting, and why would I want to? I ask, why would I do that? She pinches leaves off and drops them on the ground. She says, nettle seeds make you feel buzzed. She tells me she used to eat them on walks as a child, she'd eat them on long walks so she could keep going. And one time, she says, one time she did get lost out here, properly lost and she survived on berries and leaves and it felt like weeks but was only about twelve hours before her dad and the dogs found her wandering around like a lost lamb. He dragged her back home to her mother, who smacked the backs of her legs with a wooden spoon, then held her close and wouldn't let go.

She asks me how it feels to be so far from anything, how it feels to be somewhere so different, and I want to tell her that I don't know if I'm supposed to be here. I want to tell her that I feel like a splinter. A splinter or maybe a weed. I want to say these things, but I can't make my lips into the right shape. I say, the house is lovely, just beautiful, and yes, wasn't it kind of her granny to give it to us? And are there any ghosts? It feels like a house that would have ghosts. And she laughs but she doesn't say no. She points at things, saying, cowslip, toadflax, harebell. It sounds like a potion, I tell her, it sounds like a potion, and she agrees. She tells me about potions she made with her granny, elderberry syrup for a cough, a balm made from conkers to rub on sore feet. She tells me some of the stories her granny told her before bed, black dogs, white stags, babies being swapped. We don't talk about the other thing. She pretends that we left it behind, left it in the old flat. But we didn't. We brought it here with us.

And I didn't mind the packing, I did most of it, all while Phoebe was at work. I moved through each room, and I touched so many things that hadn't been touched since the last time we moved. So many things my hands were surprised by, but that my eyes were used to, that my eyes had given up looking at, or seeing, maybe. My mum had brought round boxes and tried to help. She packed the plates and cups and asked what she could get rid of. Nothing, again and again, I told her, don't throw that out, just leave it, please can you leave it, you're making it worse. Every day I did a bit more, I took all the pictures down off the walls and I filled in the little holes. I used the Polyfilla and pressed it in with my fingers, felt the way it caked into my fingerprints and into the wall. I packed all of the books and the cushions. I taped down the lid of the chest in the hallway. I looked at the stains in the carpet, thought about using bleach or something, but I couldn't do it. Every day when she got home, Phoebe would kiss my head and tell me I'd done a good job. I didn't have anything else to do.

On moving day, we had to get the men to lift everything, to pack up a big van and drive it all the way there. They carried out our bookcases and an armchair, we left the sofa and the kitchen table because Phoebe's granny had left hers for us. They took apart our bed, they split it into pieces so they could get it out the door. I watched their hands and how they gripped our mattress. I wished I'd covered it in something because I'm still getting these dreams about hands creeping out from under, in the middle of the night. I kept having to stand in the closet and face the wall. I kept having to go in there and stand in the dark with my eyes closed. At one point, one of the men opened the door, and I think I said something about looking for something, or maybe I said, hmm where's that thing? I said something like that probably. I didn't turn around, I didn't move, but I could feel his eyes on me and I wondered if he'd ever grabbed a woman by the back of the neck and pushed her face into a wall. He made a sound and closed the door, and it was dark again, it was like it never happened.

We checked the flat so many times. After the men had left, when they'd packed up the van and taken our things, we went through it together and then, while Phoebe sat in car outside, I went back in alone. The flat was strange without our life inside, bigger and smaller than it had ever been. The carpet was still stained and is surely still stained right now. I wanted to cut that part out and take it with us, but I wasn't allowed. Phoebe said I wasn't allowed. And I told her, I did try to explain that I didn't want to leave it behind for the landlord to bleach or to cut out and throw away. The last thing I did was lie on the floor beside the stain. I thought, in that moment, I thought I might never be able to get up again. Maybe, if I could choose, maybe I would have seeped into the carpet and never left. But then Phoebe was beside me, and she pressed the back of my hand to her mouth, and yes, her lips were warm and I could feel the places they were peeling and when she stood up, she pulled me up too and led me out to the car. I asked her, as she turned the key, I said, can we drive by her? Phoebe shook her head, not again, that was it.

When we were finally on the road, I couldn't hold my limbs in the right way and I think that was the reason – because I didn't say goodbye properly. And I felt like I had left something behind, and I couldn't sit still because my body was being pulled back. No, I couldn't fold myself properly, couldn't hold myself properly. Shifting this way and that. A leg held to a chest, then the other, and noticing the difference, the pull in the strings all up the back. And I tried with them crossed, tried with both knees held, the shape of a seed, I tried with feet up against the dashboard and Phoebe was glaring at me. If we crash, she said, if we crash your body will be crushed, your legs will shatter. And then what? I wanted to know, and then what, but I didn't ask, I just put my feet down where they were meant to be, I arranged my feet around a small fiddle-leaf fig tree.

And we had all the plants in the car because Phoebe didn't trust the men to pack them right. We had to wedge the tall ones in awkwardly and I accidentally shut a door on the parlour palm's leaf. We didn't notice until we stopped at the services, and I wanted to cry and Phoebe said it'd be fine, it would survive. I watched Phoebe in small snatches throughout the drive. Biting and chewing her lips and the insides of her cheeks in concentration. She'd turn the radio on and then off, she'd start talking about chickens or paint colours and then her voice would trail away. We kept having to stop so I could go to the toilet and I tried to make a joke about not being able to keep anything inside of me. She just looked straight ahead. When we ate lunch, it was in the car, and she wondered out loud about whether we'd get closer to her brother and his family, if he'd let us babysit sometimes. When I looked out of the window, I saw the way the blur changed colour, how it went from grey to green. When we were around an hour away, she squeezed my hand and asked me how I was feeling, I wanted to tell her that I was terrified. I wanted to say, I've changed my mind and I want to go back, please take me back. I wanted to say, I think this is a bad idea because I don't know how to be in a place like this with people like these. I wanted to ask her if this was going to be it, if this meant we had given up. But I didn't. I didn't say any of it, I told her I was excited, that it would be nice to be somewhere different. I think I said it too quickly or maybe my voice was too high. We sat in silence for the rest of the drive. The plants were breathing in what we were breathing out, and we were breathing in what the plants were breathing out, and in that moment, I wondered if we could stay forever, in the car with the plants, breathing in and out, in and out, in and out. Phoebe's chest was rising and falling, and I wanted to touch her in her aliveness, in her being and her evidence of being. I wanted to touch her face, her chest. I touched her thigh instead. Yes, I touched her thigh and she moved her arm awkwardly around mine, trying to get to the gearstick. I touched her thigh and thought about tracing down to the inside. I wanted to talk to her, but I didn't know what to say.

LAURA GRAHAM

Laura Graham was born in Norwich and grew up in Cambridge. She has a BA in English Literature with Creative Writing from UEA. Her writing is concerned with how we tell stories and convey information, and how these methods shape and are shaped by our perspective of the world.

grahamlaura01@gmail.com

The Grave of the Poet King

A Short Story

Tom is going to the grave of the poet king.

He has put on his best new dark cotton suit with the smart jacket and waistcoat, laced up his stiff new leather shoes, kissed his mother and his sweetheart goodbye, and set off. He said goodbye to his sister, too, but she just watched him, and didn't reply. He is taking with him a lunch to eat by the grave of the poet king, tracing paper and a pencil to take an impression of it. Tom will keep the impression to himself always, for that is part of the point, the journey itself, the not telling anyone else except to say, 'it's fantastic. It's like nothing else I've ever seen before. It's like nothing I ever could have dreamed of writing before.' That is what Tom's father told him when *he* went to see the grave. Tom can still remember the exact words. He mouths them as he walks.

The path to the grave of the poet king diverges from the main road which runs through Tom's town on the way to greater places. Many men of letters stop here, in the past to enquire the way, these days to apply to the council to be judged worthy of visiting the grave.

Tom has been judged worthy of visiting the grave of the poet king. His mother says his stories are very good, as does his sweetheart, as does the greengrocer who lives down the way. The council agrees with them. Tom writes stories based on his impressions of the men who come to their town, and on the history books he reads about old wars and the people who died in them. He's very convincing, almost so that you could believe it's his stories that are real, and not the men, or the history. They only lack that single spark of life required to make them perfect.

His sister says his stories lack more than one single spark of life, and laughs at him — but she's not going to the grave of the poet king, and so her opinions don't matter.

Once it was the case that to reach the grave of the poet king, Tom would have had to cross through many fields of grass, and he would have ruined his new leather boots and probably the bottoms of his new cotton trousers too from the mud and the tall damp blades, and he might even have got lost. Before he was born, though, the grave had already received so many visitors that the grass was firmly stamped down into a path that anyone could follow. This was when the council had decided to institute a guard on the grave, to prevent it being read by anyone of whom they didn't approve. By the time Tom was ten, they had also started laying down a cobbled path, because the men of letters who visited and were approved complained of the mud otherwise.

So, Tom set out for the grave of the poet king along a path that was neat and uncomplicated, but it was still a long walk regardless, barely enough time in a day to make it there and back, which was why his mother had packed a lunch for him. He would eat it, of course, a respectable distance from the grave. The poet king had transcended such lowly things as breadcrumbs and would not appreciate them falling upon the ground above his head.

The annals of Tom's town say that the grave of the poet king has been there longer than the town, although when the settlement had been built no-one knew about the discovery to be made half a day's walk away. That had been happened upon by a half-mad boy, who no-one thought would amount to much, and who had wandered away from his parents' home one morning. On the next, he had come running back to their house crying out with joy, urging them to come see the strange stone monument in the middle of a forest.

(The forest has long since been cut down, because the trees towering over the grave of the poet king made the stone look small in comparison, and everyone agreed that that should never be the case.)

After that, it's said, the boy grew into a great writer, a man for his parents to be proud of. His stories brought him renown all over the little isle. What he had written is long since lost to time; only the grave of the poet king remains, and the tale of the blessing it brings to all storytellers. Tom once wrote a story about a battle that took place near his town, hundreds of years ago. It was mostly guesswork, because so little remains, but weaved into a tale that made his mother weep. He had ended it by saying *and above the battlefield, on a hill overlooking the bloody spectacle, the grave of the poet king watched, unchanging.*

His sister had rolled her eyes. His sister always rolls her eyes at his stories. She calls them clichés, uninspired copies. But today he is going to the grave of the poet king, on the path that gradually slopes upwards, then dips, then slopes up again, the undulating hills marking out a steady rhythm for him to follow. He moves carefully, so that he does not tear his new suit by stumbling rapidly downwards, or scuff his shoes against the stones on the ground. His stomach opens up, yearning for food, but he will not eat until he is close enough to the grave of the poet king that he could reach out and touch it — if that were not disrespectful in the extreme. To take an impression is enough, and even then, he must be careful, pressing as lightly with his pencil as he can. He has promised to be careful; the guard of the poet king's grave will watch him to make sure, Tom's been told. He's been told too to keep the impression to himself, or he will have it confiscated and have to leave the town. And this is why Tom has resolved to fold it up and tuck it away somewhere he will not be tempted to show it to anyone, and his sister will not find it to steal. She has, before, stolen his pens and his paper and even sometimes his stories themselves before he is ready to share them, poring over one with a frown scratched into her face as though with a thick pencil.

Yet, Tom tells himself, of the two of them he is the one going to the grave of the poet king. He has reached the grave of the poet king, and his town is far behind him.

Tom hands his pass to the guard who stands blocking the grave from view. The pass is not a written thing but a particular mark, belonging to the town's committee; the guard has agreed never to learn how to read, in return for the honour of guarding the grave of the poet king. He steps aside and allows Tom to look at the inscription.

It is so worn with age that Tom can barely make out the individual letters. His heart jumps about in his chest, its movements reminding him of a story he once wrote after he saw a man have a fit in the town square. Still, he reminds himself, he has been invited to the grave of the poet king, he has been deemed worthy. He must prove that judgement of him correct. And so he scrambles around in his bag for the tracing paper and the pencil, at last extracts them both — must hold on tight to the paper, against a sudden gust of wind.

Tom crouches down, so that he's eye-level with the grave of the poet king. He places the paper over the inscription, pinning it as best he can with his elbows, feels the hard uneven stone imprint itself on his skin. It's sure to mark his new suit, he thinks. Then, his hand curled over the inscription, he begins to work his pencil against the paper. Grey against white, it must become easier to read. The message of the poet king. That vital spark of life, that totally new and unheard message that must be guarded at all costs. And — yes! He can see the words emerging on the paper. He can hardly wait to be done, but he must be methodical — is methodical.

Tom pulls his paper away from the grave of the poet king and stands there on the top of the hill, looking down on it. The paper displays the inscription. The inscription reads,

> Alas, poor YORICK!

and the words mean nothing to him.

Has he made a mistake somewhere? Has he missed something along the way that could have given him a clue? Or is it a message that other, more worthy men can understand without aid?

> Alas, poor YORICK!

Surely his pencil has not led him wrong — but he has no more paper with which to attempt another impression, except the newspaper his lunch is wrapped in, and that's already too marked with other writing. Tom looks at the impression; he looks at the grave. Now that he knows what he's looking for he can pick out the same letters on the stone as he can read on the paper in his hand.

> Alas, poor YORICK!

Tom retreats. He thanks the guard, who resumes his old place in front of the grave. Tom retires to eat his lunch on a grassy mound a few paces away.

He has read every book in the town, that is the problem. He has read every book, learned every history. None of them give him the key to its meaning. Yet it must mean something for it to matter so much to everyone. He thinks again of what his father told him. *It's fantastic. It's like nothing else I've ever seen before. It's like nothing I ever could have dreamed of writing before.*

> Alas, poor YORICK!

Once he has eaten, he carefully packs away the newspaper his mother had wrapped his lunch in, folding it up and stowing it in a pocket of his satchel. He steps off the mound, nods to the guard, and sets off back down the succession of hills, a frown imprinted on his face.

On the last hill before his town the wind picks up again and Tom stops, gazing down at the expectant candlelight that marks the evening air. He takes out the paper, squints at it in the encroaching gloom. The words seem to blur together because of the darkness, but their meaning remains the same. He opens his hands.

The wind stabs at the paper, shooting it away from him and from the town.

He walks down the path, towards the main road and the first of the tall brick buildings. As people register his presence, they begin to appear at their doors, despite the lateness of the day. *Tom, Tom! How was it? How was the grave of the poet king?* They gather around him, waiting for the latest of their great artists to speak.

He thinks of his father, eyes lit up; thinks of his mother and her hopes; thinks of the men with their heads held high coming back down the path. He thinks of

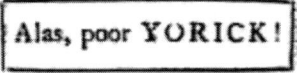

Tom opens his mouth.

'It's fantastic,' he says. 'It's like nothing else I've ever seen before. It's like nothing I ever could have dreamed of writing before.'

And rising above him, amidst the satisfied murmurs of the crowd, he thinks he hears his sister's laugh.

END

Author's Note: the image of the grave's inscription is taken from *The Life and Opinions of Tristram Shandy, Gentleman* by Laurence Sterne, volume 1.

EVAN STEPHENS HALL

Evan Stephens Hall is an artist from Montclair, NJ.

Evanhall36@gmail.com

My Report
A short story

My first thought, after the morning's oolong began to resurrect my mind, was of my report-in-progress. I felt proud of having already written two thousand words but felt, on reflection, that I had committed unevenly to the prompt. Upon re-reading my draft of the report so far, I became aware of my tendency to digress into ancillary subjects. I was unsettled by how little, in fact, the report addressed its ostensive purpose.

   Still, a part of me felt that once it could be taken as a whole, even the digressions would be seen to have their place. Some proportion of the text, I reasoned, should be centered on methodology. Far from an indulgence, recounting my state of mind, my whereabouts, and my nutritional intake would all contribute to a more honest report, and with time these personal disclosures would be considered fundamental to the effort's credibility.

   But as I swished a mouthful of tea, a concern began to gnaw. Regardless of the rightness of my subject and the rigor of my methodology, I would need a style in which to transmit my findings. That this style would need to somehow embody the details of my report was a given. But how could I choose a style before I knew the full contents of the report? This would seem to necessitate a methodology that would remain flexible to changes in the research as new facts came to light, facts which once unearthed, I realized with some dismay, might have implications on the remit of the subject itself. But to finish my research and codify my subject I would need to write down my findings, which would necessarily be laid down with the characteristic features of a style!

   I looked warily at the mug in my hand. The oolong was strong this morning. I put down the mug, hastily organized an outfit, and prepared to exit my apartment.

   This, however, was not easily achieved, due to the Shirtless Marauding Men and me being afraid of them. All morning they'd been enacting mayhem. I attempted to inflate my courage with personal affirmations, but on the threshold of my leaving I balked, my buoyant attitude having abandoned me. I paused, doorknob in hand, as my mind recounted the disturbing episode which had begun my day.

   In the early hours, hearing sounds of altercation, I rolled off my cardboard to look through the window. With my nose on the sill, I observed one dog in association with The Shirtless Men bite the ear of a smaller dog, unaffiliated, & swing it centripetally around by its ear as everyone screamed, 'No!' or 'Yes!' The latter continues to haunt me.

   Since this incident the men had been cheering, setting trash on fire, requesting to fight each other, maneuvering bicycles in ways that made me nervous. After several such hours, I'd thought their energies diminished, but an especially confident whoop exposed the naivety of this assumption. I turned from the door, grumbling, and returned to my pile of cardboard.

The material sagged sweetly beneath me. From this vantage, swiveling my view across the room, I beheld my items, and my mood began to regulate. My table, layered in papers and pencils. My upright piano against the wall. Kettle and hob in the corner. A pile of cans and loose tea leaves. Everything in one place.

I rose myself, swinging, and brewed another batch of oolong. Managing to shrink my annoyance to proportion was no small victory, and would continue to be a necessary skill as I focused my energies where they belonged: on preparing a well-researched report. I watched the oolong buds uncoil in the water, and with the first few sips I had settled back into the composure which is my natural way.

I lowered onto my piano bench, keeping mindful of my hot liquid, and played one note. I smiled approvingly at my rejuvenated position. It felt good to abandon a gripe. I bounced slightly on the bench. I would eat the Good Beans.

Back at the hob, I balanced the can on the metal grate and ignited, and then went over to choose an appropriately sized ream of cardboard. *Rejuvenated*, I whispered, in curious appreciation of how the word felt in my mouth, and once the can was sufficiently heated I put on oven mitts and pried off the top, pouring the steaming beans onto my cardboard. They spread out in an appetizing coagulation which, as the steam rose into my face, I folded in half and tipped to my mouth. The hot lumps squished down the funnel, filling my body with much needed replenishment, spreading warmth through my chest. To the remaining few beans which resisted their sluicing, I pursed my lips to suck, thus coaxing the stubborn oblongs to my nutritional benefit.

I tossed the dampened cardboard into my discard closet and regarded myself for exit.

I smiled in the sunlight.

Someone bellowed in the distance.

Returning home after my postprandial, my stomach rumbled. It was not so outrageous, given the prodigious intellectual labor I had just produced on my walk. Nevertheless I felt it odd that a postprandial should so easily elide into a preprandial. But this worry was soon overcome as the steam rose into my face. The beans were much wetter than usual and as a consequence I was compelled to use nearly twice as much cardboard to contain their spread. This is not to mention the ream I deployed for its absorptive qualities in the post-production phase of the meal.

I wiped the sweat off my forehead and reflected how much more exertion the clean up process would entail had I *not* arrived at such a convenient solution as the discard closet. My days had been so busy, what with the report, and so while a part of me resisted the discard closet as a lasting solution, its immediate benefits could not be ignored. Anyway I would not be quite so busy once my report was complete. I consciously repeated this line as a reassuring mantra, even as I noticed a certain flimse to its logic – naturally, if the report were a success, as I hoped, things would only stand to become busier after its completion. Nevertheless I knew that my present busyness prevented a thorough interrogation into different techniques of cardboard disposal, and so this and other sensible objections were likewise relegated to the closet.

I say I repeated this line of thinking, and I did, but the truth is that the discard closet became quickly normalized as a part of my routine. Each time I felt my energy dip, I would take a break from my writing to replenish with a meal of beans and oolong, and at the meal's conclusion, would dispose of my waste in a way that seemed, if not responsible, then at least private.

Throughout this period, anyway, at top of mind was not the discard closet but the composition of the above-mentioned document, a report which upon completion I hoped would be considered a helpful resource to the residents of my new city, and that as people discussed it, they would not use such terms as *dossier*, *memo*, or *note*, but rather that the text would be viewed as something in the vicinity of *proclamation*, approaching a *manifesto*, possibly, though I felt sure that if push came to shove, once the chaos of the report's reception had subsided I would not be opposed to the text being described as merely one significant public address in a long line of crucial disclosures.

But let me not get ahead of myself, for as much time as I fantasized about the project's completion and the passionate debates it would inspire, what principally occupied my time was the *research* of my subject, research which I'm afraid had led me to learn more than I'd ever intended, and to burn, I suppose, more calories than I was accustomed to. I noticed myself moving from my standard four meals a day to five, which. needless to say, produced a quarter more cardboard waste than my previous routine. I had not initially planned for such rapid usage but, consulting my figures, I found that even without obtaining more boxes I would still have enough for meals clear into next spring. I deferred concern and continued to write until my energy would flag, would eat, would dispose, would leave for my interprandial.

It was with some surprise, then, that I returned home from my walk today to discover a fairly vicious infestation at the door of the discard closet. Apparently I had been so focused on the minutiae of my work that I had failed to notice what surely was a gradual expansion of the insect community in the auspices of my own home. I marveled for a moment that, considering how elevated my reception to detail had been with regard to the report's composition, the finer points of my home environment had receded into such insignificance that a nest of alarmingly active scope could have formed next to me without my even realizing.

Where did these insects come from? It was not as if I kept my windows open. This city, for all its merits, has not yet been introduced to the window-screen, and opening a screenless window, I knew, was to invite certain entomological casualty. So they would not have entered window-wise on my watch. I stared at the festering nest, entranced by the collective activity and impressed, I should admit, by the diversity of cast who bashed themselves relentlessly against the door, drunk with the stink of rotting beans.

It was impressive, but I felt, as I turned back to my table, that it was ultimately nothing more than a distraction from my work, the details of which were growing more complicated, almost, than I could keep track of. Each remembrance of the particulars would renew my apprehension. I was gripped with anxiety over the precision I would need to wield in order to do the subject justice, and naturally over Justice itself, which I knew should be thorough but had a sense that it should also be expedient. The more I worriedthe issue, the less focused the whole project seemed. I swatted a fly from my brow. Broadly I had a basic picture. But narrowing my aperture, I had very little certainty, actually, about the particulars. Uncertainty about what it all meant, yes, but even a more literal uncertainty about events I would need to describe, their sequence, their ontological status. I felt a sting and looked at my hand.

When I looked up again I found the insects had assembled around me, an interrogative cloud. They seemed unaccountably angry, biting, stinging, demanding answers. I supposed they wanted to know, as I did, to which path I would vow allegiance.

Style or Substance?

Would I be seduced away from Justice, Purity, and Accuracy, by the frilly buntings of Style? Or would I manage to adhere to my stated goal of Truth? Representatives of both Form and Content had welcomed me in, had plied me with incentivizing whiffs. But then each, too, had left ambiguous flavors incubating in my mouth. The insects stung again: Which will it be? I cried out, for now they all swarmed at once, devouring my puffy skin. Fluids rushed into my arms and raised clusters of bumps, constituting a braille of sorts, which I tenderly consulted with the tips of my fingers, desperate to translate into some kind of guidance. Such a split allegiance could never sustain. I would need to make this right. I would face the page anew. My eyes swelling shut, I tried to stand, to stagger toward my table. Hands enormous and shaking, I cast around for a pencil as I knocked several to the floor. I wedged one in my purple hand. I was running out of time.

ELLIE HALLIWELL

Ellie Halliwell was born in London and studied English Literature with Creative Writing at the University of East Anglia. Her writing is often influenced by music, and she likes to draw on themes of neurodiversity and magical realism.

Ehalliwellwriting@gmail.com

Nell Robinson

Short Story

It was a black velvet dress with a satin bow on the front.

'Absolutely not,' said my mum.

'It's the only black dress I have.'

'It looks like something you'd wear to a party. This is a funeral, not a disco.'

'No one's been to a disco since the Seventies.'

'Don't be a smartarse! Just put on something more appropriate.'

I closed my bedroom door and rifled through my wardrobe. The room felt so empty now that I'd moved out. After shifting through old clothes, I managed to find a navy top and a pair of black jeans. Not ideal, but dark at least. I went downstairs and joined my parents in the car, my room echoing with dust and sunlight behind me.

We drove in silence out of town, past the flat-roof pubs, the red-bricked housing estates, the retail centre, the scrubby park, the industrial estate. I had a vague melancholy feeling as we drove though Shelbridge, a wandering feeling I couldn't quite pin down.

We stopped at a service station café. Generic pop music played faintly over the speakers. We sat in a booth, gazing out towards the wide Northern sky. The waiter brought three cups of tea for our table. I would have loved a biscuit too, but it didn't seem appropriate given the circumstances. Dad got a text.

'Oh for God's sake! Uncle Mick says he can't make it.'

Mum looked upset. 'Did he say why?'

'Some excuse about traffic. That isn't right. She was his aunt. I know they weren't in touch much, but you'd think he could be arsed to turn up to see her laid to rest.'

I stayed quiet. I wasn't especially bothered by Mick's absence. It was hard to resent him for missing a funeral for someone he hardly knew. None of us had been close with Cousin Nell, in fact I don't think anyone had. She always kept to herself and was rarely seen, much less heard, at family gatherings. But even when she was present it seemed as though she was never really there; nursing a glass of wine in the corner, making quiet small talk if she had to. I can't recall ever saying more than a few words to her.

Dad set his cup down and made that loud, annoying sigh that all dads make upon finishing their tea.

'Right,' he declared, 'we should get going.'

We drove deeper into the countryside. As we approached our destination it felt like Nell's presence was advancing upon us, more vivid in death than she ever was in life. Little hamlets passed us by, each one full of quiet, ordinary people, living quiet, ordinary lives. I observed them from a distance, yet I was one of them.

Eventually we arrived at the sparse village of Warren Cross. We slowed down as we drove past the modest houses and the local garage, then turned into the church car park. Our Lady Mary the Divine was surrounded by tall, whispering trees. The scent of woodsmoke lingered in the air, and an ancient stillness hung over the mossy churchyard. If I still believed in God, I would have found this a very holy place, I'm sure.

My stomach sank as I realised how few people were likely to attend. Mum opened the doors with apprehension. There was one person behind them – Nell's brother Frank. He seemed surprised to see us there.

'Joe!' he said, giving Dad a brief half-hug. 'Thank you for coming.' He gave me and Mum a slightly awkward handshake.

'Sorry for your loss,' I said. It was such a robotic phrase, but I didn't know what else to say.

He nodded, a little too vigorously.

'Thank you, Lucy. She, er, passed away peacefully, so I think we can all take comfort in that.'

He didn't want to say more on the matter, clearly feeling uncomfortable being the victim of grief. He veered quickly into bland small talk.

'How's university going?'

'It's going well thanks, I'm enjoying it.'

'What do you study again?'

'Music production.'

'Right, yes of course.'

'We're very proud, first in the family to go to uni,' Mum interjected. 'Although it's a shame she's so far away.'

Two elderly women dressed in black walked in.

'Would you be Nell's family by any chance?' asked the taller of the pair.

'We are,' answered Frank. 'I'm her brother.'

'Oh, I am sorry dear. We knew her from Mass. She didn't say much but she was ever so polite, and when one of our congregation passes we always come and pay our respects.'

'How kind of you to come. What are your names?'

'I'm Gladys, and this is Dolores.'

'Pleased to meet you.'

Just then the priest emerged. Father McCarthy was a softly spoken Irishman with blue eyes and hair white as a communion wafer. He told us in cautiously reverent tones that the service was ready to begin. Frank looked around at the sparse crowd.

'Is this all that's coming?' he asked.

'Looks like it,' answered my dad. 'Shame Mick couldn't come.'

'If you'd like to follow me,' said Father McCarthy, opening the doors to the main part of the church.

We filed in silently. Our footsteps echoed, out of tune. This was the sum of Nell's life. Seventy-four years plus one death equals six people.

In front of us was a coffin draped in plain black cloth. The smell of incense and red wine lingered in the cold air. We sat down on the polished pews, trying to space ourselves out so more of the rows were full. With muted organ music, the service began.

Hymns were sung, prayers were said, Bible stories were read. Each one of them held a fleeting familiarity, a bittersweet nostalgia for my childhood. It felt different without that earnest sense of belief, though. The words and rhythms remained the same, but the faith that made them real was gone, and they drifted to the floor like fallen leaves. Crunching over a carpet of lifeless parables and crumbling songs, Father McCarthy made his way to the lectern.

'Good afternoon. We are here today to celebrate the life and mourn the passing of Helen Robinson. A woman close to all your hearts, I am sure.'

The phrase landed like a flat note. He continued.

'Helen, or Nell as she was known, was born to Jack and Frances Robinson on the 23rd of November 1949 in Liverpool. She had a happy childhood, growing up with her brother Frank and her sister Rose. She was a shy girl, but she had great musical talent, having been taught to play the piano from a young age by her father Jack.'

I cast my mind back to when we cleared out her home a few days ago. She lived in a nondescript house on the edge of the village, a few doors along from a launderette and a Chinese takeaway. We cleared out her kitchen and threw away the old food, donating anything unopened to the local foodbank. We rooted around in cupboards and wardrobes, picking through the debris left behind by a lifetime. A few photos of family members, mostly long dead, some old books, and a collection of scarves and vinyl records. Not much at all.

Once all this was done the house was locked up, ready to be sold on to new owners. Nell left the place to Frank in her will, but he didn't want to keep it. Nobody did.

I drifted back to the present. Father McCarthy was continuing his eulogy.

'She never married, but remained devoted to her work, enjoying books and music in her spare time. She had a strong sense of faith and was a regular churchgoer. Every Sunday she would come to Mass at this church before taking a stroll through the woods, and it was on a Sunday afternoon that she passed away peacefully into the loving arms of the Lord. She was a woman of few words, but she will be remembered fondly by her loved ones and by everyone in our church community. And so, let us pray for her soul, and ask that she be granted eternal rest in the heavenly kingdom.'

Just like that, a whole life summarised in a few sentences. And then it was over. A speech finished. A full stop added. A casket closed.

***

After the service we made our way to the churchyard silently. No tears were shed during the eulogy. No relatives apart from Frank had any memories to share of her. We gathered round to watch Nell's coffin descend into the wine-dark earth. There was a distinct sense of guilt hanging over us. I couldn't help but wonder if Nell really had been the recluse we thought she was, or if none of us had paid enough attention to her. Or worse still, if she had been made to feel unworthy of that attention to begin with.

The day ended in a local pub for the wake. The Willow Tree had the same ugly patterned carpet that every pub seemed to have, but it was cosy, with wide windows and wood panelled walls. I went to the bar to order my usual rum and coke, but it seemed too cheerful for such an occasion, so I got a pint of bitter instead. I saw Gladys and Dolores, who had come here straight after the service and spent the afternoon drinking sherry. As I waited for them to get their drinks Gladys put her arm round Dolores' shoulder. The gesture surprised me with its easy intimacy. I had assumed they were friends, but perhaps that was not the full story.

'She was a nice lady,' said Gladys. 'A hardworking, honest woman.'

'But she did seem terribly alone,' countered Dolores. 'We made small talk with her occasionally, but otherwise she never spoke to a soul. Didn't seem to have any friends. Didn't know she had family till today.'

'Well maybe that's how she liked things, Dor. Perhaps she preferred to be by herself.'

'Maybe. But I'd be miserable if that was how I lived.'

'I guess we'll never know,' I said. 'Hopefully she was happy.'

It is easy to wonder why Nell lived the way she did. But perhaps it's not so hard to understand a solitary life. I wonder what it was like for Gladys and Dolores before they found each other. They must have drifted through the world thinking there was not another soul like them. Growing up I also struggled to feel that I belonged. I was strange, I was different, I was serpentine. When I lived at home I used to walk through the woods outside town, searching through Nature, trying to contextualise myself. Here was a tree whose posture resembled mine, there was a leaf with the same lined patterns as I had on my palm, there a fox whose dark irises almost matched my own. Cast off by humans, I found my place among the plants and animals, untouched by Original Sin.

Isolation seems an easy choice when trying to avoid the fate of those deemed to be different: exclusion, hatred, violence. Isolation can be a tree bearing nourishing fruit and soothing shade, but loneliness is what happens when its leaves wither and fall.

I wondered if she always meant to be alone. Was her loneliness the price of a life lived in peace? Or was it an accident, her love of solitude gone too far? Perhaps it was simply a fact she had accepted, thinking she would never find anyone else quite like her, or maybe her tree was one that had grown in the soil of shame.

I sipped my beer in silence. Cold sunlight streamed through the window. Around me people were talking, tepid English smiles under tepid English sunshine. I didn't listen to a word they said. There was a story behind Nell Robinson, that was certain. Perhaps there was more to her loneliness than there seemed.

KASPER HASSETT

Kasper Hassett is a working-class writer from London. His novel *What Parrots Don't Say* follows an autistic child's struggles with miscommunication and strained relationships as he envisions a utopian school but instead faces institutionalisation. Kasper was a 2022 Curtis Brown Creative Breakthrough mentee, and he has begun a second novel.

kasperhassett@gmail.com

What Parrots Don't Say

An extract from a novel

Most summer mornings, what woke Odie was sunlight trickling through gaps in his curtains. But before this could happen on one Thursday in late June, Candice was in his room speaking quickly as he drifted from sleep to wakefulness.

'You need to get ready. We're going somewhere.'

He heaved himself to a sitting position and blinked repeatedly. By the time he was alert, his mother was gone, and it was not long before the hissing of the hairdryer sounded from somewhere else in the house. Odie winced.

He realised he could not possibly get dressed for the occasion, so he did not do it and instead went downstairs, had breakfast and sat on the sofa, still fighting the lull of sleep.

Eventually, Candice entered, rummaging through her bag. 'Why aren't you dressed? We need to go!'

'I can't do it.'

'What do you mean you can't do it?'

'I can't get dressed.'

Candice frowned. 'Of course you can. You've been dressing yourself for years. What's the problem?'

He knew the problem. The problem was that he could not get dressed. 'I can't get dressed,' he said.

Candice breathed in, paused and bent her knees to be level with him. She said, much more slowly, '*What is stopping you* from getting dressed?'

Odie tried to avoid the intensity of her gaze which made his eyes water. 'I don't know where we're going.'

She looked away, then back at him. 'So, you can't pick what clothes to wear?'

He nodded and she stood.

'Well, we're going to visit a school.'

Odie's eyes widened.

'Not your old school. You're not going back there.'

'What's this one?'

'It's about two hours away, so wear something comfy. Make sure you use the loo before we go – be quick.'

Candice waited at the door but turned back as Odie came downstairs in his old school uniform – the green one.

'You can't wear that.'

'But it's a school, and kids wear uniforms to schools.' When she didn't reply, he added, 'I'm a kid.'

'We're just visiting,' she said. 'You don't go there. Well, you definitely don't go there right now.'

Odie picked loose jeans and a maroon T-shirt because he did not know whether he would like the people at the school, and if he did not, he did not want their gawking to ruin his favourite clothes. Maroon was a solid colour – not so nerve-shredding as garish yellow, but far from the nurturing buttery greens of jungles and forests.

It was eleven, long after Odie's father and sister had left. Candice was not at work for some reason, and Joanna had not come to look after him like she usually did. Odie clicked his seatbelt into place, and they set off away from St. Margaret's and on to roads with fewer and fewer houses.

Odie rarely sat at the front. The Baineses usually travelled individually or all together, with Odie and Rosie sitting in the back. Today he was in his father's usual space. Odie struggled to remember when he had last sat there. It was as if they had something to discuss – something big and looming – but Odie could think of little to say to Candice, so instead he read a book.

Odie glanced again at his outfit. He knew now that he should not wear a uniform for the visit. This made Odie wonder why they were visiting a school, since schools were for going to five days a week in a uniform, not for visiting. More likely, he thought, they were visiting someone there: someone his mother knew. But Candice did not know many children – she talked to only Odie and Rosie and Rosie's friends, and one time she had complained about the neighbours' children.

For a moment he thought of Joanna, studying at the Universe City school, and excitement grasped him. Maybe they were going there. Maybe Joanna was sick, he thought, and they were on their way to see her. Maybe she was too sick to travel, but she still very much wanted to look after him (this made sense to Odie, because Joanna was nice to him so she probably liked him) so he would be able to spend the day in the Universe City with her, doing lots of art and a bit of science, and a little bit of other things he wanted to try. He thought he may even get to try Joanna's *psychology,* since this was not something any of his old schools had taught.

Joanna said psychology was about people and people's minds. Joanna must know a lot about people's minds, Odie thought. He knew very little, even less than other people his age, he had been told. Candice had said it was because of 'the autism'. Odie did not know what 'the autism' was, but every time his parents mentioned it, they said that they still loved him very much. So then, he thought, it must have been something to do with loving someone, or not loving someone.

Candice said the school they were visiting knew a lot about 'the autism', which confirmed Odie's suspicions that it was the Universe City school and that it would have a lot to teach about psychology. They turned on to the motorway.

'Wait,' Odie said, after a while, 'if Joanna's sick, why is she at school?'

'What?'

'She's sick. So why is she at school?'

'Odie, what are you talking about? Joanna's sick? Did she tell you she was sick yesterday?'

'No! We're going to see her at her school, so she must be sick. But why isn't she at home?'

'We're not going to see Joanna – and she's fine, anyway.'

'Oh.' Odie sunk into the seat.

'You don't want Joanna to be sick, do you? You like her. Right?'

'I don't want Joanna to be sick,' he repeated, 'and I like her.'

'There you go, then.'

That was the last thing either of them said for a while.

The car grumbled over the tarmac. Candice squinted ahead at the horizon. Odie stared at the windscreen and every now and then felt Candice glance at him. He shrivelled up, shrinking into the seat, eventually opening his book again, holding it up as a shield. When he did this, Candice sighed, and after some minutes more of driving she pulled the car into a service station.

The engine fell silent. It was as if the car were a breathing, thinking entity (though Odie did not go so far as to imagine that it felt) and it had abandoned them at the side of the motorway. It had left behind its cold body, which had suddenly become a room, to give the two occupants a space, not for travelling but for talking. Now the engine noises had disappeared, the car needed to be filled with words. Odie did not have any to offer, so he waited, and his mother's eyes landed on him. They were heavy.

'Don't you think it's time by now?'

He did not respond.

'It's been three months, Odie. You don't miss school?'

'No. I'm better off without it.'

Candice sighed, but this time, it was a sigh of disappointment, and it made Odie worried. His mother sighed often, a good deal of the time at him, but usually he could feel it was because she could not understand him (though she would argue it was he who could not understand her). This sigh was different. It said, 'that was the wrong answer,' and 'what am I going to do with you?' These words did not need to be said as they were sighed to him very clearly.

'You need to go back soon. You can't just do nothing for ever.'

Odie felt defensive. He had been thinking about 'doing' and 'not doing', and it was as if his mother had dug into his mind just to disapprove of its contents. In principle, it was the same as reading a diary. But then he thought of Joanna and her psychology and wondered if she would be able to pull words from his mind, too. Perhaps she had been doing it all this time. Perhaps this was an expected level of knowledge about minds, and he would never be able to learn about them after all. Perhaps he could just not see the obvious, because of 'the autism' (*but we still love you very much*). Odie was angry at 'the autism'. Though he still did not understand what it was, in that moment he hated it. He felt violated. It was as if his mind did not belong to him.

Instead, Odie's mind belonged to his mother and his father and his sister and to Joanna, who he liked a little less than usual in that moment, and to all the Professionals who had observed him across meeting tables over the years. They could open up his mind, he concluded, and play with his ideas as they pleased. The disappointed Mrs. Gillingham had been reading him the whole time she had been his headteacher and could tell as he sat in that final school meeting how little he wanted to be there.

'I like doing nothing. I don't get bored.'

Cars glided past them at great speed. Odie could not help but feel like they were leaving him behind, stuck in the car as they headed in the direction of his own destination. He felt like screaming, to stop them, because how *dare* they speed past him as his mind was opened up? How *dare* his classmates continue to get older and wiser and closer to reading people's minds while he rotted? His eyes became wet and his face reddened, not with sadness, but with the rage that follows a betrayal. Odie was still ten. He thought he would be ten for a long time.

'You should be bored by now. You should be wanting to go outside every day and speak to other kids. Don't you want that? *Why* don't you want that?'

Odie felt that this was his last chance to change his mind, to say the right answer, but he could not lie. He needed to be honest because he did *not* like school and he did *not* like being told off and he wanted to stay at home with his family in the evenings, who only told him off deservedly, and with Joanna in the daytimes, who never told him off at all. Odie was facing the long road ahead of the car and he did not want to cry.

'I just don't.' He tried to hide his tears with a shrug.

They sat in silence. It lasted a long time – Odie did not know how long, but by the time his mother started driving again he thought he saw tears in her eyes. She blinked a lot, and then Odie was less sure about the tears because he could no longer see them, and once on the road again the spirit of the car returned, and Candice acted as if nothing had happened.

'Joanna told me about this school, you know. She knows all about the best schools for all kinds of children.'

Odie perked up. He liked the thought of this. 'Is it in the Universe City?'

'What? No, it's a school. You can't go to Joanna's university.'

Odie disregarded this because Candice did not say 'Universe City' properly. It was as if she had misheard it and did not really know what it was. Odie realised that she did not share his idea of the Universe City, and he resolved not to let her in on it. It would be his secret. In this moment of privacy, he forgot about the mind-dreading and the vulnerability he had felt. He was a private being again, free once more to speculate about 'doing' and 'not doing' and the Universe City and all the peculiarities he had discovered about the world throughout his childhood so far.

PIP HIBBERT

Pip Hibbert is a female writer who grew up in Birmingham. With a background in fine art, Pip has illustrated many of her short stories. Fuelled by trying to see the funny side of everything, she writes about climate change, politics, and attempting to remain hopeful in a confusing world.

piphibbert@hotmail.com

The Frogs Are After Us
The first half of a short story

The frogs lived under a small tree next to the Asda car park. It was right off the A48 and not too far from Poundland, but they didn't know what that was. To them it wasn't a small tree, it was massive. Each morning, oily leaves circled the skies as the frogs nestled beneath, making the dirty land into a fortress of warmth and protection. They spent years searching for a sustainable location, flitting between small rivers with petrol-covered surfaces and marshy bogs crowded with fish and strange worms. When the ponds became claggy and the flies disappeared, they knew they had to become experimental with their survival. When they found this tree, anchored by the ever-growing carpark, next to its boggy grass and deliciously moist soil, they knew it was theirs. From there the frogs worked tirelessly to build a series of underground tunnels beneath its roots, all leading to one another.

The frogs knew what they were doing. They were generations of builders, each a little better at creating something from whatever they could find than the last. They had to be. Every tunnel in their fortress was different and led to other tiny rooms. Each room had enough space to fit all the frogs for whenever they decided to have a meeting or discuss the weather. One room, which we would call a kitchen, they called the Moth Hole. I would tell you more about the Moth Hole, but it might scare off any of your moth friends that are already wary of the tree and its ravenous inhabitants.

Each frog had their own room, which some of the younger frogs created even more tunnels from, and filled with found treasures like bottle caps, newspaper and AA batteries. The elder frogs allowed it so long as they kept the noise down, but they had a hard time enforcing this rule. They lived well amongst each other, sharing whatever food they could find, which, some days was very little, and taking turns guarding the tree's entrance whilst some left to survey the ground or hang out with the local squirrels, with whom they were a little more friendly than frogs should be with squirrels. Plans had been made to build upwards into the tree itself; even more rooms with opportunity to survey and collect information. But first they needed planning permission, something that was difficult to get past the board of owls. The tree itself was quite beautiful, but this mattered very little to the frogs. They didn't witness its swaying, its meditative stillness, the way its wooden fingers caressed the air. They had no time to look up, no time to let themselves know its beauty. For them, the tree provided a place to live, to watch the local wildlife and of course, to survey their greatest enemy: Asda.

Every Tuesday the frogs held a meeting in the sitting hole, to discuss Asda's latest advancements. As the sounds of the trucks leaving Asda's fortress rumbled around the tree, they charted any food they were able to steal from bins and any injuries sustained in their missions. To help them, they had drawn out a small map of the area. The frogs had a history of trying to learn from the people. They'd mimic their sayings, despite never really knowing the meaning, and decipher their names for certain things, which meant some words got lost in translation. The frogs would study pieces of litter, so that they could understand their written messages and attempt to write their own. They'd listen in on conversations amongst the Asda comrades so that they could piece together what some of their equipment was used for. Two younger frogs named GreenFace and OnlyOneEye, took to the car park when the sun went down only a couple of nights prior to the meeting. They gathered what information they could on Asda's movements.

'We saw one of the Asda members pushing a line of large baskets, with silver wheels that the humans use to carry their food in, sorry, what are they called again?' asked OnlyOneEye.

'Pushchairs,' said GreenFace, with the greatest of confidence.

'Thank you. Yes, we saw a young male leading a long line of pushchairs. His face was covered with lots of small red dots, which from further investigation is common amongst younger members of the Asda force.' said OnlyOneEye.

'Hmm, interesting, anything else?' asked SpotNeck.

The frogs had created a predominantly socialist society. However, they did have a leader: SpotNeck. SpotNeck was voted as leader after his heroic altercation with a large group of pigeons many years ago. He still had the peck marks to show for it. SpotNeck had long held a great interest in Asda's advances. Their vastness of land, their huge vehicles and enormous lights that attracted the moths. Sometimes the other frogs were concerned that SpotNeck had more of an obsession than a healthy want for vengeance. As OnlyOneEye spoke, SpotNeck was reclining in his usual position at the head of the table they'd made from sticks and the cardboard from a box of Quavers.

'As the young male was walking back toward the Asda infrastructure, an older male came out and shouted some profanities at the young male. Something about his hearing devices.'

'Intriguing. It's also useful to know that there are problems amongst the rankings. We can use this information to our advantage. Very good work, OnlyOneEye,' said SpotNeck.

OnlyOneEye grinned and then turned to GreenFace to subtly pinch his fleshy little body. GreenFace let out a high-pitched yelp but the other frogs ignored him. OnlyOneEye was pleased with himself. He knew how much SpotNeck wanted information on the enemy. And he would do anything to be the one to give it to him.

'Have there been any other sightings?' SpotNeck turned towards WartLegs, another elder and the only bullfrog of the group. He and SpotNeck had been friends for as long as they could remember. They respected each other, trusted each other and most importantly, believed in their little army.

'Not much, the sightings that the squirrels gave us proved to be false again – second time this month, but I believe they've got some kind of mutiny within their own scurry,' WartLegs said, plopping his large blobby fingers at the point on the map where the squirrels lived.

'Ha! Squirrels! I told them to start rationing the acorns. Every year there's a fight amongst them. Every year.' SpotNeck reclined to sit on his back legs. As he did, he gained an extra three chins and GreenFace tried to hold in a laugh.

'So that's the only information we have? The hearing devices? Damn it, our information on Asda has been running low lately. They must be getting wise to our espionage.' SpotNeck looked concerned.

'SpotNeck, I've been thinking,' WartLegs began, 'maybe Asda aren't doing what we think they're doing. We've had no reliable information in weeks, maybe we can relax.'

SpotNeck slammed his webbed hand onto their miniature table. 'Nonsense–', he seemed to immediately regret doing this as his hand became stuck when he tried to lift it back up.

'Nonsense! Nonsense – shit, can somebody...?'

OnlyOneEye hopped quickly over to help peel his fingers from the table.

'Thank you, yes, as I was saying! I will not have you derail this operation just because you're getting tired!' SpotNeck continued.

'I'm not *tired*, SpotNeck,' WartLegs exhaled, 'but we're wasting all our resources on a battle we're not even sure is real. Hell, we sent GreenFace out the other night to spy on the humans going into their fortress and he almost got mauled by a badger looking for food! A bloody badger! Last I'd heard they were all living by the park three days away.'

'It's all going down over there! I told you they'd start acting up! One of the robins told me that the biggest badgers were ambushed by a human, only five managed to escape,' said Keith.

Keith was the only member of the army who'd chosen his own name. He'd overheard some humans speaking many years ago and thought that using one of their names would make him sound cool and threatening. Keith didn't care much for the meetings, he kept quiet for most of them. He was an elderly frog, usually slumped in the corner and happy to keep it that way. In this particular meeting, he'd been messing with the hard lumps on his legs, not really listening because he was busy thinking about how many lovely moths they had in the Moth Hole.

'Oh, shut up Keith, we all know the human-badger massacres are a myth,' said WartLegs. He was getting tired of the conversation. Lately all it had been was Asda this and Asda that. WartLegs missed being outside and not on patrol. He missed the warm breeze, closing his eyes to feel the sun's generous heat on his back as he swam amongst the delicate flowers in the pond, as he'd done with his mother when he was not even a percentage of the size he was now. He missed a lot of things that he couldn't do anymore. Half of the ponds had been covered in concrete and there was never time for rest, always something to fear. Frankly, he wasn't sure how long he could live like this.

'Stop it! You're derailing the meeting!' shouted SpotNeck, with his head in his hands. He tried to lift his face but once again his hand became stuck, this time to his head.

'Shit! Again? Somebody– can you just–'

OnlyOneEye rushed over once more and peeled his hand from his face.

'You know what I think?' Keith perked up. He started picking at the cardboard on the sides of the table, something the others had told him to stop doing many, many times.

'Oh god, what now?' SpotNeck let out an audible exhale. '*Go on* then, if you have to.'

'I think we should be concentrating all our efforts on making the tree more sustainable for harsh weather. We know what the owls have been saying, all those fires. It's scary stuff.'

'Booooorrriiinnnngggg,' GreenFace shouted from the back. GreenFace was also getting quite distracted from the meeting. He was at the age where he wanted to be outside all the time. It had just become dark enough for all the late-night creatures to come out; he thrived off the feeling of stalking around in the black, perching behind pebbles and striking any little insect that idly let their guard down. He wanted the shivering leaves that rustled whenever the pigeons were nearby, to feel the power of his own body. He wanted a fight. Or better yet, a girlfriend.

'Yes, I agree, boring,' SpotNeck said, audibly irritated by Keith, 'now can we *please* get back to the meeting at hand?'

'But even the pigeons are worried,' said Keith, 'this is really serious you know–'

Just as Keith was about to make his case, SlimeHands came rushing in through one of the side tunnels, visibly out of breath. He'd been nominated to be the watch for the evening.

'Guys, guys...' he panted, 'I saw something.'

The other frogs turned to look at him. He wasn't an attractive frog. In fact, he was the worst looking frog they'd ever seen. SlimeHands was the last to join the group, never really explaining where he'd come from, but speaking tales of destruction, dogs with dead-bodied foxes and cars, hundreds and hundreds of cars. His eyes never quite met the others and sometimes they'd hear him screaming in his sleeping hole. The frogs had accepted him, nevertheless. SlimeHands' weirdness meant they were more than happy to let him be on watch as much as he wanted, which was a lot. This simultaneously meant that the frogs didn't have to listen to his terrible singing. Even the owls complained that they could hear him repeatedly attempting several Al Green covers in the middle of the night.

LILY HYLAND

Lily Hyland writes about floating clocks, court jesters and sentient dolls. In 2023 she was published in the Eggbox anthology *Earthly Conventions* and shortlisted for the Norwich Young Creative Awards. Her stories blend the everyday with the magical realist, speculative and experimental, exploring the effects of textuality on language and language's jurisdiction over perception.

lilyhyland2001@gmail.com

Iteration

A short, short story

With the rain came a blurring for Clara. The escalator's moving bars became fractured on her way up to the office, melting into a staircase on which she was already climbing, it seemed. Perspective warped light's careful brushstrokes, blurring until there was a clearing. Wide and bright, the space held no markers, only the next few steps and, slightly beyond them, a door. Checking her watch, Clara looked ahead again and, naturally enough, proceeded. She may still get there in time, somehow. She was here, after all. And she had been almost there. So 'Here' couldn't be all too far away, in whichever direction 'There' was. It seemed only reasonable to proceed. In another moment, quite separate from the last (it may have been the next) up went Clara. Up, up, up she climbed as the stairs slowly curved themselves to the left and the walls yawned inwards. That or she was tired. She was tired.

Clara wondered if where 'Here' was, was really what mattered. This was out of her pay grade, almost certainly. A temp could only earn so much, and she only really cared so much. This seemed as good a diversion from boredom as any. This wasn't real, anyhow, not really. Still, she would have to formulate an explanation upon arrival. The induction email hadn't been particularly clear. Perhaps she had got lost somewhere along the way. That'd do.

Up went Clara, again, forgetting the particulars of place and never once considering why she was there. It wasn't the most pressing concern. How was altogether more practical when it came to return. Climbing brought her forward, that is, in relation to where she had been. That much was clear. With each step, the next appeared; if she stopped, the stairs would slide, becoming a wooden escalator down, but never reverting to 'before'. She had tried. That should be considered enough.

Either the staircase was very long, or she was walking very slowly. As she climbed, all light dissipated except some that seemed to emanate faintly from her. Clara would have tried to test the reliability of this glowing, but, odd as it was, losing all light was not a risk she could take for the sake of curiosity. Things become, in the dark, she reminded herself. The unseen bred many a monster. She had heard stories. Was it Hydra or Cyclops that blundered in the shadows? As for the light, she hoped she hadn't become radioactive. That was a thing, right?

Reaching out she felt walls, covered in an embossed fabric. There were swirls and Clara imagined they would be maroon. The banister guided and she followed. Except that the banister had long since disappeared. The paper was brighter where it had been. Clara brushed the walls aside as she climbed. Velveteen waves patterned her fingertips. She traced them, counting her steps in the dim light until one wall met another and her eyes found a curtain barely ten centimeters in front of her. Folding the curtain outwards, she found wood, indented like the paper, and a cold, glinting doorknob.

Uncertain, she checked behind her, slipping back a few steps and ending at a 45-degree angle, fingers still clutching at the door. It was safer to proceed. She turned the doorknob. The lock clicked open. Then she left it a second, waiting. Nothing awful had happened. This must be right. Gently, Clara pushed at the door, careful not to surprise whatever might be behind it. Minotaurs were a worry in circumstances such as these. The door drifted, swinging silently onto carpet, carpet and light. Warm light. Clara stepped forward, almost tripping on the top step. There was a room. Not a large room, but someone had clearly thought it sufficient for the overall profusion of stuff it contained. The walls were, indeed, maroon. The carpet was too, marked by golden, twirling bursts across the floor. There was a matching chaise longue and many, many cushions. Two rows of square windows spread, stacked one over the other, virtually continuous around the walls, leaving just enough space for significant curtains and a pelmet atop each one. The air floated with dust. Her nostrils clenched.

Clara rubbed her nose and tried not to smell the used oxygen. She thought to look at the fourth wall, then. It was behind her now, as she wandered towards the chaise longue. There were others. Three, to be precise. Women of varied ages, scurrying in front of the wall with no windows. No, not varied, varying. As she sat, the women creased and un-creased themselves, folding in and out of their features. They moved with a faint ticking, taking time to segment each movement: trace intention to action and back again, and back again, and back again. But this wasn't a film, Clara reminded herself: this was odd. The movement constituted a lulling, repeating across the wall, almost choreographed. Only almost. It was fine. Strange things were why the news existed. Strange things happened every day. This was just in front of her. No need to worry, there was almost always an explanation for these things. Damp cloth ectoplasm or Pepper's ghost, that sort of thing. Was it April 1st? It might be April 1st.

Each figure held a long paint brush; spindling away from fingers, the bristles frayed by the wall. Everything could be explained, given proper context. Sound dampened into chintz. The ticking faded, or she ignored it, and the womens' movements were only subject to the canvas' resistance. A scene was stretching itself there. All green and purple. From broad strokes a seascape appeared, rippling amongst horse hairs and shifting damply away from each dab. It grew realer, so real that, at each juncture, Clara was sure it had become what it was until a new layer was added and she became aware of the blur before. Realer, Clara wondered, not more real. Real had been superseded by some time now, though she wasn't quite sure how much. To what extent did realness extend, and could extent be extended? She was thinking too much. Maybe it was her mind that was whirring.

A woman had turned. A floor length skirt obscured her steps such that she seemed to float towards Clara. Seemed, Clara reminded herself. She had to be careful here. The woman brought a smile with her.

'Good afternoon.'

'Where are we?' asked Clara

'I am writing to inform you...' The woman glitched. Now she wore glasses.

'Hello?'

'I am writing to let you know...' The glasses were replaced with a tie.

'Just a reminder that there will be a staff meeting at four pm.

./ a compulsory staff meeting at four pm' She paused.

'Tea provided'

'Where?' asked Clara. 'Here?' She took a breath, 'and, for the record, where is here?' She was getting bold now. Dial it back, she instructed herself, rewind. Stop asking silly questions. The woman walked away. As she did so, Clara learned that her name was Rachel. She left with best regards. That was something, considering.

 Clara composed herself. The meeting must be soon, by now. She could ask all her questions then. It would be fine. She knew someone. She knew Rachel.

 Now that she was alone, though, the boredom began boring channels in her mind. The painting was still reeling her in and weirding her out and the windows were still. This vertigo was not reduced by lying down, so Clara stared into the darkness behind her eyelids in hopes of lessening the prevalence of a needless third dimension. Imitation reality, like fur, was softer and more tempting than the original, here.

'Where are we?' asked Clara.

'In time, my dear, in time,' a voice responded. 'Or now?'

'Another now'

Curiosity, though, is an inevitable byproduct of boredom. It opened Clara's eyes again much sooner than was either planned or convenient. The sense of this other floated away and she was alone again. Clara sat, clutching at the nearby windowsill. Opposing reflex, she stifled the roaring of a swallowed yawn, though she suspected carpet and curtains would have obliged just as well. Her eyes blurred.

 The window was the closest diversion.

 The glass reached upwards far further than Clara's neck could accommodate. Squirming slightly, she wriggled into a scrunched-up position, holding her knees close, tipping to press her nose against the glass. There was a constellation in the window, falling downwards into tiny oblongs with thread winding between them. It looked like a party. There were tiny people, clothed in bright fabric, running, playing tag with teams following them. Maybe these were new rules. Maybe it was opposite day. There were bursts, trick birthday candles popping up and down like whack-a-mole and Clara imagined there was music and dancing, and it wasn't fair to be up here all alone with the three facing the wall.

 She could see two panes in the glass and her reflection, if she zoomed out a little. Where the outside was and the constellation in the window began was ill-defined, pushing her into a game of hide and seek with the outside, unsure if she could find or had found it or, maybe those people were stuck in the window. She wasn't jealous anymore. Wide eyes couldn't compensate for the perspective of a kaleidoscope. The line of realer was unreeling and leaving her straining her eyes into an in-between unwilling to present itself.

Somebody behind her said something about cake or maybe bread. She liked brioche. Maybe it would come with the tea. As the others arrived they formed a semi-circle, each floating to a point and setting themselves there. Rachel's smile had stayed on that bit too long and had slipped, as though Blu-Tacked on and subjected to a hairdryer.

A very old child entered the frame, swathed in a golden threaded dress. Light warped surrounding it and refracted around the room. 'Clotho will be taking minutes', she said. 'And since it's Lachesis' day off, I will be chairing the meeting today'
'Where are we?' asked Clara, again. 'Is now the time?'
'No, the time is now and here is time. It is not in the itinerary.'
'What?'
'You shall join us for tea.'
'And then?'
'You shall join us for tea.'
'And then?'
'You shall join us for tea.'
'Who are you?'
'The outfit doesn't make the monk?'
'What, then?'
The lock snapped on the indented door. No one looked up. Clara had heard these names before, in a book, maybe.
'Are you Atropos?'
'No.'
'Where is Atropos? It is Atropos, isn't it?'
'Doesn't start till next week.'
'Where are we?'
'In time, my dear, like I said'
'Was that you?'
'Yes.'
Clara's mouth was dry. The words echoed in the absorbing room.

Her watch had broken. There was nothing to be done. Now might as well be then, and here was probably there, all things considered. As the women returned to their posts by the wall, Clara sat again. The door had locked but was ajar. No matter. Staring up she could see a face ticking its way around, staring straight back at her. Plain to see. Clara swayed back and forth, pendulumic. Some place, she thought. Some time. This had been, or would be, quite a day. This was the day. Today would become tomorrow, or already had.

Small spiders peppered the ceiling as though a nest had recently detonated across it. She made sure not to blink, squinting to keep at least one eye on the arachnid glut. Somehow it didn't particularly concern her. Novelty was no longer new. Clara noticed now that the walls were tearing, peeling, as though the paper had power to bring the wall down with it. All in the blink of an eye. Edges of light inched their way inside and Clara realised just how deprived she had been. Until then, she had thought it was bright enough. Now her eyes were streaming.

ROSEENA VERONIKA HUSSAIN

Roseena Veronika Hussain is a writer living in London. She is currently interested in exploring themes of impermanence, inheritance and extinction. ARTEFACT/S is her first novel.

roseena.veronika.hussain@gmail.com

Artefact/s

The opening of a novel

The afternoon had lost itself to evening, and the working week was done. Aaraa was the last to leave the archives, her footsteps echoing through the museum's empty halls. Only the security guard was left behind. He unlocked the door and wished her a good weekend.

Her tram was turning the corner, but she decided to walk instead. The air was cold and still; the leaves above turned copper and bronze. She made her way to Café Süssler by way of Volksgarten. When she arrived, she was disappointed to see that the dining area wasn't full. She took her seat under the smallest chandelier and waited for her sister, Ambreen, to arrive.

The staff moved swiftly between tables, their stiff shirts and black ties contrasting the diners' casual attire, although the younger waiters now wore smart black trainers instead of formal black shoes. That morning's broadsheets were no longer stretched taut in their bamboo frames; instead, their pages were smudged, and their edges curled.

Order for me, Ambreen texted, *I'm ten minutes away.*

Aaraa signalled to Ulrich that she was ready. He swooped past, chin held high, looking down through glasses worn low on his nose and held by a string. He took payment from a customer, the order from another, cleared dishes to the kitchen, and returned with three balanced plates before approaching her with a nod. She chose soup for her and her sister to start, one with frittaten, the other with knödel. For mains she ordered the usual frankfurters with extra mustard and horseradish for Ambreen, and schnitzel with yellow potatoes and a side of cucumber salad for herself. Unsure if they would drink, she ordered a bottle of sparkling water instead.

When Ambreen arrived, she was breathless. The soup was brought to the table.

'I'm so sorry. Eesa wouldn't go to bed, then I missed the U-Bahn and—'

'Relax,' Aaraa said. 'You're not late, not really.'

'Aren't I?'

'If I plan that you'll always be late, then you're basically on time.'

'I'm not always late, am I?'

'We could meet somewhere closer to you?' Aaraa said.

'You want to stop coming here?'

'Yes,' Aaraa said. 'The answer is always yes.'

'But it's tradition!' said Ambreen.

'OK, calm down. Your soup is getting cold.'

Ambreen began to eat, but the worried expression did not leave her face.

'And stop frowning so much,' Aaraa said. 'You'll get permanent lines.'

Ambreen widened her eyes and smoothed her forehead, straightening her posture as she did. 'I spoke to Pakistan yesterday. Uncle Halif is ill again. He said he has a strong feeling he won't make it into the new year.'

'He's been saying that for decades,' Aaraa said.

'I know. But when he finally does go, all three brothers will be gone.'

'Let's not forget the three sisters then.'

Ambreen broke apart a piece of knödel with the side of her spoon. Then she looked around the café, her gaze settling on a window with a view to the street outside. Aaraa observed her sister's face. Having a child had aged her. Not with wrinkles so much, but with a deep tiredness, a sallowness to the skin, the eyes betraying a mind always racing away from itself towards the needs of another. She had seen some parents recover a certain brightness after their child was no longer very young. She hoped this would also be true for Ambreen. Seeing her sister depleted somehow felt worse than when she looked at her own reflection and saw something of the same.

Are you drinking tonight?' Ambreen said.

'If you are.'

Ambreen ordered two glasses of white wine from Ulrich as he was passing.

'Oh, and Parveen wants to visit with her family. She asked if they could stay with you?'

'What did you tell her?' Aaraa said.

'You know what they're like. They probably won't actually come.'

Aaraa sighed. 'Sometimes I wish I had a studio apartment.'

'You don't want to move, do you?' Ambreen looked startled. 'Please never leave it. Sorry, I know I've no right to ask that of you.'

'It's not just mine,' Aaraa said. 'It's ours.'

Ambreen shook her head. 'You looked after him.'

'You had Eesa.'

Ambreen frowned. 'Just tell me if you're not happy there, OK?'

'We can't let it go,' Aaraa said. 'No one gives up a rent-controlled apartment. Did I tell you a couple just moved in? They're paying four times as much for half the space.'

'I don't know how you put up with the gossip.'

'I might have started that one,' Aaraa said. 'Don't look at me like that. It's not like I asked them. Besides, they think they got a bargain.'

'It will be in ten years.'

Aaraa thought for a moment. 'Isn't it strange to think Eesa could end up living there one day?'

'I really don't want him to grow into a man,' Ambreen said.

The wine arrived with their mains. Aaraa hadn't realised how hungry she was and tried to remember if she'd eaten lunch.

'Do you know what Eesa said after his birthday?' The frown had reappeared on Ambreen's face. 'He looked at me and said, "Mama, every year I get a birthday. I get presents and a cake with a candle. I am five and my candles were five. Next year I'll be six with six candles. Then I'll be seven with seven candles and eight and nine and ten. And every year I'll get a new cake with new candles, but every year is the same." And honestly, I didn't know what to say.'

'To grasp that at five is, well, it's unusual, right?'

'I'm…not sure.'

Aaraa thought for a moment. 'Maybe he's just stating a fact, and we're the ones interpreting it as a crisis.'

Ambreen frowned. 'I did think that, but it was the *way* he said it.'

'Sad?'

'Kind of.'

Aaraa stabbed at her salad until she pierced the few remaining cucumber slices onto her fork. Pieces of dill floated in the leftover dressing, the oil shimmering against the vinegar.

'Some children do see more clearly than adults,' Aaraa said. 'Lars once told me that when he was four, he turned to his mother and said, "Why do people bother talking if they only want to talk about themselves?" I mean…what do you do with a child like that?'

'Oh, God,' Ambreen said. 'You don't think Eesa is like Lars, do you?'

'No, they're nothing alike.'

Ambreen hesitated. 'How often do you speak to him?'

'As much as we both want.'

'You do know that his marriage is in crisis?'

Aaraa looked away. 'Isn't everyone's?'

'Mama's and Baba's wasn't.'

'That we knew of.'

Ambreen pinched her lips together. 'Seren is having a really hard time with him.'

'She just needs to leave—'

'They're *married*, Aaraa.'

'I was *saying*, she needs to leave him to himself a bit more. Lars wants whatever is out of reach.'

'Well,' Ambreen said, 'some of us would find that impossible to do.'

Aaraa leant back and looked into the eye of the chandelier. A cobweb draped the crystal; a few fruit flies remained stuck within its thread. The evening rush was over. Aaraa finished her wine.

'Do you think Baba would judge us for drinking here?' Ambreen whispered.

'I really don't think he'd care,' Aaraa said. 'But I'm judging you for those sausages.'

'I know.' Ambreen sighed. 'Me too.'

They chose another glass of wine over coffee and dessert, lingering over their drinks until all the other diners had left. Aaraa signalled to Ulrich; he came straight away. After taking payment, he removed their empty glasses and said goodbye.

They had known Ulrich since they were children. It was always the same between them. They spoke only the necessary words. Except for that one time, all those years ago, when their father had taken them to dine without their mother for the first time. Ulrich had offered his condolences, and Ambreen had cried. Then he'd brought them three slices of marbled gugelhupf for which he'd refused to let them pay. They knew almost nothing about him, and yet they'd watched him grow old.

The streets were quiet; an almost full moon flitted between the apartment rows. Aaraa got back just after midnight and took the lift to the third floor. She searched for the keys in her bag, thinking she would make a camomile tea and read before bed. But as she was about to turn the lock, she noticed there was no door number. She pulled the key out, horrified she was trying to enter the wrong home. She listened for signs she had woken someone and was relieved to hear none. But it *was* her apartment. This was her door. She squinted and tried to focus. The brass number eleven had been unscrewed, but its outline stood out against the faded wood, the shadowed shape like two people walking, one behind the other, each body pierced with a little screw heart.

She put the key back in and slowly tried the lock. It unbolted as she turned. Using the second key as quietly as she could, she pushed the front door open. She pressed the switch a few times, but no light came on. A mix of street and moonlight leaked its way in to meet her. As her pupils adjusted, she saw there was nothing in the hall. The telephone table no longer stood in the corner. Her coats and shoes had vanished. The mirror was missing from the wall.

Her eyes darted through the open double doors into the main living room. The furniture, the rugs, the books on the shelves, the curtains, and the lampshades – everything had disappeared. Even the lightbulbs were gone. There was nothing left scattered on the floor, no broken glass or damage done. She stood quite still, swallowing the urge to scream. Then she shut the front door and ran down the spiral stairwell to the ground floor. There had been no sound of movement within, but she could not help imagining someone lurking unseen in the dark, their silent body pressed flat against a wall.

She crept her way to the inner courtyard and looked up at her kitchen window; it remained dark and unmoving. Dim light shone from Herr Strom's apartment, but he, along with the rest of their neighbours, were most likely already asleep. She dialled without thinking, hanging up before the first ring. Taking a deep breath, she went back inside, sat down on the stairs, and called the police.

It was almost two a.m. when she heard a car pulling up and doors slamming shut. She hurried to the front entrance and opened it. The male officer lowered his finger from the unpressed buzzer. Although both he and the female officer spoke at a normal volume, in the stillness of night, their voices sounded raised. Aaraa whispered answers to their questions as she led them upstairs.

She unlocked the apartment and waited in the hallway until they shouted to her that no one was there. The officers' voices rang hollow in the unfilled rooms.

She followed them as they inspected the windows, their torches revealing sealed frames and glass intact. They opened all the adjoining doors as they moved through the space; the herringbone parquet floor flowed uninterrupted. Aaraa had the urge to race from one end of the apartment to the other as she had done when she was small. Instead, she walked calmly to the living room window. The pavement below was iced white with frost. In the sky, the moon floated behind wisps of cloud. She untangled her charger from her bag and plugged it in. With no choice but to lay her mobile to rest on the floor, the torch's glare bleached the wall like a tiny, fierce sun.

DAWN JELLEY

Dawn Jelley is a journalist from Ingatestone, Essex. Her debut novel, *The Suffolk Merman,* was shortlisted for the Adventures in Fiction Spotlight First Novel Award 2024 and longlisted for the Lucy Cavendish Fiction Prize 2024. It tells the story of a 12th century merman imprisoned at Orford Castle.

dawnjelley@gmail.com
dawnjelley.co.uk

The Suffolk Merman

An extract from a novel

Amiria lay awake in her cot most of the night, the straw of the mattress rustling with her every turn. Outside the castle walls, the Morimaru Sea whispered its constant presence, like the rattle of a timbrel with its accompaniment of songbirds from the marshes.

When the first cockerel crowed, Amiria could not rest a moment longer. Key or no key, she felt compelled to go down to the undercroft. What if the prisoner now expected her? She would whisper through the door, tell him she had not abandoned him, would come another night.

The castle was coming to life as she made her way downstairs. Amiria withdrew into the stairwells and doorways, as the odd servant passed to their morning duties, aware of the echo of her every movement, the swish of her heavy riding mantle, and the brush of her kidskin slippers on the stone floor. The new daylight aided her descent as she traced the stonework of the newel with her hand. She had become attuned to the irregularities of the steps just as her mare Frost instinctively navigated dips, cracks, and turns on a well-trodden path.

When she reached the entrance to the undercroft, Amiria found the wooden door swinging on its hinges. The air felt different – lighter and fresher than the intense damp that had hung there those nights before. She could breathe uninhibitedly, and her limbs moved with ease. In the trickle of light, she saw that the bench where he slept was bare, the stone floor swept and sprinkled with fresh reeds. Her worst fears were confirmed. The prisoner had gone; manacles and chains and all. De Glanville had disposed of him under the cover of night.

Amiria ran back up the castle stairs; its twists and turns like a warren. By the time the main hall opened out in front of her, she was breathless and craved the fresh morning air. Tiptoeing past the dozing guardsman, she slipped out of the inner keep and across the marshalsea to the castle entrance.

'Let me out at once! Queen Eleanor of Aquitaine commands it!'

The watchman jolted out of his sleep. He did not argue at the queen's name, or the sight of Amiria in her fine cloak, and swung open the gate to the high-walled bridge which led her across the outer ditch.

Free at last, she felt an insatiable urge to run towards the sea, leaving the castle well behind her. Only when she was some distance away did she stop and look back at its bastions, which resembled a resting dragon basking with the rosy crest of sunrise behind it.

As Amiria neared the Morimaru, the marshland became wilder; the waves and yelp of seabirds louder. She waded through the reeds and wildflowers that flattened and tangled underfoot. Bedstraw, chickweed, and marigolds bristled to and fro in the sea breeze, brushed against the linen weave of her skirt and the wool of her mantle. Pollen specks danced before her in the pale light and tickled her nose.

The undergrowth parted and a hare appeared in Amiria's path. It sat on its hinged back legs and twitched a velvet ear in her direction; then lolloped off deep into the marsh flowers. She had only ever seen such a creature stuffed and skinned on a banquet table and was taken aback by the sheen of its flecked coat, the blink of its timid yellow eyes.

On the spot where the hare had crouched was the start of a sandy path running towards the beach. Amiria was surprised to see some rut marks and followed the tracks until she came to the dunes. In the middle of the rolling mounds, she found a cart with two wooden wheels joined as precariously as wool spindles to a single axle. It had been tipped onto its shaft and was unladen, apart from a bed of straw and remnants of sackcloth. An ox grazed on a tuft of meadow grass alongside, unharnessed and tied loosely to the frame with a rope halter.

The sand gave way under Amiria's feet as she clambered to the top of the dunes and looked out over the grey sea. The water triggered a childhood memory – the day she did not drown. A push from one of her brothers and she had tumbled into the murky pond. The heavy drag of her gown, the stagnant water rushing into her throat and nostrils; bleared faces and muted laughter from above. The green water enclosing around her small body as it bumped against the rocky bottom with a force, then floundered and clutched at reeds and stems. She felt a chill seep through her, and swept her mantle around her body.

A breeze carrying the voices of men interrupted her thoughts. Four guards stood along the foreshore; cloaks beating in the wind like sails, flashes of red against the leaden Morimaru. They were close enough to see that De Glanville was not among them. His absence accounted for the easy behaviour of the young men, who laughed and pushed each other into the surf. Something held their attention out at sea. From her raised position, Amiria spotted a couple of fishing boats that bobbed on the waves, just like the royal galley that had brought her across the Narrow Sea to England. She could make out their crews, who held onto their nets, awaiting a catch.

'Over there!' One of the guards pointed to the water. The men on the boats moved from port to starboard, while their oarsmen paddled hard against the waves, dipping and turning the bows.

'What's she doin' up there?' One of the boatmen spotted Amiria and pointed in her direction.

A guard came marching towards her, fumbling with the hilt of his dagger, while the others returned their attentions to the water.

The guard lowered his eyes to his boots, bowing awkwardly. 'I do beg your pardon, my lady, but what are you doing here at this hour?'

Amiria had been recognised, but the guard was a subordinate, not much older than Henry the Young King, and posed no threat.

'What are *you* doing here at this hour?' said Amiria. 'And what is it that occupies you in the water?'

'That isn't any of your concern, my lady. It's not the time for you to be wandering down here alone. Let me escort you back to the castle—'

'Tell me at once, or I'll report your exploits to the governor,' said Amiria with the emboldened tone that she had heard the queen use with men.

'Ee's down 'ere!' shouted one of the boatmen, hanging over the bow of his boat.

Amiria strode past the guard onto the beach. She looked out over the water, where patches of morning mist settled, ready to be burnt off by the sun. A spume of white frothed like a cooking pot over the leaden water. It was as if the sea was about to burst.

And then, a man leaped out of the water and turned his arc of body in the air. A school of airborne silver fish swarmed around him like flies and scattered as he dived in again, disappearing back into the grey expanse, leaving rainbows dancing in sea spray in his wake. Was this an apparition or dream? Amiria questioned her wits, for she lacked sleep, and the hour was ungodly.

The guards shouted in excitement, and the boatmen rowed after him.

Amiria stumbled towards the water's edge, eyes fixed on the skyline, the wet shingle hissing under her footsteps. The man appeared again above the surface, flicking his legs behind him with a dancer's grace, so streamlined that they appeared joined as one muscular limb, like a fluke or a tail. Then he disappeared again without so much as a splash.

She studied the churn of the waves, hoping to get another glimpse of him, to reaffirm his existence. De Glanville's drunken ramblings at the banquet came back to her. *From the sea. The prisoner hails from the sea*, he had slurred over his mead. She had heard tales of sea monsters in the north: giant serpents crushing hulls like bones, sirens bewitching seafarers and leading fleets into deep mists never to return, ocean beasts that spouted water like fountains from their tusked heads. In court, travellers spoke of giant underwater shadows escorting their galleys, and limbless sea dogs basking on rocks and barking at the sun. She had dismissed all these stories as idle superstitions. Now, with her own eyes, she had just seen a man that swam like a fish. Could he even be the *merman* she had heard mention of?

The boatmen searched the surface while herring gulls circled in low, lured by the scattering fish, their wings flapping hard like heraldic flags. The guards pointed and shouted from the foreshore.

Further out at sea, the prisoner emerged again. He twisted and turned mid-air above the waves, with the stealth of an archer's bow. The queen employed all manner of acrobats and contortionists in her court; she was drawn to the curious, the *outré*, but Amiria had never seen anything – anyone – like this. She felt enraptured and fearful all at once, and, turning away from the spectacle, followed the tideline until she was a safe distance away. The guards – who seemed to have long forgotten her in their excitement – ran into the shallows, while the oarsmen turned the vessels to where the prisoner had been.

As Amiria stood and watched the disarray, she did not notice the wave encroaching across the shingle. It pushed its frothy fingers forward, then surged around Amiria's ankles, claiming the hem of her skirts, dragging her onto her knees. As the force of the water pulled her towards the sea and the shingle slipped away beneath her, one of the guards ran towards her across the beach. He helped her up by the arm and she struggled to her feet, pulling the damp weight of her gown over her shins.

'Thank you,' she gasped.

The guard's attentions were fixed on the shallows behind her. 'Get back to the dunes, my lady. Now!' he said.

There, in front of her, waist-deep in the water, stood the prisoner. He surveyed the land and the castle on its mound. The dark eyes that observed her in the cell were pools of iron gall ink in the daylight. And his face was strangely ageless, his chin and cheekbones strong and prominent, the flesh hollowed and weak. His angular shoulders and chest emerged as he rose out of the sea towards her; the bars of his ribs curved visibly under his flesh, rising and falling like gills. Away from the dark of the undercroft, his wet hair looked silvery white, and his beard trailed like Neptune or Poseidon, woven with seaweed and kelp. He walked in the shallows on two muscular legs, a castaway arriving on foreign soil. Amiria was mesmerised most of all by his flesh. Skimming her eyes across his groin, the skin on his legs looked as green-grey as the sea, and seemed to be covered in swatches of scales like chainmail, which faded in the morning light. As the waves withdrew from the shingle, she saw his large feet, which looked cumbersome compared to the rest of him. Small crabs clung onto them, then scampered off into holes between the stones. He stood taller than any man she had ever met; he would certainly dwarf the king, even the imposing figure of De Glanville.

'Come, my lady, you must return now.' The guard gestured towards the castle.

Disorientated, Amiria staggered back towards the dunes, glancing over her shoulder as the guards splashed ankle-deep into the shallows.

The prisoner offered them his wrists.

ALEXANDER KOMLOSI

Alexander Komlosi, originally from New York City, has worked as an actor, researcher, and teacher internationally. He studied political theory and performance at Bates College (BA) and authorial acting at the Academy of Performing Arts in Prague (MgA. and Ph.D.). He's looking forward to writing till the end of his days.

alexanderkomlosi.name
alex@alexanderkomlosi.name

The Dukes of Canal Street
An extract from the novel

NEW YORK CITY
July 28, 1987

Bernie's smiling contentedly behind the cash register as he surveys his store. 'Canal Street is where I run my bakery, Danny. Instead of flour and yeast, for me it's plastic and people. Instead of the whirl of a whisk, it's the padding of customers' feet, acrylic's smooth feel and its gorgeous gloss. It's the flurry of people's want to reflect, sparkle, and bend light. To sculpt the world in the material of the future. And what do I get out of all my baking, Danny?'

'Dough.'

'There you go, Danny. You're a smart kid. Yeah, gobs of dough.'

He lifts his pack of cigarettes off the counter. He smokes Pall Mall's when he's not sucking on Cubans. He taps out a cigarette, places it between his lips, flicks his brass Zippo. He pulls till the cherry burns red and glances down at me.

'You know what makes a business bustle, Danny?'

Leaning against the side of the pay counter, I take a long look around Bernie's store. It isn't the most humongous place. You can do a laid-back loop round the store in a minute — if you aren't browsing, that is. There are two customers, one in each aisle. A young lady and an old man. Not a huge crowd. Then again, it's Saturday morning. Bernie's open on Shabbos. Adam's family isn't very religious – the requisite seder and bar mitzvah; Adam just had his.

The young lady's got blue hair, except for her bangs, which are blonde. Her blue eyeliner fades into an intense eyeshadow — also blue — that reaches all the way up to her eyebrows. It's kind of Cindy Lauper-ish. She's wearing a ripped jean jacket and jean skirt. Safety pins are hanging from everything on her body, including her ears. A couple of girls in high school dress like that. Her get-up isn't so pretty, but her face, at least from this distance, is kind of cute.

She's standing in front of the shelves of wall-to-wall drawers full of translucent cubes, spheres, blocks, and cabochons. I like pulling out those drawers and playing around with them too. They're right out of some old movie, like *Superman* (kryptonite) or *Tron* (those weird pyramids). She seems to be into spheres because she keeps holding different sizes up to the fluorescent lights. She's been turning one back and forth in her hand like she's trying to see the future in a magic ball.

The old man's been in the store for a while already, in no apparent rush, like most old people usually aren't. His grey hair is slicked across and back like President

Reagan's. Mario, Bernie's store assistant, is helping the man roll and unroll different acrylic sheets. The rolls, about a yard wide each, run the length of the other wall of the store, from floor to ceiling. Mario's already shown the guy a blue one with cloudlike swirls, a silver one with spots that glitter like rainbows, and a plain matte black one. I get this funny picture in my head that they're trying to choose the right toilet paper for a filthy rich giant. It makes me laugh on the inside. The old man raises his arm and starts stroking the smooth surface of a glittering yellow toilet paper sheet. Mario mumbles something, but he's too far away for me to hear. I look back up at Bernie.

'Does business run on shiny stuff?'

'Yeah, shine is good for business, for sure, Danny. And my goods are sweet and shiny, aren't they?'

'Yeah, cool too.'

'Thanks, Danny.'

Bernie takes a drag of his cigarette, blows out a couple of smoke rings, and clears his throat.

'But the fuel, the real fuel of business, you know what that is?'

My toes tingle. Bernie's about to let me in on the secret of his business after all these years of me and Adam coming here. He trusts me, unlike my dad who's always keeping secrets from me.

I put my hands in my pockets. My right one bumps into something hard: a Swiss Army knife, the one Adam and I share. I can feel the round twirly bits of the corkscrew on the side. Is Adam's still in the bathroom? I peek behind me. The door's still closed. Maybe his butt's stuck in the seat.

'Don't know, Bernie. Do TV commercials keep a business running?'

Bernie shakes his head and taps his cigarette into the empty salted peanut can next to the register.

'Business runs on want and need, Danny. You *want* it, *you* don't have it, but *I* do. You *need* it, *you* don't have it, but *I* do. Personally, I prefer to rely on want, since it tends to be less desperate than need.'

What do I want? Comic books, a mountain bike, a lizard. Maybe to feel a girl's boob. But do I need any of that?

'And if want's ever desperate, it means that want is the manifestation of a hidden need.'

Sounds like something my mom would say.

Bernie coughs in a chesty kind of way, smooths his thinning dark brown hair. With the cigarette cherry, he points straight ahead. He leans down to me and speaks in a private voice.

'You see the skinny young girl with the blue hair? She's gotta be an art student. Probably at Cooper Union. Been here once before. Last time, she bought an acrylic sheet of orange and brown zigzags and a bag of assorted color cabochons. Took her forever to choose it. Thought she'd start spreading her roots and grow into the floor.'

I shift my feet a bit.

'See the way she's eyeing that violet pyramid? Holding it up to the light coming through the store window? She wants it, probably for some strange sculpture, or to hang from a thread above her kitchen table for her next trip. But you know what, Danny? That pyramid is mine. Mine. And when I put that pyramid on that shelf in my store, along with all those blocks, cabochons, rods, and spheres, Danny, you know what I'm doing? I'm offering it all to her. From me to her. *Would you like that, Miss?* I'm offering nicely and gently. Not like those guys out on Canal with their rickety tables covered with knock-off Casios and Rolexes, hawking their shlock to poor schmucks from Jersey. Now, I've got nothing against that those kinds of hustles, Danny. Hear me on that. Those are their goods and their style. But my style is different. It's classy. In the safe confines of these brick walls, under the protection of that cast iron roof, I'm offering shiny and smooth, opaque or translucent, round or pointy casts of creativity, along with the glue to keep it all together. I'm offering miracles of modernity. I'm offering plastic possibility. And that student is wanting what I'm offering, isn't she? Why else would she be in my store? That pyramid, it's almost hers, right? But no, no, not just yet. Even though she's caressing it softly between her forefinger and thumb now, look, weighing it in the palm of her hand, wondering if she should spend her beer money on it, it's still mine. Will her want win out? It won't be hers until she brings it up here and the register's rung. Lookie here, Danny...here she comes. She's got a nice little handful of my pretty plastic. She's accepted my offer. She wants, like we all do. She's going to make me some fine dough.'

Bernie straightens himself up, takes a deep drag of his cigarette, and exhales towards the ceiling. The smoke swirls in the currents of cold air pumped by the groaning air conditioner perched above the store's back door. It's like the smog I sometimes see over the East River from my bedroom window when I'm looking down towards my dad's place on Lex. As the student-lady walks towards us, Bernie puts his hand on my shoulder.

'Danny, why don't you stand behind the counter and ring her up? Get a feel for the joys of running my kind of bakery.'

'Really? Me?'

I turn round to the bathroom.

'Ah, don't worry about Adam. Besides, he'll be in there another decade.'

I can't help but laugh.

'Alright, I'll give it a try.'

'There you go. Stand behind the register.'

Bernie steps aside just as the young lady walks up to the counter. At the same time, there's a loud door screech behind us, then Adam's voice rings out.

'Dad!'

Adam's standing with his hand on the worn brass doorknob of the wide-open bathroom door. He's staring at me standing behind the register.

'Is Danny going to ring that lady up? How come he gets to ring her up, and I don't?'

A poop smell wafts towards us from the toilet behind him. He's left the lid up. I hope he's flushed. Bernie turns towards Adam and says softly:

'Son, first of all, please close the door behind you.'

Even after he's shut it, it still smells like toilet.

'Thank you. Now Addy, let Danny give it a go. You can ring up the next customer.'

Adam's eyes go all squinty. It's as if he's trying to aim laser beams into Bernie's forehead.

'No!'

Adam's extremely intense in his responses. It's like there's no time or space in his brain for a thought to appear before the lizard part kicks in. He makes me act like that too sometimes. It's contagious.

'I'm going to the warehouse. Me and Danny've got stuff to do back there. Danny, come.'

Before either Bernie or I can say anything, Adam spins round to the back door, grabs the doorknob, turns it hard, and smashes against the metal door with his shoulder. A cloud of hot, humid, garbagy smelling air blasts its way into the store. Adam turns back around to me.

'You got the Swiss?'

'Yeah,' I reply.

Adam nods and stomps out into Lispenard. I can't help but feel sorry for him.

Bernie, the young student lady, and me stand there listening to the air conditioner humming. It's a reassuring message: everything'll be cool again soon. The regular smell of the store – ashtray mixed with plastic – is also soothing. Bernie breaks the silence.

'My apologies, Miss. Shall we ring you up?'

It's no big deal really. You just punch plastic buttons with numbers on them. Of course, you've got to remember to hit the 'sales tax' button before you hit 'total.' You don't hit the 'sales tax' button every time – Bernie tells me after the skinny lady walks away. *It depends*, he said. He didn't say what it depends on though.

'Good work, Danny.'

He pats me on the back as the front door shuts with a ring.

'Thanks.'

Feels like I've learned how to bake a bit, Bernie style. He lights another Pall Mall with his Zippo.

'Enough baking for you today. Why don't you run across to the warehouse and play with Adam, okay?'

I nod my head and start to turn toward the back door.

'And Danny?'

Bernie scratches behind his ear with his non-cigarette hand. His shoulders are hunched. He looks tired. It's almost like he's shrunk a bit.

'Yeah, Bernie?'

'Make sure Adam's alright, will you?'

'Sure.'

I'm used to his parents telling me that. His mom said the same thing to me last week when Adam was upset about having to switch to a new school again.

'And tell him that it's his turn to ring up a customer, alright?'

'Sure, Bernie, sure.'

'Great. I'm going to help that old man figure out what he wants. Mario's a good baker, but he's no pastry chef. You run along now.'

Bernie leaves me alone facing the back door of his store. I stick my hands in my pockets. That's when I realize that Adam never said what we needed the knife for.

TOM LAKE

Tom Lake is a writer from Stoke-on-Trent, currently based in London. He holds an MA in Modern & Contemporary Literature from Goldsmiths, University of London. This is an excerpt from an epistolary novel in progress.

thomas.a.lake@gmail.com
Social media: tomlake1

The Lover

An extract from a novel

¶ What was I like in school? Do you also remember my silence? I did some things to make up for it. I have friends all over the world. I have things to say about the things that I see. I have candles for when I'm alone. But some things are the same. I let people go, drift away, especially if I don't think they're going to be around forever. What was it about you that was different? Do you remember talking on instant messenger every evening? Do you remember sending me the *Sunscreen Speech Song*? I remember rushing through dinner so that I could dial up the internet and say hello to you. You would tell me about the arguments between your parents and your sister and I would listen whilst playing your songs.

I'm at work on a break in the coffee shop. The rain just made a frosted glass wall behind the large square windowpanes. The light bulbs muffled, the cars slowed. The cyclists looked sleeker, the police cars sounded louder and more urgent. Everyone rushed inside from the tables out front. They stood around with their pints, making solo readers and writers like me taking up tables feel unwelcome.

One time, I came up with a username for a website that was an anagram of our initials, including our middle names. I moved the letters around on a notepad and felt an order in their relation to each other. I never told you about the username at the time, though you were the only person I would have shared that with. I think that's how I work: I put things together in my head before they exist. Have I been repeating the pattern of you and me for the last ten years?

¶ Recently I fell in love again. Six months ago, on the afternoon before our first date, I wrote an inscription inside a copy of *The Lover* by Marguerite Duras. It was a hardback copy with a young girl on the front in black and white, staring with such balance through a heavy plastic library cover. I had stolen it from the library years before because of its inscription inside from 1999. The person who signed off this dedication was also called Natalie. She had addressed it to a man called Jake. In a jagged blue hand, hidden under the flap of the library record, it read: *He made love, it was all he did. It was as though it was his occupation.*

The book ended up in Peckham Public Library. There was a sadness to it, but I saw my name there and it glowed. Jake must have discarded it. This copy, I thought, must have been meant for me.

I added my own line on the next page: *Why does it already feel like you're in my life in a completely unavoidable way?* It seemed so natural that he had come back into my life. I read it back ten times, thinking of my shaky handwriting, nerves. I had spent a week thinking about that evening, had booked five different restaurants in case we were hungry, and thought fifty times about whether the pub was right and where we would sit and how we would greet each other. I kept the book hidden on my shelf.

On the date, I watched him arrive. He was an elegant man, wearing a cut woollen jacket that ended at his waist, getting out of the bus and speaking into his phone, held flat in front of his mouth. He looked at me in my green leather jacket. He stepped towards me. I was nervous. To begin with he offered me a smile. His hand was unsteady. Later he asked me what my dreams had been recently. I didn't answer. There was no point in answering. What would I say? I could not reveal what my fantasies about him had already been.

¶ I first met Henry, the elegant man, at university ten years ago. I stole his cigarettes after class and let him teach me to roll. He spoke well. Others dribbled their words out in comparison, he let his lips curl quickly as he talked about the lemony pasta in his tupperware box. As he blew a raspberry when we spoke about the boring morning that had just passed, I couldn't imagine that anyone had made that motion look light before. He courted parties and took drugs without making them his personality. I felt faint next to him, this person born into who they are.

We made a habit of rolling lessons after class. He would tell me to take out a few threads of tobacco, just a smidge, or to tighten the parcel a little bit more. He always finished his own quicker. I watched his eyes as he let them focus on what he was doing. And I thought about his fingers as they gently curled the paper together.

¶ Sometimes I read the love letters of old writers. I think you would like them. Can I read some lines to you? This one is from 1945:

I pray that the said boss does not suddenly, as he leaves, give me something shatteringly long to type, and if he does I shall know the Goddess is thinking of higher things. So please lurk in your bedroom between ten and eleven, and if I don't come, leave a thwarted sign and go and have a drink. If I don't come between ten and eleven, lurk once more towards the end of lunch hour, and if once again I don't come, lurk between half past two and four. But whatever happens, at 4.30 I shall arrive, breathless and covered with ink and a furtive smile.

I stayed in the library reading. After an hour with her letters, I had seen her name written dozens of times. It didn't lose its potency. The D was always strong, in the lead. A single stroke for its backbone, probably top to bottom, followed by a curve starting to the stroke's left-hand side and curling around its front. Sometimes it looked like a sail; it was as tall as one. The often-rushed 'oris' that came after it could actually read 'aris', sometimes 'aus'. Sometimes only the D survived, followed by a small squiggle.

Was the young writer trying to collect things too? I don't think so. Lessing is calm, instructive, and already married. I am her opposite, the man. I am waiting in a hotel room for hours for her to knock. I am making no other plans should I miss her, going hungry so as not to risk leaving for even ten minutes.

¶ I am in my flat now. I am waiting for my pasta water to boil, and I can hear the tone of the conversation on the floor below me. The staired carpet between our flats, mine on the top floor, is only ever walked by me. It was ripped and frayed at the edges before I moved in, showing the plastic cream lining under the 90s pine green colour. This is the place where I've been most alone. In the spring, I think a family of ladybirds moved in. I found three within a few weeks. Sometimes I would watch them as I brushed my teeth, moving up the white wall without making a line. If I was feeling lonely, I let them stay and left the bathroom, giving them a part of my space.

I was talking about this letter in the pub last night and my friend Marcus told me that *every letter is a love letter.* Do you think that's true?

I remember the evening when you and I texted for the first time. I was fourteen, with my parents in our living room. It was a Saturday, *Who Wants to Be a Millionaire* with Chris Tarrant was on the television. My phone was a heavy Nokia that beeped twice each time you replied. You asked me if I'd disappeared completely off the face of the earth because I hadn't been online for a few days.

Earlier that evening my uncle and his girlfriend came around for dinner. We ordered Chinese food and shared it on the dining table. Afterwards I heard the girlfriend talking about me and my sister. She said *they're both quite quiet, aren't they?* My mother replied that *yes, hopefully they'll find their voices soon.* They didn't know that you were the only person I spoke to, that you had found a person.

You sent me the names of all the songs that you'd heard for me whilst we hadn't been talking. I abandoned my evening to download all of them on LimeWire. I wasn't a silent person when I played them. It's fifteen years later and I can still remember the songs that were you. This was when iTunes kept a record of the play count for each song. Sometimes I would make sure your songs were near the top of the list when they were slipping down. *You're So Vain, Big Yellow Taxi, The Reason.* I could weave the words together so that the songs were about me and you. I think I knew that this wasn't how you meant them.

¶ By the summer, three months later, I was invited to everything that Henry did. On holiday, his family rented a villa on a Greek island. You could see the sea from the swimming pool. On the island, there were herds of goats wandering around, which meant that you had to stop the car and close the gate before coming up the driveway to keep them out. His parents were there, his older sister and brother-in-law, and two other couples, friends of the parents. Henry and I made up the last couple of the eight. There was a symmetry to it.

I spent the first half of the week scared about how I fitted in with this group. I found that their conversation moved differently. They would tell stories about newspaper articles and of people they knew. They would say things like *isn't that remarkable* after telling them, and they would leave these stories hanging for the table to pick up. Someone would know to jump in.

At the start of a meal, the discussion of seating arrangement would always leave me isolated from him, as was their rule to sit couples apart. Before the third dinner I drank almost a whole glass of wine in front of Henry in two sips. He said *are you ok,* and I replied *sure.* Later I told him that I felt alone in the group of ten people with their established dining theatre and references. I told him that I felt untethered and vulnerable.

Henry was different around them, too. He knew how to blend. He had the same circumlocutory politesse as his father. I met it for the first time when I visited his parents' house. It was a different language to the ones he used with me and with his friends — a higher register. He would enquire about everyone's morning in the correct turn. He would say *that sounds like a great success* when I knew he had been indifferent to the story of searching for baklava in the local shops. I'm sure I tried to copy him too, sometimes. I'm sure this was obvious to everyone.

One time, the group debated whether talent is real. Someone had read an article which claimed that only 26% of ability could be accounted for by practice. They cited examples of things that they would never be able to do with even a lifetime of training, such as race a motorcycle or sing in an opera. Henry's mother pointed to me, *Natalie, you're creative aren't you, what do you think?* She made me forget how to speak again.

[...]

This is all for this time. Write when you can. Your letters are welcome.

N.

KARINA IC LA'O

Karina IC La'O is a Hong Kong-raised Filipina who studied Visual Studies at Lingnan University before coming to UEA. She is writing two novels; one about an LGBTQ+ relationship that begins in a religious Catholic International School in Hong Kong, and the other simulates her experience with Dissociative Identity Disorder.

Email: karinaiclao.info@gmail.com
Instagram: karinaiclao

Little Things

A Short Story

My cousin Jason flexes his thumb backwards, revealing a divot in the back of his hand created by a tensed ligament. He fills it with a fine, white powder out of a tiny plastic bag.

'Since when did you do coke?' I ask. All I came here to do was piss, but as I was leaving the stall Jason shoved past me, telling me to latch the door. In the dim light he brings his hand to his nose, sniffing so hard that I'm surprised the stall door doesn't shake. The sickly green of the walls peeks out from under the stickers plastered across them.

'Hasn't been long,' he says, then sniffs again just to make sure it's all up there. 'Co-workers do it, so. I know about you and all, but I reckon that I don't have an addictive personality.'

The bass of the music outside pulses in my chest. My nose twitches. There's a prickling running all over the surface of my brain and I stutter, 'I should go.'

'We're just hanging out,' he says. A grin breaks across his face. The bag hangs from his fingertips like fruit. My jaw tenses. Jason laughs at me, tells me that it's just coke – I should relax.

'What's it been, like a year now since your last high? Jesus.'

'A year, two months, and three days, actually.'

'Fucking hell.' His pupils are beginning to dilate.

'A year, two months, and three days,' I say again. The words are cotton in my mouth.

'I heard you.'

I close my eyes.

A year, two months, and three days. A year, two months, and four days, a year two months and five days ago, back when I was so high, I easily lost count of the days in a week.

Back when the email on my phone screen detailed a deposit from Dad. 8,000 pounds. The transaction note: 'Pls call.' My mind reeled itself back into the gaunt, lanky thing I called a body, consciousness spreading from a leak. Bile pushed against the back of my throat. I reached for a mug on the coffee table for something to wash it down. Bubbles of oil glistened on the dark surface, mold beginning to sprout on the sides, but I didn't care. I downed it. I tapped away on my phone with my other hand, settling my share of the rent before I had a chance to spend it elsewhere.

I didn't want to call him.

Back when the jingling of keys sounded behind the front door, laughter filtering in through the gaps. Vince swung the door open, a girl on his heels. His Prada button-down was open till his sternum. A Chrome Hearts chain shone around his neck. I wasn't one to show off, but Vince didn't hesitate to wear his wealth knowing he looked good doing it. Girls seemed to agree. They always fawned over him, wrapping his chain around their fingers, high off weed or cocaine or ecstasy. Their faces were a blur; he never brought the same girl home twice. I guess it helped that Vince wasn't picky. His subscribers weren't either. With the nauseating stuff he did for them, that didn't come as a surprise.

'Mi casa, es tu casa,' Vince said. The girl behind him shut the door with her heel. I stared at her – at the fullness of her cheeks and how they flushed with alcohol. Her round eyes were heavy-lidded, but her irises restlessly fluttered about the room.

Back when I thought there was no way she could be older than eighteen.

'Why thank you,' she said.

'This here is my flat mate, Seth,' he said.

I nodded at her.

'Nora,' she replied. She wore a little black dress and slick high-heeled boots. Crystal jewelry winked in the light. Her dark maroon lipstick was smudged around her mouth, fading onto her pale skin. She giggled.

'You look like shit,' she said.

'Thanks,' I replied.

Vince then told her that I didn't bite; she could sit next to me while he went to freshen up. She walked over, plopping down on the other end of the couch as Vince disappeared down the hall.

Back when I had no idea what to say to her, my brain still clogged from the comedown. My thoughts snagged and ripped, unable to complete themselves. I looked at her. Her feet flexed up and down, eyes glazed. Had she even graduated high school? How many years had it been since Vince and I were in high school? *Where did the time go, you sad sack of–*

'You live here long?' she asked. Her gaze seemed to zoom in and out on me, unable to pull my frame into focus.

'Aren't you a little young to be here?' I asked back.

She narrowed her eyes.

'Seriously,' I pressed.

Back when she had said she was old enough, her voice wavering in the air. What Vince did was his business alone. Seeing all his messes over the years, I was content having nothing to do with what he did. But she felt different.

Back when I told her she should go home, my hands were itching. I took my tin from the coffee table and unclasped the locks. My insides began to constrict within my body. A heaviness was weighing on my shoulders. Memories of the last six years began flashing in my brain like firecrackers: me on the floor of my bedroom, me puking out of a car window after a hit-and-run, me with my dealer and my hands going places I couldn't see... I lifted the tin lid and took a clouded, crystalline rock from a plastic wrap.

'Woah. That's like, *drugs* drugs,' Nora said. Another giggle left her throat as if it was pulled out of her. Weighing the rock in my hand and my metal spoon in the other, I realized I was about to shoot up again.

'Oh. Yeah. Don't do these, they're terrible.' I said it how I remembered those ads on TV usually did.

'Can I watch?' She moved closer.

Back when I was a spectacle; a magician about to perform a magic trick. I set the rock onto the spoon and grabbed my lighter. We both stared at the way the flame licked the metal, mesmerized by the rock melting into a pool.

'What does it feel like?' she asked.

I answered without my mind. The memories weren't stopping, but my mouth kept running. About floating and feeling warm. About the way my body filled up with air until I popped and became nothing. Life wasn't life then. It was pure existence. Just being. Happiness. That was what it was the first time, and I'd been chasing that ever since. The comedowns though, I told her, made me sick. The only way to get better was to shoot up again.

Back when she stared as my veins bloated and rose. With a full syringe, I slid the needle into one of the healed over craters.

'Sounds amazing,' she said. It looked as though she were about to cry.

'Nora?' Vince called out. My heart was racing so fast it was painful.

'You should go home,' I said again. She stayed still, blinking slowly and steadily. Then with a teary smile, she got up and followed the sound of Vince's voice.

Back when I thought I tried. At least I tried. I felt the weight beginning to lift off my back. The images in my mind began to blur like photographs in a vat of acid. And then I was gone, gone, gone.

A year, two months, and three days ago, back when I ate whatever rot was in the fridge when I woke. I was at the dining table, spooning something congealed and slimy into my mouth. Vince came in through the door and I learned I had 'been out for a disgusting twenty hours'. As if he wasn't high himself every other day. He placed his hands on the back of the chair opposite me, white bandages snaking around his forearms. How he wouldn't look me in the eye made me start grinding my teeth together.

'Do you... I don't know. Remember anything?' His voice came to me as though it were behind a wall.

'Like what?'

'Come on. You know.'

'I honestly don't.'

'The girl, man.'

Back when Nora's face flashed in my mind, fading into focus like a fresh polaroid photo. She was crying. I didn't remember her crying when I spoke to her. Her running mascara made her eyes look unnaturally deep in her skull, as if I had to hold my hands out to catch them in case they popped out.

Vince kicked the leg of the chair in front of him, demanding my attention. The food slid around my mouth like wet, shredded cardboard. I asked if she had hurt him.

'Stop playing,' he snapped. The image of Nora moved then, beginning to cry even harder. I saw her shake my body's arm and I couldn't understand what she wanted from me. Why was she so upset? Her mouth moved soundlessly. Her lipstick had smeared further down her chin. She was scaring me.

'Bitch had nails like a goddamn cat,' Vince sighed.

He entered the memory. There were jagged marks down his arms, gleaming a menacing dark red. He grabbed her by the hair. Ripped her from me. Her cries reverberated in my bones and as Vince spoke to me at the dining table, I swore that they were still vibrating. I didn't understand then. All I knew was that fear began to cut into my numbness and I wanted it to stop. Needed it to stop.

Back when Vince dragged her away, I fumbled for my tin.

'Is she okay?' I asked him. The air was as congealed as the food; it slid into my lungs in a paste. Chills ran down my spine.

'She'll be fine. Wasted a good two pills to calm her down, though,' he said. I wanted to vomit. I wanted to claw my face off. I wanted to punch Vince until his caved in.

'If anyone asks, you'll say that you were there, yeah? That nothing happened?' My hands were shaking so hard I had to set my spoon down. He called my name. Twice.

I stumbled out of my chair and rushed to the bathroom, throwing up splatters of food and acid into the shitter. I heaved and pushed. Sweat dripped from my temples. Her crying face was plastered against the backs of my eyelids, sharpening into focus the tighter I squeezed them shut. The bile kept coming, shifting into blood once there was nothing left in my stomach. I thought that was it. I was going die, my head halfway into the bowl, Nora etched into me. How was she going to live with herself? How had I been living with myself?

I had passed out on the floor in a puddle of my own piss and shit when Vince finally thought to check on me. He took me to the hospital, almost genuinely worried. Almost, because he'd seen this one too many times and felt sure I'd bounce back to the needle soon enough.

I woke to the crushing disappointment that I was still alive.

'Call my dad,' I told him.

'Huh?'

'Call my dad. Tell him I'll go to whatever rehab he wants.'

Now? Now. Jason is here, in this gross, green stall. His pupils are dilating, and the little plastic bag hangs from between his thumb and forefinger like fruit. He is swinging the thing in front of my face, and I feel so sick with myself. I'm so goddamn sick of myself.

'Congrats for one year?' he asks.

My hands are itching so fucking bad.
'Least it's not heroin,' he singsongs.
A chill runs down my spine.
'Sounds amazing,' Nora said, but she was frowning.
Shut up, shut up, shut– 'Just a bump. A little one,' I say.

ELSPETH LESLIE

Elspeth is a Norwich-based writer originally from North Yorkshire. She is interested in exploring modernity and mental health in fiction, and is currently working on a novel about a group of young people preparing for the rapture.

elsy.leslie@hotmail.co.uk

Notes on Equilibrium

Short story

This started as an essay about superstition. The working definition I used was: a religious, spiritual or magical belief covertly integrated with mundane, everyday, corporeal patterns of thinking. Why you can avoid cracks on the pavement and still consider yourself a rationally secular person.

My best friend is a staunch believer in karma, but of course she wouldn't call it that. I've never made her lay it out to me explicitly, but from what I gather it's the idea that suffering precedes prosperity, that our acts of kindness get rewarded and evil punished. Every time I speak to this friend—we'll call her Josie—she mentions it, specifically in how it pertains to me and her and the present moment. Any minute now, the great turntable governing our lives will grind into place, the sky will clear and we will all be well again.

Late last summer, in a Portaloo at a music festival: 'It's getting better, for real now.' Josie crossed her ankles an inch above the floor to avoid the puddles and the trampled mud-shot tissues. 'I told you it would.' *It* here in the sense of the firmament-wide *it*, as in when you say: *take it easy* or *it's going to rain*. She cited examples: the grad scheme, the new boyfriend, the panic attacks becoming fewer and further between, and finally, me, standing over her with my back to the ridged door, doing better too.

'Dude, I must have done something right to meet you,' she whispered to me once after I'd backed her up in a first-year Debate Society meeting. Before I could question her sincerity, I remembered she was one of the most intelligent people I'd ever met. Sure, why not: it wasn't so unreasonable that the universe had a way of keeping score, of issuing penalty or compensation where due. All things tend toward equilibrium. That's scientifically defensible. That's entropy. And meeting her definitely felt fated—maybe that was compensation for something I'd endured in a past life.

The day after the incident with Robbie (not his real name, obviously), I ordered Josie a pizza and for once she let me pay without a fight: 'Yeah, okay, I deserve this.' But then a week later, when I stayed over and woke up to find her crying in the bathroom: 'Why me? What did I do that it had to be me?' In second year, the student support people told us there'd be an investigation but probably not enough evidence to convict. We went back to my room and laid in my single bed for a long time without speaking, until Josie, the most vocal anti-Christian in our Medieval Theology class, said, 'Well, whatever, he's still going to hell.' At the time

I agreed, let my 21st century atheism expand just enough to accommodate a 13th century crusader's idea of eternal torture.

This is where, in that original essay, I suggest the bastardised-Westernised concept of 'karma' is a basically religious superstition: some invisible force is watching over us, waiting just beyond the visible landscape with a code of objective morality and powers of retribution. I finished that essay last week. Only on rereading do I realise how callous it comes across, pointing out all the fallacies in Josie's response to the Robbie thing, smugly sceptical of all the ways she comforted herself. It's like I'm reluctant to believe anything too sincerely, like I'm scared I'm asking to be proved wrong.

'You are so much better, dude,' she slurred in the Portaloo. I'm sure I looked better. Maybe not in that moment, with my shins caked in mud and my mascara smudged and crusting, but earlier that day, the first time in months she'd seen me in person. When she hugged me at the train station, it was tentative and precise, so that we only made contact from the collar bones up, but when she did my make-up on the floor of our tent, she told me I was glowing.

I told Josie I was better. Less tired, less unhappy, ready and excited to restart third year in September—better by every reasonable metric. The trouble is that the disorder occurs only in the absence of reasonable metrics. New metrics rush into the gap, inventing arbitrary correspondences between self-mutilation and control, and the arbitrariness only bothers you as much as you let it.

'God, exactly.' Josie was beaming at me. Her eyes were glazed over. 'You deserve this so much.' I couldn't ask why.

Restrictive eating disorders are basically disorders of racking debt. Every lapse of indulgence is worth its exact weight in remorse; every calorie consumed hovers in your peripheral until abolished by equal and opposite measures. If the goal weight is reached, it immediately inflates, and a smaller number, further below ground, inherits the status of the coveted lower bound. The sky sinks to restore equilibrium. Equilibrium is not acceptable. You need to keep digging.

There's a perversity to it. You're trying to pull one over on the laws of nature, and you know you can't get away with it forever. You do it all awaiting a kind of Faustian reckoning for the hubris of chasing these illegitimate impulses, but it's up to you whether that matters. You can choose what matters to you.

There are the body's fail-safes and ways of getting you back: calling off your sex drive and menstrual cycle, making you shit yourself in public, sentencing you to an early grave, etcetera. Cons that should outweigh the supposed pros of starving yourself, but all of that is mutable. As your dad looms over you with a fork near your mouth, and your mum sits in front of you, pleading or whatever, an extra neural pathway opens up. It reaches to a place of absolute self-sufficiency in the back of your brain, where you don't have to take anyone seriously in their predictions or worries or proclamation. You follow it back there. You may as well follow it.

My first go at third year ended halfway through the Autumn semester. I was reluctant to drop out, even when Josie, on top of everyone else, started pushing it. 'I think it might be good. If the one thing you had to focus on was just, like, getting better.'

We were in the lounge of her student house. The three people she lived with were home for reading week, and she had made me pasta. 'I'm not that bad,' I said. I'd said something similar to a doctor around that time, and he'd contradicted me.

'So you're just going to wait until you are?' said Josie.

'You never took time out.'

'So?' She'd been perched on the arm of the sofa, observing the distance we always put between us then, watching my pasta congeal in its bowl, but here she leant toward me confrontationally.

I shrugged. I wasn't going to say, *what happened to you was worse*, but we were both thinking it.

'You can't, like, weigh it, dude.' She stood up and took my pasta into the kitchen so I couldn't argue. I could tell she wasn't sure she could defend her case.

*

Late into my year out, I developed a kind of financial orthorexia. Meal deals, membership discounts, foods expiring and stamped with the little yellow stickers were automatically sanctioned, regardless of calorie or nutritional content. I rarely even needed to buy my own food, being back at my parents' house, but there was a thrill that came with receiving more than you put in. Getting away with something.

You need these substitute achievement metrics more than ever during weight restoration. When I could have been lying awake in my childhood bed, noticing the new ways my body filled my pyjamas, I started reading again. I had the bandwidth to read now, actually read, not just stare at words and flip pages to kill time. That counted for something, even if the weight gain counted against it. Pretty soon, so long as I kept this up, I could transpose my internal reward system onto uni: I'd return with more energy than ever before, with a deeper insight into the nature of suffering, discipline, recovery, all of which I could channel into seminar talking points and first-class essays. When I got the marks back, I told myself, I'd know for sure I was doing something worthwhile.

Around this time, in a Skype call with Josie, I tried to interrogate the assumption that suffering was necessarily 'bad' and that pleasure (or even a lack of suffering) was 'good'. There were any number of utilitarian philosophers we could have paged, and there was a time when Josie would have beat me to the punch, but she was about to graduate and she'd taken more applied ethics classes toward the end of her third year, so she wasn't as immersed in all that. 'That's what your dissertation will be on,' she said proudly. Wasn't it exciting, was what she meant, wasn't it self-evidently wonderful that my third-year dissertation would happen at all.

*

I remember the first time I walked back from the supermarket to my parents' house. The sun had come out while I'd been in the shop, and I didn't want to wait for the bus. A stack of discounted ready meals weighed down my rucksack, but I had energy. I walked briskly without having to force myself. Steps piled up on the concrete, unaccounted for, never to be tallied up and equated to any fraction of a calorie burnt. The sun felt good in my hair. I never stopped to measure that feeling against the vertiginous thrill of the number slipping on the scale or the pride in sustained hunger. This is because true wellness resists quantification.

Maybe. I don't know. I didn't examine it with too much scrutiny. I think I was scared it might have fallen apart.

The Portaloo stank of flowery soap, thick and dubious. Josie was talking about the next year, saying how good it was going to be, how good it already was, and how much I deserved it. I pressed my back to the door. There was another door, inside me, opening up, to that extra neural pathway of radical scepticism, and whether or not I decided to go through it I could feel the breeze on my back.

We were going to be okay, she was saying. She might have invested that certainty in anything. It felt fanatical. I didn't want to agree with her because I didn't want to jinx it.

ALEX LOUIS

Alex Louis is a French-Korean writer from London. He studied Philosophy and Computer science at McGill University then spent a year in Paris where, at times, he wrote passionately. He hopes to return there someday. Currently he lives in Norwich.

alelouis1099@gmail.com

Evening at the Fatales
Short story

Jenny stood in the Fatales' doorway as they stepped past her, tried to shut her pores to the wafting perfume which literally just reminded her of funerals.

Then Mrs Fatale turned semi-back to remind her of a few things Jenny hadn't listened to the first time, was certainly too busy counting down the pulses in her head until the place'd be all to herself to listen to this time, either. Jules was going to love it. Besides, she'd already seen the list up on the fridge of the places to find the various things the Fatales thought Jenny could find useful (of which, somehow: fire extinguisher; the fickle remote for the humidity settings), as well as all the emergency phone numbers.

In the chirruping of the late summer evening a dog walker crouched to pick up shit. Jenny hadn't even been to a funeral.

'And if there's anything else, if you have any questions about anything,' Jenny tuned back in to hear Mrs Fatale say, 'you can just ask Charles. Even about his own bedtime hours. He would never lie,' she said. 'I think you'll find that he's very much precocious.'

'A terrific conversationalist,' said Mr Fatale.

Jenny nodded.

'It's true,' said Mrs Fatale. 'His teachers are always saying how investigative his mind is.'

'That's a shame,' Jenny said. 'I think I read recently that those types are the slowest to lose their virginity. Where did I read that?' she wondered, decided to tune back out for the response. 'Anyway,' she maybe interrupted.

'Yes. Well.'

'And don't forget that we'll call you by eleven to let you know whether we'll be back tonight or tomorrow morning. All depends on old Vesuvius here—' he placed a hand on his wife's stomach, received a withering look, offered a hey-I-didn't-invent-IBS shrug in return. Silence, finally, Mrs Fatale rose above.

'Eleven's not too late, is it?' Mrs Fatale creased her brow. 'It's too late, isn't it.'

'Don't worry about me, Mrs Fatale. I'm all good,' bright as she could, uncertain about the irony in her own pronouncement as she tried to hold her smile. The Fatales exchanged with each other looks of love and assurance, shot one Jenny's way, with, what, resignation? Then Mr Fatale told Jenny to be good, took his wife by the elbow and, stately, led her down the steps and along the path through the lawn to the street, to the car, then off, away. Jenny tried to make out the sound of the car for as long as possible but before long lost it to the aural nothings of the small life, like all that coral she saw on the nature channels, watchful but unwatched, sighing away into the obscurity.

Jenny stepped back into the house and locked the door behind her, the sight of smiling houses lined up in the end for who else but her?

&&

Turning back into the house, its tessellating floorboards, mirrored console, aware too of the selfsame sneakiness she gave department stores before she shoplifted the daylights out of them. And the Fatales kind of seemed like the type for cameras, she guessed.

But, 'There aren't cameras,' came a voice from above.

Jenny turned to face Charles looming at the top of the stairs that came down into the front hall, something a little wild-westy in his stance.

'If that's what you're looking for,' he added, and began to descend the stairs.

'Oh, well. Good thing I'm not a nihilist, then?' she said.

Charles sniffed. 'Right. Nihilists.'

'People who don't believe in things being things,' she said.

'So wistful. I don't know what a nihilist is?'

'How old are you?' she asked, unsure why.

He was one of those full-bodied boys, a pudginess that imbued a sullen authority, one of those boys who sucked their thumbs knowingly, provocatively, who'd take your hat and throw it in the lake because he knew his own youth, all elbows, cheeks, huffs and scowls. Though his mouth, Jenny peered, was actually very finely pursed, and his eyes as a proportion of his facial real estate were basically oceanic, which Jenny resented, then resented resenting, blue, of course, windows in the afternoon light, absinthe blue, salmon scales in the surf and so on, loathe then to think about all the girls who would later remark it as he grew up, no doubt into one of those striking young men with abstraction in their look, pretensions in their innocence.

'Eleven,' he said, like it proved something. 'But I'm turning twelve in twenty-three days. Lots of my twelve-year-old friends call themselves nihilist.'

She was impressed, though somewhat slighted he didn't ask hers.

'So I'm not really looking forward to my birthday.' His toes probed from the beneath the hem of his octopus pyjama bottoms, a big ingratiating show of tentativeness.

'Twelve is significant,' Jenny said.

'They're mean, in fact,' ignoring her.

'To you?'

'Mostly about themselves. They talk a lot about their bad habits.'

She thought about the interaction she'd had with Charles's parents at the door, whether she'd seemed on edge. Jules was always letting her know when she was on edge, he could read her like that. She only wished she could see him more outside of her own house, and there only with the door open, house rules. Well, enter, or rather, exit, the Fatales.

'Yeah. People my age do that as well.'

'Yeah,' he said. He sniffed and looked about himself. 'I'm going to sit on the sofa and watch TV while I call my boyfriend,' and began to make his way.

'Your mother often has stomach stuff?' Jenny asked.

'Yeah,' he said, not stopping. 'Most of the times they drive over to the Dollmans they end up staying.'

'The Dollmans.'

'Who they're seeing tonight. They met them on their honeymoon. It's a whole, you know,' giving Jenny a bit of a look. 'But then again, it's true that my mom's a bit sensitive,' and paused at the door, looked back. 'TV, boyfriend, phone call,' he said.

Jenny thought about the no-lying thing. 'Yeah. Right. See you later,' she said, thinking she'd just wait till Charles went off to bed before Jules came. Right?

&&

Jenny stood in the master bedroom's ensuite bathroom, beheld herself in the haloed mirror and, when nothing occurred to her, reached for its rim to swing open the glass. Tranquilizers (she wasn't that naïve, after all) were to bathroom mirrors as car keys were to those sun flaps Jenny didn't care to know the name for.

There were two orange tubes—one for the Mrs, one for Mr—, one bottle of Advil and a couple of other bottles Jenny scanned for named labels then dismissed because everyone knew OTC stuff was pretty much just for pussies (like Jenny's own parents, for instance, who believed that ridiculous story about how Michael, still, Jenny was pretty sure, scared of the dark and everything, had outgrown babysitting. But the truth was that Jenny was hugely grateful to Jonathan and Angelina for having lied to save her skin, even if on their part it was actually kind of negligent. Now when they passed Jenny in the neighbourhood they gave her these quick half smiles which Jenny could never quite fully deconstruct, and she, despite herself, would feel as she only very occasionally felt: in fact pathetically young—turning her blush away from her parents if they were there, too. Thereby had she learnt to dilute—only a few from each bottle or box or whatever—, Jenny never knowing who'd turn out to be insanely neurotic about the daily weight of their Ambien case). Eleven-year-olds, she sighed loudly to herself and herself, the nothing girl whose hand displayed a combination of cinematic possibilities, and she stooped to cup water from the faucet. What did they know.

[It was no doubt true that in a few years' Jenny would find all this way, way less watchable. Not only that but she'd admit in the first place that a part of it *was* the watching herself, the being-displaced-from-and-looking-back-on-herself thing, good old unself-conscious vanity. Jenny previously'd thought of vanity as exhausted by looking in the mirror too much, making serious faces for the camera—a phase to eventually go and pubesce on out of. But it'd come to denote her conviction, on some level, that a serious existence(…) meant things looking seriously and that meant 1) serious paying attention, but also 2) a bit of a need to externalise things. (So vanity often got in the way of Vanity, actually, because specular or photographic images never really made anything look serious, now did they.) So if Vanity were a desire for self-seriousness, it was also a desire for self-understanding; if she could be displaced from herself for only a moment, she could watch herself, the real her, and learn, confirm to herself things that until they'd been observed could only be half-truths. And, after, if she flooded back into herself and found herself in a bad way, well, it didn't matter because at least she knew what was what and it wasn't ambiguous and it wasn't boring, because what, after all, was more boring than being at odds but only on the inside. It was like how smiling could make you feel happier – except maybe the opposite of that, but hey.]

&&

'My boyfriend's going to come over,' she said to Charlie – could she call him Charlie? – as they sat on the sofa, he cross-legged in the far corner, she with one leg genteel over her knee, upright, entertaining a suspicion that so much as a change of channel could floor her.

Charles turned to face her, crossed arms now, too, his tightly pursed lips. 'Whatever will you talk about?'

'He's going to bring a bottle of port. He says it's very old. His dad's,' Jenny explained. On the TV a man with funny hair was walking down an institutional-looking corridor and gesticulating. Jenny couldn't make out the words but whatever she heard was definitely more involved than silence.

'Right, sure. Have my parents met him?'

'Jules,' she said. 'I've known him for years.'

&&

'The phone's ringing,' came Charlie's voice, later, not all that impressed-sounding.

Jenny couldn't make it out. She felt she'd been there, on the sofa in the living room, between quiet and words, for a while, but she couldn't've said what had happened since earlier. And the phone was ringing, apparently.

'What time is it?' she spoke out into the room, hopeful that Charlie was still there.

'A bit past eleven.'

'Is Jules here yet?'

'The doorbell went off some time ago. But I didn't open it.'

Good boy. 'How long?'

'An hour, maybe.'

'Okay. That was the right thing, I guess,' Jenny said.

'I think you should get the phone.'

'What?'

'It's past my bedtime.'

Her eyes open, the room was much darker than it'd been before. She stood just in front of the sofa and looked around herself. 'I can't see anything,' she said.

'Jesus.' A scurry of movement and then something poked at her side. 'Here. They're just going to tell you that they're staying at the Dollman's. I don't know why they think—' he looked up at her. 'Never mind. Listen. Just press this button, see? and say OK until they ask you whether I'm in bed and then say Yes, he is, he's so cute when he snores. OK? OK, here.'

Jenny took the phone and pressed the wrong button, realising when the phone just beeped into her ear.

'Jesus. What the hell are— One sec.'

Jenny didn't say anything while he tampered with the phone, then handed it back to her and when she brought it to her ear she could hear ringing.

'Say you accidentally hung up,' whispered Charlie.

Jenny looked at Charlie as the phone rung and wondered whether Jules was going to come back with the port. She wanted to be known, not that she needed him to see, even if didn't matter either way.

MARY LOWTH

Mary Lowth is a doctor, writer, and *Private Eye's* human rights columnist. She lives on the tiny island of Bryher, twenty miles off Land's End, where her current stories are set. They explore the risks of isolationism and othering, the meaning of solidarity, and how and why resistance begins.

mary@lowths.com

The Watchers

The opening of a novel set on Scilly in 2084, 20 years after the AI-triggered release of a bioweapon decimated Europe. The UK is a closed authoritarian state – intelligent mines police the sea against refugees, and secrets are deemed subversive. But on Scilly, resilient and remote, both secrets and resistance endure.

CHAPTER ONE

The tide is turning, and the sea is restless. Her paddle slices the surface cleanly, the kayak cleaving smooth as a fish. She's close now, but so are they.

Help me.

Is it because he's dying that his voice fills her head? It makes even the full-throated roar of the waves pounding the Retarrier Ledges seem distant.

She steers into the uneasy swell, its restlessness growing as she approaches the Western Rocks, Rosevean now to her left, Rosevear ahead. She knew he was out here the moment she woke this morning to find him inside her head. She didn't understand, then, how she knew, which worried her almost as much as his voice getting louder when she put her fingers in her ears. Now that she does understand she is no less worried because the SOS he is broadcasting is reaching her through the sense she shouldn't have, the one she can no longer pretend is some variant of normal. That she is in Forbidden Water, on the other hand, doesn't worry her. Magda first brought her out here when she was ten, ostensibly for bigger lobsters but really because Magda saw the word 'forbidden' as challenge rather than limitation. Brae has been coming ever since, maintaining both Magda's lobster pots and Magda's defiance, the least she owes the fierce, crazy-haired grandmother whose mantra was that as long as you keep resisting they can never win. But she has never taken the kayak to the far side of the Western Rocks – she promised Magda she wouldn't. The sea over there once hurled half the British navy onto these brutal granite teeth, drowning two thousand men and the Admiral in the process. Last winter it flung a huge, rusty iron stair wrenched from some ancient wreck twenty feet up onto Rosevean – she can see it from here (after a brief territorial standoff with a peregrine the gulls have taken it for their own). Even on a calm day it's no place for a sealskin kayak – but she is going to break her promise all the same. She must find the Swimmer before they do. And they are coming.

The grey boat must have reached Scilly during the night because the Watchers on Land's End didn't see it leave, but those on St Agnes saw it at first light, hunting out here. It missed him that first time, which provided her chance. By the time the Watchers signalled Bryher she was already preparing *Eel*, stowing her gear and erecting the small upwind sail. She crossed Broad Sound whilst the grey boat searched the back of St Mary's. Annet shielded her from view for the last leg, and now she has taken the sail down – it is unpredictable enough out here without trying to second-guess the wind.

This is as far as she has ever come alone. Through the neck between Rosevean and Rosevear she can see the lighthouse on the Bishop's Rock some half a mile away – Magda took her there once, but then unaccountably placed it off limits forever. It is still beautiful, pale and elegant as a swan. In her mind it's Magda's lighthouse, because Magda was as proud of it as if she'd built it herself. It should have been impossible, she always said, to build anything on a submerged granite pillar beset by monstrous waves, yet men had lashed themselves to iron posts, drenched, battered and half-drowned, fixing block after block till it was done. Small wonder that, one June evening, a dazzle of petticoated ladies and shining men had rowed out here and danced all night in celebration. The lighthouse they called the Bishop shone for nearly two hundred years, a beacon of solidarity in a world where saving those in peril on the sea was actually encouraged, whoever they were. The world before the Incident.

I am hanging by a thread, my friend.

She worries they will hear him too, and find him the way they find radio operators that transmit for too long.

Stay quiet. They are hunting you.

The first time she tried to reply to him she produced only squeaking in her head, but as she focussed mind on meaning she found the way, like flexing a muscle she hadn't known she had. Now, barely three hours later, she can form words that curve round his, birthing communication in thought. She thinks it must be like this the first time a baby seal slips into water and the vast dimensions of possibility unfold. It should be wonderful, except that normal people can't do this. And whoever is not normal is not safe.

They are closing in. She feels the unease of the Rosevear gulls even before they start rising anxiously from their perches, feathers ruffled and minds akimbo, screaming edgy warnings into the wind. She wedges *Eel* against rock, drapes bladderwrack over her, then slips into the sea. He is just through there, but so are they. She breathes in.

The grey boat appears so slowly from behind Rosevear that the antennae that sprout from its hull seem to blossom from the granite itself, as if Rosevear is coming alive. By the time two dozen baby shags come swimming frantically towards her in a tight-packed group she is low in the water, dark wet head the colour of the seals that breed yards away on Gorregan. The shags are taken in at first

– they have nearly reached her when they stop, milling in comical confusion. She feels their anxious, simple minds shift in unison from surprise to anxiety as they turn and hurry back the way they came. The movement catches the attention of a drone, and she drops beneath the surface as it whirs into the neck. Water closes over her head, the sea gathers her in, but she can still feel the cold purpose driving the hunt. The hull blots out the sun.

She stays like that, one hand steadying *Eel* and the other gripping tethered oarweed, moving with the wash till the light returns. After years of practice she can hold her breath for five minutes – she comes up only when the grey boat is beyond Rosevean, drones buzzing round it like flies. She is glad of her wetsuit. This water unnerves her. It comes from very deep, surging up monstrous underwater cliffs just beyond these rocks, sometimes dragging huge squid up with it, and its cold pulses round her, an ancient rhythm from perpetual darkness. She tries not to remember the story of the drowned woman found right here, grasped in the tentacles of a giant cuttlefish, and so thinks of it all the more. So many others have drowned just here too, she tells herself, the echo of their dying voices lingers in the waves, but there is only one cuttlefish story, which surely means it's ridiculous. (And hearing the dead isn't? Magda would have said. But it isn't hearing in that sense, is it?)

A young grey seal nudges against her, making her jump – she's glad of his friendly company. The grey boat has moved away, but not for long. Once it rounds Gorregan it will come in behind her, right to the spot where she and the seal now wait. It's time to move.

Breeze and spray whip the nauseating smell of rotting weed and diesel through the neck at her, but she begins edging forward, assessing the heaving water, listening with every sense. She wants to know if they spot her, and she thinks she will – because barely a second after the probes find her trace, exclude seal, dolphin, flotsam or corpse, and conclude girl, alive she will feel their excitement. Then she, too, will become quarry, because there should be no girl, alive out here.

She emerges on the other side into bright sunlight, a twisting breeze, and a fitful sea. Spray stings her eyes, there is foam everywhere soft as snow, and the roar of the Retarrier Ledges is close, sullen and menacing. A sudden, sharp undertow catches her by surprise, and she braces the paddle to keep from being sucked out, feeling the urge to abandon kayak for rock. She is too experienced to heed it – it's rarely safer to be out of a boat than in it, something proved here a thousand times by a thousand dead – any of these granite points could pierce her right through. She conjures Magda's words from memory – concentrate, listen, act. The sea has no pity, but she must hold her nerve. A man's life depends on hers – and besides, the seal is still with her, his placid fearlessness reassuring. And just for a moment she sees it all with his mind – the limitless open ocean, the heaving joy of the tide, the pure exhilaration of freedom.

She focuses on the moving water. The state of the sea out here has little to do with the bright, breathless weather above, the groundswell is born of storms miles away and days ago, carried by current, whipped by wind, magnified by the sudden change of depth. She is watching for a pattern, looking for a route. There are rhythms here, if you can find them. Two heavy waves in thirteen counts, one respite in eleven, but next time seventeen, an eddy on the twenty-fourth beat. There is a maths to it, if you know what you're doing, a maths of instinct. She feels it as she might predict the next note in a complex piece of music. There will be a moment and a place where the water is briefly stiller, the undertow paused. She must find it.

Are you there?

I am close.

She can barely hold him in her mind. He is fading, and she needs all her concentration for the water. It's harder to stay calm, even, than she expected. If the grey boat comes back round here again it will be over. People say that to be taken by them is worse than death. Nobody ever explains what can be worse than death, but it doesn't matter, Brae tells herself, because she isn't going to be taken.

Count. Wait.

A flash catches her eye over on the Bishop. Odd. She squeezes her eyes against the sun to see better, but the lighthouse looks as empty and dead as always – it was probably sun catching broken glass on the old lamp. Around it, though, the sea is irritable, white crests on the tops of the waves and a dark line on the horizon. Storm coming in. Shaking water from her face, she expels the large and angry crab that a passing gull drops onto her lap.

The seal dives for it.

That's it.

Now.

She takes the moment, follows him into cleft between whirl and trough. A pull, a thrust, and she reaches the far side of Rosevear. She hears a drone, faint, on the other side. At last.

Even though she has known exactly where he is all day, she would have missed him if the seal hadn't found him, its surprise flicking her mind like a child with an elastic band.

His pale hair is spread on the water like seagrass. He's on his front, almost completely submerged in a patch of channelled wrack, its bulging fingers wrapping him like a child. His face turns slightly to one side, the weed holding his nose above the waterline as he rises and falls with the surge. He is alive, but barely. How the grey boat missed him she can't imagine.

I am here.

I knew you would come. My strength is gone.

DARIBHA LYNDEM

Daribha Lyndem is a writer from Meghalaya, India. She is currently working on her second novel that explores the fault lines in India's Civil Services Examination through the lives of three aspirants in North Delhi. Her debut novel *Name Place Animal Thing* was shortlisted for the JCB Prize for Literature in 2021.

daribhalyndem@gmail.com

Obituaries

Flash Fiction

The morning after his father died Vivek sat down and scanned the obituaries. Getting it published had been harder than he had expected.

'You can't write Pankaj Kumar *died peacefully* in his sleep,' the man said over the phone.

'Why not?'

'Because you need an autopsy to establish the cause of death.'

The thought of getting an autopsy to write two throwaway words was too much for Vivek. There was no real need for people to know how his father had died, after all he had always been such a private person. He would have hated all the fuss, the relatives crawling about the house, so many of them Vivek did not know. It was surprising to him how their small house could accommodate so many people as if it had taken a big inhale and expanded to allow all these people to fit in.

He flipped through the advertisements and headlines until he found it on the last page–a rectangular insert among the other pixelated portraits of dead people. His father glared back at him, his face saggy, pale and unsmiling. Vivek remembered that the photograph had been taken the day they had had a spat about carving up some of their ancestral property and selling it. The money from that deal could have paid off the mortgage for their home in Lucknow. It meant that he could finally buy a Jeep and a reduction in his monthly deductions. But his father, who was unnecessarily attached to those two acres in Manikpur, was not ready to let go. Even though he would never go back, there was a feeling that a connection to this piece of land meant a connection to his family's history. 'Land always appreciates,' he had always said.

Vivek looked at the printed image, followed the lines on his father's face, the worn out formal shirt and the acetate glasses resting crookedly on his nose; perhaps he could have looked for one that was more flattering, but there had been no time. Between taking care of his mother and making sure that there was an endless supply of food and tea, these smaller details had been ignored. He could imagine his father being disappointed about this decision. Even now when he was lying in a casket in the other room, Vivek felt like he was being rushed into making a choice.

As he was about to put the papers down, he spotted something odd. If he had been less careful, been distracted by his mother calling him from the other room, or by his Auntie crying right next to him, he would not have noticed it–another obituary for his father. There it was, the same name under the same face, but in this case the face beamed up at him and the testimonial ran twice as long.

Pankaj Kumar, C.A

Husband of Usha Srivastava

Father of Rohan Kumar

These were names Vivek had never encountered. It could be a misprint, a typographical error. The newspaper would be able to clear it all up. He read through the obituary again, it described his father in endearing terms—inspiring, family man, zest for life—terms he would never have used. This was a man he had never met. He looked at what he had written—left for heavenly abode, cremation on 3rd May—these were sufficient for his no-nonsense father. He counted eleven lines of text. It was what he would have liked, probably. This extra eulogy led with *I did it My Way,* a song Vivek was unfamiliar with. Of course, there had been rumours about another family; he had ignored all of them. It was not possible, not his father who spent most of his time hunched over balance sheets.

Vivek had to make sure his mother did not see it. It was annoying that there was one more thing to worry about (he had to make sure the pandit would be on time to perform the last rites). The newspaper should have known better than to place them next to each other. It felt as if they had done it on purpose. Others would also see it, nosy neighbours, malicious relatives, his mother's friends at the workplace, they might mention it to her. He knew there was no way to stop the news from getting to her eventually. All those years, his father had been so discreet, and now everything was laid bare in a column of print. And what if *they* showed up here, how would he stop them from barging in? From laying before the body? From also calling his father Baba?

Loving family man, no, this eulogy was not for the same man. Vivek had never spent time with his father outside the dinner table. One Diwali, when he was ten, his father had taken away the three hundred rupees his Chacha had given him. Vivek had not been allowed to exchange gifts with his Christian friends at school. Three years ago during Holi, his father had drunk a glass of bhaang and he had mentioned another son, but everyone had ignored it. His Bua said: '*it's the bhaang, the bhaang*, and he had believed her.

Apart from this one time there had been no other clues to indicate this other life and Vivek felt that he needed to extend the lie as long as he could. So the newspaper had made a mistake, the obituary was describing someone else. This Pankaj Kumar C.A with unfurrowed brows, who wore floral patterned shirts, and looked like he enjoyed having his picture taken was someone Vivek did not recognise. He put the paper aside and walked up to the casket where his father lay with a scowl on his face, having died peacefully in his sleep.

POLLY MANNING

Polly Manning is a writer from South Wales. Her work has appeared in VICE, *Planet Magazine*, the *Western Mail*, *The Welsh Agenda*, and *Spacecraft*, amongst others. She is the 2023/24 Annabel Abbs Scholar at UEA, and currently working on her first collection of short stories.

pollylizmanning@gmail.com

Did You Hear About Paul?

An extract from a short story

It had been an accident, the first time.

Paul had been delivering parcels for six years by then, and mostly liked the work. It was honest and kept him slim, and strong. He enjoyed talking to people on the doorstep, and when women opened the door they often seemed pleased with his looks, and offered him a drink of water if the day was warm. Some of the regulars on his route knew him by name, and asked after his wife and baby. He liked that, and exaggerated the truth out of thanks. They're great, he said. They're doing really great.

In the last few months he'd been having fewer of those conversations. The courier company had put a tracker in the delivery van that beeped his phone when he spent too long on a delivery, and if it beeped twice within one hour the shift manager would call and ask him to explain why. The first time the shift manager called, Paul had laughed but the shift manager hadn't.

The van he hired from the courier didn't have air conditioning. They'd given him a discount for that, but it was turning out to be a very hot summer. For the first time he found himself accepting the women's glasses of water. He didn't like to drink in front of them but he did, sometimes so quickly the water dribbled down his chin. He'd point at the stain on his shirt and laugh, make sure to see that the women laughed along with him so that they wouldn't be embarrassed.

One afternoon, early in the summer, he was driving over the speed limit through a small, leafy village on the outskirts of the city. He'd fallen behind schedule on his last stop. The man was old and had a tremor in his hand, and asked if Paul could write an address on an envelope for him. Paul had written the address and taken the letter, said he'd post it at the next box he came to so the man didn't have to worry about it.

The tracker on his phone was beeping now, a trio of ascending pips every few seconds. He was tired, and hungry, and his T-shirt was slick to his back with sweat. It was the hottest day of the year so far, almost 35°C, and there hadn't been time to stop for lunch. The baby hadn't slept the night before, and neither had Paul. His wife Bethan had shouted at him for forgetting to warm a bottle, then cried. Paul had touched her arm then and she said that she thought she might not be very well, might not be coping with being at home all the time. She maybe didn't feel like a real person anymore.

They couldn't afford childcare, and their parents didn't live close by enough to help, but something would have to be done. Paul was thinking about this as he came around a bend in the road and saw something white flash across the tarmac. Too late, feeling the thump of it under the wheels, he slammed down the break. The van lurched to a stop. There was a ringing in his ears. A cry.

'Fuck.'

For a moment he sat without moving in the driver's seat. Then he turned on the hazard lights and got out.

Under the front left wheel was a mop of blond curls. Paul retched, almost stumbled. A wave of terror shuddered though him like an orgasm.

Then he saw the collar, the paws, and it was over.

The dog, a small white terrier-type thing, was bunched up behind the wheel. Its eyes were open, glassy. He squatted and reached behind the wheel and laid a hand on the soft curls of its stomach, which was still warm.

Footsteps behind him.

'Oh, my god.'

He could tell from her voice that the woman was the one who'd cried out. He craned his neck to face her from his spot on the ground, squinting against the midday sun. The woman was perhaps in her early sixties, with wrinkled, tanned flesh. Her hair was bright blonde and curled and so much like the dog's fur that Paul had to look away for a moment. The woman opened her mouth. There were tears in her eyes but she didn't move, just stood there in the road looking down at the dog. He noticed now the loop of a leash in her hand.

'He just slipped right out,' said the woman, showing Paul the leash. 'He's never done that before.'

Paul stood. He wanted to console her in some way but thought it might be wrong to touch her.

'I'm so sorry,' he said. 'I didn't see him till he was under me.'

The woman shook her head.

'Just slipped out. Never done it before.'

'I'm sorry.'

The woman looked at him now. She blinked.

'It's not your fault. He just…'

Her lip trembled then. Paul touched her shoulder. She patted his hand.

'I had him nine years.'

'I'm so sorry,' said Paul.

He wanted to say something else but couldn't think what.

The woman shook her head again. They both stood looking at the dog for a moment.

'I think you've got a call there,' said the woman.

It took Paul a moment to register the beeping in his pocket. He took the phone out and silenced it.

'It's nothing.'

As carefully as he could, he reached behind the wheel and picked up the dog, and set it down on the pavement. The woman knelt down beside it and stroked its head. Paul saw now that the middle part of its stomach was so crushed that it was almost level with the pavement. There was no blood, at least, but he wished he'd left it behind the wheel, or at least asked her for a bag to put it in, so she didn't have to see.

He climbed into the van and parked it at the side of the road and got out again. A small group of people had formed around the woman and the dog. A teenage girl was patting the woman's back.

Paul looked around at the street, a terrace of pebbledash houses with tiny front lawns and net curtains in the windows. In some of the gardens there were pots of flowers, little stone fountains, a bike on its side. The sound of a radio drifted from an upstairs window and down into the street. Beneath the smell of hot tarmac was a sweet, earthy smell of freshly mown grass.

Paul went to the woman and apologised again, asked if there was anyone he could call for her.

'That's alright,' she said. She'd stopped crying now, was looking down at the dog in calm disbelief. 'You probably need to be getting on.'

He took all the notes out of his wallet and tried to hand them to her, but she waved him away. He wrote his name and phone number on the back of a missed-delivery card and gave it to her. He looked at her and the dog and the girl, and thought there probably wasn't anything else to do.

As he drove away, Paul looked in the wing mirror and saw the woman lift the dog and put it in a shopping bag that the girl was holding open.

He drove for a while and then pulled into a quiet side street. He took out the phone and saw the notifications, and called the shift manager.

He explained what had happened.

'How many deliveries d'you have left?' said the manager.

'Eleven.'

'Alright. Any damage to the van?'

'No.' Paul wiped his forehead. 'It was a small dog.'

'Were you injured at all? Or anyone else?'

'No. I mean, the woman was upset.'

'Alright. You probably won't hit quota today. If you come to the depot and drop off the rest of the deliveries, I'll have another courier take them out tonight.'

Paul looked out at the street, at the heat lines rippling along the tarmac. There was a patch of grass the other side of a fence. He imagined how it'd feel to run his fingers through it.

'Thanks,' he said.

At the depot, the shift manager took the parcels and said he might as well go home.

'No point hanging around with nothing to do. Just check back in the morning so I can get your signature on an incident report.'

Paul thanked him and went outside. Crossing the car park, he blinked his eyes against the molten light reflected in the car windows and tried to work out what it was he was feeling. He thought about the woman and the dog and understood that he should feel guilty. He did feel bad for her, if he thought about it. Nine years. It was a long time to care about something that you suddenly couldn't have anymore.

This was more of a thought than a feeling. That was always a distinction in Paul's mind, one that had been useful to him over the past few years.

Climbing into the van, all he felt was relief.

Bethan opened the front door as he came up the driveway, and Paul knew she'd been waiting and listening for him even now, two hours before she should have expected him home.

'You're home early,' she said.

He kissed her and went inside. The hall was cool and dark, and he peeled off his shirt with a sigh.

They went through to the kitchen. The baby was in a highchair, watching a children's show on a tablet Bethan had balanced on the counter. They'd named him Jack after Bethan's father, who'd been a machinist at the steelworks in Port Talbot and who'd died when she was young. At four months old the baby was just beginning to lose the watchful look in his eyes which had made Paul so nervous those first few months. Paul kissed the top of his head and sat down at the table.

Bethan went to the fridge and brought him a beer and sat down.

'I'm letting him watch too much,' she said, looking at the baby, which was laughing at something on the tablet. 'Nothing else was working.'

Paul rubbed her shoulder. After a while she asked him what'd happened. He told her about the dog, and the woman, and the girl holding open the shopping bag. He didn't mention the woman's hair looking like the dog's fur.

'That's horrible,' she said.

She reached over and touched the side of his face. He leaned into it and felt the weight of his head in her palm, closed his eyes. The beer was cold and good. He looked at her. She smiled. He thought about telling her how good he felt, better than he had in a while. It would be difficult to find the rights words. And she looked so tired.

'It's a shame about the dog,' she said. 'But it's nice to have you home early.'

He often worked until late in the evening and found himself, now, unsure of what to do with the time he'd gained. He played with the baby a while and ran the vacuum around the living room. It felt good to vacuum his own carpet. The warm dusty smell of it mingled with something Bethan was cooking in the kitchen.

Bethan put her head round the door.

'Pasta bake alright?'

He grunted approval, his mouth full of beer, though of course she wasn't asking. He didn't like her pasta bake much. It felt good to have that secret from her. He felt grateful to be married each time he remembered it. Paul understood that he'd entered into something larger than himself. It had been surrender, and a relief.

CHARLOTTE MARAR

Charlotte was born in London and has a BA in English and Related Literature from the University of York. Her writing often interrogates the unstable relationship between the mind and body, addressing themes like family dynamics, sexuality, illness and trauma.

charlottemarar@hotmail.co.uk

Small Differences

An Extract from a Novel

Note: Erin (the protagonist) and Mae are identical twins. This extract is from early in the novel.

The white rectangle of light that framed the blinds in my room glowed strangely bright, considering it was dark outside. I mused on this for a while, hoping to bore myself into unconsciousness. I really needed to get some sleep if I was going to handle tomorrow's shift. Otherwise, I would have to tolerate Adam's remarks about the dark circles under my eyes; the ones he pretended were jokes. He was good at that. Pretending he was joking. I heaved my body to the other side of the bed.

Then came the noise. A plasticky rustle, unnaturally loud, as if someone was opening a crisp packet on the other side of the room. I pulled the chain on my bedside lamp, squinting in the sudden wash of yellow.

Rustle.

It sounded like it was coming from the wicker bin next to my desk, the one I stole from Mum. I stared at it for a moment, then realisation dawned. All the moisture evaporated from my mouth.

A mouse. It had to be. Or, God forbid, a rat.

Blood thudded in my ears as I scanned the room, one, two, three times over. Everything was undisturbed. The wooden chest of drawers, the white desk, the barren bookshelf and the abandoned paintings resting against the wall all stared back at me. My hand lingered on the chain. The idea of something breathing, crawling, sleeping in my room brought a cool nausea to my throat. Something dirty and quick and animal. I listened hard. Silence. Maybe I had imagined it. Or maybe it was just a gurgle coming from the radiator.

'This is ridiculous,' I said, then louder, 'I'm being ridiculous.'

Rustle.

'No, I'm not. Nope. No, thank you,' I said, darting out of the door. 'Goodbye. Goodbye, sir.'

I left the door open behind me to give the mouse a wide exit route and leaned against the wall, trying to decide what to do next. I still needed to sleep, though the thought now seemed absurd. My whole body shook as if I had been sprinting for hours. I peered into Mum's room. She was sleeping as she always did, flush to the edge of the bed so that if an emergency occurred in the night that needed her attention, she was already on her way. Perpetually poised for a catastrophe. I decided against it. She would be even more frightened than I was.

I tiptoed instead towards Mae's door along the hall, pressed my ear against the wood and listened to the low sound of snoring. Mae snored chronically, ever since I accidentally broke her nose in one of our bigger fights when we were children. Any memory of the reason behind the fight was replaced by the blood and the white lights of the emergency room. She had forgiven me for it – it was many years ago – but the snoring issue meant it was never quite forgotten.

I traced the chipped paint on the doorframe with my finger. My hand was still shaking. Surely it wasn't fair to wake her up either. Although, on second thought, I was the one who had to do a full day of work tomorrow. Really, I needed sleep more than she did. Maybe I could sneak into the room without her noticing. I cracked the door open and, as quietly as possible, slipped inside. The air smelled musty and stale, and a dark mass of hair was just visible on the far side of the bed. As I sat, the mattress sank under my weight, though the snoring continued uninterrupted. Encouraged by this, I lay down. The mass of hair catapulted itself upright.

'It's me!' I whispered. 'Sorry! It's me! It's me!'

'Erin?' Mae hissed. 'What are you doing?'

'I'm sorry, I didn't mean to wake you.'

'What! Why did you get in my bed, then?'

'There's a mouse in my room. I'm, like, ninety per cent sure of it. No, ninety-five.'

Mae fell back onto her pillow and rubbed her eyes. 'Jesus Christ, Erin. Don't do that again. You scared the shit out of me.'

'I know. I'm sorry.' My eyes began to adjust to see Mae's toes poking out from the bottom of the duvet. I felt the urge to laugh at the image but restrained myself. 'Do you mind if I sleep here?' I asked.

It was hard to read her expression in the darkness. Her breath smelt like the toothpaste we shared.

'Fine,' she said. 'Just don't steal the duvet.'

'I won't,' I said, folding the pillow in half to give it more height. 'Sorry,' I said again, for good measure.

As I settled down, I tried not to move too much so I didn't accidentally prod her with a knee or an elbow. She wasn't moving either, but the heat that emanated from her side of the bed reassured me of her presence. I wondered if she was worried about prodding me too or if keeping still came naturally to her.

Swaddled under the duvet, a pleasant heaviness settled over me, as if my body had suddenly admitted to itself that it was tired. Even if the mouse found its way into the room, I wouldn't be scared, I decided. It would be outnumbered here. I tried to imagine what would have happened if I had come into Mae's room when we were teenagers. Maybe she would have thrown something at me. Not that I would have ever come to her in the first place. But now, as Mae's breathing turned to snoring, I was surprised by how comfortable I felt, lying beside her. Occasionally, images of the pub, of Adam's face and his travelling hands, of the mouse, floated in my mind, but each time Mae's snoring got louder, they melted away.

Mae was gone in the morning. On the bed lay a stray hairband, which was knotted with her hair. I snatched it on my way out and put it on my wrist. I wasn't sure where she went in the daytime, but I knew she preferred to be out of the house, especially in the heat of the summer. Perhaps she just wandered the streets aimlessly, going into expensive shops, trying on clothes, and leaving without buying anything. Maybe she saw friends, people I didn't know. Because of my hours in the pub, I rarely saw her. Or Mum, for that matter.

I was tired that day as I filled and drained the sink over and over in that sweaty kitchen; after all, I had spent more of the night awake than asleep. But it was a different sort of tiredness. A peaceful kind, not the bone-drying exhaustion I was used to. This peace carried me all the way through my shift. Even when Adam looked at me with those expectant eyes, I felt that he was very far away. Or rather, that I was. I kept Mae's hairband on my wrist. Every so often, I would glance under my rubber glove, see it there and feel soothed.

When I got home, I shovelled down an under-microwaved mac and cheese, went upstairs to bed and paused outside my room. The gaping doorway seemed to pulse as if on the verge of explosion, and I bit my lip. Maybe I could just sleep in Mae's room again, just for one more night. This time, I knocked.

'Yes?'

'Do you mind if I sleep here again?' I whispered through the door.

'Is the mouse still there?' she replied.

I poked my head into her room. 'I think so.'

A pause. 'Okay,' she said. I entered and crawled into my side of the bed.

'We need to get, like, mouse traps or something,' Mae said as I pulled the duvet to my neck. 'Have you told Mum?'

'Not yet,' I said. 'I'll tell her tomorrow.'

'Good. But put it gently. You know how she gets.'

'Yeah, I know,' I said. 'And you're sure you don't mind me sleeping here?'

'Erin, it's fine,' she replied. Her voice had a firmness that approached exasperation. It reminded me of when she used to walk me through my maths homework, and I was too slow to reach the answer. She yawned. 'There definitely *is* a mouse, right?'

'What?' I replied. 'Yes, of course. Why would I make that up?'

'I don't know,' she said. 'Whatever. Just go to sleep.'

I did have a history of lying, it was true, but not since I was a child. She liked to use my past against me, sometimes. It was in these moments that I felt most distant from her. As far as I was concerned, the past wasn't relevant to today. I rolled over to look at her, but she was already facing away, so I turned back to stare at her room instead. There was no clear surface in sight. Her messiness used to disgust me; the towers of unwashed clothes, the abandoned tea slowly shrinking as it evaporated and stained the mugs, the books strewn across the floor. Not that my room was perfect. But now, I found I was comforted by the clutter. I was not only lying beside her, I was surrounded by her. I began to feel that warm heaviness again. If someone put me on a scale, I would have weighed more, I was sure of it.

The heaviness didn't last long. As the night grew older and the room, paler, Mae began to toss and turn beside me. Her breathing became ragged at the edges and the bed squeaked under us. My eyes flicked open. She was never a restless sleeper back when we used to share a room.

'Mae?' I murmured. She whimpered and what felt like an arm struck my own, hard. I sat up, grabbed her shoulder and shook it. 'Mae? Are you alright?'

Her face loomed clearer in the grey light. With her eyes closed tight shut and her mouth twisted, she looked like someone else. She rolled back and forth like a bat trapped in a bag.

'Mae, I'm here,' I said.

I leaned over and folded myself around her, whether to embrace or restrain her, I wasn't sure. Her skin was damp and hot and smelt of new sweat. I felt enormous as I enveloped her shuddering, bony body. It had been a long time since we hugged. If she's lost weight, I'll kill myself, I thought. Then I pushed the thought away and held her closer, so close that I could feel her heart thud in my chest. A strange part of me wanted to smile. After a while, her body stilled itself and she began to snore again.

Like the day before, she was gone in the morning. I expected this, but I was still disappointed. I wanted the chance to ask if she was okay. On the never-ending bus ride on the way to work, I thought about sending her a text, but I couldn't think of how to phrase it. Besides, she had been asleep. She wouldn't even remember the night before. The thought made me sad; that I was thinking about her, and she probably wasn't thinking about me. Later, I decided, as I scraped a stubborn yellow stain off a frying pan, that I would speak to her when I saw her that night. But when I finally reached her bedroom, with my tired muscles thrumming, I was met by cool sheets and an empty bed. She was gone.

REYAH MARTIN

Reyah Martin is a Scottish writer whose work explores the endless complexities of the human condition. In 2020, she won the Commonwealth Short Story Prize for Europe and Canada. She is currently working on her debut novel about the power of memory and storytelling during the Great War.

reyah.martin@gmail.com

Laid To Rest

A novel extract

Sometimes it is best leaving a mother to what she knows, and if not what she knows, then at least what she believes. For instance, Lily Lacey believes that Michael will be sensible, given that it is a Wednesday, and he will leave early for the market tomorrow. She believes that her eldest will come straight home when the Reverend has finished spreading the Word. He will put the war out of his mind and fill his head instead with stories made for his younger brother, for softening the world and keeping him safe on the inside, fearful whenever they walk together along the cliffs.

Lily is so certain of what she believes that she begins preparing for the birthday party on Sunday, humming and stringing up rows of colourful paper chains. She clears the morning's mess from the table, scrubbing crumbs and stains away, convinced that by evening they will be sitting together. They will be eating together. They will be together after sunset, trying to make things right. Wrapped up in believing, she promises herself, promises her youngest, promises the walls closing around them. Doubt takes hours to tighten its hold on her, tucked in the corners of every room, waiting like a held breath for evening.

The Lacey house lies so far out from the church, from everything in Stoor-Brig but the east-side sea, that Lily never catches the tiny smoke plumes rising from beside the graveyard wall. She never spots the signs of a well-kept secret, a conspiracy near the cemetery, where the young men gather, and the old yew tree hangs its head. Alma is the only one listening. She is the only one to hear dozens of lads' voices, making plans behind their hands in pantomime whispers. At every turn, she catches them. She matches them to mothers, to brothers and sisters and homes on the island. Their voices mark stirrings of desire; these boys will be the first in generations to up and go, to seek and find.

Into the city. Tomorrow. No, we mustn't wait. Wait and it'll be over.

Don't you want to be there? You might come home with a medal and all.

A medal for what? I wouldn't want to go killing a man, German or not. Besides, I've got no reason to. What have they ever done to me?

You ought to be careful, saying things like that. It's practically treason, now we're at war.

Treason, is it? Alright. Next time you meet the King around here, be sure and let him know.

Look, all I'm saying is, it could be us they come for next. What if some Hun was after your mother? Your sister? You'd kill him then, wouldn't you?

Leave my sister out of it. She's fourteen, for God's sake.

Makes no difference to any of them. You heard what they're doing to the nuns over in Belgium. And that sister of yours...well, she's pretty enough. They wouldn't think twice about –

Alma listens until it pains her, stars behind her eyes. She passes, head bent, gaze to the ground. They jostle each other for space, throwing their voices and their bodies, their plans flying up on the dense August air.

'Get me home, child,' she mutters to Beth, her bones stiff and aching from too long in the hollow chill of the chapel. The old witch swallows a shiver at the bottom of the church steps. 'Home, and quick about it. Before I fall to the ground.'

'Don't be so dramatic, Granny. It's no more than a mile away.'

'Dramatic, indeed. Five minutes more and I'll hit the floor.' Alma's eyes narrow to slits. Her grip tightens at Beth's elbow. Beth hardly notices. She is caught up in searching for girls her own age, craning her neck to see the faces of the ones she went to school with, who are making their own conversations beneath the murmur of their mothers.

These girls are beginning to fall in love, to style themselves after the fine ladies of the city, over the sea on the mainland and scattered as far off as London. They are still wearing their brightest colours, their softest expressions, not one widow among them. Their youngest brothers, too young to sign up, too high-pitched in their spirited yells, pinch their sisters' wrists and squirm to be free. Little sisters just like them are staring up into their faces, watching their lips move and wondering what it means. Most of these almost-women are practised already in raising children, babies on their hips since before they can remember. Despite their rouged lips and cheeks, they are, beneath it all, daughters working to keep things as they should be.

The styling business began with the likes of Millie Naismith – Millicent, after a dead aunt – who's been going steady for a year or more with the eldest Crook lad. Alma can't remember his name. Millie spends Wednesday mornings helping with Mrs Stark's reading lessons and hounding her for advice on how to look pretty, first for God and second for the lad she is courting. On Sundays, she doles out her answers like chicken feed, and the girls of the village scrabble around for the scraps. No matter how far forward she sits, Beth never hears from the back pew. She guides her grandmother, by the elbow, through the thickening crowd.

'You knew it would tire you, being on your feet for so long. Nobody made you get up, Granny.'

Alma scowls. 'Nobody makes me do nothing, child. There'd be hell to pay if they tried.'

The watchers are all Stoor-Brig women, huddled with their heads bent together, their words the last thing to keep them tied to this moment. To the final days before the village is marked forever. Before their fresh-made soldiers spill, shouting and singing and crushing rose petals under their boots, onto the station platform.

For now, these women are wives. Sisters. Sweethearts. They can reach for a wayward son, pat down his hair, make sure he eats enough. They can cross their arms over the body of an unsuspecting husband, fresh from the fields or from the sea, startling him from some faraway thought, rooting him to the spot where he has everything, where there is no need to see more of the world, to answer the call of a king who will never visit.

Alma's gaze follows Beth's and lands among the gaggle of gossiping girls. Her voice rises, barbed.

'You're prettier than every one of them. No need to go changing yourself.'

'I'm not changing. I'm wondering, that's all.'

'Wondering what, exactly?'

'How they manage it. Where they find the means to make themselves up as they do.'

It takes a while for Beth's attention to return. She is in the habit, on Sundays and whenever else she is alone, of stealing glances at these girls. When she was little, she stared because of their mothers. How attentive they were. How present. How strange it felt to go without a mother of her own. These days, she lingers for tips on how to wear her hair. How to give herself the look of a lady and not a tawdry star of the stage.

The secret, revealed in snatches, lies in how much rouge to use. How much to dab on the eyes, the cheeks, the lips. It lies in the faces of women like Helena Stark, a well-to-do wife who once travelled as far as the capital to keep up appearances. Besides Mrs Stark there is nobody with enough silver to paint their face every day. Of course, there is no point in telling a quiet village girl what she already knows. Especially not a good, sensible one like Beth. She never gets further than the edge of the trees. The market on the shore, where Michael glimpses her in the crowd and stutters in his haste to keep her a while longer, offering the ripest fruits. Alma is thinking of him when she turns.

'You're a lot like me, you know. Nobody can make you do anything, either.'

Beth is waiting for one of the other girls to turn and see her hopeful, hankering on the edge of the crowd. 'And what am I being made to do, Granny? I won't be going to war, if that's what you mean. They want the men. The horses. The old boats, perhaps.'

'They'll want more and more, you mark my words. In fact, they'll want every one of us, one way or the other, *for King and Country* and all. But it's not the war that bothers me now.' Alma inches forward, one hand pressing against the pain at the base of her spine. 'For God's sake, get me home, child. Before I get down on my knees and crawl there.'

'Alright,' Beth sighs, 'we're going.'

The girl measures her steps so that they fall behind the tap of the cane. She is watching her feet as they approach the graveyard wall. Michael Lacey sits on the stone by the rusted gate, swinging his legs and smoking. The cigarettes, hanging from his hand in their own silver case, have summoned a string of lads. A scramble for his attention. Alma counts all four Crook brothers, tossing a light between them. Beside Michael, there is Earnest Stark. His laughter arrives before his face. His fingers are raw, cut open with rope-burns from ringing in the war.

'Afternoon, Missus Cairns.'

Earnest goes so far as tipping his hat, parading his best manners while he sneaks a stolen Woodbine behind his back. Alma follows his voice, thick and muffled in her one good ear. She squints, but he is hard to make out in the afternoon light. More shape than certainty. Longest shadow of them all, stretching across the churchyard.

'*Missus Cairns* indeed. Seems we've become strangers, Earnest, what with you bringing out my Sunday name.' She lifts her head, following a trail of tell-tale smoke into the branches of the yew tree. 'Either that, or you're hiding something.'

'From you? Never, Alma. I know better than that.'

'I should hope so.' She steadies herself against the stone, her fingers spread where Michael has stopped swinging his legs, fumbling in his haste to stow his cigarettes in a pocket. He sits straighter at the sight of her, making the other boys pay attention. Earnest is the last to look her in the eye. 'Meanwhile, hiding things from your mother is somewhat your speciality.'

He is the sort to blush from the neck up, going puce to the roots of his curls. It is the one thing he got from his mother that Alma can count on. She waits for the colour to seep into his cheeks, for the moment before he tosses his cigarette into the grass. His mouth is already shaping into *sorry*, the laughter-light leaving his eyes. She waits long enough that he fidgets, pleading with her on the quiet. By now, the Crook brothers are watching. Michael sits smokeless and still, cigarette case snapping shut on the wall. Earnest blanches.

'You won't tell her I'm smoking, will you? Please, Alma. She'll go mad.'

'Tell her? What do you take me for? If I ever thought of telling her, it would have been last spring. Back when you had me swearing on my life. Do you know how many years I've lived, child?'

Before Earnest answers, the old woman winks. She is performing, holding the boys' eyes and hearts. Alma becomes the convincing witch of bygone days, her hands capable of any curse. Her wisdom hanging in the air, the stuff of star-pricked evenings and cautionary tales. She smiles, showing the pits in her gums where teeth have sunken to stumps, or tumbled out over the years.

'Do you know how much life I've lived? How many years it's been?'

One of Alma's secret church-going pleasures, keeping her mind from the pain in her spine, is watching Earnest Stark flit from answer to answer, snagged between plain honesty and the good manners that raised him. Now that he is seventeen, she is keeping a hoard of his secrets, each one a memory she can still recount.

LUCY MAY

Lucy was born in Sheffield and works for independent non-fiction publisher Pen & Sword Books. Her writing combines the literary with fantasy and over the course of the MA she has been focusing on her novel, a love story that transcends time, death, and other worlds.

Lucy.May.98@icloud.com

Déjà Vu

An extract from a novel

She woke gasping like a newborn, flat on her back on a wooden floor. The ceiling above her was collapsing in on itself. Daylight streamed through half-boarded up windows.

She sat up, vision splitting double. A pain throbbed at her temple as if she had recently hit her head. She shivered in a thin cotton dress, trying to get her bearings: a house, derelict. There was the sound of children outside. Something tapped against the outside wall. *Tick, tick.*

She couldn't have guessed where she was, but that wasn't new. She was used to waking up and puzzling it out. It didn't scare her. What scared her were the bones.

Her eyes came to rest on his skull. She couldn't have said how she knew it was a *him*. Something about his gaze. Watching her, balanced on the arm of what might once have been a sofa. She tipped her aching head to one side, looking into the holes of his eye sockets, and felt an odd sense of familiarity. She had definitely seen him before.

Her mind crawled. Once, she recalled, there had been a thick granite window-ledge in a low-ceilinged room. The only light was candlelight. No glass in the windows, cold seeping into her soul. The skull, in this memory, observed from a window ledge. Much like now.

Hello again.

She jerked to her feet, making her head spin stars. She glanced around frantically for who it was that had spoken.

'Hello?'

Only her own voice, thin from disuse.

As her breathing slowed, it occurred to her that she hadn't actually heard the voice aloud. It had been *inside* her head, like a thought that wasn't hers. She stared at the skull until she was convinced that she had misheard. Misthought?

There were only two rooms: this one, where she had woken, and another that led out to an empty yard. She couldn't explore the upper floors because the staircase hung crooked from the floor above, a gap ripped up the middle of the house. The window in this other room – possibly once a kitchen – had been smashed from the outside. The remaining pane was poised delicately in place, cutting her view into triangles: an isosceles of red brick wall. A shard of sky.

She tiptoed through debris with her arms folded. Something gave a gentle crunch underfoot, making her cry out. Her animal whimper echoed through the gutted building.

It was sharp, like seashells or broken crockery. When she lifted her foot to see, there were fragments pressed against her skin. She pulled a piece away, straining to identify it. White, smooth as a tooth.

Careful now.

It was bone. Immediately, she could see bones scattered across the space in a delicate network: a femur resting beneath the cracked sink, a pelvis nestled in the fallen stairs. By the window where she had been standing was the intricate scaffolding that once been a hand.

She gave another cry, brushed her foot clean in a frenzy. Something had destroyed this house, killing a person in the process. In her imagination, she saw them crushed by the fallen staircase, dying and rotting alone, and put a hand over her mouth. A sob burst in her throat. She felt the urgent pull of her heart, its muscular pump while this person's had stopped.

Time to go. Her stomach was empty, her feet bare, but before food and shoes she needed courage. That, and any supplies her surroundings had to offer. She shuffled through the debris, trying to discern if there was anything of use, and found a dented butterknife, a frayed carrier bag and half a box of matches. Wedged beneath the corpse of the sofa was an enormous book with its cover torn off. She leafed it open. Its writing was tiny, the pages spitting dust. She left it resting there despite her curiosity, this book having far too much story to bring along with her.

She gathered all the bones and arranged them respectfully before the skull, where she liked to think he could see them. His hips, his hand. The more she looked at him, the less sinister he became. The bones looked almost endearing now, and they were very clean. This skeleton had been a skeleton for a long time.

When she had exhausted her surroundings of anything helpful, she paid one final visit to the skull. Daylight was beginning to fade and if she were going to explore beyond the house, she should do so before dark.

'Bye-bye,' she murmured.

Off so soon?

She glared at the skull. Of all the oddness she had experienced, talking bones weren't the least of it.

'Pardon?' she said, indulging either the skeleton or her crumbling mind.

You're leaving.

It wasn't a voice at all. It was distinctly a thought; it was the same voice in her head that read the little letters on the butterknife and told her where it was made.

'Have we met before?'

You usually ask that.

This settled it. She sat cross-legged on the floor beside him.

'I remember you. Were you on a windowsill?'

There's been a lot of windowsills.

'How do you know me?'

You could say we've crossed paths a few times.

'When?'

There was a pause, roughly the length of a sigh. *Let's not do silly questions. I wouldn't bother with* who are you *and I won't do* how can you talk, *either. I just can. Don't frown at me, that's not fair. You're going a funny colour. Put your head between your knees.*

Now he mentioned it, she did feel faint. Bones wriggled across her vision. She hung her head and breathed deeply.

It's okay. Are you going to be sick?

'No?' she muttered, although she didn't feel right, it was true. 'Who…' she stopped herself. 'What should I call you?'

You tell me.

She snorted. 'I don't know my own name, never mind yours.' She could barely recall the names of anyone she'd met before, not concretely. Only sensations, images. She needed to hold on to more of her selves, retain things somehow.

The book she had found under the sofa was about a prince. His was the only name she could summon at that moment; it shone in her mind like a pearl.

'Genji,' she said. It felt good to speak it aloud. She had someone, and he had a name.

That'll do for now. What about you?

'Did I have a name, when we met before?' She tried to cast her mind back. Letters floated in her mind like a crumbling tombstone. She made out an A, an N.

Last time I saw you, they were calling you Anastasia. Bit of a mouthful.

'You don't have a mouth.'

I have all my teeth.

She considered picking him up to check, but worried that that this might offend him. Anastasia. She remembered a feeling along with that name, a taste of metal.

How about Ann?

'Okay.'

So, Ann. Where to?

'I don't know.' She crushed her eyes with the heels of her hands. 'I'm so hungry. And I need something for my feet. Did it hurt when I stepped on you?'

Not really. I've had worse.

Ann was starting to feel trapped in the little rooms. 'I might go. Before it gets too dark.'

Can I come?

She supposed it wouldn't make sense to leave behind the one friend she'd made so far. Even if he did turn out to be imaginary. 'Can you walk?'

Genji was silent.

'I said, can you walk?'

Obviously not.

'But you can speak,' she said. She wouldn't have been surprised if he had somehow assembled himself and walked about.

I don't make the rules.

She put Genji's skull into the flimsy carrier bag. 'Is this alright?'

Yes. Inexplicably, his thought-voice became muffled. *Don't forget the rest.*

Ann cluttered the puzzle that was Genji into the bag, knuckle bones jingling loose in the bottom. She considered leaving his pelvis behind, not wanting to strain the weak material. She turned it over in her hands, an awkward an awkward figure-of-eight.

Don't even think about it. You'd be distraught without your pelvis.

'Sorry.' She tucked it in beside his skull. She hadn't noticed any other bones lying around other than these scant few.

'What happened to the rest of you?'

I'm not entirely sure.

'Shall I look for…more?'

Genji was silent again. It almost made her repeat the question.

I'll manage.

Ann set off, not wanting to haunt the derelict property any longer than she had to. The alleyway leading to the street was empty, the children gone.

She passed red brick houses, squat and identical, lit up yellow from within. In the streets were tall metal lamps with hooked, swan-like necks. When they blinked on they made her jump, darting on the balls of her feet. Dandelions reached for her through cracks in the pavement, vivid in the twilight.

'Do you know where we are?' she asked Genji.

Nope. It's all new to me as well.

'How did you get here?'

I don't know. I woke up and I was here, with you.

'Are we the same?' Her chest fizzed with excitement. 'Do you wake up in a different place every time, too?'

Not quite. Look at you, you're all fleshy and alive.

'I suppose.' It was terrifying to think she might never escape this ordeal, of waking and waking and waking. 'How did you die?'

Murder.

'Really?' she paused, but he said nothing more. She assumed he was serious. 'Are you immortal?'

I wouldn't go that far.

'You must be. You died and then you woke up. How long have you been dead?'

It's hard to be sure. Centuries, possibly.

Her mind couldn't help but linger on the idea of being killed, but not dying. 'Did you…rot?'

Of course.

A flash in her mind's eye showed a living corpse. Bones draped with peeling flesh.

It wasn't pretty. People would scream, run, cry, et cetera. It's nice to be good-looking again.

A shudder wracked Ann's spine. She tried to imagine what Genji might have once looked like with a body. It was impossible to guess. He was a handsome skull, it was true. She imagined him with a twinkle of humour in his eye.

She followed the strange, tall lamps, keeping to where it was lit, and gave oncoming pedestrians a wide berth. The area was steep and looping. Genji insisted he be taken out of the carrier bag so that he could help her cross the road.

No...no...still no. Stop stepping out! You have to actually look around.

'You know an awful lot for somebody who's never been here before.'

I've seen cars before. Unlike you, clearly.

It was hard to snap out of the spell cast by the cars. She had assumed they were fixed, like buildings. When she saw one move, she had to stifle a scream, and picked across when told it was safe to do so, cradling Genji in her elbow.

When she saw a brightly-lit street in the distance, she decided this was their destination.

'Do you think they speak English?' she asked Genji. Then she had a thought. 'Do *you* speak English?'

I'm speaking to you, aren't I?

'Well...no?' She couldn't be bothered with the logistics of it all. It was bad enough that she kept waking up in bizarre new places. It was far easier to go along with everything as and when it happened, no matter how strange.

SAROJINI J. MISRA

Sarojini J. Misra grew up in Hyderabad and spent her childhood traveling between north and south India. She studied English Literature with Creative Writing at UEA. Her debut novel explores the complexities of family dynamics, generational trauma and examines the variable nature of truth.

appsagni2020@gmail.com

The Fall

The opening to a novel

We're flying over the Indian Ocean, cruising at an altitude of forty thousand feet when the turbulence begins.

There's no warning over the intercom. The seatbelt signs turn on and a moment later the plane shudders, beset by heavy winds. We jerk and pitch and sway, the more nervous among us beginning to pray. Beside me the old woman in the brown-gold kurta jerks awake, then proceeds to chant the Hanuman-Chalisa in an endless litany. She winces every time there's a bump, contorting into herself like a tortoise.

'We'll be alright,' I say, unable to stand another second of her recital. 'It's just turbulence – planes are made for this. Sab theek hai.'

'Lekin they didn't make an announcement.'

'They probably couldn't get to the intercom.'

She uncurls slightly, eyes fixed on her window like she's expecting it to break open. They've dimmed the lights in the plane, but the small light above her head is switched on and it catches the embroidery of her kurta, little golden glints over her saggy bosom. She's slept through most of the flight, head rolling from side to side, a deranged sort of pendulum to keep time by.

I wish she was still asleep, both for her sake and mine. I'm not a nervous flyer, but her terror is unsettling. She's so certain we're going to plummet to our deaths it makes me entertain the possibility. I offer her my hand to hold, like I did during takeoff, and she latches onto it immediately. Her hand is soft against mine, so pudgy that the feel of it is unpleasant.

'We're going to crash,' she mutters as the plane jerks sharply. 'Jai Hanuman…'

'Nahi, nahi. We're perfectly safe.'

'This is just horrible. I'm never doing this again.'

I let her move closer to me, stroke her withered fingers. Her skin is loose and almost transparent, thick ropes of blue-green veins jutting out from her hands. The flesh sinks in on itself like it's rotten, like there is no form to it. She reminds me of my grandmother—her hands could be my Nani's hands, trembling and liver-spotted. It makes me feel tender, forgive the sourness of achar on her breath. We shared her parathas and achar earlier when the British Airways meals proved inedible. Aloo parathas made with ghee, smeared with fragrant Punjabi pickle.

'What did you think of London?' I ask to distract her. 'Didn't you say your daughter lives in Shoreditch?'

'Haan.' She brightens immediately. 'My daughter Sheila, with her husband Bablu. They have a very nice house, two-storey.'

She tells me all about the house, her doctor daughter's practice and establishes Sheila's superiority to her cousins. Sheila's her only child, and the old woman can't help boasting a little about the one egg in her nest hatching so satisfactorily. The terror of turbulence is set aside in favor of making me understand just how caring Sheila is, how polite, the perfect daughter in all matters except for her lack of progeny.

'Chintu already has two children – Chintu is Sheila's cousin, on her father's side. Oh, I can't wait to be a Nani.'

She picks at her nail polish, the red flaking off into translucent bits. It looks like she's picking her skin off. In the white overhead light her face looks forlorn, makeup creased into the divots of her skin.

'Grandmothers are important,' I say. 'I've really missed my Nani.'

I don't know why I said that. My grandmother is a private grief, the kind you bury deep into the psyche to preserve sanity. This woman reminds me of Nani, and my sympathy for her is tempered with the natural dislike of facing things one wishes to avoid.

The airplane stabilizes, and the seatbelt signs turn off. My co-passenger stands up, a little wobbly, and makes her way to the washroom. I don't know her name, and she doesn't know mine. We introduced ourselves by the places we are from, Hyderabad and Delhi, and that was enough.

When she returns, I help fasten her seatbelt and she dives into her purse, searching through its compartments with great focus. Her purse is my mother's purse, bursting at the seams with all the things she'll never need, begging for respite from her overpreparation.

She extracts a little plastic bottle from it, filled with fennel seeds. Shaking half the contents into her mouth, she holds it out to me. 'Saunf?'

I empty the bottle into my mouth. The woody, acrid taste of fennel is so sharp it almost numbs my tongue. My mother softens the taste with sugar. Amma used to steal sugar-coated saunf from the dessert plates served so often in Indian restaurants, giggling as she wound up paper napkins into stuffed pockets and buried them away in her purse. Papa always scolded when he caught her doing it. He thought it made us look poor.

'Thank you,' I say. 'Are you OK now?'

'Yes, yes.'

Leaning back in my seat, I munch on the saunf. We're going to be landing shortly. On the digital flight map I can trace our route and watch as we get closer and closer to India.

'Your Hindi is very good,' the woman says. 'I thought you were from Hyderabad.'

'Most people from Hyderabad can speak Hindi.'

'Oh, accha. Are you Telugu?'

'My grandparents are from Kanpur.'

'How wonderful! My husband is from Lucknow, you know – we might as well be neighbors.'

I've spent very little time in Kanpur, and the distance between Kanpur and Lucknow is about a hundred kilometers. Still, that won't matter to her – to mention it would upset her. I smile and listen as she praises Thaggu Ke Laddu and Kanpuriya chaat, lists her relatives both living and dead who have spent time in Kanpur.

'Are you visiting Hyderabad after a long time?'

'Yes. Almost seven years.'

'Baap rey!'

Seven years. It feels like an age, like no time at all. I remember being on the opposite route of this flight, flying from Hyderabad to London instead of the other way around. It seemed like an impossible journey then. Now it's just inconvenient.

'Well, it's good that you're going home. Your family must be desperate to see you.'

'Yes.'

'Is it a happy occasion? Someone's wedding?'

'No. My grandfather – my Nana is very sick.'

I should say *my Nana is dying*. But I can't bring myself to speak the words. I've got to trick my mind, say *he's very sick* like there's hope of his getting better.

There isn't. My grandfather is ninety-six, his legs mapped by lurid varicose veins and his arteries corroded from almost a century of living. He is not going to get better. Amma wouldn't have called me home unless he was dying.

Old hands envelop mine, cool lac bangles pressing uncomfortably into my wrists. 'It will be alright,' she whispers. 'You poor child, he will get better.'

It is a lie, but such a kind lie. I let my hands rest in hers, her ugly rotting hands that have likely been softened by Boroline and years of Vicks Vaporub.

Attention, passengers, we are thirty minutes away from landing. Cabin crew, prepare to begin descent.

The flight crew makes their way down the aisles, checking on overhead baggage and urging people to put their seatbelts on. We're descending rapidly, and my ears ache. I see Surat appear on the screen-map in front of me, followed by Navsari. We aren't over the ocean anymore.

The plane tilts to the right, and the old woman's hands clench tightly around mine. They feel even more unpleasant this time, clammy and wet with the sweat of her fear. We're over Valsad now. The flight crew has retreated to their stations, strapped into their seats with landing imminent.

We fly past Malegaon. Sangamner. Shrirampur.

I've never been to these places. I can't picture them in my head, can't see them outside of names on a map. But somehow through the exhaustion of flying they bring relief, a sort of homecoming in the sky. I am over the earth that I came from. I can say these names like locals say them. They are populated by people whose skin is like mine, who share parts of my culture, who can speak my name as it is meant to be spoken.

And then the world stops. It feels like the engines beneath my feet have ceased thrumming. The lights inside the plane are even dimmer than they were before, and it is completely dark outside. We are suspended in a capsule, thousands of feet above ground in an empty void.

The old woman has her eyes screwed shut in terror, lips moving again in silent prayer. I am not afraid. I am ecstatic, weightless, poised like a bird mid-flight.

We begin to fall.

It's a slow, controlled fall, but a fall nonetheless. Forty-thousand feet, thirty thousand, ten thousand.

Five. Four. Three.

The lights of the city appear below us. The plane tilts again, to the left, and the woman screams. We level out, hovering, and then the wheels slam into the ground. The force is enormous, and it slams us back into our seats. Slowly, the airplane eases into taxiing on the runway.

I look outside the window, at the end of a six thousand mile journey, and find myself home in Hyderabad.

After the first perfect silence of landing, cacophony explodes. Phones are switched on and start pinging – people begin to unload their overhead baggage in defiance of the flight crew's instructions to remain seated. The woman is still praying, heaving great big breaths, fingers trembling. I wait in my seat till the hubbub has died down, then pull my backpack out from under the seat, checking to make sure my passport is tucked safely inside. My mind is occupied with the trivialities of immigration and the journey to Nacharam when the old woman pulls at my sleeve.

'Do you need help with your luggage?' I ask, though I'm desperate to get out of the plane.

'No, Sheila booked for special assistance. They'll come with a wheelchair.'

'That's good.'

She hesitates for a moment, then smooths her hand over my hair. It smells of milk and ghee. 'You're a good child,' she says. 'Thank you for all the help.'

'I didn't really –'

'Thank you,' she insists. 'I was very scared.'

'You won't be so scared next time.'

'Mmm.'

I strap my backpack to my shoulders, checking my seat and the storage space with it for anything I might have left behind. Finding nothing, I prepare to leave the plane, smiling one last time at the old woman.

'It was lovely to meet you,' I tell her. 'I hope your journey to Delhi is smooth.'

She blinks, rheumy eyes watery in the overhead light. 'I will pray for your Nana,' she says. 'I will pray tonight.'

'Thank you.' I have to thank her, but somehow I resent the presumption, kindly though it's meant. If I could I'd pray for Nana myself. I stand up to leave the plane, but the old woman takes hold of my hand again. Irritated, I look down at her. 'Yes?'

'You should come home more often.' There's a strange fervor in her eyes. 'Your Nani must miss you. And your parents – fathers always miss their daughters.'

I don't know what makes me say it. Maybe I'm fed up with her after eleven hours, maybe I feel betrayed by what she says after all the help I've given her. I think it's the anonymity of people on a plane, the knowledge that this is the last time in Hyderabad that I can speak without watching every word I say.

'My Nani is dead,' I tell her. 'And I hate my father. Goodbye.'

DENISE MONROE

Denise Monroe is a London based writer. In her contemporary fiction debut, *And the Grass Still Grows*, a park in South London talks to the lost soul of a young man as a community reels and recovers from the tragedy of his death.

denise@denisemonroe.co.uk

And the Grass Still Grows

An extract from a novel

Mel sat at the kitchen table holding a cold cup of tea. There was a smudge of lipstick around the rim, which was odd because she hadn't bothered to wear make-up since the funeral – and that was weeks ago. Lentil nudged his nose under her arm. She really ought to take him for a walk, but he was getting on and the garden was big enough. She pushed herself up from the table and opened the double glass doors into a shock of fresh air. The buzz of next door's mower carried across the boundary wall, loaded with the verdant scent of spring; she used to love that smell. The dog leapt across the decking and onto the grass as a squirrel scuttled over the back fence. She'd need to clean up after him but that could wait. Everything could wait.

Lentil returned to her side. She held his head and looked into the same eyes that had adored Adam, touched the same fur that he'd stroked. She wanted to speak but no words would come so she made a little humming noise and he cocked his head in reply.

The bell rang and Lentil's bark shuddered through her body. He skidded across the kitchen's quarry tiles, gaining traction on the hall's floorboards, and launched himself at the door. He didn't usually do that. Maybe he did need to go for a walk.

Mel had no intention of talking to anyone but knew she could be seen if the caller peered through the letterbox. That was how Louis had known she was home the other day. Whoever was there now must have lifted the brass flap and be talking to Lentil because his tail was wagging desperately. It must be someone they knew.

She hid by the sink and stared into the bowl of cold, scummy water. A ring of orange fat lined the surface, probably from the spaghetti Bolognese that Louis had brought over. This is what she'd become: the old mum, living alone, being given ready meals by her surviving kids who had their own lives to be getting on with.

It wasn't that she was a complete hermit. She'd been out since the funeral, but only when she gauged that the rest of the world was safely at home. She'd started walking in the park at night, tucking her pyjamas into her wellies, sneaking in through the gap in the fence that the kids used after dark, standing under Adam's tree, talking to him, wanting him to know how sorry she was. She'd taken Lentil a few times but he whined at the shifting shadows and pulled to get away. Last night, she'd gone alone but as she'd approached the lodge, unfamiliar shapes loomed out of the darkness. The entire site had been fenced, blocking her access to the tree. She'd come home to her old dog and an empty house.

Lentil ran through the kitchen and straight into the garden. Too late, she realised the visitor had let themselves in at the side gate. Now there was nowhere to hide.

'There you are.'

She flinched and a little squeal escaped her.

Roddy stood at the back door and Lentil jumped up to him. He hooked the dog's paws around his waist and swayed a little from side to side as though dancing with a child. 'I hope you don't mind,' he said, 'but I heard the mower and thought you might be working in the garden...' His voice petered out and she felt the concern behind his searching gaze.

She was wearing Adam's grey towelling dressing gown which was much too big for her. There were pulls in the fabric where Lentil's paws would have caught in their play fights, and a stain of something that could be coffee by the front pocket. She couldn't bring herself to wash it, not while it still held the essence of Adam. Her feet were bare, the skin pale and dry, and she couldn't remember the last time she'd brushed her hair or looked in a mirror. Teeth? Had she cleaned her teeth recently? She licked her tongue around the inside of her mouth in search of any debris and flattened her hair with her hands.

'Hi Roddy.' Her voice cracked so she coughed and tried again. 'How are you?'

'I'm good, Mel. How are you doing?'

She reached for the kettle, as though she'd been planning to make tea all along, and registered three empty wine bottles on the counter which was strange. She was sure Louis had emptied the recycling before he left.

'I'm fine,' she said. 'You know how it is.' She turned the cold tap on with force and water bounced from the side of the kettle and into the sink.

'Here.' Roddy stepped into the kitchen just like he'd done a hundred times before. 'Let me do that.'

She felt the pain of his kindness and blinked back useless tears. 'Yes, perhaps,' she said.

'I've tried calling you a few times.'

When Louis had come over, he'd chastised her for not having her phone on. She hadn't been able to find it when he'd asked, and it had finally turned up under the pillow in Adam's room. She couldn't remember how it'd got there.

'I lost it' – she couldn't be bothered to find more words – 'but I have it now. Was there anything in particular?'

'Just checking in.' Roddy uncovered a red teapot from under a crumpled tea towel and rinsed it under the hot tap. He emptied the bowl and squirted washing up liquid under a stream of steaming water. 'And I wanted to tell you that we've started work on the café.'

Mel picked at a loose thread on the sleeve of the dressing gown as she envisaged Adam's tree, trapped behind fencing and no longer hers. She'd thought the café idea had been something in their past, surely it wouldn't be in their future.

'I wanted to make sure you were okay with it.' Roddy brought two mugs of tea to the table and sat opposite her. Lentil settled at his side and stared up hopefully.

'I know.' Mel's voice was quiet even though she felt like screaming. 'I mean, I saw that things were happening. I sort of thought it wouldn't. Not after –'

'Yeah,' he said. 'That's why I had to see you.'

She nodded her head, still worrying the thread between her finger and thumb. She wanted to be angry, to tell Roddy to leave the site alone, that it was the only place she could go and talk to Adam. But she knew it was useless. If Roddy pulled out of the project someone else would take over. At least he was her friend.

'When did you last leave the house?'

She couldn't tell him about her night time visits to the park, he'd think her mad. 'Not for a few days.'

'And Lentil?' The dog looked up at the sound of his name and thumped his tail on the floor in a slow steady rhythm.

'Louis took him out when he was here. He's fine.'

They drank their tea quietly. It was time Roddy left but he seemed content looking out onto the garden. It was March now and the daffodils had popped up along the borders. It used to be her favourite time of year, seeing the buds appear, the colour start to infuse the garden, the lawn thickening into its deepening green. Now she felt it was mocking her. All this new life carrying on, moving forward, growing up.

'Spring's arrived,' said Roddy. 'The lawn could do with a trim. Shall I give it a quick mow while I'm here?'

'It's fine,' said Mel. 'I can do it.'

He stroked the dog and she stared into her cup because she didn't know where else to look. She didn't want his sympathy and didn't want to see the world outside.

'The thing is, Mel,' – Roddy seemed shy and started drawing circles of spilt tea on the tabletop – 'I could do with some help.'

She was confused. Surely he'd mistaken her for someone who could function.

'The trouble is, with Lisa out of action, I'm kind of on my own with the build.'

'What's wrong with Lisa?'

'Didn't you hear? She had the baby.'

'Is she okay?'

'She is, but she ended up having a caesarean.'

'And what was it?'

Roddy paused for a beat too long.

'I see.' She squeezed her eyes shut against brimming tears and bound her arms into the dressing gown sleeves, holding onto herself as she rocked against the sudden images of baby Adam that flashed across her mind in a torrent of torment.

'Shit.' Roddy grabbed a kitchen roll and passed her a piece. 'I'm so sorry Mel. I didn't think.'

She slowly unwound herself and took the paper towel, pressing it into her closed eyes. She wanted to clear the pictures that taunted her but at the same time never wanted them to go. 'It just keeps hitting me.' She sniffed. 'I'll be alright.'

'Why don't we take the dog out?' said Roddy. 'A bit of fresh air will help.'

It was the last thing she wanted to do but at least it would get Roddy out of the house. She took a deep breath and stood up. 'Come on then. Before I change my mind.' She locked the back door and walked to the hall where her wellies stood, next to Adam's running shoes.

'You might be better off in jeans,' said Roddy.

She looked down at the grubby pyjama legs that flapped around her ankles, suddenly ashamed of what she'd become. She felt weak and propped herself up against the wall of the hallway. 'I can't go Roddy. Look at me. I'm a mess.'

Roddy didn't seem to know what to do and, for a moment, she felt stupid. Although they'd known each other a long time, he'd always been Hamish's friend. She might have kissed him on the cheek after the occasional dinner party but nothing more and certainly no excessive signs of emotion. He stepped forward and held her and, as she rested her head on his chest, she felt the comfort of the years of their friendship; remembered him in the garden at Adam's fourth birthday party; Hamish and Roddy waving goodbye as they cycled off to Brighton, promising Adam he could join them next year. She wept.

Roddy didn't speak or tell her it would be okay or that the pain would go away, and she was grateful. They stood in the hallway until her sobs subsided.

'Right.' Roddy released her. 'New plan. I'll take Lentil out and you're going to run yourself a bath. I'll get Sally to come over. You can't go on like this.'

She wiped her runny nose on the sleeve of the dressing gown. It really did need a wash. She found the dog's lead on the coat hook and crumbs of mud fell as she attached it to his collar.

'Will you be alright for half an hour?' said Roddy.

She nodded and opened the door. He kissed her on the cheek as though it were an ordinary day and walked down the path with Lentil chewing his lead in excitement.

NIC O'KEEFFE

Nic O'Keeffe is a prose, stage and screenwriter from Sunderland. Her short film *Sparklers* (BBC iPlayer) won a 2021 Broadcast Digital Award, and she was shortlisted in the final round of Penguin WriteNow 2023. Nic's work centres queer, northern and working class identities, exploring themes of disconnection and loss, often through a speculative lens.

nicokeeffewrites@gmail.com

Starved

An extract from a short story.

Jamie pulls a bowl from the cupboard. When did she last speak aloud? There was a moment, at the shop this week—or last week, maybe—when the self-service checkout glitched, double scanned. She dithered, debated going to the till, speaking to the uniformed teenager: masked and face-shielded behind her plastic pane. Lump in her throat. The cashier noticed, fixed the error from afar. The wonders of technology.

    She opens her mouth, as if to test her voice, then closes it again, suddenly fearful that nothing will come out.

    She pours Frosties, lets them sog in the milk, sits and scrolls. Chews, swallows. Something squeaks between her teeth and she chews harder, thinking it's a particularly crunchy flake. It bends and springs back between her molars and she freezes, tongues it into her cheek, raises a hand and spits. She searches the palmful of orange mush until she finds it. A ragged half-moon of bitten off fingernail. Her stomach lurches, mouth flooding with hot spit and she struggles not to be sick. Swallows. Swallows again.

    She rinses the cereal off her hand, then peers at it. Gnawed shred of thumbnail. Saliva thickens around her tongue and she pulls out her phone, takes a couple of pictures of it. Takes a photo of the cereal box, its barcode, then dumps the whole lot into the bin. Scrubs her hands. Brushes her teeth. Drinks a glass of water, then another. Swishes, spits into the sink.

    'What the fuck.' Her voice startlingly loud, surprisingly intact. Not rusted or withered, like she expected. 'What the *fuck,*' she says again, savouring the shape of it on her tongue.

    Her skin crawls. She paces. She can't stop feeling the sensation in her mouth, the creak and bounce of it against her teeth. She feels unclean. The window is still smeary – she's been meaning to sort that since...when? The sink crawls with fingerprints. The dust behind the TV is pockmarked with them, footprints in snow. The countertops too, though she wiped those down at least, just the other day, after she brought the groceries home, she's certain she did. She hoovers, dusts, wipes. She blasts music, same song over and over until it becomes just a thumping in her blood. She feels almost good. She sweats from the effort, invites the non-existent breeze in through open windows. The irony of a gorgeous summer spent indoors. She longs for barbecues, sunburns, beer gardens, walks by the Thames hand in hand.

    Her stomach gurgles but the thought of chewing is nauseating. She drinks a beer. Forces down some toast, carefully inspecting each slice. Two beers become three become four: cells multiplying. She retreats to the bedroom. The world shrinks, her bed a tiny swaying boat.

She feels restless, like her skin is on too tight. She windmills her legs, slides a hand into her underwear. She tries to masturbate but it's not taking, she just feels sticky and over-warm instead of wet, rubbing herself with uncomfortable friction. She squinches her eyes closed, tries to think of sexy things. Red, wet mouths, tongues and fingers. When did she last see anyone's mouth, touch anyone's hand? These have taken on sinister, dangerous connotations: contagion, death. She tries to shift her thoughts. Featureless, imagined someone. Think of breasts and cunts, buttocks and thighs, pliable flesh, kneading the meat of an anonymous arse under her hand, breathing hot, open-mouthed breaths against their neck, sliding fingers up and in, damp, slick body heat. The image slips, and it's Soph's neck she's panting against, Soph she's fucking, familiar shivers around her fingers, familiar moans against her ear.

Scrit scrit. Jamie grinds her teeth, the reluctant orgasm cresting, then retreating. She stills the motion of her fingers, wipes them on her shorts. She turns on her side, sour taste in her mouth, gluey feeling between her thighs, and lies there, eyes closed, feeling vaguely sad, vaguely ashamed, still vaguely horny.

Something touches her leg. A little drunk, a little sleepy, for just a moment she thinks it's Soph, running a finger up her calf. Soph's love language: tactility. Pressing kisses to the backs of knees, chasing a trail across the soft flesh where belly meets hip. Jamie sighs into the touch. It really does feel just like Soph, gentle fingers tracing the whorl of her leg hair. But Soph isn't here. Jamie jerks upright, searches the peaks and valleys of the crumpled sheets. Something slips off the end of the bed, startlingly pink, and she blinks woozily. A tail? Too thick, maybe, but that's all it can be. She shudders. As if they're getting bold enough to climb onto the bed, crawl on her legs now.

She climbs out of bed, checks all the traps are set. She still hasn't caught a single mouse.

***

Unhook mask, dispose of mask, wash hands. Unpack packages, wipe packages, wash hands again. Milk, eggs. More beers. Extra mousetraps. One at the foot of the bed, one by the front door, another in the kitchen. Dig the peppermint oil out from under the sink. It's half dried up but she smears what she can on the skirting boards, paint flaking, strange little scratches.

***

Sticky, mouth-open, toss-turning sleep. Beer bottles congregating on the bedside table. She dreams about Soph, memories mingling with imagined realities. She wakes fuzzy tongued, a dark mood simmering. Opens Whatsapp, ignores the little red number in the corner, larger every day. Soph smiling and pretty in her picture. Jamie drafts a message, deletes, clenches fists, nails biting into the meat of her sore palms. Anger thuds, dull and nauseous in her belly. She pads to the kitchen, laps water from the tap like a dog, retreats to the bedroom, stares again at the tiny, smiling Soph. Puts down her phone and instead fetches a bin bag, moving to the wardrobe.

When Soph left she was frenetic, unchoosy. Cramming clothes into the case, one of those miniature ones that can walk by your side, companionably. They'd bought it for a holiday in Rome. Wheeled it across dusty, heat-cracked cobbles, underestimating the distance from the train to the AirBnB, sweating under the unrelenting Italian sun. A wheel broke, they bickered, then Jamie picked it up, soldiered on with it banging against her hip. After showering, cooling under the air-con, Soph apologised and kissed Jamie's biceps, kissed the bruise purpling on her side, called her strong, tumbled her onto clean linen.

Some of her dresses hang alongside Jamie's shirts and jumpers, nestled close, open armed, lovers waiting for a song to dance to. Jamie opens the wardrobe, feeling bilious. Here, the yellow scoop neck Soph wore on their first date, sunkissed collarbones and freckled shoulders. Here, the dress she wore to David's wedding, frothing lace, pink-cheeked and pretty after too many mimosas.

One by one Jamie plucks them out. Not folding, not even de-hangering, shoving them deep into the bag so hard one snags, rips, fabric puffing through black plastic. Her throat thickens, and she tries to cry. A frustrated, chest-heave of a sob sticks in her throat like a cough. Tears won't come. She pushes the hanger back through the hole, piles more clothes on top, widening the ragged tear.

Afterwards she feels worse than before. She hefts the bag into the corner where it sighs, crinkles, leans. She snaps a picture of it and, before she can think better, sends it to Soph with the caption *Ready whenever you want to collect.* One tick, then two--grey, then blue. No reply. She slams her phone face down onto the bed with a muffled thump. She feels hungover, dried out and clammy all at once.

The restaurant up the road is doing deliveries, contact free. She orders pizza on her phone. Still no reply from Soph. This restaurant was a favourite of theirs. Anniversaries and birthdays, feeding Soph a mussel from her fork, giggling at how they look like tiny vulvas, sharing garlic bread, kissing, sharing garlic breath. The restaurant started doing deliveries a week or two before Soph left.

Shall we order something? A date night. Proffered hopefully.
I don't think we should eat something someone else has touched.

Soph wasn't leaving the flat at all by then, getting Jamie to strip off her outside clothes in the hallway and shower as soon as she returned with the groceries. She slept with her back turned, shrugging off any attempts to spoon. Moved from living room to bedroom and back again, a metronome, stopping only to watch the news, eat the dinner Jamie cooked. If Jamie could convince her to watch Netflix, she sat at the opposite end of the sofa, cross-armed, the space between them cavernous.

Jamie didn't mind running the errands. Going out. Started buying cigarettes on her shopping trips, walking a slow, circuitous route back, soothed by the rhythm of inhale, exhale, smoke coiling deliciously in her lungs, podcast burbling in her ears. She'd spritz perfume after her back-home shower, brush her teeth, chew gum. Needless gestures. Soph hadn't kissed her in days.

Soph found the pack in Jamie's jacket pocket, crumpled and strewn with tobacco threads.

Are you taking any of this seriously? A crack through the middle of her voice. The buzzer shouts. Jamie permits entry to the grainy figure on the screen, masked and high-vised, insulated package in hand. A strange thrill up her spine: a person, acknowledging she's real, she's here. Not a recorded voice reprimanding, *Unexpected item in the bagging area.* An actual, living, breathing person. She watches through the peephole, pulse thumping along with each dull thud of boots on carpeted stair. He turns the corner, comes into stark relief. Raps sharply at the door, then unsheathes the pizza from its bag, places it on the doormat.

'Hi,' she says, almost breathless, mouth pressed to the grain. He straightens up, gives a small, shoulder height wave. She raises her own hand, pushes it to the door, echoing his gesture. If he leaned forward just a little it would be as if they were touching. 'How are you?'

He gives a thumbs up, turns, his figure becoming smaller in the warped, fisheye view of the peephole. Then he's around the corner. Then he's gone. Adrenaline recedes. Her teeth ache. She waits a breath, then two, then three, then retrieves the pizza. Decants it from box to plate, washes her hands, Soph shouting in the back of her mind about caution, despite his thick gloves, his mask. It's gone lukewarm already, so she microwaves it.

She burns her mouth, shovelling it in, folding slices, barely chewing. She drinks beer with dinner. One, then two, then three. Cheese congeals to fat, claggy threads on the plate.

She retreats to bed, her phone for company and *Friends* on the TV. Her soft palate feels raw and stringy, she tongues at it. Throws an arm over her eyes, static dancing against the squint of her eyelids. The mice *scrit-scrit* in the walls, behind the headboard, the sound cresting, a wave pouring down and across, chittering behind the skirting board, towards the door frame. If she tries hard enough, she can almost imagine Soph is still here, just in the other room, hunched over her laptop and the scratching actually the tap of keys. If she just tries hard enough she can almost hear the creak of her foot in the hallway. Feel the bed dip as she climbs in. Her breath against Jamie's neck, hairs rising on her arm. She can almost feel fingertips brush her cheek, the shell of her ear, thumb pressing against her lower lip. With a gasp she opens her eyes, presses a hand to her mouth. She blinks in the sudden brightness of the room, skin tingling with the aftershock of touch. It felt so real. Her throat thickens. She checks her phone; still no reply. She worries at the sore roof of her mouth. Wonders what it would take, what she could say, what she could do, to bring Soph back.

GAYATHRI SANKAR

Gayathri Sankar was born in India. She studied English Literature with a minor in Creative Writing at Ashoka University. Her current novel deals with the violence of memory, disintegration of the self and queer desire.

gayathri.sankaran1999@gmail.com

Katha Block

An extract from a novel

I've taken to calling you my caterpillar. Tucked into your cocoon of blankets, you look serene in your hibernation. I'm not sure where your chrysalis begins – sheets or skin or sweat – but I can sense the non-stop activity underneath the surface. Do you ever get any sleep?

You told me you enjoy running the same scenario through your head, like a film stuck on loop. You like to imagine waking up a hundred years in the past. This impulse doesn't arise from misplaced nostalgia or the sense that you were born in the wrong era. You had a more sinister goal. Plagiarism, you whispered, with eyes that lit up so brilliantly they looked like headlights speeding towards me. A special kind of plagiarism where you steal the work before it has been created. You would go into the past and write all the books of the next fifty years. Forfeiting smartphones and computers and the internet, you would crouch over a typewriter or write with a fountain pen. You liked to flesh out the minutiae of this dream, as if this obsessive attentiveness to detail would impose it onto reality.

When I saw Yuki yesterday, I braced myself for a question about your absence. But perhaps she doesn't remember you anymore. She tries to hide her forgetfulness, as everyone in Katha Block does, but I could see the blankness in her eyes.

I wonder if you'll emerge from your blanket with no memory of yourself. I'm even more concerned you'll have no memory of me.

But I'll keep the records, just in case.

Should we begin with the first time we met?

It was summer and Katha Block's spiralling snail shell streets made me dizzy as I followed them to Yuki's house. Each step I took towards the centre, the posher the houses became. Once I was at Yuki's front door, I adjusted my dress. It was fancy, branded. I chose the dress for two reasons. The first was its lack of sleeves. As you know, I can't bear the embarrassment of pit stains and worry that I sweat too much for a girl. I know that it's psychosomatic – that I sweat when I'm anxious and the regulator exists somewhere in my mind. But I just can't access the switch. The second reason was the bustle, the crinoline-like material that expanded the skirt and made it resemble a ballgown, so I could pretend to be a character from a Victorian novel.

Yuki opened the door. Her gaze swept over my clothes and an uncertain smile budded on her mouth. Then her eyes reached my face and widened.

Vivek was right – you look *just* like…

Yuki's excitement swallowed the rest of the sentence. She grabbed my hand and tugged me through the doorframe. We glided through a long hallway adorned by a lone painting: two figures in dramatic shades of red and green interlocked in intimate battle. The artist, who I identified as Tyeb Mehta, left some of their thrashing limbs uncoloured, so you can hardly tell them apart. I wanted to show off my analysis of the piece, but Yuki towed me along with too much haste.

In the dim living room, Yuki called everyone to attention. It took them a while to compose themselves. They moved towards her like sluggish moths to a flame. As they registered my appearance they began fluttering excitedly. From amidst their folds they offered you up, placing you next to me.

This one's taller —

No, the other one slouches. And her face is rounder.

The shape of their eyes are the same but...

Her eyes are lighter —

Hey, what is your name? someone asked. My lips moved, outlining my name, but no sound came out.

Hi Yaminah, you said, extending your hand like you were tossing me a lifeline. I took it.

It's exciting to meet my doppelganger, I said, trying not to stare.

Your palm was wet inside mine, though I couldn't tell whether it was my sweat or yours. Were our bodily functions facsimiles as well? Your eyes were glasslike, reflecting me back to myself. As you looked around, laughing at everyone's excited reactions, I was perturbed to see my face in your profile. There were details I hadn't accounted for: the hint of a double chin, the wispy sideburns... I wondered to what extent we resembled each other. But then there was the way your eyelashes curled upwards, hair flanking your face like velvet curtains waiting to be drawn. I thought you were beautiful, so I must be as well.

Vivek stood with his arm around Yuki. They watched us like a couple admiring a diptych.

You seem much less impressed than Yaminah, he said to you.

I just have a common face, you said. This is like the third doppelganger of mine I'm meeting.

Despite your aloofness, you seemed to feel some sort of obligation towards me. As you worked the room, you kept me involved in every conversation. We stayed linked, elbows touching. Both of us were outsiders – I had moved to Katha Block a month prior; you had moved here only a week ago. But you were already more at home than I was, charming and articulate and acquainted with everyone.

The next time we met was at another party, someone's birthday, a month or so later. We messaged each other erratically during the time in between. I felt as though I knew you intimately and not at all. Initially, I could not find anything of you on the internet besides your Instagram, which was a wasteland containing no profile picture and a single post (*The Two Fridas* by Frida Kahlo, with no caption). Eventually I tracked down your Spotify, where I scoured your playlists, followed by your Letterboxd, where you kept track of the movies you watched. I went to the second party feeling like you were a test I had studied for.

These things sometimes make me feel like I'm in *The Symposium*, I told you as I lit your cigarette. You know, a room full of people all having intellectual conversations while sipping liquor.

The Symposium is one of my favourite books.

Oh! I said, as if I didn't already know this from your Goodreads account. Mine too.

Who's your favourite speaker from the book?

I had not read the whole book, only the SparkNotes summary in college. My only recollection was the speech of Aristophanes, so I blurted out his name.

Why him?

I thought his speech was… funny, I said lamely. It's a pretty absurd visual. A time where human beings had four legs and hands, two faces, two sets of genitals. And they *cartwheeled* everywhere? I simply can't imagine an army of gymnastic primeval humans being *such* a threat to Zeus that he needed to split them in half.

You laughed at this.

Well, Aristophanes was meant to be a comic character after all. With his persistent case of the hiccups.

I nodded knowingly.

I was worried you'd take the speech seriously, you continued. I don't know why so many people seem to genuinely resonate with it.

I shuffled around guiltily. Well, maybe it comforts us, in some way, to believe our original nature has been cut in half. It helps us make sense of our yearning, why we feel incomplete.

Our *original* nature, you murmured. Do you feel that way?

I blushed. I do, I confessed. When I really like someone, it's like I want something from them, but I don't know what. I just want to… absorb them sometimes. Anything less just isn't enough. Who's *your* favourite speaker?

My namesake, obviously, you said. Diotima.

We've only ever had one argument, do you remember? It began when I heard from someone that you had dyed your hair green.

I'm just surprised you didn't *tell* me, I said to you on the phone. I had to hear through someone else. I surprised myself with my entitlement to you, considering I had only known you three months.

I was pacing my room as I spoke, resentful of how nagging my voice sounded. I could hear a strange amalgamation of noises in the background. It sounded like a busy kitchen – water flowing, whistles screaming, meat sizzling.

Should I dye my hair too then? I asked.

What? you laughed. Like the *same* colour? Why are you behaving like —

Because it's *not* just hair, I snapped. Or it'll start with hair, and then it'll become… everything else. What is that sound?

What is this really about?

I sat down on my bed and took a deep breath.

Remember when you told me about your doppelgangers? Your... your *three other* doppelgangers? Since they all look like you, it would only make sense that they look like each other, right? So, I looked for them on Instagram, but they... *don't*.

I paused, giving you a chance to call me crazy.

They all look drastically different and I just don't know how they could *all* look or have looked like you if...

The noise in the background abruptly ceased. Now I could hear a horrible, raspy retching interspersed with deep breaths, like someone was drowning.

I don't feel well, you said. Your voice sounded huskier, hoarser.

I'm coming over.

When I arrived at your flat, the front door was unlocked. You were squatting on your haunches on the bathroom floor, gazing at the vomit bubbling sordidly inside the toilet. Your green hair was slick like seaweed.

Yami, I don't think the hair suits my current skin tone. Your voice was unsteady. I'll have to change that. Maybe the shape of my face too.

I rushed to your side, lifting you into bed where you gradually returned to life, a light flickering behind your glassy eyes.

Do you know why I'm so obsessed with plagiarism? You asked me once you were wrapped safely in your cocoon. Your eyes were two pinpricks of light inside your canopy of blankets.

Why? I perched at the corner of your bed.

I think someone stole my face, you said. I get little glimpses of it every now and then, but then I forget. I'm just this useless, drifting chameleon. I can't even remember what I look like.

You can look like me, I said. You can keep my face. Until you remember.

You emerged from your blankets and stared at me – your face a patchwork of my features sewn into others. Your eyebrows, which were sparser than they had been a few days ago, shot into the green fuzz of your hair in disbelief.

Why are you okay with me stealing from you like this?

It's not stealing if you ask, I shrugged.

It has been a month now and I can sense that you are almost done metamorphosing, slipping back into my face. But I need to see you. I can't wait.

Can I... join you in there? I whisper.

A hand reaches out from the folds of blankets. It is rosy pink, smooth like a baby's. I take it. Slowly, you draw me in. Inside your cocoon the heat is almost suffocating. I start to cough. Then I feel my body melt into yours. For a second I am in agony, my skin burning, falling apart at the seams. We cry in pain and ecstasy, collapsing into each other, ears ringing and eyes swimming with tears. I clench my fists and we scream, laughing as we become monstrous, outrageous and – finally! – complete.

SAM SAXTON

Sam is a writer and producer in the television industry. Their fiction has appeared in various journals, including *The Rumen*, *Ambit* and *The Phare*, and is forthcoming in Foglifter. *Binaries* is a literary novel that uses the structure of a Choose Your Own Adventure to force the reader to navigate life as a person struggling with their gender identity.

sosjones@gmail.com

Binaries

The opening of a novel

I

Well, you've already made your first decision. You're here, right?

Seconds ago, the cataclysm you didn't know you'd been waiting for hurled you out of near-certain oblivion. The vast white universe tremored and dissipated into a fantastic new darkness, and you, along with three hundred and twelve million, seventeen thousand, eight hundred and fifty-four like you, began shimmering towards an imagined light.

Many didn't even make it this far. Some dissolved instantly in the hostility of the blackness. Some fell over themselves, went wayward before they'd even had a taste of hope. But you're still here. Your chances might be infinitesimal, but they're an infinity better than they were yesterday.

And when your next decision comes, it still doesn't feel like one. Two tunnels loom, but only one seems to beckon. Hesitation is death, and the swirl is unfazed. Half swim one way, the rest the other. But the one way feels like just that: the one Way. It seems to be subject to an irresistible pull; the other is surely some kind of transgression of the intended. Hadn't you better follow that pull?

To go the one way, turn to II
To go the other, turn to III

II

Good. You're on your way. But a good start is only a start. You're still little more than a tadpole in a blizzard. You're going to have to get a wriggle on.

You shimmy your behind with vigour, answering the siren song that eddies you forwards, if there even is a forwards.

It's a good thing you don't have eyes yet, because if you did, you'd see legions of your sisters liquefied by the substance that's supposed to be carrying you. They didn't have your constitution. Others, brilliant misshapen heads betraying them, tug themselves off in the wrong direction, backwards even, like they know yesterday held more promise than tomorrow. The rest gallivant around you like they're high on life, when they're not even life yet (not as we know it).

That's their lookout. Yours is the race. And something about being near the front feels like it's your right.

And now, at a reach that feels at once like an enticement and an impossibility, a great blank globe, suspended planet-like, like an orb, like a crystal ball that knows your future.

The distance between you and it halves and halves again with each new pulse. You pound onward. But it's exhausting, this keeping on keeping on thing. It's taking everything you've got. And will it forever require this constant, relentless input? Will it forever be a kind of agony?

Cessation glimmers tantalisingly. Imagine it. You *could* just stop. The pain could be abandoned along with the struggle. The weight of the will to go on is almost unbearable, but only almost. And you have the power to stop it all.

Only that might be…

The End

Is that what you want? Because if you're learning anything it's this: that it's your will that's omnipotent here.

Yes? Then turn to IV
Not yet? Turn to V

III

OK, you're a disagreeable type. Good for you. That could serve you well here. And disagreeable might not be the right word. Questioning, perhaps. Sceptical. Cynical, on a bad day. All admirable qualities in the right quantity. But you're going to have to trust some of your instincts if you're going to get ahead in this game.

And is some preconscious voice already trying to tell you this isn't the time for dissent?

As you double your push, the great black fluid redoubles its pushback, more viscous, more hostile still.

There's still time to follow that pull, still time to switch course. No one likes to change tack, but humility sometimes asks more of us than determination.

And what, really, has so far been determined?

Hadn't you better follow that pull, after all?

For yes, turn to II
For no, turn to IV

IV

You can't say something didn't warn you.
 You can't say anything, it turns out. Because The End is nigh.
 But the end of what?
 The end of the progress, yes, the end, even, of hope. But the end, also, of the struggle. The end of it all.
 Fair enough, maybe. It's a way out. One of many. And no one is going to judge you here.
 So, you stop. And in the place of struggle – in the place of the embrace of it all – there is another kind of embrace: the embrace of surrender. The embrace of…

The End

V

BOOM!

You've made it.

You burrow your head through the globules that sentry the globe's surface, and you're in. Your membranes fuse, and in a few seconds of alchemical brutality those other losers are sealed out. Victory is yours. And yours alone.

Twenty-three strands unspool from inside you, and the orb produces a partner for each. This is it: the stuff life is made of.

Queued up behind this moment are ten trillion unchangeable moments more: a universe bursting into being; stars exploding into luminescence; the ice, the rocks and the dust coalescing; the planet forming; the seas boiling; cells answering some inalienable call to multiply and specialise; to bask in the sun and drink in the air; to crawl from the water and colonise the land, adapt; a meteor setting everything back, telling the planet to rethink; the continents drifting; the land freezing and thawing; the apes falling out with the monkeys and going their own way; social orders forming; trees abandoned; savannahs crossed; we had to learn; to walk before we could run; to grasp tools and ideas, with opposable thumbs and with brains growing larger and curiouser; to light fires and sharpen spears and trade and fish and paint and speak – of movement and of building and of working and of life and of death. And through it all, above all else, we had, unavoidably, to fuck, generation after generation after generation, fucking and fucking and fucking again, until one day (seventeen minutes ago) your dad fucked your mum, and you came bursting forth, asking yourself only this:

X or Y?

What matter? The two are so very alike. A Y is just a X with its legs together.

And yet.

In similarity there lies difference. In proximity there is distance.

One X is predetermined, immutable. But do you want another? Or something different?

Which is it to be?

X?

Or Y?

For X, turn to VI
For Y, turn to VII

VI

Ah. Things appear to have taken a turn. Not for you – there's no room for that in here. When you're unhappy with the way things are going, you can only express your frustration in a kick. But your existence has always been on a knife edge.

And your mother has just parked outside her second medical facility of the week.

The first was more routine. She watched you wriggling in a snowstorm of blacks and greys that could have been anything (an insect? An alien?) and asked if anything could be determined.

The sonographer smiled, as if he cared.

'Well,' he said, 'if you look at this area here, you might be able to errrr...'

She was confused. He was pointing at something, so–

'It's a boy?'

'No, I don't think so. See this sort of hamburger shape, well that's the clitoris and the labia, so I think it's safe to say...'

An answer was on the cliff edge of his tongue. But it wasn't safe to say it. Because in a hospital, where the bureaucracy of identity is first conjured into existence, saying a thing can make it so.

It may be a girl, but for now it's still an it. And your mother can do with it whatever she wants.

She thanked him quietly, but busied herself gathering her things, so he wouldn't see the storm brewing in her eyes, though it could have been for anything.

When the drops did fall, though, in the car, on the way home, they weren't for the traffic, which felt like a rebuke, or the yellow diversion sign, which felt like a pathetic fallacy. They were for you.

She still thinks of you as a lemon. Even despite what she saw on that screen. When she first figured out the IUD device had failed, she tried to remember when the last time had been, and checked the book Ruth from church bought for her when she had Adam. It said you'd be around the size of a lime. When she booked one of this week's appointments, she checked again. Now it said lemon. What difference? But don't limes sink and lemons float? She double-checked in another book. No, you couldn't float, not for weeks, not without her.

Whenever she thought about you, though, it was as she would think about a lemon: a forbidding combination of bitterness and sunshine. But when life gives you lemons... Not a gift in themselves, but the potential, if you squeeze and sweeten...

But they'd talked about this. Adam was enough. They'd both wanted a boy and they'd got one. So, she didn't talk about you, not to your dad, not to anyone. Especially not to God.

She hesitated, though, didn't she? Rebooked this next appointment three times. Then she booked the scan. She knew it was strange, but she wanted to get just one look at you. That's what they make them do in America. And aren't we all pro-life, really?

She parks the car in the clinic carpark now, checks her reflection in the windscreen mirror, and blinks away any gathering moisture. What a cliché it would be to enter a place like this teary-eyed. This had always been the plan, and nothing has changed. No, she didn't want a girl, but she didn't want another boy either. It's all the same to her. Lime. Lemon. Boy. Girl. Float. Sink.

It's comforting, when she arrives at the reception counter, to be told (by a woman) to fill in another form, take a seat, wait to be called. And when the doctor (also a woman) spools through the list of potential side effects from the anaesthetic (nauseavomitingdizzinessheadachemuscleaches) and the very rare complications from the procedure (infectionhemorrhagetearingoftheuteruscervicallacerationinfertility) they, too, are a comfort. Because she's part of a system now, and systems have a compulsion to plough on, one cog caught in the teeth of another, until they produce the desired output. In this case? A woman, looking to all the world like any other. Without child.

'You shouldn't feel anything,' the anaesthetist says, as he puts the spent needle away, and she flinches at the accidental double meaning.

He's right, maybe, but even the disinfectant-laden too-cold air of the surgery room, even the scratch of the sheets, even the fluorescent light blinking down on her, it all conspires to feel like something: like a punishment. For what? For not being careful enough? For not telling anyone? Or for that most unoriginal of sins: for being a woman?

No matter. You're gone now. And no one need ever know you were here.

The End

VII

'Well done!'

That was the midwife.

He's smiling, as if he cares, telling your parents, 'It's a boy.'

Your dad is not crying (because he's a boy too?) but he might have gently shining eyes, as he wraps his hand around your mother's wrist, and tells her, 'Well done love.'

Your mother is sort-of-crying because she feels every bit the feeble little girl right now, especially after the episiotomy ('a surgical incision of the perineum and the posterior vaginal wall,' the doctor explained to your dad, who'd never even heard the word).

Lord knows you're crying though. You're crying like there's no tomorrow, though you've a terrible, ineffable sense that there's something like ten thousand tomorrows on the way.

ISAAC TAN

Isaac Tan was born in Subang Jaya, Malaysia. In 2022 he completed his BA in English and Creative Writing at the University of Nottingham, Malaysia. His writing has appeared in a few anthologies and journals. After completing his MA at UEA he intends to pursue a career in the UK.

isaactan153@gmail.com
@isaac_hj on Instagram

Edifice

An extract from a short story

That we spent seventy minutes waiting for each other at different terminals did not make our reunion any less meaningful. I had been waiting at Terminal 4 when it was supposed to be 3, where he was, and having just arrived I had neither the battery nor the signal to contact him. When we finally met, owing to a string of guesswork and luck, we did not hug or exchange one of those cheek-to-cheek hellos I kept seeing here, but it's not like I would've felt natural about it from him either. We never made such a display of greeting in Kuala Lumpur, so why would we now? The way he tapped my arm lightly and no more, saying, *Eh*, was just enough. Ma, it's me. Ma, it's good to see you again – that's what it meant.

    I swear I didn't mean to jump, and I can't imagine the fuss if I had screamed. But, for a moment, I did think him someone else – a man I hadn't given birth to, much larger than my memory of him. A security policeman perhaps, there to arrest me for some wrongdoing I didn't know why or whether I'd committed. But, to my relief, it was just Kevin. It must've been the jacket, the ubiquitous one here in England – the North Face, whose label I could see prominently on the left of his chest, right above his heart – putting such breadth on his shoulders he looked entirely like someone else. Still, it did quite suit him, even if he seemed a little imposing in it.

    How much is this? I asked, poking at the black, puffy fabric.

    He said I don't want to know.

    Tell me.

    Two hundred pounds.

    I had my opinions but held my tongue. This was our first Christmas holiday together in two years since he came to study here, and I wasn't about to disapprove of him as a first thing. It didn't matter that the coat I was wearing cost fifty ringgit, and his about a thousand and two hundred (I could never think in sterling), we were not going to argue.

    Instead, I said he looked really good in it – a truth.

    Kevin gave a wink and said he knew I'd like it. Since when he started winking I had no idea, but it was a pleasant surprise. I'd never seen such exuberance coming from him back home, and felt myself mean for having even thought about money. Two years of studying History here seemed to have instilled an ease into him, and I should be feeling happy about it. Ease not just about life in England, but about, from what it seemed, whatever life might throw his way. His voice, neither gentle nor obtrusive now, was somewhat like his present posture: hands in pockets, standing firm in one corner, content with taking no more space than he needed, and not being in anyone's way.

Admittedly this newfound confidence made me feel slightly uneasy, but I'm not sure why. What mother would question her son for growing into a man knowing his place in the world, unflinching in its vicissitudes? If anything, he even seemed ready to start his own family some time soon, and it can never be too early to start thinking about these things. He was on track to get a good degree. A house could be next, then a wife, then of course children to fill the house, for what good is one without the merriment of children running in it? Or, as I'd been warned not to assume too comfortably of individuals educated in England, I know it might be a husband he'd want with the house, which I'm more than fine with.

I genuinely am, as long as he's happy.

Kevin himself once said he didn't know; we'd just have to be prepared for anything. Pansexual, that's the word he used, and even after looking up the word multiple times, I can't say I've ever quite understood what it meant. Being into men or women or both, I can understand well enough, but with Kevin, there will always be these details seemingly destined to go beyond me, no matter how hard I try to understand them.

That's all right, he always said, without offering another word.

It never felt right to me, but well, what could I do about it?

When you are a tourist, you sometimes forget there's a before and an after to where you are that might look quite different to how it appears to you at the moment. You have to tap into your imagination to picture some festivities you are in the wrong season for, or else picture the red and gold leaves that have been up there before they fell and were imprinted on to the ground, leaving the trees bald and bare.

Autumn is, in fact, my favourite season, and Kevin said he was sorry I couldn't see it this time. I said it was fine; I came here for him anyway.

It wasn't a particularly cold winter, he insisted, and I pretended to agree. Only eighteen hours ago the sun set at seven for me, not four, and my idea of December was all sunshine and coconut water, not scurrying for a heater because it felt to me too cold to do anything else. Kevin asked if I didn't feel too warm under all those things – the bobble hat I had on, earmuffs, gloves, a jumper under the fifty-ringgit winter coat – but if anything, I thought I was missing a scarf matching my bobble hat. All these I'd ordered on Taobao and got delivered to KL before coming here, but never had the opportunity to put them to use, so what's wrong with seizing my chance now? I didn't mind them. I found them affordable and decent in quality, but I knew better than to mention it to Kevin.

Once, I tried to do him a favour in a similar way. He'd been looking for an out-of-print book that he couldn't find anywhere, and it happened to be available on the platform, because I searched it, because I am his mother and mothers do such things, and it ended up with him awkwardly declining and thanking me and telling me I should have the right to do whatever I want and not let his consuming preferences deter me.

What was it he said were the preferences?

Ethical consumption, that's it. Something about fakes and copyright, sustainability and work conditions, sweatshops and the like.

I asked how he knew it was going to be a fake.

He didn't. But it could be.

And the work conditions?

He didn't know either. But that's the point; he couldn't be sure.

It was already dark by the time we found each other, so we decided to go straight back to the hotel and do the sightseeing proper the next day. I thought it wasn't such a bad idea. We were tired from our respective travels – me from Kuala Lumpur to Abu Dhabi to Heathrow, him from trips he made to Manchester and Cambridge prior to meeting me – and we must have a lot to catch up on.

At the hotel the lifts were suffering from a malfunction, so Kevin had to grab both our suitcases and walk up three flights of stairs. He seemed to do that with ease.

How are your studies? I asked as he held the door for me. The room was pitch black and it wasn't until I fumbled around for a while that I found a switch that only lit up the area near the doorway, where Kevin was standing. He was holding the door so the light outside could be let in before I found the switch that finally brought the whole room into full view. It was a clean and tidy room, smelling faintly of disinfectant only just applied and wiped away, and for a second, I didn't know why, I pictured a heap possibly just here moments before, one so unmanageable housekeeping had to spend ages clearing it away.

It's all good. His studies.

Had he made friends?

Yeah, they were nice. I'd like them, probably.

He must like it here then?

Yeah, very much so. Would I mind if he opened the window? Felt a bit stuffy in there.

I said no.

No, why on earth would I mind that?

What was revealed – when he pulled the blinds and lifted the pane up – was a building sitting across us I could only describe as being unnervingly sophisticated, stately, perhaps a little ancient, and frankly, beautiful too. I could see why he liked it here, every sight in every corner seemingly rich with a history and legacy he could somewhat participate in, even if only as an observer, always at one remove away. What I felt instead was a common impression of being intrigued – by its essence I recognised as being English, its character unlike anything I'd seen back home, but not so much that I'd be stopped in my tracks so I'd marvel at it, the way Kevin would. But that's only natural; I wasn't studying History as he was. Kevin, on the contrary, would feel something more urgent, as he must be feeling now, his back turned towards me. He'd have to spend a good few minutes absorbing the edifice as if his life depended on him knowing anatomically every part by heart, taking in every spire on every steeple, all the weight redirected by each buttress, and the way the arches formed the vault to total the grandeur he was seeing before him, all of which mattered immensely to him.

'What do you think of it?'

For a moment I thought he was talking to the building, but his face had turned to me.

'It feels European, and English.'

A chuckle.

Was it my imprecision? In my limited vocabulary for distinguishing between types of architecture, let alone of that not found in where I – where *we* were raised, it was my best guess.

'You're right.'

'You think we could build something like that?'

'We?'

'Malaysians.'

'Oh.'

'Or Asian, whatever you identify as.'

'Identify? Mum, how can I identify as anything other than Asian?'

I don't know why I said it, but it came to me as something I couldn't stop.

'No, but if we learn how it's done, you think *we* can actually build something as grand as this?'

Couldn't have stopped that either, or how it sounded like I was mocking him when I hadn't intended to. I was expecting an argument, another chuckle at my ignorance, or a puzzled look questioning what I could possibly mean by it; not that I had any clue.

But to my surprise he just smiled, and in that instant I saw not the Kevin I'd mistaken for a broad-shouldered security policeman, but the boy whose little hand I used to hold before he found a life here so far away from home.

He really did smile. Not the tense and polite kind I'd intermittently caught on our way here from the airport to this room, to this redeeming moment, but one that harked back, unwelcome, to something I thought had been lost to me for ever, never again within my reach. Then to an even bigger surprise for the both of us, a yelp escaped my throat before I began to bawl so impossibly that all I knew of what happened next was a long, muffled blend of *Okay! Okay! Mum! Please stop!*, the sobs I didn't know why I was making, the thud made by him knocking the suitcase over on his way to put his arm around me; all these interfered by knocks on the door and Kevin having to reassure the curious guests everything was all right – he wasn't abusing a woman incapable of defending herself, neither physically nor verbally, which was the truth, which I confirmed and then affirmed, before they finally left, satisfied, as I must've been too, for I had decided to stop my hysteria.

EVA TANG

Eva's writing explores themes of attachment, disconnect, and release through the lens of nostalgic documentation. She is currently working on her first novel, *The Big Sulk Pharmacy*, and monthly art column for *Delude* magazine. Her prose has been displayed in bookstores and gallery spaces across Shoreditch, Peckham, and Baker Street.

Violetsrglue@gmail.com

Lump in the Throat Falling Through to the Stomach
Excerpts from a short story

First, the morning after your twentieth birthday.
You fell asleep beside me several times and begged me intermittently to lie with you. I refused and waited patiently for your next alarm to sound so we could continue the next few sentences of our hilariously delayed conversation. 'These are like intervals in a really shit play,' you said, face pressed into the mattress, both arms gripping a pillow over your head.

I laughed, the sound swelling, before finally falling down beside you; my hot forehead pressed and screaming against your shoulder blade, my eyes knuckled into the soft, inflated flesh just underneath it. With my mouth half-open, the coarseness of my bottom lip brushed against the softness of your armpit hair.

What had become the familiarity of your scent hit me in the stomach, the drop in it akin to the millisecond that you miss the handrail or the step, making the next landing of your hand or foot onto metal, wood or cement, essential. Before slipping you pray for deliverance from the monotony of walking, of placing one foot in front of the other, of commuting and living. And after its avoidance, your skin feels stroked from the inside with the flush of relief, embarrassment, adrenaline.

Bonfire Night.
A lock of candy floss on the back of your neck from where I'd stood too close behind you. You explained that when a metal salt is burned the electrons in it move to a higher shell level. They become excited. But when returned to their original shell the energy gained is released as a form of light, a form of emission. Lithium produces a red-pink flame, calcium an orange-red, strontium a bright crimson.

'They're the colours we're seeing in the fireworks now,' you repeated to me over the whooping crowd.

'Would you say my jumper was lithium or calcium red?' I asked.

You tilted your head to one side like a photographer and waited for the next flurry of rockets to hit the sky to produce the perfect lighting. 'Probably calcium,' you said, 'I should call you Cali for short.'

And the backs of my ears warmed, even though the bonfire was in front of us, a hundred metres in front.

The closing comets rapid streaks of chalk on a kid's blackboard, the air the musty scent of chalkboard water, too. The soil wet enough under our boots for me to want to bury whatever I couldn't say yet in its lumpy, fertile belly, with a hope for you so hungry it would've chased cold mud right up to the elbow.

The first time I took the morning after pill.
'How do you feel?' you asked.

'Better,' I said, 'Do you want to lie down with me?'

You: 'Do you want me to get you some water?'

For an entire morning we spoke in questions, and it made me feel stupid and my stupidity made me feel like I needed to hold you.

'Are you still worried about the side effects?'

I knew you had asked me this hoping I'd say no, and because I loved you I did you one better.

'Of course not.' I tucked both hands underneath my knees, my palms flush against the hundreds of little bits of synthetic carpet beneath me. The effect was a light eczema flare-up. I focused on the idea of my skin and the areas that were furry and hot; the back of my neck felt licked, like the envelope of a passionate love letter. I thought of Sartre and de Beauvoir, Miller and Nin. You were talking again about some famous American baseball player, and I realised then how far apart our reference points were.

My stomach jolted and I made it to the bathroom just in time.

You put both hands in my hair as I retched, tucking it behind my ears with slow, petting movements as you told me to 'get it all out'. When you removed my dressing gown a cascade of crumbs descended upon the shower mat like hungry locusts, and you stroked my pale cheeks and called me your Little Ghost.

The effects of the pill coincided with a twenty-four-hour, online assessment. Below the toe of my favourite slipper – steel-capped with a rim of white computer light – a new patch of eczema. The rash, rubbed raw by the previous hugging of sock and shoe, creased with an almost reptilian effect when the toe was pointed or flexed. The intense bunching of red skin contrasted to the thin layer of pink jam on the slice of toast sat by the foot. The jam – chosen by you and not yet confirmed by me as being strawberry or raspberry – was mostly smooth. The one clump of jelly that had ducked the butter knife batted the screen light into my eye like a champion baseball player, and when I turned the plate slowly, the gleaming, white light ran around the centre of the toast like it was performing a homerun.

The silent date in the café.
We'd agreed to work side by side on a long bench rather than opposite each other, so our laptops could enjoy the separate space of their own, adjacent tables rather than bumping heads. This arrangement reminded me fleetingly of free-range chicken farms; I hoped our increased, independent surface areas would produce some benefit in the respective essays we were birthing. *Happy hens lay happy eggs.*

A feature which made the coffee house less nondescript was a tan, metal bar which allowed those sitting on the high bench a place to rest their feet. For me it meant that although I could not see your expressions head-on, I could feel the vibrations whenever contact was made with the bar. At first I was reminded of telephone lines or two empty cans with a string between them, but this technique dismissed the necessity of attempted speech. We sat in ten, fifteen-minute silences while those around us made the actual effort to converse. I saved a note of your unconscious processes on Word...a four second drumming meant the internet was struggling. A single, contemplative tap was likely to be followed by a pause in keyboard tapping, and a minute-long jitter indicated that in the next minute you'd be ready for a cigarette. I also documented my hope that apart from a childhood music teacher (or therapist potentially diagnosing you with anxious tremors (the contrast made me want to laugh and cry)), I was one of the first to forge a pattern from your vibrational movements.

At four o'clock, a Yorkshire terrier jumped onto one of the seats to our right and declared the science experiment over. I stroked its grey beard while you tipped the barista on our way out.

At nineteen years old it'd become difficult to find shared 'firsts'. I knew you'd lost your virginity two months after I did, although your first kiss had taken place ten days prior to mine. At twenty it felt like we were practically bunny hopping over the adolescences we'd barely buried, although sometimes these reared their heads in the form of parental visits or accidental run-ins with exes. But I hoped my paying such close attention to your various bumps and rattles in the poorly lit, poorly heated café would be love enough in its own context: like one newborn animal soothing the caged anxiety of another.

'Stop pushing against the bar,' I'd told you, eventually. 'You'll hurt yourself.'

Christmas Eve.
My period is three days late. The weather forecast said it would snow this morning, but it hasn't. I play a game of Uno with my brother and lose.

Boxing Day.
My period is five days late. I pull up my trousers and tug down my red jumper and call you.

'Do a test,' you tell me, 'Don't freak out.' You play me a new song you've been learning over the phone; it starts in D Minor, and I tell you that it sounds awesome.

New Year's Eve.
Loose tendrils of hair stick to the back of my neck like when you lift a plant pot and see the two or three worms writhing in the gritty space underneath. I try to sleep but can't.

Besides the family house's heating and plumbing, I'd always sworn I could hear my room's heartbeat. Like the room knew. Like it always knew when I'd be lying there, sad or angry, adult or child; the first time I'd begged for a renovation at ten or to sleep over at a friend's at eleven, and when I'd finally cleared it to go to university at eighteen. Like it still knew, now, everything about me – could smell it on my skin like blood.

New Year's Day.
I've been home fifteen days now. The nearest river to our house looks like it's about to burst. My mother's mouth goes weird when I tell her, and our old tabby jumps out of my arms and into hers.

The sluggish middle of January.
Meat tastes disgusting; sugar tastes worse. Even in my dreams I dream about the nausea, the backache, the dandruff, you.

The day of the consultation.
'Can I get you anything to drink?' the GP asks me.
   'No, thanks,' I say, counting the ceiling tiles.
   The form she gives me states that the termination will take place on a Friday, and I expect her shoes to squeak when she walks away, but they don't.

Two months post-abortion.
While completing crosswords, I liked to pick out the words within words. For example, the one letter difference in 'God' and 'good', which I thought sweet and would happily give as an example if asked to define the word 'nuance'. Another was the entirety of 'stance' in the noun 'distance'; it reminded me of how I'd always thought the physical stances (and distances) employed by soon-to-be-separated TV couples overly dramatic.
   When you first start distancing yourself, usually to a window where you stare out at a sticker-clad lamppost, I hardly notice. It isn't until you start picking up extra shifts or spending entire weekends at your family's house two hundred miles away that fear gradually fills my head like water, and my pockets like heavy stones.

Three months post-abortion.
Some days I listen to the weather forecast knowing that in your hometown my lips would be four degrees colder. Some weekends I take day trips into conversations I had months ago. An unreliable drip-feed of a thousand different colours and lines and bad sensations: the rude prickling of baby tears in your eyes when you're losing an argument, the salty wet at the back of your nose when you're sorry. I wonder five times nightly if I should have kissed your hair with what was admittedly self-assuring firmness, although it felt good to be firm and I would have regretted performing the action with any lesser velocity. *I mizz you zo much*, I write, because the keypad is broken.

Three months post-you.
He draws the curtains of his blistering living room and we sprawl across a velvet couch each, chewing his father's Diazepam until he decides we are relaxed enough to make love. It's not the heat that makes my skin crawl in the unfamiliar room, but still; I fantasise about the shape of his jawline, watch his tongue slide over his

teeth when he pauses in conversation, and have to scrunch my own face up hard to stop crying. And so, something that I can't decipher but know exists continues to splinter directly above my head in the near perfect darkness, and when somebody asks if I know you, I say, no — no, I don't know him at all.

ALEXIA TOLAS

Alexia Tolas is a Bahamian writer who explores the intricacies of small-island life, drawing heavily from local folktales and mythology. Her writing has been shortlisted for literary prizes including the Commonwealth Short Story Prize, and her stories have been featured in journals like *Adda, Granta, The Caribbean Writer,* and *Podcastle*.

alexiatolas@gmail.com

Pretty Mollies

The opening of a novel

SUNDAY, AUGUST 25TH, 9:12 P.M.

This is a night for a ghost story. I can hear it on Daddy's tongue. He speaks with a weight in his throat, like a sinker at the end of a fishing line dragging along the seabed. Snagging on coral. Snapping on the words he chooses to hide that something's wrong.

Nights like these are good for ghost stories. Rain batters the bougainvillea around my veranda. Frogs croak from windowsills. I step out onto the wet porch, holding my cell phone between my ear and my shoulder, and take a seat in an old wicker chair.

I can barely hear Daddy over the receiver. He mumbles something about newborn lambs, but that's not why he called. Only bad news comes after eight. But Daddy knows that bad news needs some sugar. Some Carnation cream to cut the bitterness. I picture him at the Bonny Breeze Lodge watching the sea from his porch, a story as long as the cigarette between his lips. I wonder if it's raining there too.

'Mummy tried to call.'

I know she did. The number I never bothered to save in my contact list has been flashing across the screen all evening.

'You heard about Molly?'

I brush a rain ant from my arm. 'Who?'

'Molly Singh. Our cook.'

It's hard to conjure Molly's face at first, but, slowly, she comes to me – cutting coconut tart in her grandfather's restaurant. Shuffling to Mrs. Pinder's math class behind the rest of her grade. Mopping up sky juice from the bar floor as her cousin Marvin shouts at her.

'She missing.'

Dread sinks to the bottom of my belly, but it lands on the fading image of Molly's face. Like everything else from Long Island, Molly's image is oxidised, crusted white with pain and regret.

'How long she been missing?'

Daddy's sigh crackles through the receiver. 'Must be twelve hours.'

'A few hours ain't nothing. Give her a day or two.' That's what I'd learned working the Nassau crime beat. A schoolgirl will turn up after a few days of galivanting with her lover. Your local drug dealer will return to his corner once the white Hondas lose his scent.

'Her car still home, Jory.' Daddy's voice is crisp. Curt. 'Tea on the table. Molly missing.'

There's a disquieting logic buried in this island ethnology. For Daddy, 'disappearing' is a choice. But no matter how far you run, you leave traces. You drop breadcrumbs at the airport when your neighbour books your flight. You leave clues at the dock when your cousin helps you onto the ship. By the time you shut the door on the life you're leaving, the whole island knows where you're going.

Nine years ago, when I disappeared, my aunt Tina watched me from the airport's parking lot as I boarded the plane. I should've known she'd be there spying on outgoing passengers. It's what she and her best friend did every day at 3:30 p.m.

But no one had seen Molly. In island vernacular, Molly hasn't disappeared. She's missing. That means she's gone.

'Maybe you could mention it in the paper,' Daddy says.

'No,' I say. It's just a rumour. I need it to be. If it isn't, my editor will make me cover the story. I can hear him now: *You're local. You'll know who to talk to. Where to go.* 'She could turn up any minute.'

Daddy sucks his teeth. 'There's only so many places Molly could go.'

A balloon of silence fills the space between my ear and the receiver.

'Mummy say hi.'

The silence pops.

'I gotta go, Daddy.'

I can hear Daddy gnawing on his sun-chipped lips as I hang up the phone. I play out the scene on his side of the line. Daddy will avoid my mother's glare because, of course, pitching a rumour to a national newspaper was her idea. He will shake his head when my mother storms off to the kitchen to take out her fury on the dishes. She may even try to call me again, and her number will flash across my phone's screen like a hungry ghost.

'Who's that?'

Darrell pushes through the screen door, shirtless. Jeans unzipped. A younger me would have savoured the slickness between my legs. A younger me would have released the bulge inside Darrell's pants. Instead, the me that sits in the old wicker chair fights the urge to throw up.

I won't lie: Darrell's personality does to a libido what salt does to a slug. But he's not the problem. I haven't been on good terms with desire in nearly ten years, and her persistence makes me sick. When I saw Darrell at the bar earlier this evening, I'd only meant to apologise for embarrassing him in front of the Minister of Tourism. But after his fourth round of Hennessy, Darrell mentioned a cousin who sold tourists Rohypnol and GHB, and I realised I wanted something more.

Darrell kneels at my feet. Cups my hips. Grins impishly as he peeks at my phone.

'Daddy? I thought I was your daddy tonight.'

I never humour Darrell's poor jokes and tonight is no exception. If we were at a press conference or a crime scene, he'd repeat the quip in case I hadn't heard him, but not now. Darrell coaxes my legs further apart. He kisses my hands as I pretend to text. His breath, thick with over-ripe fruit, lingers under my nose. He pries the phone from my hand and tucks it into his open fly.

My stomach turns.

I ease my hips from his grasp and slip out of the chair, shoving Darrell off in the process. I thought that would discourage him, but he follows me into the house.

'I'm tired,' I say. I take a can from the six-pack of Johnnie & Coke that Darrell bought for us at the pharmacy. I pat my pockets, looking for my phone, sure that I had it a second ago. But then Darrell saunters over to the kitchen counter and grabs the bottle of pills he'd purchased along with the whiskey. He gives me his best Regé-Jean Page smirk.

'Then let's wake up.'

A part of me says let him have it. Don't stop him as he shoots an eszopiclone with a whiskey chaser. Set him up on the couch when he drifts into a ten-hour coma. When he wakes up, have a note on the coffee table thanking him for the Vitamin D that he didn't give me. Make him feel like he should do this again. Bar. Pharmacy. Sex so good he doesn't remember it never happened. A part of me says that I must do whatever it takes to keep this plug. I'm not lucky enough to know two people with pharmaceutical-dealing cousins, let alone a plug so eager to please. Darrell didn't ask me to repay him for the pills – not that they cost him much. He'd gone for the generic.

But a kinder part of me says kick Darrell out.

Darrell trips as I shove him through the front door. I throw his shoes and shirt at him to make the message clear.

'Cockteasing bitch!' he cries, juggling his belt and his left shoe.

'Cockstain,' I say before slamming the door.

I don't answer when Darrell bangs on the door. I ignore the call of my name as I walk upstairs to the bathroom with the six-pack of Johnnie & Coke. I listen instead to the promise of sleep in the bottle that rests so gently in my hand.

I shouldn't need the pills. I've done everything right. Followed all the doctors' orders to cure my insomnia. I have the thousand-dollar ergonomic mattress. I crank the air conditioner every night and then cry over the electricity bill. I don't eat or watch television or use my phone before bed. I haven't had alcohol or coffee since I got out of rehab. Not even a cup of fucking tea. And for a year, it worked.

Until last night when the nightmares returned.

It started with a whimper from my closet. A small, wet sob. And then other voices, susurrating like casuarina pine needles in a soft breeze. The women gazed at me from the shadows, their broken jaws hanging. The empty black sockets of their eyes leaking rancid brown sludge. Like marsh mud. The women grew in the dark corners of my bedroom. *Jordan*, they said in thin, high pitches.

Last night, my sheets moved under many bone-white hands. The cotton hissed as breasts like dried pawpaws dragged across the length of the bed. The corpses gathered around me and wept. This is how they've always spoken to me – in agonised keening.

Jordan...

Jordan...

And then from the shadows came the water, salty and cold. It filled my mouth, my nose, my lungs. So much water that it filled my room to the ceiling. I struggled against the hard, corned hands clasping my neck. They shoved me into the seabed, and I gagged on the sand. I thrashed against the weight pressing into my back until I couldn't fight anymore. I let the water drag me down.

And all around me were sepulchral eyes and gaping mouths whispering, *Jordan, Jordan...*

I swallow last night's nightmare and reach into tub to turn on the hot water. Then, I grab the eszopiclone, the only thing that keeps the nightmares away. I slosh back three pills as the steam fogs up the bathroom mirror, each with their own can of Johnnie & Coke, and undress. I'm dirty. So dirty. I smell sweat that isn't mine dripping between my breasts. Taste a mouth I haven't tasted in years on my tongue. Feel fingers that should never have touched me slip between my legs.

And I'm panting.

Because it feels so good, my mother's voice says. Always her voice. *Don't it feel good, Jory?*

It always does.

I sit in the tub and let the hot water rain over my naked body. The water stings, but then the eszopiclone takes over, and that sweet, familiar heaviness I've missed so much sinks in. Electricity courses from my fingers to my toes. The rhythmic spasms between my legs dissipate. Soon, a delicious numbness takes my body, and I can breathe again.

I close my eyes and lay down in the tub. The droplets from the shower paint white phosphenes in the darkness under my eyelids. I search between the beads of water, but too much whiskey and pills have blown those drops into a maelstrom.

The swirling current under my eyelids draws me
>   down,
>   down,
>   down...
>   And in the whirlpool
>   a face...
>   Molly's face
>   fights the water,
>   skin dimpled,
>   grey,
>   like fish left too long to defrost.
>   Mud in her hair—
>   her long black hair...
>   She opens her mouth—

Jordan...
Like an eddy—
Jordan...
her words suck me down.
I know this pressure—
felt it
the night I gave my body to the sea.
Molly,
so close now,
I can smell her—
the sargassum on her tongue...
I can touch her—
sunken cheeks,
streaked with mud
blood?
No.
Tears...
I touch her cheek,
Jordan...
the skin breaks—
wet like sponge—
I pull away,
her flesh in my hand.
Please, Jordan!
Molly reaches for me,
eyes sinking
into her skull,
mouth collapsing
into a black hole.
She reaches for me, her voice
a hoarse rattle,
a cacophony of dry bones,
scaling to a feverish pitch.
She reaches for me.
Grabs my arm—

And my scream breaks the water.

LIAM VAN DEN HOEK

Liam van den Hoek graduated in 2020 with a Bachelor of Arts in English from Duke University, and in 2022 with an MFA in Screenwriting from Emerson College. He is a 2023 Academy Nicholl Screenwriting Semifinalist. His novel depicts a tainted American Dream and a fatal love for Las Vegas.

liamvdhoek97@gmail.com

The Outskirts of Paradise
The opening of a novel

CHAPTER ONE
July 1981

Scarlett crawls over the gravel, then uses her last strength to prop herself against the 'Welcome to Fabulous Las Vegas' sign. Her pain is constant and chilling, and the desert breeze only makes it worse. Bright lights above reveal how dark blood is. But instead of focusing on that, she distracts herself with her surroundings. Planes sleep to her left at McCarran, and it's early enough on Tuesday for the Boulevard to be clear. The few cars that pass drive fast and don't spot her. She guesses their eyes are drawn to the sign. She doesn't blame the drivers; she'd be looking up at it too. Besides, it's too late for her. And that's why she placed herself here – to make sure Douglas would find her. She can relax now. So she leans back, and then spots something.

In the depths of the night sky, beyond the silhouettes of palm trees and mountains, her life rushes by like grainy and unfocused frames of a film. Suddenly, the reel catches, snagging on a recent Thursday. She smiles, seeing herself up on that stage holding the microphone. The road around her fades, and she can taste the stale and smoky air again. Her body's pain persists, yet she hopes she'll last long enough to relive her downfall.

Her desire was gorgeous – but her love for this city was fatal.

CHAPTER TWO

June 1981

The stage was just a stool, a cassette player, and a lamp in front of a black wall. Yet in the dimmed light, Scarlett recognized some of the faces in the small crowd – faces rusting with the bar.

The Copper Tail was a crumbling water hole right by her apartment, closer to Henderson than the city limits, which meant it was right by nowhere. The regulars were like her: unable to afford a place in Sin City but living close enough to be webbed in its promise. Between dulling sips, their bitter conversations repeated themselves on loop. She'd overheard enough to know that they all worked in the city and felt expendable. Yet they couldn't give it up, and their lives seemed to be part of the cost of making it shine. There was something contagious about their downbeat talk, so she kept her distance from them, and sipped on drinks in concealed corners before and after her song.

With the mic in her hand, she was comfortable. This was her most sacred time of the week. She got paid, and needed the money, but it was the chance to express herself that really appealed to her. She had to admit, it was the attention too – and it was no ordinary attention. She was noticed for what she could share, what she could offer this world, and it was essential. When all else in her life wasn't where she wanted it to be, her songs, her three performances a week, allowed her to escape from her forgettable days, the ones she chose not to think about, and the ones that just slipped away. She'd sing, and raise her spirits back up, and bring her soul to the surface to know she still existed. She'd been doing this for a couple of years now, after she'd moved from Southern California to Vegas – or not quite Vegas. When she'd auditioned for the slot, Crim, the bar's owner and only bartender, had said she sounded hopeful. He'd offered her fifty bucks a week for a song on Tuesday, Wednesday, and Thursday nights. She'd been a feature of The Copper Tail ever since.

In other parts of her life, she performed too: at work, on weekends to score free drinks, even at home to get her creepy neighbor off her back. But lately, her acting had taken over, and now, even when she sang alone at home, the lyrics sounded false, like her real voice had been swallowed by a stranger. Still, every time she sat on that stool in front of the black wall, she could perform from somewhere honest, and heard herself again.

She was a decent singer, nothing spine-tingling but nothing to wince at either. Everyone seemed to say there was something raw in her notes, like they could know her heart from her sound. They heard her truths too.

She placed her tip jar at the edge of the stage and was ready to give Crim the usual nod, but he was already looking at her with something unfamiliar in his expression and waved her over. She met him at the bar.

'Yeah?'

'I wanted to tell you earlier, but you went right up on stage,' he said.

'Go ahead.'

'This is the last week I can pay you.'

'You barely pay me.'

'I don't have fifty bucks a week to spare.'

'I bring in that much on drinks.'

'Believe me, you don't.'

'Is it the singing?'

'It's not the singing. You know how much I like your singing. It's me. It's money.'

'I bring that much in. I know I do.'

Crim just huffed, and she knew he'd somehow made his mind up. It was up to her to change it.

'I'll prove it. Back in five.'

She marched out to her car. In her glove compartment, under a pile of unpaid parking tickets, she found her *For You* Prince album. She knew that her best performance would be something tragic, something dealing with loss, something she could sing more honestly than anything else, and 'So Blue' was it.

Up on stage, she fast-forwarded the cassette and tried to find the beginning of the song. She could hear the audience starting to grumble. Then she found the opening notes. The backing track played.

When the guitar started, she cleared her throat. Though she shut her eyes, she felt the gazes on her through the darkness. She knew the lyrics, and it meant she didn't have to think or worry when she sang. The words just poured out. It was mindless, outside of her body but also deeper inside it, and she let that unknown space take over. Each verse, each chorus, each tender note, slipped out without thoughts crossing her mind. Usually, during the middle of her performances, something brought her back – but not this time. Nothing disturbed her. She was joined with the song, and the audience was silent even when she paused.

Through the lyrics, she saw her younger self, the one who'd grown up without much but enough. The one who used to smile a lot and figured things were going to work themselves out. She saw her plastic trinkets, and her lilac-walled bedroom, and her carousel music box which she'd made her own song for. Those days in the car park in front of their apartment, her mother spraying her with the hose, and the water making the concrete slick. Popping dish-soap bubbles with friends, the shifting colors mesmerizing her before breaking and stinging her eyes. The weightlessness of her giggle. That ease of joy and her caring only for the moment. She wasn't that girl anymore. Now, she wasted away in decaying spaces and, for all her memories, couldn't access that feeling she used to know or who she used to be. The drop was seismic.

As she held the final note, her listeners erupted. They clapped and whistled, and some stood in ovation. It was more than she could've ever anticipated. Something like an itch rose at the back of her throat because there was sorrow and pity in their downturned mouths. She'd planned to call for them to go and order drinks but was too overwhelmed now. Instead, she nodded a 'thank you', hurried out of the lamp light keeping her back to everyone she could, and returned to the bar.

She hated how well she'd done without understanding why. The intensity of their reading her was too much. They'd seen a piece of her she'd never shared before, not even with herself. They had no right to witness what she'd only just accessed. Crim awaited her with an excited look, like he'd just seen a new side of her too, one so sad it must've made him feel better about himself.

'Great job,' he said.

'Yeah, thanks.' She couldn't keep eye contact with him, it was too intimate.

'Really, that was amazing. People never stand up for anything but a drink in here.'

'I know.'

'I still can't pay you though. I'm barely scraping by. Here.' He slid her over a glass of red wine. 'On the house, and you know what, maybe I can pay you in drinks instead.'

'I need the money, Crim. Do you want me to beg? Do you want me to tell everyone here you're firing me after that performance?'

'I don't have the money, Scarlett.'

She took a sip. Crim was about to leave her there in defeat when he noticed someone behind her.

'Excuse me, miss.'

She turned to find little green eyes shining back at her. The skin around them was worn thin; he must have been in his seventies.

'I loved your performance.'

'Thank you,' she said.

'Do you perform here regularly?' the older man asked. 'I want to bring some of my pals to watch you.'

'Well, unfortunately –'

'She does,' Crim interrupted. 'Tuesdays, Wednesdays, and Thursdays.'

'Oh yeah?' Scarlett asked.

'Yeah, for thirty bucks a week.'

'Forty,' she snapped back.

'Done,' Crim said.

Scarlett took a celebratory swig.

'Great. Here, take this.' The older man handed her a ten. 'I could feel how lonely you are. Everyone could. It was amazing. Goodnight.' He headed off.

She was struck still, the glass remained an inch away from her mouth.

'You just got saved,' Crim said.

She put her drink down.

'Scarlett?'

'Keep your forty bucks,' she said, and left the bar as quickly as she could.

The crowd hushed as she left the room, like she was some kind of zoo animal going back into hiding. It wasn't just her suspicions, she used to be hopeful – now she was authentically tragic. All the misalignment she sensed: the distancing of her own skin, the past dragging down her steps, the heaviness of sleep and the struggle to wake, all became fully known to her in that instant. She beelined through the parking lot and hurried into her car and slammed the door.

When she first came here and left behind her mother, backstabbing friends, and the assholes in El Centro, she'd thought living on her own terms would be enough. But then the dizzying pleasure of Las Vegas made her realize how utterly bored she'd been for twenty-one years. Thanks to her friend Kimmy, she'd been able to spend more hours there, even nights sometimes, but now it wasn't enough, and neither were these songs.

She couldn't stay where she was, with her money problems, creepy neighbor, shitty job, and the pain of sitting with who she'd become. Nor could she depend on three performances a week to claw her out of this. Things had to change, and fast.

She had to be a part of the good life, the glitz and glam of the city so tantalizingly nearby. Countless people treated it like a playground – celebrating, careless and free. She could be one of them. She'd find a way to live where the thrills didn't stop or slow, and where there was no such thing as a still room. Then she'd own that something. That yellowness. That spark. She'd make it happen this weekend, she thought, and her spirit lifted a little.

She put her hands on the steering wheel and looked out to a wide night and made a promise to herself to only return here after making it. She'd come back and sing with joy in her voice, enough to get booed off stage for failing to hit a single note of 'So Blue.'

ZABU WAMARA

Zabu Wamara (she/her), is an up-and-coming writer who uses her writing to capture the magic of everyday experiences. Zabu was part of the Uganda cohort for the 2021 International Chair of Creative Writing project, where her short story 'Cracking' was chosen as the title story of their anthology.

yvonne.zabu@gmail.com

Contextual Note

Ugandan weddings typically consist of three different functions. This story takes place during a version of the second function, known as 'okuhingira' or the give-away ceremony. During this function, traditional customs are usually performed to signify the union of the couple, such as a meeting of both families' elders, and the exchange of gifts. In Kampala, the capital city and a melting pot of Uganda's many cultures, families often blend customs. One recent popular custom is 'sooka omunonye', the search for the groom, who sits hidden among his relatives. To directly translate this, the bride has to 'find him first'.

Find Him First

An Extract from a Short Story

Nyanjura is the last to step onto the raised aisle between the two families. Seth's heart misses a beat and then stutters into a run. She is glorious, Seth thinks, and it hurts more than he expected to see her like that for someone else. She has chosen a kinyankore that is a cascade of greens and burnt orange. Gold threads sparkle in the light. Seth can almost feel the warmth of her skin through the sheer veil that covers everything but her face. He tries to console himself with the fact that it is not her, not the Nyanjura he cares about. This Nyanjura is a perfect copy of the original. The beauty spot on her chin is gone, the small, jagged scar just beneath her right eye invisible. The lie he's telling himself shatters as the emcee makes a joke and her face transforms with a grin he often dreams about.

Seth's throat is tight as Nyanjura moves to her place – a low love seat a step above everyone else on the stage. If the aisle is a boundary between the sides of the tent from which the two families face each other, then the stage she is perched on is a bridge. The enshagalizi settle around her, butterflies floating down to rest.

Seth's friends begin to gather themselves as the emcee welcomes the bride. Nina and Hawa pat at their hair. Odur asks a waiter to clear the table. Bbembe pulls his phone out of his pocket one last time and begins typing furiously. As Seth takes her in, Nyanjura stands, and unexpectedly he is reminded of his father who used to joke that in the olden days, the bride could pick anyone out of the crowd to be her husband, anyone at all. Seth pauses. He allows himself to think it. She could choose *me*. A faint hope blooms.

A trumpet sounds, a pause and then an electric guitar solo blasts through the speakers, joining it. It can only be one song. The elders ululate and the younger generation whoop as a soukous beat older than their time drops. Everyone at Seth's table begins to sway and sing along to the soprano belting out the opening verse. Seth claps and sways. He knows the words too but he's too tense to sing along. His pulse is picking up, his mind running away with the maybe.

His attention stays on Nyanjura, whose focus is on her heavily beaded dress as she navigates the steps back down to the ground. She stops at the emcee's side as the chorus starts.

'Nyanjura, first find for us this man!' the emcee shouts. His voice rings out over the music and singing guests.

The crowd chuckles. Seth laughs because of the thrill that comes with the possibility of possibilities. Nyanjura begins to weave through the guests. Some of the people stay seated as they clap to the beat, cheering her on. Many stand to follow her progress, tracking her with their phones' cameras.

Seth peels his eyes away from Nyanjura. His table is pretending to be too busy to notice what is happening. James adjusts his tie. Bbembe dusts his shoulders, straightening his suit jacket. One of the wedding photographers perches at Odur's side, ready for Nyanjura's arrival. Hawa and Nina exchange lip gloss. Seth cannot help it. He finds himself looking Nyanjura's way again.

Nyanjura makes her way slowly through the crowd. Whoever did the décor left enough space for her to pass comfortably. Another wedding photographer shadows her, his lens, like Seth, pinned to every movement she makes. Nyanjura lights her way with every step, leaving a smile as she searches the faces at each table, mouthing a hello to those she knows. She sees James first, but Seth cannot blame her – James is a big man in any setting, but he always seems bigger at weddings; the bulk of him contrasts harshly with vases, muted colours and delicate chairs. Nyanjura's focus narrows and then she takes them all in.

Seth is transfixed as Nyanjura's pace picks up; still graceful but swift as well now. He allows himself to be carried away by what he is feeling. It is real. She is coming, he thinks and swallows a laugh at the giddy feeling rising within. There is sweat on his palms. He realizes this because the bushera slips in his grasp. He places the calabash on the table and wipes his hands on his lap. The silk of his kanzu is smooth against his callouses. The closer she gets, the brighter the light becomes, until, at last, she is there, standing in front of them.

For a moment, Seth is blinded. Everyone is cheering. Light flickers and blinks as the flashes go off. He notices all and none of it. She holds out her hand and the movement makes her shuuka slip slightly. Suddenly he can see the full curve of her shoulder, the swell of her chest as she breathes in. Her hand is soft. She pulls him gently out of his seat. Her smile brightens as he rises to join her, and he cannot help it, he smiles back. The music transitions into something more modern, something they have danced to in clubs on nights long since passed. He holds her close.

'She has found him!' the emcee shouts, startling Seth. Reality resets. Nyanjura is standing in front of Bbembe. Seth tries to make sense of what is happening. His smile falters as, within him, feelings battle for centre stage. The guests continue to cheer, oblivious to his upheaval. Seth's mind is a bedlam as he rushes to rise with the others. He watches Bbembe embrace Nyanjura. The pit within him gapes furiously.

Seth is fighting himself when he feels Nyanjura's eye on him – over Bbembe's shoulder as she hugs her fiancé – and she smiles when she sees he's noticed her. Acid misery fills Seth as he contemplates the reason behind that smile. He forces his face into a smile back, but it does not matter because Nyanjura isn't paying him any attention. Their hug has ended and now she faces Bbembe smiling so wide you can see the pink of her gums.

Bbembe dislodges Nyanjura's shuuka. The loose material slides down, held in place by a wish and the crook of her elbows – giving Seth a view of the loose bun at the nape of her neck, the tiny pearls someone seeded carefully within it and the glow of her skin under the lights. Everything he has imagined since he first met her. Everything he has dreamed in the rare moments he allowed himself to believe he still had a chance. The view vanishes as Bbembe helps Nyanjura settle the shuuka back over her head and around her shoulders.

Seth claps hard, along with everyone else, as Nyanjura leads Bbembe away, his hand firmly clasped in hers. His mouth is dry, and when he swallows to ease it, bitterness floods his tastebuds. He blinks away the echoes of lights, thankful the cameras have followed the new couple as she introduces her chosen to her family.

Seth's hands hurt from all the clapping, and he hisses a curse under his breath as he sits back down. Luckily, no one is paying him any mind. Nina and Hawa are looking at each other's phones, admiring the photos they took of Bbembe and Nyanjura's staged meet-cute. Odur has turned so he can follow the couple's progress. James is looking at his phone.

Seth goes to take a sip from his bushera but the gourd is empty. Disgusted with it and himself, Seth pushes the calabash roughly across the table, releasing some of the anger he is stifling. A hand rights the gourd and then places a bottle of stout in front of him. When Seth follows the arm up to the attached face, James does not smile at him.

'Have mine.'

The stout fizzes slightly with the motion as Seth pops its top off with the edge of the table. He takes a deep swig. With the bottle in one hand, he squeezes the bottle's metal top into the other. The sharp edges bite into the flesh of his palm so hard that when he lifts the metal, there is a thin circle of blood. The physical pain is a relief, cutting through the chaos that threatens to overcome him. It is done now. Seth takes another chug and smiles wryly at his idiocy. It has always been done.

Seth cannot help himself. When he looks up, he finds Bbembe and Nyanjura seated on their throne. Cameras click around them; their light is a halo over the couple. The lines of his mouth pull downwards.

'You're staring again, my guy,' James says, 'Are you sure you're good?'

Seth nods. He doesn't know why James asks. They both know he is not okay. It is James who found Seth staring hungrily at Bbembe and Nyanjura on that fateful prom night back in high school as the couple slow-wined to a dancehall beat. Seth had been confused the whole night about what to feel. You know it can't work if you like her too, James had said. Seth had tried to deny it, but James had shaken his head before he could string words together and left. They'd never talked about it again.

'Just hungover, that's all,' Seth manages now. The years have not yet given him the words for this conversation.

'Hmm.'

Seth centres his attention on the exit. He wants to be done with this. Clouds squat like sulky toddlers, their sniffles making for an insistent drizzle. He fidgets with his collar's stranglehold on his throat, made worse by the humidity from the afternoon's rain.

'Babes,' Nina is talking to him. She has turned fully in her seat, so her back is to Hawa. He wonders how long she tried to get his attention. There is a question to her smile as she searches his face. She weighs him. He wonders what she thinks. Hawa, just beyond her, shakes her head slightly in his direction, signalling something. He blinks. Nina's hand waves her phone hypnotic-slow at him.

'Take a photo of us.'

Nina has both hands held out toward him. One hand offers her phone, camera app open, while the other rests on his forearm; has she been nudging him to get his attention? Seth's gaze travels the length of her hands. Nina's hands are freshly manicured, and the rose dusk nail colour matches her mushanana. She rarely wears jewellery but today her wrists are a tangle of bracelets and bangles. A ring cradles every finger but one.

OLIVIA WATSON

Olivia previously worked documenting human rights abuses in war zones and is now a writer at the UN. In her first novel, *SAUSAGE*, a dog attempts to write a philosophical treatise but is constantly interrupted by the misadventures of his owner. Her writing has appeared in the *Guardian, Literary Hub*, and elsewhere.

olivia.watson@cantab.net

SAUSAGE

Opening of a novel

Once upon a time, let's say around twenty-five thousand years ago, the wolves made a bargain. We – I mean *Canis lupus familiaris* – call this bargain 'The Great Bargain'.

Picture those wolves, stalking the unseen depths of the forest. Picture their prey, *Homo sapiens,* huddled thin and frightened around the fireplace. See how the humans shift and shuffle their bony hindquarters, how they draw their stolen furs more tightly around them. Watch them dart their strange, white eyes to the right and to the left, sensing danger. Watch the wolves watching them, sensing dinner.

'Let's eat them,' says the first wolf to her friend.

'I'm not that hungry,' replies the friend, examining his claws.

'Still, it seems a shame not to eat them, since they're here,' says the first wolf.

Before they can come to a decision a pointed spear is thrown from behind, there is a tussle, and in another moment the two wolves are gazing at a clutch of slack-jawed *Homo sapiens* from the wrong side of a net.

'Well done,' hisses the first wolf, 'Now they're going to eat us. Turn us into sausage. Are you happy?'

'Not so hasty,' says the second wolf. '*Homo sapiens* are famously weak and not as clever as they think they are. Let's see if we can't reach some kind of an agreement.'

So the two wolves chat a little to put the humans at ease and after some relieved laughter on both sides, a conversation ensues.

'We know you're sentient and political animals,' say the *Homo sapiens*. 'That's clear enough for anyone to see. But unfortunately there's no opening for that right now. What we mean is that it would suit us much better if everyone pretended that we are the only sentient and political animals. It makes us feel strong, and brave, and knowing. There is however a vacancy for a sort of bodyguard, defender-type something or other. As you can see, our bodies are naked and cold, our snouts are useless, and our teeth are feeble. We are frail and vulnerable, compared to you, king among animals.'

(One suspects that the tale has undergone some embellishment over the years.)

The wolves, so the tale goes, exchange a look.

'You want us to pretend not to be sentient so as to prop up your wavering sense of self-esteem?'

'Precisely.'

'And what do we get in return?'

'Well, we can promise the vast majority of you a lifetime of comfort and safety and the scraps from our table.'

'That sounds good,' whispers the first wolf to her friend, 'They have sausage.'

'Still, our sentience?'

'That just means looking the other way when they do something stupid.'

'How can we protect them if we are always looking the other way?'

A pause, and then, 'How will we communicate with you,' says the second wolf loudly to the *Homo sapiens*, 'If we are pretending to know only how to fornicate, bite, eat, and excrete?'

'You can communicate with the one you have a special bond with, and there will be other humans capable of reaching out to you.'

'Sounds a little vague.'

'It's not like they're asking for our undying love,' reasons the first wolf, 'It's just a practical arrangement. A steady stream of food. What's not to like?'

'It is dangerous to trust. Who can tell how this will shape us?'

The first wolf rolls her eyes. 'Will you have a little optimism for once? Come on, I'm getting really hungry now. Anyway, if we don't agree they're going to kill us.'

'Loyalty must trump freedom,' say the *Homo sapiens* with a warning note in their voice. 'Forever.'

'Fine, fine,' agree the wolves at last. 'Loyalty before freedom.'

And so it was that the two wolves were given sausage and the Great Bargain was struck.

A rattling, phlegm-filled cough from the other side of the living room interrupts my thoughts. Deep in the hollow of the sofa, carefully curated over the course of many long years, Man shuffles his hips. He fumbles for the cane leaning against the faded floral armrest and makes an initial effort to stand. It fails and he falls back into the trough. Then he peers at me through the gloom, through air that is thick with years of moulting hair and flaking skin: a half century of his and nearly a dozen of mine.

'Saturday, Dog,' he says, the sound of mucus lingering in his throat.

He leans forward with difficulty to pluck a half-eaten sausage from the coffee table. Correction – it is not just any sausage. It is botifarra sausage, the finest type of sausage you will find in all of Europe. A sturdy cylinder of compressed meat: long, pink, pale, and tubular as a turd. His breakfast, lunch, and dinner. He is a magnificent man – one to be admired in all respects. He takes a large chunk out of the end of the botifarra with his teeth and then clears his throat again. Gristle spatters the table in front of him.

'We had best start getting ready, yes. I have a good feeling about today.'

I could tell him that I am right in the middle of the opening chapter of my philosophical treatise, but he tends to glaze over when I discuss my work.

Man shifts his hips again and then sighs, and a thick, luxurious stench fills the room. It is almost liquid in its density. Few things make the heart sing like being in the service of a flatulent *Homo sapiens*. He twists his face into an exaggerated expression of disgust, waving the remains of the botifarra at me.

'Dog, I have asked you before. Could you try for one blessed day not to fill our living quarters with the rotten smell of your intestines?'

I know from long experience that it is better not to answer. I gaze at him. I try to convey a deep sense of pity.

Now he plants the rubberised tip of his cane down on the dull, stained tile at his feet. With a jerking, rolling motion, he propels himself out of the hollow, leans heavily on the cane, and hauls himself upright. He stares around for a moment as though taking in for the first time the bare walls of the living room, the solemn mahogany furniture that seems always to observe us with a disapproving gaze, the stacks of yellowing newspapers that cover every surface, the piles of junk – old lightbulbs, rusted tools, dead batteries – that have for reasons of convenience or lethargy decided to see out their days in our company. There is a bucket catching a few solitary drips of water, a sagging bag of compost loaned to us by Montse and never touched again after its initial foray through the front door, an unruly heap of bags designed for the collection and disposal of my excrement, a bulky, shining Zimmer frame given by Man's well-meaning health worker. He takes it all in, and then he looks down at me across the pock-marked coffee table, surveying me as I lie calmly in the only available space in the entire room – on my cushion in the Rest position.

'We had best start getting ready, yes,' he says again, hitching his trousers up awkwardly with the hand holding the botifarra. There was a time in my life when such a statement would have sent me into a frenzy of excitement. No longer. My life now is the humble life of the mind.

Man shuffles from the living room, tracing a narrow path past the bucket for the drips and the bag of compost propped against the wall, talking as he moves down the dark corridor towards the kitchen.

'I do have a good feeling, Dog, that today is not only Saturday but a final Saturday, a last Saturday. Perhaps it is hard to believe after all these years, but don't lose faith. There is a beginning and an end to all things, and I believe we are almost at the end, Dog, after all these years of searching and hunting. Yes, I do have a good feeling.'

The rest of what he is saying is lost to me as he enters the kitchen and begins to clatter things around in the sink, so I return to my cushion and to my thoughts.

The Great Bargain, passed down to all dogs through our ancient lineage. Whispered by every exhausted, sleep-deprived mother to her pups as they suckle in the earliest days of life. Thanks to the Great Bargain, I and all my fellow once-wolves have been stretched, tucked, nipped, squeezed, shrunk, moulded, tweaked, and plucked into every shape and size imaginable, at the expense of some mobility and a great deal of dignity. Now, instead of a wolf, I am what is known in common parlance as a Basset Hound.

Few of our sages, until now, have had cause to question the ethical hierarchy established at the time of the Great Bargain – loyalty before freedom. The human sages question all kinds of things, leaving proof of their thinking in the billions upon billions of words that adorn the pages of the books lining Man's shelves and which I have been at liberty to peruse while his attention is turned towards the television. But how is it that so many of my kind have accepted this bargain? And what has it done to us? I have often wondered while cleaning my most sensitive parts if there wouldn't be a better way of handing down the story – a way that would more thoroughly address the advantages and disadvantages of such an agreement. What was gained, what was lost. The costs to our kind of concealing our sentience. Whether, all these thousands of years later, we should still choose loyalty over freedom. In the tragic absence of a progeny of my own, and with a mind to interrogating more closely that which has shaped our lives for so many millennia, I leave this treatise – my life's work – to whomever may follow. Man has agreed, albeit reluctantly, to take pen to paper on my behalf.

'Oh what a sight it would be, Dog!' calls Man from the kitchen. 'What a sight it would be to see Montse finally freed from that prison of her own making, what a thing it would be to see her out in broad daylight with the rays of the sun shining down on her as they once did and catching in all the very many shades of her hair, getting in her eyes and causing her to twist up her face in that peculiar, particular manner she has.'

I stand and begin to move slowly in Man's direction. My armpits chafe. My legpits, too. Oh, how they chafe. It is worse on warm days, but it must be said that it is also a problem on the cooler days. Oh, every step is a misery. Not just a misery but a bitter humiliation: that the limbs made for the very purpose of locomotion should be the cause of such pain. What cruel god made me in this mould? I think I know. And to add insult to injury named me 'Basset', etymology French: 'rather low.' Oh, misery. And my ears, especially my right ear. Don't even get me started on my ears.

NAYELA WICKRAMASURIYA

Nayela Wickramasuriya was born in Sri Lanka and spent most of her childhood in Scotland. She studied Persian at the School of Oriental and African Studies in London. She writes fiction that explores identity, belonging and postcolonial legacy whilst using writing as an anti-colonial tool and means of resistance.

nayela.wickramasuriya@gmail.com

This Tender Soil

An extract from the opening of a novel

I have been here for some time now. When did I arrive? Hmm. It's hard to say, really. Sometime just before the 1800s. I'm not sure, it's been such a long time since then. I came on a boat, that I can say with certainty. A creaking, hulking, wooden thing, filled with the stench of vomit and greed.

Very happy to come, of course! Delicious little place, this. Hot days, cool evenings. Jungle, beach, rainforest, hill country. Seas that are sometimes a thundering surf, sometimes like glass, full moons, no moons, monsoons, heat so dry it crackles. Joy, fear. Variety is the spice of life, as they say.

I so enjoy raking my claws over the soil, feeling the little snags here and there as I tear furrows in the earth. Such red earth, beautifully stained. The night here is wonderful, a velvety blackness that blooms like a flower, laced with scent. That metallic smell gets me going, girds my loins! Can you smell it? Not yet, not yet. Can't cut straight to it now, can we? Sometimes the real pleasure lies in the anticipation, so let us anticipate. Myriad pockets of darkness for me to feed on; the meat lingers in the shadows.

Things are beginning to heat up now. They've been ramping up for years, this smorgasbord, this feast, laid out just for me.

You should see me now. I've filled out, I'm no longer the tiny slip of a thing I was when I arrived.

And here I am. At your service, yours truly, pleased to meet you. So pleased to meet you. You look like my kind of person, you do, you do. But we'll come to that in time.

1929 – COLOMBO, WESTERN PROVINCE, CEYLON

The little girl stood outside the black, iron gate, sweating in the mid-afternoon heat. It was locked, an aberration for which she was not prepared. She did not have a key for the gate, only for the main house, for the front door, the only door that she needed access to during the day. Being eight, she was never out at night.

She was calling into the house when she heard footsteps behind her and turned to see her older brother walking down their road, his black leather shoes raising puffs of dirt. He neared her and gave her a frown.

'Why are you outside?'

'The gate is locked.'

He examined the chain and padlock. The little girl saw that the blue shorts of her brother's school uniform were smeared with dirt.

'Amma's going to punish you.'

He ignored her and began shouting into the house.

'I already shouted.'

'My voice is louder than yours.'

They called into the house for an interminable amount of time, their little stomachs growling in the absence of their after-school snack. Their siblings, an eldest sister and a youngest brother came home too, having finished their tuition classes. The four of them puzzled over what to do. The boys wanted to climb the gate but the eldest sister, seventeen and aware of the weight of responsibility on her shoulders, pushed them away, mindful of the black spikes at the top. They were squatting by the gate when their neighbour's car pulled up. She cranked down the window and asked them what they were doing, and the children told her their gate was locked. The woman motioned for the driver to park the car in their driveway before returning to the street and ushering the children into her house.

It was a hot afternoon and, as they sat on their neighbour's sofas in her formal sitting room, the little girl felt sweat beginning to drip down the back of her legs. It was her first time in the house. Their neighbours seemed to her to be eternally on holiday, and she ached to run through the rooms and see the tasteless furniture her mother had spoken of but squashed her hands under her thighs instead. The maid brought them little glasses of thambili, and their neighbour sat with them and asked questions, none of which they knew the answers to. Why was their house locked, why wasn't the maid at home, where was their mother? The little girl wondered whether their neighbour might give them something to eat but did not want to ask, for reasons she could not pinpoint other than she had a faint sense that her sister would be embarrassed if she did. So she sat with her sweaty knee creases and coughed quietly every time she felt a rumble brewing.

As the sky began to fade from blue to peach and the cool breeze rolled in, their father arrived from his work at the hospital. He spoke with their neighbour too quietly for the four hungry children to hear, though not for lack of trying, eight little-ish ears straining to make out the adult murmurings in the adjoining room.

He then entered the room they were seated in and summoned them with a sharp sweep of his hand, making sure they thanked their neighbour as they trailed past. The expression on the woman's face perplexed the little girl. It was an adult expression, one she had seen adults make before, a tightness in the mouth that she had tried and failed to replicate in the mirror.

The four children watched their father unlock the gate. They let themselves in as their driver rolled the car into the garage. The house was cool and dark, all the windows shuttered and doors bolted.

On the dining table lay a cream envelope, with their father's name on it. He picked it up, opened it with a knife and read the words on the paper in silence. When he was finished, he slipped the letter back into its envelope and put it in his pocket. That evening, they sat down to dinner and ate, ignoring the now-empty space at the table. The children forced food into their mouths, their hunger replaced by a thin fear, for they had only ever known their parents as a single entity. The man who sat with them at the table felt like a stranger, someone who wore the skin of their father but whose movements and impulses now came from an unknown, invisible source.

As the years passed, the little girl began to wonder whether she had had a mother at all, so complete was the silence around what happened that day. Her father never mentioned it again and took down the framed photograph of him and the children's mother on their wedding day and her image began to fade in the girl's memory.

The men who brought me fed me rather well. I remember one fellow called Maclaine, a rich feeding ground if ever there was one. He was endowed with an ego that was vast and fragile in equal measure, exactly the kind of person I can follow around for years in the knowledge that I won't go hungry for a single day.

Well, this Maclaine, he lived in the rolling hills. Endless undulations of green, mountains that are misted in the morning, a breeze so cool that you feel you might weep if you went there following a few days in the heat of the lowlands. Tall trees with firm boughs, leaves that whisper gently as the wind moves through.

Every morning, Maclaine liked to have his breakfast laid out for him on a brass platter. He ate fresh fruit and two eggs on two slices of toasted bread. And a cup of tea, of course. It would be criminal not to, being so close to the source. The eggs had to be laid on the toast slices at the very last minute, as he liked his toast hot and crisp. I like a man of particular tastes. If the toast was soggy or a little cool, Maclaine would have the cooks beaten. Fear is no good, tasteless and insipid. As if it were something I might have liked, had it not been so watered down. Anger is marginally less bad, it'll do in a pinch. I'd have to be rather desperate to go with anger and, even then, it takes quite a lot of it to sate my appetite. But it can be the seed from whence a rich and bountiful harvest grows, so I mustn't complain! There was a lot of fear and anger around Maclaine, but, as they say, if you cast your net wide enough, you're bound to catch a fish. When Maclaine beat the cooks himself, it was not so interesting. Lots of anger, some fear. But when Maclaine made them beat each other – my goodness. The thing that I like to eat the most is that black, curled thing, gnarled, an irregular shape. Comes in all sizes, depending on the source. It is beyond fear, beyond anger. It happens when those things have curdled, become something darker, more sinister. Hatred. It tastes exquisite.

So, each morning I'd linger in the kitchen and try to ruin Maclaine's toast. There's not much I can do – what I have in enthusiasm I lack in form, alas, but that doesn't mean I'm impotent. I might extinguish the flames over which the bread sat, or perhaps nudge a plate off a counter if it protruded far enough over the edge. And then I'd pray that he would make them beat each other, so that they hated him more.

This one morning I wasn't even all that hungry, so I didn't mind when I saw that the toast was perfect, but I knew something else was afoot. Flickerings of fear, silver and quick and a hum in the wood of the house, as if the trees already knew, had known when their roots were still in the ground. As if they had always known. I was excited, of course. Ever ready for a snack, I am. I was lounging on the veranda next to Maclaine as he ate his breakfast. I remember the crisp crunch of his knife as he cut his egged toast first in half, then in quarters, then into smaller, bitesize pieces that he ferried to his mouth with slow relish. Some of his underlings brought out a string of natives, one after the other. I could see the whites of their eyes from where I lay, bright, so bright. One in the middle started speaking to Maclaine. He didn't shout, spoke softly but firmly, and said some words that were translated for Maclaine by one of his men. Something about not having done anything, that they weren't involved. Maclaine continued eating, crunch crunch. By this point I was alert as the feast was multiplying before my eyes. The other natives began talking too, nodding at the one who first spoke, but Maclaine gave a little wave of his fork. The men who worked for him began leading the natives up a little platform that they'd built the evening before, underneath the trees in the garden. They lined them up on the platform and Maclaine leaned back in his chair, looking up for the first time. My god, I could barely keep up. So many fat, succulent nuggets, I feasted as fast as I could. Maclaine himself was oozing something, something new and viscous and sweet, something I had to lick directly off him it was that delicious. He continued eating his toast, then his fruit, then sipped his tea while the natives were hanged from the tree, one by one. The last one's body stopped twitching in the breeze just as Maclaine drained his cup. I remember the way he clicked his fingers and pointed at his tray when he was finished, while I, little glutton that I am, rolled around in ecstasy beneath him, gobbling up what I could.

Breakfast has been my favourite meal ever since.

ACKNOWLEDGEMENTS

Non-fiction

This anthology contains work by the 2024 cohort of UEA's MA in Biography and Creative Non-Fiction. We are grateful to the UEA School of Literature, Drama and Creative Writing in partnership with Egg Box Publishing, without whom this anthology would not have been possible.

First and foremost, enormous thanks to Nathan Ashman. It was his first year in charge of the anthology and we appreciate his willingness to answer all our questions. His patience and organisational ability ensured the successful production of this year's anthology.

Our deepest gratitude to our course tutors—Ian Thomson, Stephanie Bishop, Andrew Kenrick and Helen Smith—for their mentorship in the discipline and possibilities of creative non-fiction writing.

Thanks goes out to Ian Thomson especially, who took over as course convener this year. His trademark wit and exuberance animated our seminar discussions and Ian was also kind enough to write the non-fiction anthology's introduction. Further gratitude goes to Stephanie Bishop, who taught several of us for our autumn term's module. Her breadth of knowledge and infectious curiosity were inspiring for many of us. We are similarly appreciative of Andrew Kenrick, who joined the faculty this year. His dedication and enthusiasm, bolstered by his expertise as editor of the creative non-fiction magazine *Hinterland*, was invaluable.

We would also like to thank Birgit Breidenbach, Thomas Karshan, Jean McNeil, Jos Smith and John Steciuk for their instruction and insight during our multistrand optional modules.

Many thanks to the 2024 Editorial Committee for their collective support as we worked through the submissions and proofing processes. We are grateful to the non-fiction anthology's team of editors in particular—Helen Adcock, Charles Bliss, Julia Hollingsworth and Manasa Tantravahi—for their work in seeing the anthology editing process through to completion.

Finally, we would like to express our appreciation for each and every graduate of the 2024 Biography and Creative Non-Fiction MA course, all of whom provided encouragement and support to each other and the editorial team, as everyone developed their submissions from initial drafts to the completed works in this volume.

The editorial team are incredibly proud of the literary and artistic achievements of our peers. We are grateful for this precious opportunity to develop our writing and look forward to growing the creative community we have built with everyone we have met during our degree as we move into the future.

Prose Fiction

This anthology contains work by the 2024 cohort of UEA's MA in Creative Writing: Prose Fiction. We are very grateful for the support of the UEA School of Literature, Drama and Creative Writing. Thank you especially to Nathan Ashman for undertaking the mammoth task of supervising the whole process, without whom we would have been lost. Many thanks to the people at Egg Box Publishing, who made this anthology possible.

Special thanks go to Priscilla Morris, for generously writing a foreword to the anthology.

We would also like to thank our course convenor Julianne Pachico, with Jean McNeil in the Autumn term, for making the course an incredible experience for the whole cohort. Both of your hard work, dedication and passion has not gone unnoticed. We could have not wished for better people to lead the course.

A huge thank you to our tutors: Julianne Pachico, Jean McNeil, Tessa McWatt, Nick Bradley, Giles Foden, Trezza Azzopardi, Stephanie Bishop, Philip Langekov, Ashley Hickson-Lovence, Jacob Huntley, Naomi Wood, Michael Lengsfield, John Stecuik, Ian Thompson, Thomas Karshan, Jos Smith, Rachel Potter, Clare Connors, Stephen Benson, Iain Robinson and Kiare Ladner. You have each inspired us in countless ways. Your insights, expertise and support have been invaluable, and we leave the course changed writers because of you.

Thank you to the authors who have run the masterclasses this year: Nalo Hopkinson, Mallory Tater, Eleanor Catton and Alexander Chee. Thanks also to those who have contributed to the salons: Priscilla Morris, Stephen Buoro, KJ Orr and Ashley Hickson-Lovence. Each salon and masterclass were greatly insightful and memorable experiences that enriched our year.

Thanks to our anthology editors: Alexia Tolas, Godess Bvukutwa, Siobhan Horner, Sophie Chapman, Giulia Da Re, Elspeth Leslie, Eleanor Halliwell, Reyah Martin, Gayathri Sankaranarayanan, and Charlotte Marar.

Finally, we extend our deepest thanks to everyone who contributed their work to the anthology. Each of your submissions demonstrate the unique, diverse and rich talents that make this year's cohort. You should be very proud of what you have achieved, and we wish you luck in all your future endeavours. Write on!

UEA MA Creative Writing Anthologies: Non-Fiction and Prose Fiction

First published by Egg Box Publishing, 2024
Part of the UEA Publishing Project Ltd.

International © retained by individual authors

This book is sold subject to the condition that it shall not, by way of trade or otherwise, be lent, resold, hired out, stored in a retrieval system, or otherwise circulated without the publisher's prior consent in any form of binding or cover other than that in which it is published and without a similar condition including this condition being imposed on the subsequent purchaser.

A CIP record for this book is available from the British Library
Printed and bound in the UK by Imprint Digital

Designed by Emily Benton Book Design
emilybentonbookdesign.co.uk

Distributed by BookSource
50 Cambuslang Road
Cambuslang
Glasgow
G32 8NB
+44 (0)141 642 9192
booksource.net

ISBN 978-1-915812-60-5